WALKING THE TALK
THE BUSINESS CASE FOR SUSTAINABLE DEVELOPMENT

Charles O. Holliday, Jr, Stephan Schmidheiny and Philip Watts

CHARLES O. HOLLIDAY, Jr
Chairman and CEO, DuPont

An industrial engineer by training, Chad Holliday parlayed a summer job at DuPont into a full-time position in 1970. In his 30-year DuPont career, he has touched virtually every aspect of the business—from fibers and chemicals to agricultural products and biotechnology. His diverse assignments have spanned nearly all key functional areas, advancing through various manufacturing and supervisory assignments to product planning and marketing positions and, more recently, to executive responsibilities and his current role as chairman and CEO. Chad is the first DuPont chief executive with extensive experience outside the United States, having been based in Tokyo for seven years as head of the DuPont Asia Pacific operations. Chad is a former chairman of the World Business Council for Sustainable Development. He also serves on the board of directors of Analog Devices, Inc. and Catalyst; and is a senior member of the Institute of Industrial Engineers.

STEPHAN SCHMIDHEINY
Chairman, Anova Holding AG

Swiss industrialist Stephan Schmidheiny founded the Business Council for Sustainable Development (BCSD) after he was named in 1990 Principal Advisor for Businesses and Industry to the secretary general of the 1992 'Earth Summit' in Rio. He was principal author of the 1992 book *Changing Course: A Global Business Perspective on Development and the Environment* (MIT Press, 1992), which was published in 15 languages. Mr Schmidheiny is now honorary chairman of the World Business Council for Sustainable Development. His business interests are centered in the GrupoNueva holding company of more than 40 companies (30 production plants) in 15 Latin American countries. Companies on whose boards he has served include the Union Bank of Switzerland, ABB, Leica, Swatch, and Nestlé. He is also founder, funder, and president of the AVINA Foundation, which promotes sustainable development in Latin America.

PHILIP WATTS
Chairman of the Committee of Managing Directors of the Royal Dutch/Shell Group of Companies

Philip Watts has been chairman of The 'Shell' Transport and Trading Company plc and of the Committee of Managing Directors of the Royal Dutch/Shell Group since July 2001. He has been a managing director of Shell Transport and a Group managing director since 1997. His functional and geographical responsibilities as a Group managing director are: Finance; Human Resources; Legal; Planning, Environment, and External Affairs; and the United States. He joined Shell in 1969 and worked in Indonesia, the UK, Norway, and the Netherlands. In 1991 he went to Lagos as chairman and managing director of the Shell Petroleum Development Company of Nigeria, returning to The Hague as regional coordinator Europe in 1994. From the beginning of 1996 until becoming a managing director, he was director of Planning, Environment and External Affairs for Shell International in London. Philip Watts was born in 1945 in Leicestershire, England. He graduated from Leeds University with a BSc in Physics and an MSc in Geophysics. In between these two degrees he taught in a secondary school in Sierra Leone for two years. He is married and has a daughter, a son, and two grandchildren. His interests include reading and gardening. He is the current chairman of the World Business Council for Sustainable Development and of the UK chapter of the International Chamber of Commerce.

WALKING THE TALK

The Business Case for Sustainable Development

Charles O. Holliday, Jr • Stephan Schmidheiny • Philip Watts

Greenleaf
PUBLISHING

BK

BERRETT-KOEHLER PUBLISHERS, INC.
San Francisco

2 0 0 2

Published by Greenleaf Publishing Limited
Aizlewood's Mill, Nursery Street
Sheffield S3 8GG, UK
Tel: +44 (0)114 282 3475   Fax: +44 (0)114 282 3476   www.greenleaf-publishing.com

Published simultaneously in the United States and Canada by
Berrett-Koehler Publishers, Inc.
235 Montgomery Street, Suite 650
San Francisco, California 94104-2916, USA
Tel: +1 415 288-0260   Fax: +1 415 362-2512   www.bkconnection.com

Printed in the United Kingdom

Printed and bound, using acid-free paper from managed forests, by
The Bath Press, Bath, Somerset, UK.

British Library Cataloguing in Publication Data:
   A catalogue record for this book is available from the British Library.

Library of Congress Cataloging-in-Publication Data is available.

Greenleaf Publishing edition ISBN 1-874719-50-0
Berrett-Koehler Publishers edition ISBN 1-57675-234-8

First Edition
07 06 05 04 03 02   10 9 8 7 6 5 4 3 2 1

Contents

4. Corporate social responsibility 103

5. Learning to change 125

6. From dialogue to partnerships 150

7. Informing and providing consumer choice 174

Foreword

Björn Stigson, president,
World Business Council for Sustainable Development

It was with a great deal of hesitancy that we entitled our book *Walking the Talk*.

We do not want to claim that our more than 160 member companies are already doing precisely what many of their mission statements say they are trying to do: run their companies in the best interests of human society and the natural environment, now and in the future.

However, as provocative as the title might sound, it is what the book is about. What will it take for our CEOs to put their companies on a sustainable path? What progress has been made in the decade since the 1992 Earth Summit in Rio? Which companies are trying what? What works? What does not? Where do we need help from governments? Where do we need help from other stakeholders?

The book is about dilemmas faced by companies trying to walk their talk, and the opportunities and problems in doing so.

Walking the Talk offers a 'Foundation' chapter in which we discuss how the business case for sustainable development has grown and changed over the past ten years. We are now more convinced than ever that companies can do themselves good through doing right for society at large and the environment.

This Foundation is followed by ten chapters we call the building blocks of sustainable progress. Each of the chapter overviews comes from our publication *The Business Case for Sustainable Development: Making a Difference toward the Johannesburg Summit 2002 and Beyond*, which we published as a statement to inject some business vision into the planning for the 2002 World Summit for Sustainable Development.

The Council also partnered with the World Resources Institute (WRI) and the UN Environment Program to publish *Tomorrow's Markets: Global Trends and their Implications for Business*. This report documents 19 powerful trends that are shaping worldwide markets. It is meant to help companies spot opportunities and risks, and better understand their roles in sustainable development.

Walking the Talk itself sees the globalization of the marketplace as the best path toward sustainable human progress—but only if business, governments, and citizens' groups can cooperate in creating a market that maximizes opportunity for all.

I would like to thank our three authors: Chad Holliday, Stephan Schmidheiny, and Philip Watts, and would like to thank the editorial team that backed them up: Amy Brown and Andrea Spencer-Cooke (editorial consultants); Lloyd Timberlake (editor); Claude Fussler (project director), Samantha Chadwick (case study research), Shelley Hayes (project coordinator), and Cherryl André de la Porte (editorial research). I would also like to thank the many WBCSD members and staff who gave generously of their time and effort to produce the book.

Of great interest in this publication are the 67 case studies, which were researched specifically for the book. In addition, a great many of the insights and comments from business leaders and experts from around the world appear here in print for the first time. All quotations not directly attributed fall into this category. We feel this adds tremendously to the book's value as a precis of current leading-edge thinking. Thanks are due also to those who have contributed in this way.

GAINING PERFORMANCE INSIGHTS

In the following chapters we will chart specific implementation indicators. They are derived from the 2001 yearly corporate sustainability assessment for the Dow Jones Sustainability Indexes (DJSI). This assessment is conducted by SAM Research Inc., the research company of SAM Group Holding in Zurich.

Our charts cover 996 companies analysed by SAM and grouped in nine main economic sectors. This is how the selection process operates:

Number of companies

- Start from the Dow Jones Global Index (DJGI). It represents 95% market-capitalization coverage of developed markets and 80% coverage of emerging markets.

5021

- Select the largest companies on 31 December 2000 and invite them to participate in the written SAM survey.

2552

- Create a sample including survey respondents (450), and other companies that publicly declare an interest in sustainable development (546). This reduced universe is verified as statistically representative of the total DJGI. It is the basis of the charts in this book.

996

- Apply a performance scoring system to this sample. The top 10% companies in terms of corporate sustainability in each of 62 industry groups are selected for inclusion in the DJSI World.

312

Member of
Dow Jones STOXX
Sustainability
Indexes

- The SAM scoring system is verified for replicability by a third-party auditor. SAM publishes this ranking in 18 market sectors and highlights the top-scoring companies (*ex aequo* in 2 sectors).

20

Source: **sam**

Part 1
THE FOUNDATION

The business case for sustainable development

> ❝Yet in the end, sustainable development is not a fixed state of harmony, but rather a process of change in which the exploitation of resources, the direction of investments, the orientation of technological development, and institutional change are made consistent with future as well as present needs . . . Painful choices have to be made. Thus in the final analysis, sustainable development must rest on political will. ❞

WCED 1987, *Our Common Future*

The World Business Council for Sustainable Development (WBCSD) emerged from the vision and concerns of a small group of business leaders during the two years leading up to the 1992 Earth Summit in Rio de Janeiro. This is why we feel a responsibility to update our views before another Earth Summit (the 2002 World Summit on Sustainable Development in Johannesburg).

Much of this book looks ahead, into the first decades of this new millennium. However, we begin by looking back at where we have been, what issues prompted us to act, and how those concerns and visions have played out over the decade.

To do that, we need to go back yet another decade, to the early 1980s. Then, 'development' seemed to be failing. Large parts of the globe were stagnant economically and falling heavily into debt. The 1980s is known in Latin America as 'the lost decade'. At the same time, the environment was being mismanaged, if managed at all. From a United Nations viewpoint, neither the UN Development Programme (UNDP) nor the UN Environment Programme (UNEP) seemed to be very effective.

With both development and environment in crisis, citizens' groups championing either cause argued fiercely over which 'comes first'. Against this background, the UN General Assembly in 1983 adopted a resolution to establish a commission to seek ways forward. A total of 21 members, mostly from the developing world, composed this World Commission on Environment and Development (WCED), and former Norwegian Environment Minister Gro Harlem Brundtland chaired it.

The Commission did two things that had a lasting impact. In its 1987 report, *Our Common Future*, it developed and championed the concept of 'sustainable development' and, in the final pages of that report, it called for preparations for 'an international conference' on sustainable development. That conference was eventually held as the 1992 Earth Summit.

Why no one likes sustainable development

In calling for such a conference, the Commission wrote (1987):

> When the century began, neither human numbers nor technology had the power to radically alter planetary systems. As the century closes, not only do vastly increased human numbers and their activities have that power, but major, unintended changes are occurring in the atmosphere, in soils, in waters, among plants and animals, and in the relationships among all of these.

That rhetoric is interesting because it demonstrates the WCED's environmental motivation. It tended to have much more to say about environmental management than about meeting human needs. Yet in defining the term 'sustainable development' it gave equal weight to both concerns:

> Sustainable development seeks to meet the needs and aspirations of the present without compromising the ability to meet those of the future. Far from requiring the cessation of economic growth, it recognizes that the problems of poverty and underdevelopment cannot be solved unless we have a new era of growth in which developing countries play a large role and reap large benefits (WCED 1987).

So, sustainable development is partly about social justice. Debate about what constitutes a fair and just distribution of wealth, rights, and opportunities is nothing new. In the past, debates about social justice tended to focus on distributional issues within a particular generation. However, with the rise of concern about environmental issues over recent decades, increasing attention is being given to future generations and considerations of justice between generations (Starkey and Welford 2001). This is one aspect that makes sustainable development seem so challenging. Another aspect is the systemic nature of the concept. Sustainable development cannot be achieved by one nation alone. It cannot be achieved in only one sphere, such as the economic sphere. It will require types of partnership never before witnessed in human history. The Commission argued that the conditions of the present poor must be improved, a fairly radical argument considering how low this goal was on most political agendas.

The WCED's key concept of sustainable development has informed environment and development discussion since 1987 but it has never quite caught on to become a mainstream, unifying, rallying cry among the general public or even among environmental and development groups. We suggest this is because of the following reasons:

- Environmental groups do not appear to like the concept because they did not 'invent' it and because it has the word 'development' in it.

- UNEP seemed to take a similar 'not invented here' stance, offering alternative expressions such as 'environmentally sustainable development'. They resisted its use in the official title of the 1992 Earth Summit, which became the UN Summit on Environment and Development.

- Developmental groups do not appear to like it because they see it as being too green, feeling that all the emphasis is on the needs of the future rather than the needs of the present.

- Governments seem to shy away from it because it does not fall to any single ministry or department. It requires levels of integrated thinking and acting that governments have thus far failed to achieve.

- Academics tend not to like it because it can be made the property of no single discipline. Finding its definition vague, they endlessly redefine it, so that today there are many competing definitions. Academics also point out, rightly, that the concept does not really help one to know what to *do* about issues such as climate change and species loss.

- The general public also has trouble with the concept. After all, its main message is that in thinking about environment and development issues, as in thinking about one's own life, one must figure out how to live off interest and not capital. One must not eat one's seed corn, burn down one's house to keep warm or use one's drinking water to wash the car. The public is not excited by such thinking. Thus it is unlikely to read about sustainable development in its newspapers or hear about it on radio or television. Surveys in the USA found that few had heard the expression, but, on hearing it, they took *sustainable* to mean *static*—requiring that one always drive the same car, have the same amount in the bank, and live in the same house. So the term *sustainable development* is unlikely to rally millions to the cause of sustainable development.

The business connection

Thus for the past decade or so we in the WBCSD have been championing a term that is unknown to most of the world's inhabitants but is universally known among environment and development actors and thinkers, where it seems to mildly annoy them all. Whether this will change now that the 2002 summit has been titled the 'World Summit on Sustainable Development' remains to be seen.

Why are some of the world's major corporations drawn to such a problematic concept? First, we must admit that sustainable development is still largely unknown among most businesses around the world. Nor do those who know about it necessarily accept it readily or understand what it means for their companies. Yet some business leaders were drawn to the concept as they realized that not only was it not anti-growth but also it called for serious economic growth to meet the needs of the current population. Also, some warmed to the idea as they compared the issues involved in sustaining a planet with those involved in sustaining a corporation. Both require balancing acts between managing for the long term and managing for the short term. Companies can fail spectacularly—and become 'extinct'—if they get this wrong in either direction. Companies that live only in the present may not notice disruptive technologies coming their way, as happened when some of the big computer makers missed the advent of the personal computer. Yet companies that base their strategy on meeting future needs—as did many of the dot.coms in the late 1990s—may burn through their resources before a market based on those perceived needs emerges. Thus business leaders may have an experimental understanding of sustainable development that governments and citizens' groups lack.

Also, financial markets expect companies to grow or be taken over. But many corporate leaders have realized that there is little growth potential in using the same strategies of the past 30 years. As they search for new strategies, they find that sustain- CASE STUDY 1
Norsk Hydro
page 32
able development thinking opens new ways to grow.

However, this is not to claim that it is easy to sell sustainable development within the ranks of a company. Paul Tebo, vice president for safety, health, and environment at DuPont, finally created the term *sustainable growth* to get the message across to colleagues:

> Growth was very important. I tried *sustainability* and the business leaders saw it as status quo. I tried *sustainable development* and they viewed it as environmental sustainability. I tried *sustainable business* [but] growth is what organizations want—either you're growing or you're not and not growing is not a very good sit (Spencer-Cooke 2000).

When the Earth Summit came around in 1992, business wanted to be involved, partly to protect its own interests. The quotation at the beginning of this chapter says that sustainable development is about changes in resource exploitation, investments, technological development, and institutions. It is not surprising that business there-fore decided to take a keen interest in what was to transpire at Rio and to make sure that it was business-friendly.

The Business Council for Sustainable Development (BCSD) emerged after one of us, Swiss industrialist Stephan Schmidheiny, was asked to serve as the principal adviser for business and industry to the secretary general of the Summit, Maurice Strong. Not knowing quite how to fulfill such a responsibility, he rounded up some 48 other CEOs of major companies to create a group with two functions: spread the sustainable development message among business and produce business input for the Summit. Schmidheiny promised the BCSD group that they were a 'mission', not an organiza-tion, and would disband after Rio (see page 16). The International Chamber of Com-merce (ICC) also prepared business input for Rio. In 1993, a group of ICC member companies formed the World Industry Council for the Environment (WICE), which, in the beginning of 1995, merged with the BCSD to form the WBCSD.

The BCSD had its first meeting in the spring of 1991 and had to produce something by June 1992. This was a tall order for people who had not worked together before

Stephan Schmidheiny *it all started . . .*

66 It all started in 1990; I had come to a resting place in a decade-long job of turning a global construction materials business into a diversified portfolio of companies: banking, electronic instruments, watches, forestry, water systems, and some very different types of construction materials. Resting from the rat race of business, I could afford to think about such 'luxury' issues as a safe and clean environment.

I was in an introspective mood. The 1980s had been a bad time for the environment; we were told that rainforests and whales would not be with us much longer and that the climate was changing beyond recognition or predictability, but that none of this would matter because we would soon all be dead of skin cancer because of the hole in the ozone layer. That, at least, was the way the message came through to an industrialist not paying close attention.

However, the 1980s had been fairly kind to me and my attempts to change my business holdings. So I wondered privately, and then aloud in a speech I made in 1990, how we could create a world in which what was good for the planet was good for business, and vice versa.

Not many people heard my short address, made in the L-shaped hold of a noisy, creaking wooden ship tied up in Bergen, Norway, where the wealthier countries of Europe and North America were meeting to plan their approach to the 'Earth Summit' two years off; but one of the few who heard me was Maurice Strong, designated secretary general of the Summit. He was pleasantly surprised to hear someone suggest that perhaps gains for business did not necessarily have to be losses for the environment, and, again, vice versa.

My family later claimed, half-jokingly, that Maurice Strong invited himself to our house in Switzerland and would not leave until I had agreed to do his bidding. In truth, Maurice is far too shrewd and diplomatic to have to resort to such tactics. And what he wanted me to do attracted me. He wanted me to coordinate a message from business to his Summit and at the same time to spread the message of sustainability among business leaders. He was challenging me to put my efforts—and, as it turned out, some of my money—where my mouth had been in Bergen.

To spread those efforts, and any blame attached to the results, I began flying around the world signing up members for a group of chief executive officers (CEOs) we would call the Business Council for Sustainable Development (BCSD). I found it hard to get many developing-world members and hard to find many women as they were—and alas still are—under-represented at CEO level.

But eventually we had about 50 members, including the predecessors of my co-authors from DuPont and Shell. I had made prospective members only two promises. First, I would pay all expenses, as there was no time to negotiate dues—especially as we did not know what we were going to do. Second, I promised we would disband after Rio; I certainly was not starting a permanent organization.

In this chapter, we three offer a more sober account of the work of what is now the WBCSD. I wanted to counter that with my personal view. After their experience at Rio, most of the members decided that business had an important role in forging paths toward sustainable development and insisted that the council continue. So I insisted that members pay dues. Today, as Honorary Chairman, representing no company, I do not even pay dues.

So my two promises lie in ruins, but the WBCSD continues to seek ways by which companies can achieve economic vitality while helping the planet toward environmental and social vigor. 99

and who were busy running their own companies. One member actually suggested that, as they were living in a world of acute scientific, economic, and political uncertainty, they ought to issue a call for further research and then all go home. However, another member argued that what they all had in common was a trust in the workings of the marketplace. Indeed, the marketplace is pretty good at reflecting short-term economic realities: scarcity raises prices; demand raises prices; etc. However, it is not so good at reflecting environmental realities and longer-term economic realities. In fact, given the perversities of subsidies on such things as water and carbon-based energy, or the lack of ownership of certain crucial resources such as deep-sea fisheries, markets can send exactly the wrong signals. They can signal abundance of environmental goods and services when in fact the supply is dwindling dangerously.

As the economist and champion of free trade Jagdish Bhagwati (2000) wrote:

> Adam Smith's Invisible Hand will guide you to an efficient allocation of resources only if markets yield prices that reflect 'true' social costs. If there are market failures, as when a producer pollutes the air but does not have to pay for this pollution, then the invisible hand can lead you in the wrong direction. Or, to put it in flamboyant terms, it can immiserize [impoverish] you.

Not surprisingly, the member's description of a flawed market led to heated debate and got the council off and running in producing its report to the Earth Summit: *Changing Course: A Global Business Perspective on Development and the Environment* (Schmidheiny 1992). (See Chapter 1 for our concerns about today's market flaws.)

Given our initial focus on market and government failures, we called in *Changing Course* for:

- Progress toward full-cost pricing

- The use of economic instruments such as environmental taxes and charges and tradable permits instead of command-and-control regulations

- The phasing-out of perverse subsidies

- Changes to standard national accounts (such as gross domestic product [GDP]) to reflect environmental scarcity. (On market framework conditions, see Chapter 2.)

These are controversial issues about which CEOs are rarely required to speak out, much less to fight for. In fact, the WBCSD's speaking of them occasionally gets us into trouble, because critics complain that we may favor full-cost pricing in principle or before a summit but that our companies do not lobby for such a change in 'normal' times.

There is truth in this criticism, and it brings us to a point that we need to make early on. Business is as much a part of society as fish are part of the sea. We cannot swim too hard or for too long against prevailing currents. The prices of goods ought to reflect all the costs—financial, environmental, and social—involved in making them, using them, disposing of them or recycling them. The prices of services ought also to reflect their full costs. That way the market reflects environmental and social as well as financial realities. It reflects scarcities. It requires less government 'tinkering'.

Leadership companies would be happy with full-cost pricing because, being cleaner and more efficient than other companies, they would be producing goods and services for less.

However, business is only one of three pillars of society, the other two being civil society and government. We are not particularly happy with this so-called 'tripartite world', which is a fairly recent way of looking at the world. We feel that business is part of civil society and inseparable from it. But the point here is that all three sectors must progress at about the same speed. No one sector can get out ahead of the other two.

Today each sector waits on the others. Politicians tend not to run for office on promises of making the prices of goods reflect their real (higher) costs for the sake of sustainable development; consumers tend not to demand to pay such higher costs; business tends not to lobby lawmakers for higher prices.

We in the WBCSD feel we have been able to promote the goal of sustainable development in many helpful ways, often ahead of the demands of civil society and the regulations of government. However, there will not be real progress until business, government, and civil society team up in new and dynamic partnerships. (For a discussion of such partnerships, see Chapter 6.)

Getting practical; taking a stand

The early council began to search for a phrase that would pull sustainable development into the business agenda and make it more immediate and practical. A contest was held to find that phrase, and the winning phrase was *eco-efficiency*.

We want to save our discussion of eco-efficiency for later (Chapter 3). However, it was this conceptual breakthrough that began to convince us that a business case could actually be made for sustainable development. Before this, we had acknowledged that it was an important moral concept: ethically driven people have a responsibility to be concerned about the welfare of both their own generation and future generations, but we worried over whether this ethical duty could be linked to good business practice.

The concept of eco-efficiency began to suggest that such a linkage is possible. The notion does not cover the entire territory of sustainable development; it lacks a social side. It means producing more (goods and services and value-added) with less (resources, waste, and pollution). It is not a new idea, but by packaging it in terms of *eco*—referring both to *economics* and *ecology*—*efficiency*, which appeals to most business people, we had a new way of expressing the idea. It does not set limits, but it does encourage businesses to use less—making more available for other uses, now and in the future—while producing more. It can also make companies more competitive.

As we discuss in detail in later chapters, if resources are highly subsidized and waste and pollution go largely unpunished, then eco-efficiency may not improve the bottom line. Thus it makes sense for business leaders who feel that the world would be a better place, and that their companies would be more competitive if markets were to reward eco-efficiency better, to join organizations such as the WBCSD and call for such things as full-cost pricing and economic instruments to discourage waste and pollution.

A reviewer of one of our earlier publications concluded, admiringly, that the WBCSD was much like an old bait-and-switch confidence game. We told fellow business people that eco-efficiency was good for business. They began to take the bait. Then they thought better of it and complained that they could get along pretty well being dirty and wasteful. Yes, the council replied, but that is changing, and you had better get ready for changing times and, once you get ready, you may as well join us in fighting for those changes so they benefit your company.

This brings us to the point that members of the WBCSD—and of other business organizations promoting eco-efficiency and similar concepts—are not taking a short-term stand. Most feel they see the writing on numerous walls in the shape of various global management trends. They want to prepare their companies to take advantage of those trends—whether these trends be toward eco-efficiency, corporate social responsibility, transparency, or new partnerships with civil society and governments and so on. Having thus prepared themselves, it is in those CEOs' interests to advocate societal and governmental changes in the right direction to speed up the trends. Thus smart CEOs not only are going to orient their companies toward sustainability, but also are going to try to orient society toward sustainability.

Changing priorities

In its earlier manifestations, sustainable development was largely a green agenda. In the mid-1990s, this changed. It was not that companies suddenly noticed that they were ignoring the social side of the concept; it was more that many companies' problems were shifting from being environmental to social. There were charges of exploitation because of their use of child labor and because they were running sweat-shops, were union bashing, and were being particularly nasty neighbors 'out in the bush' where a mining or oil company might be the most powerful institution around. Whether as an effect of various scandals or as a cause, polls were showing that con-sumers were becoming as concerned over companies' worker-rights records as their records on environment and animal welfare (Gallop 1995).

Thus it was in a problem-solving mode that council members noticed that the social side of sustainable development was becoming as immediate and pressing an issue as its environmental side. In fact, given that the social side focuses on the needs of the *present*, it began to seem even more pressing. The council started work on how to integrate corporate social responsibility (CSR) issues into business strategies and everyday business activities. (For a discussion of CSR, see Chapter 4.)

The Royal Dutch/Shell Group of Companies (better known as 'Shell') was particu-larly hard hit at this time by environmental and social concerns. It had been criticized for planning to dispose of the Brent Spar oil storage buoy by sinking it in the North Atlantic and of being insensitive to minority rights in its operations in Nigeria. These challenges led Shell to change many of its ways of doing business. We asked Tom

CASE STUDY 2
SC Johnson
page 33

CASE STUDY 3
Shell
page 34

Philip Watts *the social side*

I have been involved with the WBCSD since 1996. At that time I had the feeling that work on the financial and environmental aspects of sustainable development were well advanced. There was certainly more to be done in both fields, but I felt that business had not been taking a hard enough look at the social side.

So I volunteered to help lead the Council's look at corporate social responsibility (CSR). We took the WBCSD into the heart of 'stakeholder dialogues' for the first time, listening to NGOs, religious groups and others in places like Taiwan and the Philippines. We heard what these people—not business people—thought of corporations' responsibilities.

We produced two reports to help companies create their own CSR strategies tailored to their own needs by offering policy and strategy approaches as well as basic inventory and implementation tools. We found a market, in that the Council has had some 20,000 requests for copies; the second report was translated into several languages, including Chinese and Portuguese and is being used by Harvard's Kennedy School of Government.

As WBCSD chairman for 2002 and 2003, I believe this is a good time to look at our past achievements and future challenges and have started systematic discussion with members on 'the way forward'—work we shall need to do if we are to begin live up to the title of this book and 'walk the talk'.

Profound change in the world now has business facing new scrutiny, risk, and challenge. As never before there is pressure for us to be profitable while keeping a 'human face'. Our stakeholders, including our employees, shareholders, and neighboring communities, demand increased transparency. The requests are consistent: show more, deliver more, and do it all quicker and more responsibly.

I believe the WBCSD has served business well in helping address the sustainability challenges of the past ten years. Our member CEOs continue to reaffirm their commitment to this leadership by 'walking the talk' in their own companies.

The Council and its members will keep on articulating the business case for sustainable development, informed by a deeper understanding from our projects and practical successes within our companies.

Getting down to specifics more and more typifies the WBCSD approach. Some projects explore sustainable development issues through the whole value chain in challenging specific sectors of industry such as forestry and cement. The Sustainable Mobility project, which looks into the state of transport systems worldwide, goes further. The report we issued last fall, *Mobility 2001* (CRA *et al.* 2001), tells us that significant action is needed now, as our own commercial future depends on our ability to adapt and meet these challenges. A feature of this project, and a hallmark of the WBCSD, is the use of stakeholder dialogue. We speak with people, inside and outside business, to deepen and broaden our understanding of the sustainability issues that face us all.

These projects provide insight into the WBCSD's past and future successes. They are directly in line with my conviction that business is not divorced from society. Rather, profitable and responsible business is a necessary contributor to a better world for all. I am confident that we can build on these successes and am sure that the WBCSD has the drive and purpose necessary to help us meet the challenges of the next ten years.

Delfgauuw, who retired in 2001 as vice president for sustainable development at Shell, what he thought was the most important of those changes. In his view it was:

> the transition to a listening mode, which is shorthand for a lot of underlying activities—the way we broke the corporate mold in reporting. I am very proud of that. We demonstrated that transparency works, as does sharing dilemmas and difficult and sensitive issues where we were not certain how to proceed. Sharing this with the outside world was not a sign of weakness but a sign of strength.

Delfgauuw was clear and eloquent about what had gone wrong, and about what can easily go wrong for any big company in a transparent world. He said the error we can make is:

> Insufficient listening to signals from the world around you: every single multinational in the world has a tendency to become too introspective, too internally focused, take things too much for granted. And one day you hit a brick wall and find out the world is moving much faster than you thought. We discovered there are no more 'local' issues anymore.

Delfgauuw regards the mid-1990s problems at Shell as 'the best things that ever happened to us, first because we've come out of it much, much stronger as a company, and second because it accelerated a great many needed corporate developments'. He finds the very frank *Shell Report* (Royal Dutch/Shell 2001), which catalogs the company's financial, environmental, and social strengths and weaknesses, to be 'just as important for internal as external reasons. We give insufficient attention to the need to capture the hearts and minds of our own employees.'

Looking at the social side of sustainable development is more important in countries with many social challenges. According to Carlos Poñe, head of ABB's operations in South Africa and Southern Africa, 'corporate social investment has been a priority for many years in South Africa because of the disparities in society':

> In recent years, environmental legislation provided a legal framework for companies in South Africa to comply with and is it speeding up this pillar of sustainability. We see more and more business involvement in sustainable development, making us believe that this is not only a question of persuasion, but also a question of businesses wanting to do things the right way for the right reasons.

He added that 'progress has been made mainly in South Africa thanks, in part, to voluntary agreements from business and public–private partnerships':

> A major barrier is that the economic climate in which we operate is not conducive to taking major steps in the area of sustainable development.

> We think our strength lies in initiating projects that will improve the quality of life of people living in the communities in which we operate. We place a high focus on involving community leaders in the project and empowering them to take leadership roles in the project.

Transparency and innovation as sustainable development issues

Rising public pressure in the 1990s around issues related to human rights and the impacts of globalization forced business to take a closer look at sustainable development, particularly its social dimension. Companies such as Shell, Nike, and BP were unprepared for consumers' ability to get their concerns into the boardrooms. In a globalized and transparent world, managing a company's reputation becomes a central element in managing a corporation.

Today, what a company does in a remote part of Africa one day may be headline TV news in the industrial world the next, so a company might as well make a virtue out of corporate frankness and transparency. In the long run, it is simpler and, like anything simpler, it is also cheaper and safer. Frankness and transparency get the attention of the staff, and gaining this attention makes it much easier to change corporate ethos. (On how companies learn to change, see Chapter 5.) Any company electing to follow such a policy of openness will also choose to be as responsible as possible in its social, environmental, and legal activities so that transparency is not a constant embarrassment.

To be socially responsible, a company must have open dialogue with those who have a stake in and are interested in the fortunes of the company. Share-owners, employees, customers, and suppliers are obviously 'stakeholders', to use the jargon, but so are neighbors, citizens and citizen organizations, and governments in their various forms. One cannot have a dialogue for long with all these groups and be secretive successfully; and being more transparent makes it hard to be environmentally careless or anti-social. So transparency becomes an issue for a sustainability-driven company.

Realizing this, many companies have begun to change the way in which they report to the public and shareholders. First, some have started adding environmental sections to their annual reports, if only a formal policy statement. Some have gone on to produce separate, annual environmental reports which, in turn, has led some companies to begin to report on social issues. Now some companies offer 'sustainability reports' that cover financial, environmental, and social progress—the 'triple bottom line' of sustainable development (see Figure 1).

These reports reflect what companies want to say, so the indicators used and the presentation of performance data vary a great deal and make comparisons between companies difficult. The use of auditing firms to check environmental and even social data, as well as financial data, can be of some help. Yet many see these reports as being limited in terms of the help they can provide for those trying to assess the risks associated with the operations of companies. These problems are being addressed as reporting companies are beginning to relate their performance against such indicators as volume of emissions or waste per unit of volume or value of production. The Global Reporting Initiative (GRI), in which UNEP, the non-governmental organization (NGO) the Coalition for Environmentally Responsible Economies (CERES), the WBCSD and individual companies are all participating, is trying to bring rigor and comparability to such reporting. The reports, being global in nature, are also of limited use to communities trying to find out the local effects of corporate activity, so companies will need to seek ways of adapting their reports to meet different needs.

CASE STUDY 33
Global
Reporting
Initiative
page 163

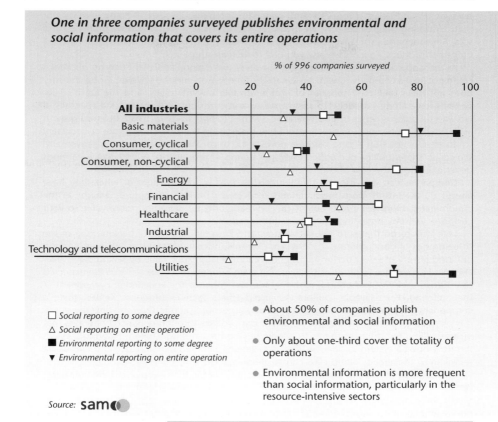

One in three companies surveyed publishes environmental and social information that covers its entire operations

Figure 1 **ENVIRONMENTAL AND SOCIAL REPORTING**

Innovation is also a sustainability issue. First, sustainability requires new products and services that are less greedy of natural resources, create less pollution and waste, and are more affordable to poor people. (On innovation, see Chapter 8; on making markets work for all, see Chapter 10.) Second, given the transparency imperative, innovations of a radical nature—especially those affecting basic human concerns such as food, healthcare, and reproduction—can no longer spring suddenly from corporate headquarters but must be developed with stakeholder advice and buy-in. There is a tricky balancing act between transparency and maintaining a company's competitive advantage.

Sustainability's business case is strengthened by the ways in which thinking of sustainable human progress encourages us toward innovation. It offers business opportunity, and it pushes companies toward thinking about more 'sustaining' forms of energy, agriculture, construction, mobility, and forestry. The relatively straightforward concept of eco-efficiency has already encouraged some companies to make radical

Chad Holliday *less is more*

DuPont is 200 years old in 2002. For most of our first century we were a manufacturer of explosives. At the start of the 20th century, however, we had begun the shift to what would become a world-class chemicals and materials company. Like most companies in our industry during the past century, we measured success by how much stuff we produced and sold. Revenues and profits were directly tied to throughput of energy and raw materials and output of product. To increase one you had to increase the other.

As we approached the 21st century, however, we recognized that such an approach could not lead a company toward sustainability. One reason was the obvious: global industry does not have unlimited supplies of non-renewable raw materials, and the Earth's eco-systems have limited capacity to absorb waste and emissions. But, more fundamentally, if we wanted our *businesses* to be sustainable, we had to find a way to create business growth as measured by revenues and earnings while minimizing the pounds of product necessary to do so. Our solution was to devise a new metric to measure performance improvement. We call it 'shareholder value added (SVA) per pound of production' (where SVA is earnings generated above the cost of capital).

Companies can increase the numerator (the SVA) by doing more of what they have always done—selling more products and services. However, with pounds weight as the denominator, then real improvement can be made only by delivering more value to your customer without increasing the pounds produced.

One way to do that is to sell knowledge, and knowledge intensity became one of the three prongs of our corporate strategy. For example, our safety resources business is taking our long history of safety performance and creating shareholder value by selling our knowledge and experience to other companies. But even business units that sell *stuff* are expected to improve their SVA per pound, and they too can enhance the knowledge component of their offering. For example, DuPont Advanced Fibers Systems produces Kevlar® fiber, a component of protective clothing, among many other applications. Over the next five years, it is planned to double the SVA per pound of this product through enhanced offerings that include selling hazard assessments to people buying the clothing. DuPont Flooring Services has developed a system to offer certified installation, patented maintenance and end-of-life recycling to the already world-class carpet offering of DuPont Antron®.

The concept of SVA per pound is a revolutionary metric for a manufacturing company, but it is not our only way of driving toward sustainability. Another prong of our strategy is productivity improvement—really basic eco-efficiency. In a general sense, most productivity improvements in manufacturing contribute to sustainability. Whenever you can maintain or increase production with lower levels of input or capital investment you are probably moving in the direction of sustainability, one way or another. By the end of 2001 we had over 5,500 of what we call Six-Sigma projects in place that are focused on eliminating defects in all aspects of our operations. What is key, though, is that we have come to consider waste and emissions, in and of themselves, as *defects* in our production processes. One business unit, White Pigments, estimates that 70% of its Six-Sigma projects result in environmental footprint reductions, including reduced energy and water use and reduced waste and emissions.

Our third strategic prong is integrated science. We have for over a century made products and profits by integrating chemistry and physics. Now we are focusing on integrating chemistry, biology, physics, and information to create products that can make a difference in people's lives. One new product line, Sorona® fiber, will soon use a biological process to obtain a key intermediate. Essentially, we will be fermenting corn sugar, a renewable resource, to create a key component of a recyclable polyester fiber. Previously, such ingredients would have been produced from petrochemicals. Our Qualicon business is integrating chemistry and biotechnology to create commercial tests that can rapidly detect and fingerprint pathogens in food.

We at DuPont have a long way to go in the journey to true sustainability, but we believe it can be done. There are many companies operating profitably today without giving sustainability a second thought. However, we believe that such companies will encounter major obstacles to growth and acceptance as the new century progresses. For us at DuPont the question of whether sustainability improves the bottom line is not asked anymore. We are committed to sustainable growth. That is how we will get our bottom line, and that is how we will create value for our shareholders and for society.

shifts from maximizing sales to selling no *thing* at all—and being cleaner and more profitable in the process. Instead of selling things, they sell services, or they lease things, or both. Companies that once sold auto paint to car companies now sell the service of painting the cars. So where once they improved the bottom line by maximizing cans of paint sold, they now improve the bottom line by minimizing the use of paint per car.

Manufacturing companies have the best opportunities for using eco-efficiency thinking to innovate toward cost savings, but service companies can also benefit, often in surprising ways. When Salomon Smith Barney (SSB) prepared to furnish new offices in London's Canary Wharf, the information technology (IT) department wanted to give its traders sleek, flat-front liquid-crystal display (LCD) monitors, which take up far less space than ordinary cathode-ray tube (CRT) monitors, but the cost was difficult to justify. LCDs cost about $3,000 each, whereas CRTs are only about $500. By digging a little deeper, the company found that LCDs use one-third the energy of CRTs. The fancy monitors also emit much less heat than CRTs, which means that SSB did not have to pay as much to cool the new building. These cost savings were enough to justify the purchase.

Business guru and Harvard Business School professor Michael Porter argues that well-framed environmental regulations can encourage innovation and thus make businesses and nations more competitive (Porter and van der Linde 1995a). They can improve a firm's competitive position in a number of ways. They may direct the firm's attention to the cost of inefficient use of resources and encourage the collection of more information about waste—for example, by increasing the number of activities that are monitored or by installing higher-quality systems and devices for monitoring and reporting. When companies improve their measurement and assessment methods to detect environmental costs and benefits, they raise corporate awareness and increase the incentive to encourage and reward innovations that enhance resource productivity.

Taking eco-efficiency and the environment seriously can, and should, lead to strategic corporate innovation. According to Stuart Hart (2001), a professor of strategic management and director of the Sustainable Enterprise Initiative at the University of North Carolina's Kenan-Flagler Business School, 'The environmental revolution has been almost three decades in the making and it has changed forever how companies do business.' He adds that:

> those who think that sustainability is only a matter of pollution control are missing the bigger picture. Rarely is greening linked to strategy or technological development and, as a result, most companies fail to recognize opportunities of potentially staggering proportions.

(For a discussion of business-like responses to global environmental issues, see Chapter 9.)

The bigger picture

The new paradigm of sustainable progress has changed the ways in which some companies think about doing business. These changes range from:

- Moving from seeing only costs and difficulties in the concept of sustainable development to seeing savings and opportunities

- Evolving from using end-of-pipe approaches to pollution to using cleaner, more efficient technologies throughout entire production systems and, further, seeking to make sustainable development integral to business development

- Changing from linear, 'throughput' approaches to systems and closed-loop approaches

- Moving from seeing environmental and social issues as the responsibility of technical departments or experts to seeing these issues as company-wide responsibilities

- Changing premises of confidentiality to ones of openness and transparency

- Changing from narrow lobbying to more open discussions with stakeholders

A vision of sustainable development as opportunity rather than burden is proving to be a source of competitive advantage. Bill Ford, great-grandson of Henry Ford and now chairman of the namesake company, stated at a CERES meeting that his company's participation in environmental programs has confirmed his 'strong belief that—in addition to being the right thing to do—preserving the environment is a competitive advantage and a major business opportunity' (in Mitchell Moore 2001).

By capitalizing on these assets, a company stands to gain customer success, brand strength, first-mover advantage, motivated employees, and potentially more profits. The first step, however, is recognizing that both the political agenda and the business

CASE STUDY 4
MeadWestvaco
page 36

agenda are driving the move toward sustainability and its inherent opportunities. The business case must be made persuasively by business itself to win the commitment and support of line managers. Only with that kind of support can business win the confidence of the markets—the ultimate judge of how well business is exploiting opportunities.

The new entrepreneurs

Michael Porter (1980), Gary Hamel and C.K. Pralahad (Hamel and Pralahad 1984) have all made powerful distinctions between two management types. The classic managers, the majority, aim for their business objectives at the lowest cost. They are 'denominator managers'. Their pride is in achieving results at low cost or below budget. They tend to adopt realistic objectives, proven approaches, and incremental improvement.

Meanwhile, the innovators or shapers drive for the highest impact out of a given investment. They are 'numerator managers', a minority of leaders in their sectors. They often exceed their goals and sometimes their budgets. Both types of manager confront the same challenge with similar budgets but their different world-views influence the results obtained and competitive strength in extremely different ways.

With regard to sustainable development as with other areas, it is the innovative manager who can be described as the entrepreneur, capable of seeing the next point on the curve and moving quickly to gain a competitive advantage. Such individuals keep abreast of rapid changes and potential markets by anticipating trends in regulations and standards, becoming familiar with international environmental agreements and monitoring rapid technological advances, such as those now taking place in electronics and photovoltaics. They also watch for economic and social trends that are 'pulling' the development of sustainable technologies. These include higher, market-based prices for many resources and a move by governments away from regulation toward the use of economic instruments and performance standards (Andersen 2001).

The person with an entrepreneurial vision also extends his or her attention to the social dimension of the triple bottom line by constantly evaluating relationships and spotting the need for engagement with a wide variety of stakeholders—including his or her own employees. As with the environment, DuPont's Paul Tebo views social issues through a tightly focused business lens:

> Corporate social responsibility? That's the right to operate and grow. Influencing customers and suppliers? That's improved efficiency along the value chain. Products and services that make lives better and reach a greater percentage of the world? Expanded markets and new customers.

Another entrepreneur who has fought the mainstream to bring forward his sustainable development agenda is Pasquale Pistorio, CEO of the Swiss-based STMicroelectronics. His vision is to turn the company into a 'zero-equivalent carbon dioxide emission company' by 2010—while still maintaining a leading market share. Pistorio intends to do this by continuous improvement of energy efficiency in company processes (a 5% annual reduction of energy per unit of output) and increased use of alternative and renewable energy sources. The recipe also includes compensating for the company's remaining carbon dioxide emissions by planting about 35,000 ha of land with trees (Pistorio 2001). 'If we achieve those goals, we calculate that we shall save close to $1 billion on our energy costs between 1994 and 2010', reported Pistorio.

Pistorio has math behind his vision. In 1995, the company began to devote an average of 2% of its annual capital investment—a total of more than $3 billion a year in 2000—to improving STMicroelectronics' environmental performance:

> Thanks to these measures, the planet has been spared the burden of another 100-megawatt power plant; the water we have saved could quench the thirst of 50 million people a year. We are using 28% less electricity and 45% less water than in 1994 for the same output. This translates, with a large increase in volume today, into a saving of $50 million in 2000 alone (Pistorio 2001).

On average, says Pistorio, investment in energy conservation pays back within 2.5 years, adding that 'this proves the validity of the stance we have taken for years: ecology is free'.

Tebo and Pistorio demonstrate the three fundamental skills of the entrepreneur: creation of far-sightedness, increasing one's ability to act in time and make an optimal change in behavior. Entrepreneurs do not accept the world as it is. They do not follow others' maps. They look at the world as components of what they can create from the various parts. They are creative destroyers; they lean on the system in order to outperform it—a highly desirable quality in a competitive and quickly changing world.

The bottom line

'Businesses are ultimately interested in one thing: profits', *The Economist* stated in an article on globalization:

> The business-bashing NGOs are right about that. If businesses think that treating their customers and staff well, or adopting a policy of 'corporate social responsibility' or using ecologically friendly stationery will add to their profits, they will do it. Otherwise they will not . . . If firms have to compete with rivals for customers and workers, then they will indeed worry about their reputation for quality and fair dealing—even if they do not value those things in themselves. Competition will make them behave as if they did (*Economist* 2001h: 4).

The question remains whether a profit or shareholder value case can be made for the corporate pursuit of sustainability. This is a crucial question for the WBCSD, which exists partly to make 'the business case' for sustainable development (WBCSD 2001h).

First, it is worth pointing out that, contrary to popular opinion, companies tend to get involved in activities long before they can prove the business case for doing it. As Paul Gilding, director of the sustainability consultancy ECOS Corp. of Australia, points out:

> You couldn't make the business case at the beginning for the total quality management movement in the 1970s or the IT movement in the 1980s. This is true of any major trend in the history of business over the past 20 to 30 years. Before an idea begins to gain traction among the leadership of companies, there is always a fierce debate on the business case.

Gilding believes that many people in a variety of industries are coming to the same conclusion: a sustainable development approach brings value to the company. He adds that:

> That is important, because, ultimately, this is about judgment. Business is all about judgment. It's not about an analytical framework, because, if every-thing were proven, competition wouldn't exist. For instance, if a company changes CEOs, you get a different strategy, but the only thing that's changed is one person's judgment. It is not because that person had a different way of adding up the numbers.

'The business case is still more anecdotal than factual', says Wayne Visser, the director of sustainability services for the international auditing and business advisory firm KPMG's operations in South Africa.

> While good sustainability practices are increasingly being associated with good management practices, especially in terms of corporate governance, the link is still tentative. The business case also varies by country and region.

Among the factors that determine the business case are: strength of sustainable development legislation, degree of enforcement, extent of litigation, empowerment and activism of communities, and awareness of financial analysts. These elements tend to be more lacking in the South than the North.

However, a growing number of studies show a link between the profitability of a company and its pursuit of social and environmental goals. But no study can 'prove' that pursuing sustainability goals makes a company more profitable. First, there are too many variables. Second, it is impossible to prove the direction of the flow of causality. Does a company become profitable and thus enjoy the luxury of being able to worry about environmental and social issues or does the pursuit of sustainability make a company more profitable for all the reasons we have listed earlier in this chapter?

The London-based group SustainAbility was willing to only go so far in a recent report as to admit that 'sustainable development performance does not detract from a firm's obligation to its shareholders. The impact of sustainable development performance on shareholder value is neutral at worst and in some instances has been shown to add considerable value' (SustainAbility/UNEP 2001). It argues that the sustainability performance of a company matters a great deal in that shareholder value is driven by brand value and reputation, risk profile, and customer attraction—all of which are among the 'intangible assets' that define sustainable development. According to SustainAbility, 'the impact of sustainable development performance on shareholder value is likely to be long-term. Day traders won't be looking for companies with strong sustainable development performance.' It adds that 'The more a company can demonstrate the anticipated benefits of sustainability activities and/or investments, the more likely the markets will recognize these links. If investors believe it to be true, it will be true.'

Visser of KPMG argues that 'Financial markets are broadly more aware of unsustainable corporate practices and the effect these could have on company performance, through attracting liabilities and reputational damage':

> We have seen a marked increase in awareness of sustainability issues in due diligence investigations associated with various financial transactions. In addition, there is a niche in the financial markets that is growing exponentially, which specifically targets investments in sustainable companies, through a variety of sustainability funding mechanisms.

Innovest Strategic Value Advisors, an international investment firm specializing in environmental finance and investment opportunities, is trying to develop some hard numbers for the environmental side of sustainable development. It uses up to 60 environmental criteria to develop its EcoValue21 ratings of AAA (outperform) to CCC (underperform) on over 1,000 domestic and international equities. Depending on the sector, companies with above-average EcoValue21 ratings have consistently outperformed lower-rated companies by 300 to 2,500 basis points per year. Innovest claims that it is able to uncover hidden value and risk potential among companies using evaluation techniques often ignored by mainstream Wall Street analysts. Its methodology has been both back-tested and β-tested by Morgan Stanley and Pricewaterhouse-Coopers. According to Peter Wilkes, business development managing director of Innovest:

> Innovest has found that corporate management teams that are dealing with their complex environmental issues on a proactive and profitable basis are also usually running the rest of the business well. Therefore, our research can be used to further define superior management, which of course is a creator of long-term value and appreciating stock prices.

For example, in 2001, top environmental performers in Innovest's annual survey of the global metals and mining industry posted accumulated returns over 60% higher than environmental laggards over a three-year period. Total returns per share on equity and earnings were also found to correlate positively with environmental leadership (*PR Newswire* 2001).

Going mainstream

CASE STUDY 5
Dow Jones
page 37

Since its launch in 1999, when the Dow Jones Sustainability Index (DJSI) began tracking the performance of the leading sustainability-driven companies worldwide, the index has consistently outperformed the Dow Jones Global Index (DJGI) World.

Reto Ringger, CEO of Swiss-based SAM Sustainable Asset Management that co-founded the DJSI along with Dow Jones & Company, says that the success of the index makes it clear that sustainability is moving into mainstream asset management, stating that 'a growing number of investors now share our conviction that integrating economic, environmental, and social success factors into business strategy can result in competitive advantage'.

However, Ringger is willing to admit that sustainability funds represent less than 1% of the entire market, and indexes such as the DJSI still have to prove their worth to a skeptical mainstream financial community. He points out that 'sustainability doesn't have a track record. It is very new, at least for the financial markets. A track record of just two to three years is too little to bring many assets into the process', predicting that 'it will take another few years before we gain substantial interest'. He goes on to say that 'most players have the perception that all that goes along with green and sustainability is losing performance and giving up some of the upside. Losing that perception takes time.' Making progress will depend on coming up with some of the numbers that financial analysts value so highly. The triple bottom line, says Ringger, is a challenging concept to measure and quantify:

> A lot of our criteria are qualitative. A lot of financial markets are used to juggling numbers and it is very difficult to come by hard numbers with sustainable development. How can you measure the reputation that comes out of sustainability? Or the satisfaction of employees? Or the innovation that comes out of eco-efficiency?

Yet Ringger remains optimistic that the proactive approach of sustainable development performance will pay off, not just for corporations that take that approach but for investors as well. The GRI (see page 22), which has set itself the task of standardizing the elements contained in a sustainability report, should go some way in helping analysts make sense of the information that lands on their desks.

Between September 2000 and September 2001, there was a doubling of the number of asset managers who use the DJSI for a variety of investment products, including mutual funds, equity baskets, certificates, and segregated accounts. Today there

During the past five years the DJSI consistently outperformed the DJGI in bull and bear market situations

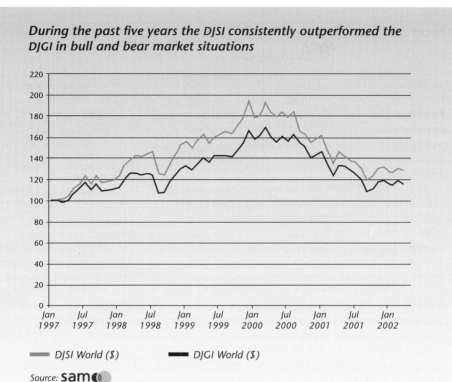

DJSI World ($)   DJGI World ($)

Source: **sam**

Figure 2 **PERFORMANCE HISTORY OF THE DOW JONES SUSTAINABILITY INDEX (DJSI): WORLD**

are about 40 well-known financial institutions in 12 countries that have licensed the DJSI to manage sustainability-driven portfolios.

Increasingly, companies are jostling for an opportunity to be included in the index. They like being able to attract long-term shareholders, being seen as industry leaders, improving their reputations with legislators, customers, and employees and attracting customer and employee loyalty.

CASE STUDY 1
Norsk Hydro
a business case for sustainable development

Norsk Hydro operates globally in environmentally sensitive and technically complex fields such as plant nutrients, offshore oil and gas, aluminum, magnesium, and petrochemicals. Because of the company's size in Norway—essentially a large fish in a small pond—and because of Norway's early resolve to rectify environmental ills, and exceptionally diligent regulatory authorities, the company was an early target for the green movement. Norsk Hydro has been extensively regulated, monitored, and challenged.

In response to these and other emerging pressures, Norsk Hydro's environmental and sustainability work evolved in four phases. In Phase 1, the 'repairs' phase, efforts were concentrated on cleaning up local pollution and amending 'sins of the past'. In Phase 2, the 'preventive' phase, the focus changed to developing and installing 'cleaner technology'—technology that prevents pollution from occurring in the first place. Phase 3, the 'business development' phase, concentrated on analyzing and minimizing the environmental impact of products throughout their entire life-cycle, from raw materials, through production and use, to their subsequent recycling or deposition. In Phase 4, the 'globalization' phase, Norsk Hydro began addressing the challenges of globalization of economies and markets, as well as global environmental issues such as climate change and the Kyoto Protocol. Each phase has provided Norsk Hydro with organizational experiences and knowledge.

The first ('repairs') phase did not result from a business strategy, nor were its projects closely linked to business activities. In fact, the opposite occurred, with the individual projects adding up to become the environmental strategy. These projects were managed internally as a functional-driven process and implemented on an ad hoc basis. However, when the media, NGOs, and authorities highlighted some of the environmental issues, it became clear that top management would have to become more involved. Norsk Hydro had long been a 'closed' company regarding environmental issues. A change of direction and openness was necessary.

The second ('preventive') phase made environmental work a key part of operations, to be integrated throughout the organization. Clear lines of responsibility were established, goals set, reporting improved, results analyzed, and organizational expertise developed. Systematic work on quality management was undertaken in the 1980s, and the company experienced, as did many others, that 'what gets measured, gets done'. Pockets of excellence were emerging; however, organization-wide performance improvements were not yet strong enough. The challenge was to identify best practice internally and externally and to facilitate rapid adoption throughout the company.

In the third ('business development') phase, the focus extended to applying experience and expertise to the life-cycle aspect of products. Environmental care, in its broadest sense, was being transformed into an important strategic business issue. Environmental issues took on a firm position as an important part of the strategic decision-making process. Through life-cycle analysis, Norsk Hydro gained insights that enabled application of the most advanced knowledge. The company also sought to establish closer links between customers, business needs, and research and development activities. It worked to stimulate creativity within the organization and in external research institutions. This extended across traditional organizational barriers and traditional scientific disciplines to enhance conceptual and technological innovation. It was recognized that the potential for new commercial opportunities would arise from new combinations of existing and emerging technologies.

The fourth ('globalization') phase shifted the focus to bringing together the three pillars of sustainable development: economic, environmental , and social responsibility. This ongoing phase addresses more broadly the issues of globalization, and many new emerging issues in addition to the previously recognized environmental concerns. Ethical challenges are more pronounced when companies establish operations in regions with clear cultural differences and in developing countries. Themes such as human rights and considerations for the indigenous population and other questions related to values are raised. Coming to developing countries with a background in Norwegian culture and industry is difficult.

This phase has required greater collaboration and increased openness. Norsk Hydro recognized that, if a company were to create business value from its efforts, environmental and social issues could not be handled in isolation. 'As a business, we have shifted our focus from tackling individual issues to the systematic integration of sustainable conduct into our business operations and our management systems', states Egil Myklebust, president and CEO of Norsk Hydro. He goes on to say that:

> In the course of my ten years at Norsk Hydro, I increasingly recognized that development trends, in connection with population growth, environmental hazards, social differences, globalization, greater transparency in industry and society in general, plus ever-increasing competition, lead to the emergence of a new agenda for managing the industrial enterprises of the future.

CASE STUDY 2
SC Johnson *sustainable communities*

Racine, Wisconsin, is the world headquarters for the 116-year-old SC Johnson family enterprises. By 1996 Racine was experiencing many of the same problems of other mid-sized, industrialized US cities at that time: growing crime rates; rising unemployment (largely because of the lack of skilled labor); poorly performing public schools; and increasing concerns about pollution.

The local economy and businesses felt the pain: Racine was less attractive to new businesses and top talent; factories were being vacated, leaving brownfields behind; and the local tax base was stagnating. The situation was hard to square with SC Johnson's core value: 'Every place should be a better place because we are there.'

Around this time, the US President's Council on Sustainable Development (PCSD), in which SC Johnson was active, was focusing on local communities and their critical role in 'advancing prosperity, opportunity, and a healthy environment' across the nation. Through its study of local sustainability efforts, the PCSD found that an energized and engaged citizenry—as opposed to local government officials—were the primary drivers of change for the better. Further, successful communities had embraced sustainability as a process of collaboration among all stakeholders. Importantly, the PCSD realized that sustainability happens one community at a time and that it does not look the same everywhere, reinforcing the characterization of sustainability as 'think global, act local'.

Spurred on by this movement in other local US cities, SC Johnson became the catalyst for Sustainable Racine, a local movement that grew into an organization to ensure civic and citizen engagement in helping to make Racine an even better place to live. Within a year, a long-term community vision, key local priorities, and defined action plans were supported and were being implemented by the broad spectrum of stakeholders representing the community's rich diversity.

Today, for the first time in two decades, local teachers and parents are working together for better student performance and teacher training. Commercial vacancy rates in downtown Racine have fallen from 46% to 18%; and four municipalities in the Greater Racine Area have forged a landmark agreement to share water and sewer costs and services, which will mean lower costs for residents overall.

Sustainable Racine is the company's first civic approach to sustainability and builds on its heritage of sustainability efforts in local communities worldwide. For instance, in South Africa, SC Johnson has reduced solid wastes by 68% and air emissions by 33% since 1990. Socially, it identifies and supports community leaders; provides a teacher for 40 HIV-positive orphans and daily meals for 300 children; and funds the Good Shepherd Sisters to operate an adult education center where more than 1,000 women have achieved certificates for employable skills.

As multinationals move forward on the road to sustainability, SC Johnson's global commitment to living its core value of 'every place should be a better place because we are there' provides an inspirational successful model of sustainable development leadership.

CASE STUDY 3

Shell *community development in Nigeria*

Operating in Nigeria has required a shift in approach for Shell. It is not simply ecological sustainability that needs to be addressed; the business case for sustainable development in Nigeria rests heavily on social elements. Shell has recognized that community development is required for both the company and the region to develop in a sustainable manner.

The Shell Petroleum Development Company of Nigeria Limited (SPDC) is the largest oil and gas company in Nigeria, accounting for some 40% of the country's oil production and about 53% of Nigeria's hydrocarbon reserve base. SPDC is the operator of a joint venture involving the Nigerian National Petroleum Corporation (which holds 55% of the venture), Shell (30%), Elf (10%), and Agip (5%).

The company's operations are concentrated in the Niger Delta, the population of which is about seven million people, largely drawn from some 20 different ethnic minority groups. There are around 1,600 long-settled communities in the area. There is a history of ethnic conflict in the region and also a long-standing feeling that not enough of the Nigerian government's revenues from oil have been invested back into the Niger Delta. Both these factors combine to make the area a challenging place in which to work.

SPDC has had a long history of assisting the communities in which it operates. However, discussions with NGOs, resulting in part from contacts made during the Ogoni crisis—a crisis that led to the execution of Ken Saro Wiwa—convinced the company that it needed to change its approach—from community assistance to community development. The main objectives of this change in approach were to:

- Help communities to help themselves develop in a more sustainable way

- Adopt a participatory approach to the selection, development, and implementation of community projects

- Work in partnership with others

- Adopt an open and consultative way of working

With these objectives in mind, SPDC began in 1997 by commissioning an external review of the way in which it assisted communities. This led to the formation of a new community development department, staffed by development professionals. This in turn led to new ways of working with the communities—with the adoption of participatory techniques to help communities decide their development priorities.

New ways of delivering community projects also began, using partnerships formed with local community-based organizations, NGOs, developmental agencies, and government departments. Furthermore, a spirit of openness and transparency was encouraged by:

- The publication of an annual report on the company's social and environmental performance (the SPDC *People and the Environment* report)

- A yearly stakeholder consultation workshop to review SPDC's programs and performance

- The co-hosting, with the UNDP, of a partners' roundtable in the Niger Delta

- SPDC's participation in the World Bank's Business Partners for Development program

- Annual appraisals of community projects implemented during a given year (the 2000 appraisal was conducted by independent, external experts, and future appraisals will follow this practice)

The 2000 appraisal of SPDC's $60 million community development program commended the company for its openness and observed that the company demonstrated a number of best practices. The number of community-based project management committees continues to grow (200 in 2000), as does the number of international and local partners providing expert help and implementing projects (49 in 2000).

Much has been achieved, but much more remains to be done in terms of spreading good practice and raising project success rates. The Niger Delta remains a difficult place in which to work but, in partnership with its stakeholders, SPDC will continue its drive to improve the lives of its host communities and increase its business in the region.

CASE STUDY 4

MeadWestvaco *its Brazilian subsidiary Rigesa*

Rigesa is a wholly owned Brazilian subsidiary of the MeadWestvaco Corporation. A family-owned business established in 1942, Rigesa had become financially over-extended by 1953, at which time the former Westvaco Corporation acquired it. The company consisted of a pulp mill making about ten tonnes of pulp a day from bagasse (waste sugar-cane fiber), which was then used to make corrugated con-tainers. Land ownership was limited to the factory site in Valinhos, São Paulo State, in south-eastern Brazil. A total of $2.8 million was invested to purchase the business and provide working capital.

Solely on its own earnings, Rigesa has developed under Westvaco's and Mead-Westvaco's nearly 50 years of ownership into the most profitable producer of corru-gated containers and folding cartons in Brazil, basing its operations on environmental and social sustainability.

A global code of conduct is reviewed and signed each year by each salaried employee and is discussed with workers employed by the hour. Environmental excel-lence in operating manufacturing facilities and sustainable forestry practices is a key element of the code and other company policies.

Profits from the mill have been used to expand production capacity and to develop the forest resources that replaced bagasse. With new thinking about plantation sustainability and the need to protect ecosystems, Rigesa designed a forestry program to plant high-quality trees on acquired depleted forests and farmland. In conjunction with its parent company, Rigesa began forest research with the evaluation of more than 100 hardwood and conifer forest tree species to find the best combination of fiber productivity and adaptation to the local environment.

The forest estate began with the purchase of lands in Santa Catarina and Paraná States, over 1,600 km from the Amazon rainforest. In 1974, a new pulp and paper-board mill was established in Três Barras, Santa Catarina. The company's 48,000 ha of ownership now includes over 13,000 ha of native woodland managed as bio-reserves. MeadWestvaco's award-winning Ecosystem-Based Multiple Use Forest Man-agement™ concept is used in conjunction with Brazilian plans to integrate water, habitat, and biodiversity goals across the landscape, while supplying 100% of the fiber required and supporting the local forestry industries with high-value pine saw-logs to export value-added products to the USA and Europe.

In recent years Rigesa has implemented a landowner assistance program with private farmers in the area. Future wood supplies will increasingly come from private farmers. Investments in new technologies were aimed at minimizing fiber use while at the same time turning out products that meet stringent quality-control tests. Today, Rigesa is a leading supplier of distinctive packaging for domestic and export markets. It has grown to include two paper mills, four box plants, two folding-carton plants, and one micro-corrugated plant, all using advanced manufacturing technol-ogies.

Rigesa's 2,000 employees constitute a significant part of the local workforce and economy in which the plants are located. The company has maintained a strong 'people focus' since its beginning, offering training and professional development to local employees, including assistance schemes to promote the health of employees and their families. Rigesa established supplemental schools, producing many high-school graduates among employees and their families. Rigesa has also worked with more than 26,000 students and 1,100 teachers in recent years to raise awareness of conservation through the Project Learning Tree, a program developed by the American Forest Foundation and introduced to Brazil by Rigesa.

When Rigesa bought land near Três Barras, the region was fairly impoverished. The timber had been cut without regeneration in the 1920s. When the Três Barras paper mill was built during the period 1972–74 the roads were of dirt, and most employees walked or cycled to work. Electricity and running water were sparse. Today, roads are paved; workers' homes have electricity, running water, and satellite TV; and ancillary businesses have arisen to generate additional employment. Unionized employees earn salaries that are above average for the region. Factory and forest operations, measured by US Occupational Safety and Health Administration standards and Brazilian safety rules, have lower accident levels than most comparable US operations.

Rigesa now stands as an example of a business with the principles of sustainability clearly woven into its fabric, with its operations based on the three pillars of economic, social, and environmental progress. The company proves that sustainable development did not begin at Rio.

CASE STUDY 5

Dow Jones Sustainability Indexes

In August 1999 Zurich-based SAM Sustainable Asset Management joined forces with Dow Jones & Company to establish the Dow Jones Sustainability World Indexes (DJSI World), the first major benchmark tracking the financial performance of sustainability leaders on a global basis.

The launch of the Dow Jones Sustainability Indexes (DJSIs) was a milestone in proving that corporate sustainability performance is a concept in which one can invest with confidence. Two years later, the two partners were joined by leading European index provider, STOXX Ltd, to launch the Dow Jones STOXX Sustainability Indexes (DJSI STOXX) as benchmarks for European sustainability investments.

DJSI World is made up from the top 10% of the biggest 2,500 companies in the Dow Jones Global Index (DJGI), including 307 companies from 62 industries in 26 countries, with a combined market capitalization of $5.5 trillion as of 31 January 2002. The DJSI STOXX tracks the leading 20% of the companies in the Dow Jones STOXX 600 index.

As sustainability concepts move into mainstream asset management and as the demand for sustainability funds increases, investors are looking for indicators of a company's value creation beyond economic parameters. The DJSI provides a global, rational, and flexible index to benchmark the performance of investments in sustainability-driven companies, identifying those firms that create long-term shareholder value by embracing opportunities and managing risks deriving from economic, environmental, and social developments.

Companies also benefit. Firms in the index are recognized by important stakeholder groups as being industry leaders in strategic environmental, social, and economic dimensions. In a growing 'stakeholder' world, such an index acknowledges those industry leaders based on reliable in-depth analysis and publicly available information; companies are then entitled to use the official 'Member of DJSI' label.

The DJSI is based on a three-tiered analysis, evaluating companies on their economic performance as well as environmental and social indicators. Identification of companies for the DJSI is based on the corporate sustainability assessment conducted by SAM, through the SAM corporate sustainability questionnaire. Research at SAM begins with the assessment of industry-specific trends and driving forces impacting each sector. The use of industry-specific driving forces and trends means that sustainability is not assessed in terms of past performance but that the focus is on assessing the future sustainability potential of industries and individual companies. Through these trends and driving forces, sustainability criteria are identified with which sustainability opportunities and risks can be assessed.

All indexes of the DJSI family are assessed according to the same corporate sustainability methodology and respective criteria. Therefore, the DJSI methodology facilitates the design, development, and delivery of customized sustainability indexes; for instance, there are indexes covering different regions and segments of the leading sustainability companies, there are indexes with exclusion criteria, and indexes denominated in different currencies.

Increasingly, as investors are diversifying their portfolios and investing in companies committed to corporate sustainability, this analysis is required to identify those firms that are profiting from sustainability and proving to be attractive investments. The DJSI is reviewed annually in September to ensure that the index composition accurately represents the leading sustainability companies in each of the DJSI industry groups. The selection of index components follows a rule-based process and is regularly verified by the auditors PricewaterhouseCoopers.

Comparative analysis of the DJGI and DJSI World conducted by SAM between January 1997 and April 2002 (with backcasting analysis) demonstrates statistically significant outperformance of the DJSI. There is growing evidence that corporate sustainability leaders create long-term shareholder value by gearing their strategies and management to harness the market's potential for sustainability products and services while at the same time successfully reducing and avoiding sustainability costs and risks.

Currently, the SAM analysis is applied by many mainstream institutions to manage funds and derivatives. More than $2.2 billion of assets are under management by licensees in 12 countries on all continents. The SAM membership logo is granted to more than 300 surveyed companies.

Part 2
THE TEN BUILDING BLOCKS

1
The market

> **The market economy, if utilized rather than worshiped, is the best mechanism available for pursuing both economic dynamism and desirable social goals.**
>
> *Adair Turner, vice chairman, Merrill Lynch Europe*

Sustainable development is best achieved through open, competitive, rightly framed international markets that honor legitimate comparative advantages. Such markets encourage efficiency and innovation, both necessities for sustainable human progress.

Business remains the most potent force for wealth creation. The extent to which that wealth goes toward poverty alleviation depends largely on societal choices. Countries do not have low incidences of poverty because of their welfare programs but largely because they have created frameworks that encourage business enterprise. These enterprises offer people tools—business opportunities, jobs, wages, investment possibilities, training, and pensions—with which to build secure lives.

Governments that make it hard for business to do business and that try to take the place of business in meeting people's needs keep their people poor. There is a striking correlation between the national scores on the Index of Economic Freedom and on the Human Development Index: roughly, the more economic freedom, the higher the levels of human development. Markets are human constructs based on human values, laws, and norms. They must be built, and they can always be improved.

Today we witness a virulent debate between those opposed to the so-called global market and those in favor, yet there is no true global market. There exists only the badly flawed, shaky beginnings of one. Many of those opposed are unwilling to work on improvements, and that unwillingness is also shared by those who benefit from the flaws.

Business should contribute and play a role in building a free and equitable international market—a market in which trade is not distorted by subsidies, tariffs, and non-tariff barriers.

Denying poor people and countries access to markets is planet-destroying as well as people-destroying. Some 80% of people live in developing countries and have to live off 20% of the planet's goods. To survive, much less to thrive, they need more. If they cannot get more, or even the basic necessities, through market access, they will be forced to destroy natural capital to support themselves.

Speaking for the market

Business leaders are often chided for not regularly calling for the creation of a free global market that is also fair to all players. When you consider the business benefits in such a market, our silence may be seen to be surprising.

In November 2001 the 144 members of the World Trade Organization (WTO) surprised everyone, including the delegates attending the Doha meeting, by agreeing to an agenda for a new trade round. Based on that agenda, one excited newspaper editorial writer estimated that 'Up to $700 billion in tariffs and trade-distorting subsidies may eventually disappear, possibly generating $2.8 trillion in global economic activity by 2015' (*International Herald Tribune* 2001). Surveys of companies around the world showed that most welcomed the new trade agenda.

If the financial benefits of trade liberalization are so high, why is business not fighting fiercely for it? The reason is that, in a political sense, there is no such thing as 'business'. There are many individual companies and enterprises, farmers, street traders, and artisans who collectively form business. So, while most business people are for freer trade in the abstract, individual companies may find themselves opposed to specific market liberalization policies that throw more competition their way. And it is to individual companies that governments listen.

However, we in the WBCSD are a group of business people who feel we have a duty to speak frankly about the need to build a better global market to offer as much opportunity as possible to as many people as possible. This market should be largely 'free' of entangling rules that could diminish its usefulness as a tool for human development. Of course, the term 'free market' is more an idealistic than a realistic expression. Officials have been on hand to check the scales since the earliest markets. Rules and respect for those rules are the foundations of markets, which cannot function without them. The agreement under which China joined the WTO, thus becoming a member of the 'free market', is some 1,000 pages long.

Since its beginnings, the WBCSD and its members have repeatedly stressed their conviction that the most effective way to achieve sustainable development is through the market. From *Changing Course* in 1992 (Schmidheiny 1992) to *Sustainability through the Market: Seven Keys to Success* in 2001 (Holliday and Pepper 2001), we have argued that the market offers the most effective method for harnessing human creativity in favor of more sustainable production and consumption. Properly framed markets founded on respect for certain basic rights and obligations promote the most efficient and cost-effective use of resources. They encourage innovation and competition, they offer freedom of choice and greater transparency and they are a primary vehicle for wealth creation and the improvement of quality of life (see Box 1). Accord-

Ten ways by which the market can help us toward sustainable development:

- It encourages **efficient use** of resources
- It delivers the most **cost-effective** solutions
- It offers **freedom of choice**
- It encourages **competition**
- It fosters **innovation**
- It spurs human **creativity**
- It offers **flexibility**
- It promotes **transparency of information**
- It helps in **wealth creation**
- It opens up new opportunities for **improving quality of life**

Box 1 **THE MARKET DECALOGUE**

ing to *Changing Course*, 'open and competitive markets foster innovation and efficiency and provide opportunities for all to improve their living conditions' (Schmidheiny 1992: xi).

Written as it was in the wake of the fall of communism, *Changing Course* was quick to acknowledge that sustainability through the market was not a foregone conclusion. Rather, it argued, 'market economies must now rise to the challenge and prove that they can adequately reflect environmental truth and incorporate the goals of sustainable development' (Schmidheiny 1992: 15).

Over the ten years since the Rio Earth Summit, governments have been slow to introduce the policy frameworks needed to help markets support sustainable development (see Chapter 2). To encourage governments and business, the WBCSD published *Sustainability through the Market*, which identified seven critical preconditions, or 'keys', for markets to work effectively (Holliday and Pepper 2001: 8). The first three keys addressed areas where business can take a lead and deliver further progress— innovation, eco-efficiency, and stakeholder partnerships. The remaining four keys related to how markets can be improved to foster sustainability: better information flows, sound market framework conditions, full-cost pricing, and a more inclusive global market system. The latter four keys tend to require action in partnerships.

'It is clear that today's rough approximation of a global market has some significant limitations', the report argued. In particular, inadequate framework conditions, exacerbated by persistent trade barriers, perverse subsidies, corruption, monopolies, and deficient property rights serve to perpetuate unsustainable practices. Add to these factors concerns over the carrying capacity of the Earth and a chronic lack of market access suffered by the world's poor, and the scale of the challenge still before us as we prepared for the Johannesburg World Summit on Sustainable Development (WSSD) was clear.

The demonstrations against free trade and market globalization have thrown down a challenge for those of us who believe firmly that markets offer the most promising means to achieve global sustainability. Protesters have leveled varied, often colorful and, we believe, mostly misinformed criticisms at multinational companies and international organizations such as the WTO. Among these criticisms are legitimate concerns that must be tackled if markets are to succeed in helping to deliver social and environmental progress.

What is globalization?

As is often pointed out, there has long been a global market. International economic exchanges have been taking place for thousands of years—from the sea routes of the ancient Phoenicians to the medieval commodities trade in spices and porcelain. International trade flourished as never before just prior to the First World War. Indeed, the linking together of disparate locations on the globe through extensive migration, communication, and trade and the resultant interaction between the local and the global is a central driving force in world history (University of Pennsylvania 2001).

In its widest sense, globalization refers to the rapid acceleration in the global exchange of information, ideas, goods, services, technology, values, people, culture, microbes, weapons, and capital. It implies a rising level of broad-based interdependence among nations in the three areas of sustainable development: economic, social, and environmental (Gladwin 1998). Thus the 'global market' is only a subset of globalization.

What is new about this current phase of market globalization is the sheer speed and scale with which it is taking place and the pace of technological change that contributes to this speed and scale. This time around, there are far more players, as the colonies of the earlier rapid phase now participate as nations (Sachs 2000). This latest spurt of economic globalization is also different because it is fostering linkages that make it unlikely, but not impossible, that we shall face a reversal of openness and trade integration such as that which followed the First World War.

Innovations in transportation and communication technologies have been key elements of the market dimension of globalization. The widespread availability of cheap telecommunications and the spread of the Internet are fundamentally transforming the way we do business, lowering costs, removing barriers to entry, and merging previously inaccessible parts of the globe into a fledgling single 'borderless' market. The information revolution allows small entrepreneurs to reach distant markets, and it allows markets—for goods and information and beliefs—to reach distant individuals.

The implications of these changes for business are enormous. According to Harvard's Jeffrey Sachs, a 'veritable economic revolution' has occurred. He states that, 'as a result of changes in economic policy and technology, economies that were once separated by high transport costs and artificial barriers to trade and finance are now linked in an increasingly dense network of economic interactions' (Sachs 1998). Thanks to the removal of barriers, the value chain of production can now be divided up, with different elements of the production process for a single product being undertaken in different regions of the world, according to the comparative advantages of each region. Thus, describes Sachs (1998):

> Semiconductor chips might be designed in the US, where the basic wafers are also produced; these are then cut and assembled in Malaysia; and the final products are tested in and shipped from Singapore. These cross-border flows often occur within the same multinational firm—an estimated one-third of merchandise trade is actually composed of shipments among the affiliates of a single company.

The result is enhanced competitiveness, greater economies of scale, falling costs and a presence in new markets.

One of the key policy changes driving the move toward a global market has been the so-called 'liberalization revolution' in international trade policy occurring under the auspices of the WTO. This process includes decreases in trade and foreign investment barriers, decreases in exchange controls, the adoption of a rules-based system of regulation and the promotion of policies encouraging financial stability (Cable 1999: 15-20).

Trade liberalization carries a number of benefits. It encourages productivity and efficiency gains from specialization, it helps to build economies of scale, it spurs efficiency from increased competition, and it lowers the costs of production—benefits that are passed on to consumers and shareholders in the form of lower prices and higher profits (Cable 1999: 23). In addition, liberalization favors trade creation, boosting employment and investment, increasing consumer choice, and encouraging the spread of knowledge, technology, and best practice.

It also tends to decrease corruption. First, the growing transparency that accompanies globalization makes corruption more visible to all. Second, bribes and kickbacks complicate deals and raise transaction costs, so investments are more likely to flow where deals are cheaper and cleaner.

From a sustainable development viewpoint, trade liberalization offers our best hope for meeting the needs of the present generation while safeguarding those of future generations. Opening up access to markets can empower people and can offer greater opportunities to the poor to improve their lot. The result can be that odd, much sought-after, situation in which both sides of a contest win. *The Economist* (2001f: 10) claims that 'both [*sic*] sides—exporters and importers, borrowers and lenders, shareholders and workers—can gain'. That view is shared by Jeffrey Sachs (1998), who argues that more liberal global markets stand to improve living standards for rich and poor alike:

> Both sides of the great income divide stand to benefit from globalization, the developed countries by reaching a larger market for new innovations, and the developing economies by enjoying the fruits of those innovations while sharing in global production via multinational enterprises.

Critics of freer global trade claim that nations that embrace the global market lose sovereignty and compromise their ability to govern effectively. This, we would argue, is nonsense. As in signing up to any other treaty or joining any international organization, joining the WTO implies abiding by rules and regulations, but these rules and regulations are changed only by consensus; all must agree. So the WTO does not have the ability to ride roughshod over the interests of any group of nations or even of any nation. However, as we argue later, wealthier states can field much larger, more powerful, teams of officials, experts, and lawyers than can be mustered by smaller, poorer states. The wealthier states can therefore better negotiate the rules to their advantage.

New York Times journalist Thomas Friedman (2000: 105) has written that nations find their choice of policy options constrained by a 'golden straitjacket' of fiscal and economic measures which liberalization entails. He is referring to the core elements considered necessary to establish market confidence in a particular government and its economy: privatization, reduced regulation, balanced budgets, and moderate taxes to name but a few. But this is a little like arguing that people committing themselves to a healthy lifestyle—regular exercise, wholesome diet, rest—are tying themselves into straitjackets. Nations in Europe and North America that have achieved the core elements of economic health do not seem to be straitjacketed.

Claude Martin, director general of the World Wide Fund for Nature (WWF) International, worries that:

> one of the effects of globalization is to limit the powers of governments and their social partners to deal with the problems arising from an international tide of pressure on their natural resources. Sovereignty over such resources is called into question by expanding market demand for timber, beef, or palm oil from converted forests; or for cotton, grain, fruit, and flowers produced by depleting freshwater ecosystems; or for fish harvested by over-capitalized and heavily subsidized fleets (Martin 2000).

It may be easier to sell food and natural resource products in a global market, but there is no reason why governments cannot regulate this at source, individually in their laws or collectively through multilateral agreements. Besides, by moving technology and innovation to poorer countries, a global market offers these countries an opportunity to export more manufactured products rather than remaining caught in the trap of seeking prosperity as an exporter of cheap commodities. It is this trap that degrades the environment of so many countries.

Some critics see governments losing power as business gains power. Harvard's Dani Rodrik (2001: 16) maintains that:

> globalization has made it exceedingly difficult for government to provide social insurance . . . At present, international economic integration is taking place against the background of receding governments and diminished social obligations. The welfare state has been under attack for two decades.

In fact, governments throughout the Organization for Economic Cooperation and Development (OECD) have increased the percentages of GDPs going into public coffers. In the North, countries politically committed to equality, environmental protection, and workers' rights while remaining open to globalization—such as Australia, Canada, Denmark, Iceland, the Netherlands, and Sweden—have successfully done so (Cable 1999: 23-24). It is harder for poorer countries to do this. However, the problem is not globalization; more often the problem arises from the inequalities of the present version of a global market. As argued in *The Economist* (2001h: 4) in its 2001 survey of globalization:

> the liberal case for globalization is emphatically not the case for domestic or international laissez faire . . . markets have their limits, for instance in

tending to the supply of public goods (such as a clean environment). A liberal outlook is consistent with support for a wide range of government interventions; indeed a liberal outlook demands many such interventions.

The pooling of sovereignty that is taking place in return for the benefits of globalization is both calculated and rational (Bhagwati 2000: 335). Governments that sign up to the freer trade regime have chosen freely to do so, essentially because they see this to be in the interests of their citizens. Markets are, after all, voluntary human constructs. Moreover, if individual governments wish to restrict the scope of free markets, they may do so. As the vice chairman of Merrill Lynch Europe (and ex-leader of the Confederation of British Industry [CBI]), Adair Turner, maintains in his book, *Just Capital*, 'the common belief . . . is that developed economies face severe constraints on social choice, that either we must accept the economic imperatives of the global economy or . . . break entirely from the philosophy of free market'. But, continues Turner, we are 'free to limit the application of free markets in specific instances where they are undesirable and free to combine flexible market economies with . . . levels of provision of collective goods and redistributive welfare nets' (Turner 2001: 274-75).

Democratic governments have the responsibility to see to it that the societies that elected them have the education and health facilities, infrastructure, environmental protection, and other amenities the voters reasonably expect and are willing to pay for. It has become all too easy for governments—in the North and South—to blame globalization for their failure to live up to their election campaign promises.

Democracy

Globalization accelerates the pace of change and produces winners and losers. Thus when shocks come, such as the 1997 Asian crisis, people feel that neither they nor their governments have control over what the market is doing to their lives.

Thomas Friedman (2000) describes the impact of such economic meltdowns as akin to being trampled by an 'electronic herd'. This vulnerability to sudden market fluctuations, combined with the pooling of national sovereignty, leaves some people feeling a loss of democratic control. As Friedman (2000: 12) explains:

> the defining anxiety in globalization is fear of rapid change from an enemy you can't see, touch or feel—a sense that your job, community or workplace can be changed at any moment by anonymous economic or technological forces that are anything but stable.

This feeling of powerlessness is not restricted to individuals; entire nation-states can experience a sense of loss of control at the hands of what appear to be unelected, uncontrollable forces.

However, globalization has actually exerted a democratizing and empowering influence worldwide, partly through liberalized telecommunications markets and the advent of the Internet. The financial markets' hunger for transparency is also fueling a democratization of information. According to Columbia University Professor Jagdish

Bhagwati (2000: 339), former economic policy adviser to the director general of the General Agreement on Tariffs and Trade (GATT), far from undermining it, increased trade and investment have actually improved the quality of democracy.

Clearly, citizens must feel that they have both the voice and the power to help shape the process of globalization if they are to accept and not reject it. And it is equally important that nation-states develop improved governance to cope with the inevitable ups and downs of the world market, supported by a strengthened international financial architecture that helps avert, or neutralize, the worst effects of that market.

Thomas Friedman (2000: 46) identifies three so-called 'democratizations' that are spurring greater global connectivity: the democratization of technology, of finance, and of information. These, Friedman argues, are empowering citizens worldwide, stating that 'the days when governments could isolate their people from understanding what life was like beyond their borders or even beyond their village are over' (2000: 67). By dissolving technological and informational boundaries, globalization can promote better, more accountable, government and empower individuals, activists, and companies better to shape the emerging global order.

Competing successfully in the global market requires nations to make the best use of their human resources. Nations that deny education and jobs to women will not be successful; nor will nations that marginalize religious, ethnic, or tribal groups. Neither can governments that deny their people free access to information succeed; such policies put too big a handicap on entrepreneurs and companies.

In the joined-up, wired 'CNN world', we are becoming acutely aware of glaring inequalities and injustices previously hidden from us (Elkington 2001: 28). Globalization gives those treated unjustly the ability to communicate and organize themselves. It also gives those opposed to globalization the ability to air their concerns to a wider audience; ironically, globalization makes possible more effective protest *against* market globalization. Thanks to the Internet, for example, globally organized environmentalists can quickly shine a spotlight on how a multinational is behaving in different countries.

Inequality

That globalization can deliver benefits is rarely disputed. What is more controversial is how those benefits are allocated and distributed. Although trade liberalization undoubtedly creates wealth, skeptics of the growing market claim that it tends to widen rather than close income gaps, concentrating wealth in the hands of the rich at the expense of the poor, both within and between nations. According to British economist Vincent Cable (1999: 40):

> Globalization rewards the many but also a few in particular. The disparities in rewards thus produced have enormous implications for domestic politics, feeding the politics of envy, and creating a new class of individuals and companies with exceptional leverage.

Losers in the market globalization process tend to be the low-skilled workers in industrial and developing countries and, in the developing world, farmers who must compete against subsidized farm goods from wealthier countries.

Also, whereas wealthier nations and developing nations adopting market-oriented approaches, such as Singapore, have quickly become more wealthy, those in poorer nations have gained more slowly. Western European incomes have multiplied 14 times and Japanese incomes 17 times, but African and Indian incomes have only roughly doubled in over a century and a half, to $840 and $1,350 respectively (Cable 1999: 27). However, those countries that have developed economically more slowly seem to have suffered through staying relatively out of the market rather than entering into it.

Globalization provides tremendous opportunities for those in developing nations in a position to seize them. The personal odyssey of Eugenio Clariond, executive president of Mexico's Grupo IMSA, is a good example. When in 1986 Mexico joined the precursor of the WTO and opened up its markets, Grupo IMSA, which produces batteries and steel goods, was focused entirely on the domestic market. 'I thought my company would disappear,' recounts Clariond:

> But instead of fighting, I adapted, focused on our key strengths, and my company now boasts revenues of over $3 billion per annum, with over half our sales outside Mexico. I have gone from employing 2,500 people to a workforce of 17,000—all of this thanks to globalization. And, thanks to the North American Free Trade Agreement (NAFTA), I now have 5,000 Americans working for me!

The challenge is to minimize the pain of the losers—and to help them find a place in the new economic order. In developing countries, the key goal is to bring people *into* the market. Unskilled workers in developed countries, particularly those in sectors such as shipbuilding, steel, apparel, and agriculture, are another vulnerable group who may stand to lose from economic liberalization—and who is therefore actively resisting it (Hufbauer and Warren 1999: 17-18). In North America and Europe, foreign investment and trade may increase the demand for skilled labor and decrease the demand for less-skilled labor. This increases inequality. *The Economist* (2001e: 9) argues:

> Some people in rich countries do lose out from the combination of trade and technology. The remedy lies with education and training, and with help in changing jobs. Spending in those areas, together perhaps with more generous and effective help for people forced to change jobs by economic growth, addresses the problem directly—and in a way that adds to society's economic resources rather than subtracting from them, as efforts to hold back either technological progress or trade would do.

The economic integration that globalization pressures are encouraging is perhaps the only way for poor countries to move toward prosperity, and most developing-country governments realize this. As Jagdish Bhagwati (2000: 332) argues:

> The fears of integration into the world economy are being heard, not from the developing countries which see great good from it . . . [but] it is the North that is now fearful . . . In particular, the fear has grown . . . that by trading with the South with its abundance of unskilled labor, the North will find its own unskilled at risk.

We may indeed see more protectionist responses in the North as uncompetitive industries are opened up to competition. According to Henry Paulson (2001), chairman and chief executive of the Goldman Sachs group,

> Liberalization, domestic and international, is good for economic growth, and economic growth is good for everyone, especially the poor. The great irony is that anti-globalization activists are attacking a phenomenon that is an essential part of the solution to world poverty.

Foreign direct investment

This liberalization of flows of goods and capital has led to.a sharp rise in foreign direct investment (FDI), mainly by companies, in physical assets such as factories, facilities, and utilities or in infrastructure located in nations other than their home countries. Worldwide, the foreign assets of multinational companies are valued at some \$2.6 trillion (Cable 1999: 7-8), and this figure is growing. The World Bank estimated that FDI in transition and emerging economies virtually tripled between 1990 and 1996 (World Bank 1997). During the 1990s, whereas official overseas development assistance (ODA) hovered at around \$50–55 billion, FDI in developing countries grew steadily from \$25 billion to reach almost \$200 billion in 1999—four times as high as official flows (World Bank 2000).

The increasing role of FDI in global trade and production is emerging as one of the key consequences and drivers of globalization, rapidly replacing ODA as the chief vehicle of development (Cable 1999: 48). However, FDI does not flow in big streams to the poorest countries but to the better-off and better-managed developing countries—and to the wealthy countries. The USA has been the largest recipient of FDI recently.

These trends refute the argument that there is a 'race to the bottom' in progress in which companies are setting up their plants in the least-regulated, least-governed nations where they can get away with pollution and sweatshops. The opposite is happening: investments are going to what may be perceived as better-run countries, where the companies will be safer and more productive. By and large, companies do not want to invest for the long term where their people will not be secure, where communications are unreliable, where corruption is the norm and where contracts and legal recourse are erratic. A number of commentators have argued that there is actually a 'race to the top' in progress, a trend toward tighter regulations everywhere (*The Economist* 2001g: 24).

FDI tends to have a long time-horizon; when a company invests in, say, a factory in China, it does so because it plans to establish a long-term presence in the region, both as an employer and as a supplier of goods. Consequently, the role of business in relation to development is changing. This growth in cross-border enterprise implies a greater engagement with—and therefore a greater sensitivity to the social, environmental, and economic concerns of—local communities, regulators, and consumers. As companies move into new markets in developing countries they are often faced with social and environmental challenges that must be tackled if the investment is to succeed. In the words of BP group chief executive, Lord Browne (2001):

Globalization and the end of the Cold War have taken companies into a wider range of countries, some of which have fragile social structures and limited experience of the workings of a market economy. We're an example. In 1995, our business was dominated by our interests in the oil in the North Sea and Alaska. Now our interests are global. We're one of the largest foreign investors in China, and in more than 20 other significant economies around the world, from Azerbaijan to Angola. In many places we are the vehicle for development.

The adoption of minimum environmental standards in 996 surveyed companies is illustrated in Figure 3.

Protesting and listening

The globalization of the market is facing a crisis of legitimacy. To get the popular support it needs to succeed, it must give due consideration to the hopes and concerns of the world's citizens. The past few years have seen a groundswell of anti-globalization feeling, exemplified by demonstrations in Seattle, London, Prague, Stockholm,

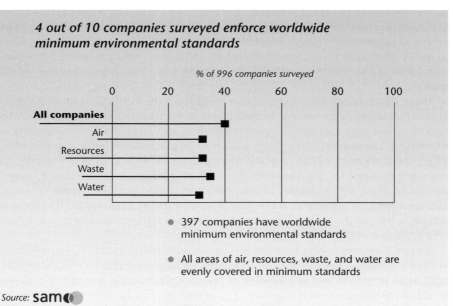

Figure 3 **USE OF MINIMUM ENVIRONMENTAL STANDARDS**

Davos, and Genoa. The demonstrators' arguments are summed up by Lori Wallach and Michelle Sforza, of the NGO Public Citizen's Global Trade Watch, as follows:

> The world has been buffeted by unprecedented global financial instability. Income inequality is increasing rapidly between and within countries. Despite efficiency and productivity gains, wages in numerous countries have failed to rise, while commodity prices are at an all-time low, causing a decrease in the standard of living for a majority of people in the world (Wallach and Sforza 1999: 63).

They go on to argue that:

> there is a growing consensus among NGOs worldwide that the WTO must be pruned back to ensure: access to essential goods, such as foods and medicines; access to essential services, such as safe water, sanitation and other utilities, education, transportation and health care; respect for basic labor and other human rights; product, food and workplace safety; a healthy environment and conservation of natural resources; the availability of information, such as the accurate labeling of the contents and charac- teristics of goods; choice among competitively priced goods and services; representation of citizen interests in decision-making; and an avenue of redress, including the ability to hold accountable corporations and govern- ments that undermine core citizens' rights (1999: 65).

This list appears to us to be a perfect summation of the flaws in the protestors' argu- ments. Unless the WTO is successful in its efforts to help poorer countries gain access to markets and to fair competition in those markets, then people in developing coun- tries will not be able to afford 'access to essential goods, such as foods and medicines; access to essential services, such as safe water, sanitation and other utilities, educa- tion, transportation and health care'. Leaders of most developing countries under- stand the basic fact of life that most goods and services have price tags and they know that they cannot develop them by printing money to buy them. The provision of other, less material benefits, such as respect for labor and other human rights, depends in democratic nations on laws passed by governments elected by people of those nations, not on procedures within the WTO.

We applaud the protestors' efforts to improve the market, but we believe that they neither understand its real flaws nor acknowledge its real benefits.

A global market for all

We would argue that protestors should fight for trade rules that lead to equitable access to the market for poor people and poor countries. There is a groundswell of people demanding access to markets and wanting to share in their benefits (Friedman 2000). Developing countries are rushing to join the WTO and are beginning to make their voices heard more effectively in its deliberations. UNDP administrator Mark Malloch Brown (2000) argued that:

> Unless we can build a global consensus around the principles for managing global integration that ensures the benefits of growth include and empower

> the poor and women; protect the environment; reinforce rather than under-
> mine human rights, the rule of law and national institutions; and regulate
> transborder activities through a set of modern and accountable international
> institutions, the clashes of Seattle will continue . . . Unless we realize the
> possibility of a progressive alliance around such an agenda, the current
> trade liberalization process will degenerate into a new protectionism.

In the light of the terrorist attacks on the USA of 11 September 2001, forging a broad global alliance around inclusive globalization becomes all the more urgent. Says Henry Paulson (2001):

> Let us have no illusions: globalization will not transport us into a world of
> democracy and peace overnight—or even in our lifetimes. But it remains
> perhaps the most effective tool we have to make the world not just more
> prosperous, but also a freer and more peaceful place.

Gary Sampson (2000: 3), former director of the Trade and Environment Division at the WTO, argues that the collapse of the Seattle meeting can in large part be attributed to developing countries' unwillingness to rubber-stamp a process in which many of their principle negotiating objectives were not being addressed. In many instances, claims Sampson (2000: 124), trade-and-environment-related proposals tabled at the WTO have:

> lacked sensitivity to [least-developed-country] needs; they frequently don't
> pay due regard to core principles such as common but differentiated
> responsibility, the right to development, or even the right to basic human
> needs such as food, health, and education that industrial countries take for
> granted.

As the chief executive of Procter & Gamble (P&G), John Pepper, and P&G president, A.G. Lafley, wrote in the foreword to their 2001 sustainability report:

> Sustainability is an important way for us to leverage the power of innovation
> and global markets for the benefit of everyone—not just those in the
> developed world. We cannot condemn developing countries to a life of
> poverty so those in the developed world can maintain their lifestyles. But
> neither do we have to presume that the only alternative is for the developed
> world to reduce its quality of life (Pepper and Lafley 2001).

Realistically, if the people of the developing world, where over 95% of population growth is expected to take place, are excluded from market opportunities, then the developed world's 'lifestyles' would certainly be under threat. One could expect increases in instability, failed states, terrorism, and civil wars. Industrialization can be hard on the environment, but not as hard as large populations forced to seek survival by mining topsoil and water systems to produce cheap commodities or to cut into forests to clear farmland. If industrial development in huge nations such as China, India, and Indonesia is largely carbon-based, as was development in the North, then we should expect the climate of both the developed and the developing worlds to become more unpredictable and destructive. For nations to compete in a global market, they need more efficient manufacturing equipment, and more efficient equipment is almost always cleaner and less wasteful.

So, building a better global market is not only about fairness but also about the wellbeing of global civilization. Many business people do not like the expression 'fair market'. They assume that this refers to a market burdened with rules attempting to create a better environment and better conditions for everyone: labor, women, minorities, poor countries, etc. The freer the market, they argue, the fairer. But the present market is largely unfair because it is 'unfree', burdened by policies and conditions that hinder the poor from freely competing in it.

Toward a fairer free market

The poorest countries remain excluded from the trend toward increasing economic integration for any number of reasons. Many lack the institutional and regulatory capacity and mature governance structures needed to foster a vibrant economy. Wars, political instability, disease, endemic poverty, and corruption have also taken their toll. But there is a vicious cycle at work whereby the trappings of poverty limit market access, and lack of market access keeps countries poor.

The very structure of the global trading regime itself also limits poorer countries' abilities to benefit from world trade. The WTO, quite rightly, is a rules-based organization, but these rules are complex; negotiating them and setting up the appropriate legal and technical regimes to honor them are expensive in terms of financial and human resources. For example, it is extremely expensive for a nation to set up the types of national intellectual property right (IPR) regime demanded by the wealthier countries that are producing the bulk of the patented products. Moreover, OECD countries are almost always at a negotiating advantage in trade negotiating forums—perpetuating an imbalance that undermines these institutions' credibility and effectiveness. The UNDP's Mark Malloch Brown (2000) argues that 'the present unevenness [in international trade] . . . works for nobody. It denies to the global trade negotiations their indispensable universal legitimacy.' This unevenness of representation has translated itself into trade policies that favor the interests of developed countries above those of developing nations. Largely to blame, in the opinion of economist Jagdish Bhagwati (2000: xvi), has been the drive of the more powerful negotiating countries for preferential treatment, rather than their providing leadership aimed at creating a regime that benefits all. The result is that industry sectors in which the South holds a clear competitive advantage—agriculture and textiles, for example—remain among the least liberalized and are characterized by persistent high and price-distorting subsidies.

According to Eric Neumayer (2001: 17), lecturer in environment and development at the London School of Economics:

> The very fact that liberalization in agriculture and textiles remains rather limited and has been delayed to a later period than most other liberalizations shows that developed countries successfully managed to shield themselves to some extent from increased competition in the markets that were most relevant to developing countries.

The wealthier countries also tend to place higher tariffs on goods with higher degrees of processing and manufacturing. This means that in forestry, for instance, companies are encouraged to ship quantities of low-value logs rather than higher-value products such as door frames and furniture, putting great pressure on the forest environments. Given that little value is added by processing, maximum bulk must be exported—'rip and ship', in the graphic parlance of the critics of this syndrome.

Whereas the South tends to lose out on what it is good at, the North tends to win on what it is good at. Thus the Uruguay Round of trade negotiations made great progress on IPRs, investment, services, telecommunications, the strengthening of anti-dumping measures, and increased access to developing-country markets.

Eliminating perverse subsidies

When it comes to running a global economy, the acid test of successful policy inter-ventions, in the view of Theodore Panayotou (1992) of Harvard University, is the elimination of policies that distort markets. Yet today's global market is beset by the persistence of subsidies and trade policies that actively distort markets and can con-tribute to unsustainable forms of production and consumption. These markets are not free in the sense that they are rigged by the more powerful nations. It is not that subsidies and tariffs exist only as industrial-nation policies; developing nations engage in these policies as well, but their impact on trade is nowhere near as great. Ironically, industrial nations are the ones constantly urging developing nations to rid themselves of 'market-distorting' policies.

As the OECD observes, government intervention in agricultural production in domestic and international markets is nothing new. Much of this intervention, how-ever, takes the form of production subsidies and trade barriers, the net result of which is to 'impose costs on consumers and taxpayers, reduce economic efficiency, distort production and trade, impede growth in developing countries, and . . . damage the environment' (OECD 2001a).

Subsidies are not inherently evil. They are a powerful policy tool and can be used for good—as in subsidizing shifts toward cleaner energy sources. It is the 'perverse', environmentally damaging, subsidies, the effects of which are described above, that are our concern here. They are usually implemented in stopgap, short-term fashion to please a sector or a group around election times, but over the decades they turn into vast 'entitlement' expenditures demanded as rights by small sectors of society or of the economy.

Perverse subsidies inhibit the marketplace's normal ability to ensure the most efficient use and distribution of goods. Members of the WBCSD argued in 1994 that all subsidies are inappropriate if they are 'economically inefficient' or where they 'distort markets and generate negative side-effects' (de Andraca and McCready 1994: 45). According to the International Institute for Sustainable Development (IISD 1998a), some $700–900 billion is spent annually on subsidies to agriculture, energy, water, and road transportation. By far the bulk of this occurs in industrialized coun-tries, in sectors such as agriculture, energy use, mineral extraction, logging and forestry, fishing, water, and road transportation.

Let us look at one example of just how vicious subsidies can be in development terms. Most African capitals were constructed by colonial powers as ports to aid commerce between Africa and Europe. The wealthier, political and economic elite tends to live in the capitals, but the vast majority of Africans are poor farmers living on small farms inland from capitals, separated from them by bad or non-existent roads. Thus they cannot get their goods to port markets. These food markets are fed largely by grain offloaded from freighters from European and North American countries.

OECD countries subsidize their domestic farmers' production at a rate of about $365 billion a year, or $1 billion dollars a day. Total OECD official development assistance has been running at about $50–55 billion per year (World Bank 2000: 58).

Thus, under the present agricultural trading regime, the governments of some of the wealthiest farmers in the world are paying those farmers vast sums to help them compete against some of the world's poorest and hungriest farmers. These subsidies undercut their own or other countries' aid programs aimed at poor rural areas.

As argued in *Changing Course*, the dismantling of such market-distorting policies is a fundamental precondition for a shift toward more sustainable trade: 'before new instruments can be put in place, instruments already in place that actually encourage resource waste and environmental degradation should be removed' (Schmidheiny 1992: 27).

Progress at Doha

The developing nations feel that they gave a lot during negotiations over the Uruguay Round: they agreed to lower their own agricultural and industrial tariffs, opened their borders to some international service companies and agreed on new IPR regimes. Later, they felt that they had made a poor bargain, in that commitments on issues such as IPRs have proved more expensive than they anticipated; also, they had made strong commitments in return for weak commitments from the North on agricultural subsidies and textile tariffs. Accepting their point, the WTO and World Bank are using the term 'development round' to describe the next round of trade negotiations (Watal 2000).

The agenda of that new round was agreed in Doha, Qatar, in November 2001. It is only an agenda; there is no guarantee that the goals it contains will be realized. However, we cover its key points here because it provides a good description of the sort of global market that governments need to construct as well as some steps in that construction process. Given the broad consensus achieved, there may even be some political will and reality behind the agenda.

In Doha, WTO members signed a declaration covering a broad range of issues of interest to developed and developing countries, opening the way for a new round of multilateral trade negotiations to conclude in 2005. Among the issues on the official agenda at Doha were six key areas of contention in international trade policy:

- *Implementation*, including improved market access for textile products from the South, action on the abuse of anti-dumping measures, and the correction of imbalances in the subsidy rules

- *Rule-making*, including reform of subsidy and anti-dumping rules and fisheries subsidies

- *Agriculture*, focusing on the opening of Northern markets by means of tariff reductions, quota removal, the long-term elimination of export subsidies, and the scaling-back of domestic support

- *Environment*, clarifying the relationship between the international environmental and trade regimes

- *Intellectual property rights and public health*, including access to medicines

- *'Singapore' issues*, including new items on the trade agenda such as competition policy, investment, trade facilitation, and government procurement

The resulting Doha Ministerial Declaration managed to address all six issues, with varying degrees of success. Most significant from a developing-country perspective were the agreements reached in relation to future WTO activity on development-related issues. Among those flagged explicitly were (ICTSD 2001):

- Capacity-building and technical assistance for developing countries

- A work program for the fuller integration of small economies

- A work program for least-developed countries

- A framework for WTO activity in the area of technical assistance

- An agreement on the establishment of working groups on debt, finance, and technology transfer

The agricultural mandate, by far the most politically sensitive, included: improved market access; reduced trade-distorting domestic support; and, finally, reductions in—and the eventual elimination of—export subsidies. And, critically, the declaration undertook to eliminate tariffs, tariff peaks and escalation, and non-tariff barriers affecting 'products of export interest to developing countries', stating (WTO 2001):

> We are convinced that the aims of upholding and safeguarding an open and non-discriminatory multilateral trading system and acting for the protection of the environment and the promotion of sustainable development can and must be mutually supportive.

This endorsement of the need to seek out win–win trade and sustainable development objectives marks an important step forwards for the WTO.

Uncharacteristically, *The Economist*, which can be regarded as one of the most non-radical of publications, closed a major survey of market globalization by offering advice to the protestors on how to do a better job at protesting. It called on them to narrow their concern to addressing 'the scandal of third world poverty'. They would do this by demanding that:

- Rich-country governments open their markets to all developing-country exports

- Rich-country workers hurt by globalization be given more training and education and their economic losses be cushioned

- Spending on foreign aid be increased, taking care that it benefit the poor and the diseased

- There be an end to all subsidies that promote the wasteful use of natural resources

- Pollution taxes be introduced, including a carbon tax so that the price of energy reflects the risk of global warming

With some quibbles, we would largely agree with this list.

Writing of the perverse policies that distort global trade and keep nations poor, *The Economist* said that 'all these policies owe much to the fact that corporate interests exercise undue influence over government policy'. Historically speaking, there is fairness in the charge; corporations, acting in their short-term interests, have been responsible for many of the subsidies, tariffs, and 'beggar-the-poor' policies reflected in the present trade regime. However, a growing number of companies are taking the view that policies that lock billions in poverty are not going to create a global market that is going to be much good to anyone, even over the medium term. It is time for a change of course.

2
The right framework

"Governments have to stop pretending that they can exhort people to make changes when the prices people pay tell them otherwise,"

Simon Upton, chairman, OECD Roundtable on Sustainable Development

Badly framed markets cannot encourage sustainable progress. In its 1992 report to the Earth Summit, the then BCSD called for:

- A steady, predictable, negotiated move toward full-cost pricing of goods and services
- The dismantling of perverse subsidies
- Greater use of market instruments and less use of command-and-control regulations
- More tax on things to be discouraged, such as waste and pollution and less tax on things to be encouraged, such as jobs (in a fiscally neutral setting)
- More reflection of environmental resource use in standard national accounts

Other bodies, such as the US President's Council on Sustainable Development, made similar calls. Yet there has been very little political support for such moves from governments, civil-society organizations, or, frankly, most of business. If basic framework conditions push us all in the wrong directions, then that is the way society will go—until extreme, vociferous forces compel a change.

Other conditions for sustainable development include:

- Democracy and the accepted rule of law
- Effective intellectual and physical property rights
- Reliability of contracts

- Lack of corruption

- Equitable trade terms and respect for comparative advantage

- Ordered competition among businesses

- Fair and transparent accounting standards

- Accountability and predictability of government interventions

- Investment in education and enabling technologies

- Reform of taxation so that it funds collective investments rather than penalizes income

There has been progress in many countries in some of these areas.

The World Commission on Environment and Development (WCED 1987) listed as preconditions for sustainable development:

- Access to information

- Access to decision-making

- Access to justice

These are also framework conditions for economic development. These and the other conditions listed above tend to attract investment. Nations simply cannot compete effectively in international markets if they deny any of their people these rights of access based on their sex, race, religion, ethnicity, or culture.

We do not intend to wait for perfect conditions before pursuing more sustainable development. We do, according to our mission statement, intend to work with governments and civil-society organizations to 'promote the role of eco-efficiency, innovation and corporate social responsibility toward sustainable development' (WBCSD 2001h).

Many companies are willing to be held accountable for their actions and are working to be more transparent. They expect governments and civil-society organizations also to become more accountable and transparent.

The framework

In 1994, BCSD members Roberto de Andraca of the Chilean holding company CAP SA and Ken McCready of the Canadian utility TransAlta found that, despite their very different origins and types of business experience, they were so in agreement about how markets *ought* to work that they wrote a Council report about it: *Internalizing Environmental Costs to Promote Eco-efficiency*. Their conclusion was that companies can go only so far in delivering sustainability; sooner or later they are constrained by the policies and framework conditions governing their operating environment: 'While businesses can do much to encourage eco-efficient practices in their operations, they are ultimately limited by the government-established policy and regulatory frameworks within which they operate' (de Andraca and McCready 1994: 7).

Optimum frameworks would have as their core objectives the generation of economic value, the regeneration of the environmental resource base, the reduction of poverty and inequality, and the improvement of standards of living—all within an open and accountable system of governance (Robins 2000: 56). Chief among the characteristics of a sustainable development market framework, according to the OECD (2001b: 48), are long-term planning horizons, appropriate pricing, delivery of public goods, cost-effectiveness, environmental effectiveness, policy integration, precaution, international cooperation, and transparency and accountability.

Ideally, market frameworks should reflect a nation's sustainable development strategy. However, few nations have such strategies, and most market frameworks have grown up ad hoc and uncoordinated through years of scuffling by special-interest groups. Most existing regulatory and policy frameworks are awkward hybrids of policy tools that do not serve the sustainability strategy and of outdated, entrenched instruments that serve instead as barriers to change. This sends the wrong signals to market players and perpetuates unsustainable practices. If markets are to deliver sustainability, this policy and regulatory architecture must be overhauled and streamlined to encourage behavior that fulfills, not hinders, the aims of this strategy.

CASE STUDY 6
BCSD–GM
page 80

In addition, to ensure the market mechanism is harnessed in favor of sustainable development, these instruments should establish the full-cost pricing of goods and services, personal security, freedom, and democracy (see also Table 1).

Back in 1994, de Andraca and McCready called on governments to integrate more flexible, market-based approaches into their national sustainable development strategies. Persistent framework problems were hampering the market's ability to deliver more environmentally sound forms of production and consumption. To correct these, de Andraca and McCready (1994: 8) advocated the use of economic instruments, tax shifts, the internalization of environmental costs, the reduction and removal of harmful subsidies, the encouragement of voluntary agreements with industry, the reform of existing regulation, and an expanded program of education and information to enhance public understanding of the issues. By resorting to a combination of such tools, governments could ensure that environmental values were efficiently and cost-effectively integrated into the market.

During the 1990s a number of new social and developmental issues moved quickly up the business agenda—new views of corporate social responsibility, the need to address the developmental needs of the South, and the question of how to tackle the gap between the 'haves' and 'have-nots'. As a result, designing the right framework has become not simply an issue of ensuring greater eco-efficiency but a complex balancing act of securing progress across the economic, social, and environmental bottom lines—without cluttering the market with rules and regulations that hamper efficiency.

In designing the right frameworks for sustainability through the market, national governments need to operate more effectively on multiple levels: the global, the regional, the national, and the local. Although this does not alter the fundamental characteristics of a sound policy and instrument mix, it does make the task of streamlining and dovetailing different tools more complex.

Legislation and regulations should promote:	Otherwise . . .
Competition among enterprises	Innovation and productivity will lag, resources will be used inefficiently, and quality of life will stagnate
Effective intellectual and physical property rights	There will be no benefit for those who develop better, more sustainable, products and services
Reliability of contractual terms	Fraud and short-sightedness will pervade, challenging economic and social equity
Fair and transparent accounting standards	Corruption will thrive, draining resources from the economy and increasing the gap between the rich and the poor
Accountability of government intervention	Perverse subsidies will encourage unsustainable practices
Predictability of government intervention	Entrepreneurs who could create jobs and wealth will be deterred from investing
Freedom and democracy	Social exclusion will grow
Full-cost pricing of goods and services	Undervalued resources will be wasted

Table 1 **MARKET FRAMEWORK BASICS**

Source: Holliday and Pepper 2001: 29

The instrument mix

So what policy tools are needed to create a market that encourages sustainable development? To encourage companies to go beyond regulatory compliance, the WBCSD has long advocated the greater use of market-based instruments such as taxes, charges, and tradable permits that reward sustainability-oriented behavior and discourage pollution by making the polluter pay. Regulations, necessary as they are in so many cases, are like requiring everyone in a school class simply to pass an exam; good economic instruments encourage everyone toward excellence. Such instruments have a number of advantages over other command-and-control regulations: cost-effectiveness, a lower administrative burden, greater flexibility in the choice of means, and stronger incentives for improvement and innovation. In addition, economic instruments tend to increase transparency, are more easily adaptable than regulation, can be harnessed to achieve multiple objectives, and, critical for competition, pose less of an obstacle to market entry (de Andraca and McCready 1994: 45-47).

The most important feature of market-based instruments is that they harness companies' creativity and self-interest to achieve environmental and social objectives. The flexibility inherent in market-based instruments plays to the strengths of business—namely, competition, creativity, and innovation—harnessing these qualities in the search for solutions. Less-flexible, regulatory approaches can stifle innovation, removing the incentive for continuous improvement and can result in technological lock-in.

CASE STUDY 7
Dow
page 81

The optimal mix of policy instruments for sustainability is listed in Box 2.

Key actors need to form policy partnerships to make instruments work. On their own, economic instruments will not stimulate change where informational, structural, and political obstacles impede them. Market instruments, regulation, and voluntary initiatives each have their role to play, but any sound mix of these needs so-called horizontal measures that support their use. These include education, capacity-building, infrastructure, institutional and regulatory reform, and the empowerment of citizens and consumers to play their part in shifting markets toward more sustainable forms of production and consumption. Most importantly, governments need to work with key actors to streamline government policies and dismantle those policies and instruments that hinder sustainable development.

Sending the right signals is a good start, but changing market behavior also means changing culture and attitudes. Effective policy partnerships, together with the approaches discussed above, form what the WBCSD has dubbed a 'smart' hierarchy of policy tools (see Box 3). Within the right framework, an optimal combination of command-and-control regulation, economic or market instruments, and voluntary initiatives or self-regulation by business, combined with horizontal support mechanisms such as education, information, and research, are by far the best means to achieve sustainable development objectives through the market (Schmidheiny 1992: 19).

Ultimately, the choice of tools will also be guided by administrative feasibility, political acceptability, and by the urgency, nature, and complexity of the problem being addressed. As Figure 4 indicates, there is a policy continuum whereby the choice of tool can be seen to evolve in keeping with the nature of the issue being addressed.

An optimal mix of policy instruments should be determined by:

- Environmental effectiveness

- Economic efficiency

- Flexibility of response

- Administrative feasibility

- Confidence in the regulatory environment

- Gradual introduction and progressive implementation

- Fiscal neutrality

- Equity and a level playing field

- Transparency of compliance

- Acceptability

- Simplicity and complementarity

- Shift from 'goods' to 'bads'

Box 2 **INSTRUMENT CHARACTERISTICS**

Sources: de Andraca and McCready 1994: 49; Schmidheiny 1992: 29-30

- **Voluntary initiatives** should be preferred, since these often provide the most flexible and, ultimately, overall most cost-effective way to achieve a desired result.

- **Negotiated agreements** can provide high operational flexibility if focused on what is required rather than on how it is to be achieved.

- **Economic instruments** can provide incentives but must be carefully designed to avoid unintended, unwanted consequences—such as the creation of perverse subsidies.

- **Command-and-control regulations** are needed to outlaw unsafe and unacceptable behavior and to provide the framework within which innovation can flourish. Alone, however, they cannot deliver continuous improvements, since the most effective solutions cannot be predicted or prescribed in advance.

Box 3 **THE 'SMART' HIERARCHY OF PUBLIC POLICY TOOLS**

Source: Holliday and Pepper 2001: 33

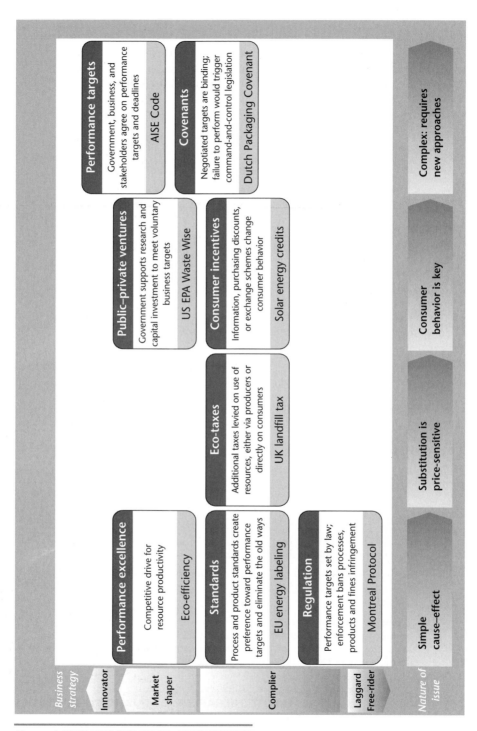

Figure 4 **THE POLICY TOOL CONTINUUM**

Source: Holliday and Pepper 2001: 31

This figure shows, moreover, what type of business strategy each choice of tool is likely to favor. In addition to these considerations, instrument choice should be guided by equity and by the need to create a level playing field and to promote more open and competitive markets.

Non-market measures

Non-market measures are needed to support the market measures, especially in developing countries and economies in transition to market systems.

Niall FitzGerald (2001b), chairman and CEO of the Anglo-Dutch food and home products company Unilever, maintains that in addition to market liberalization 'the means and the will to provide schooling, prevention-oriented healthcare and stable legal regimes for individuals and property rights rank as high'.

For developing countries lacking the resources and institutional infrastructure to implement and enforce complex regulatory systems, market instruments offer a promising alternative (Panayotou 1992). But the pace and manner of their introduction will be critical in determining their success. Before such instruments are adopted, adequate governance structures must be in place and the capacity-building and institution-strengthening necessary to the smooth functioning of the market must occur.

So, in addition to fiscal and economic measures such as full-cost pricing, tax reform, subsidy shifts and elimination, and the creation of sound property rights, we believe that a number of fundamental social conditions must prevail: democracy and governance, human rights, the elimination of bribery and corruption, and greater transparency and accountability. These are dealt with in the following sections.

Full-cost pricing

Full-cost pricing can be a frightening concept. First, that term 'full cost' makes it sound very expensive. Second, the implications are unsettling: in places where water is scarce and costly for a government to provide to its people, must it be priced so high that few can afford it?

Full-cost pricing is not necessarily expensive nor does it place resources out of the reach of the poor. It is not some fixed mathematical goal but a direction of movement. It is also the most fundamental way, and the most cost-effective way, in which the market can encourage, rather than discourage, sustainable development. De Andraca and McCready (1994) concluded that 'increasing the visibility of all costs associated with waste and pollution will encourage businesses to design products and services that reduce impacts on environmental systems and add value for consumers'.

The policy framework implications of such costing are twofold, according to Germany's Wuppertal Institute. First, at the micro-economic level, environmental 'externalities'—namely, the neglected social costs of environmental damage—must be 'internalized' into business and consumer budgets to encourage more sustainable production and consumption patterns, through the application of pollution charges, tradable pollution permits, fees for natural resource use, or by establishing property rights over natural assets (Bartelmus 1999). Second, at the macro-economic level, governments should establish what the Wuppertal Institute dubs 'environmentally adjusted aggregates', such as a green GDP or satellite accounts, like the Yale sustainability indicators or indexes launched by the World Economic Forum (WEF) in 2001. UNDP's composite human development index (HDI), meanwhile, addresses the social aspects of sustainability. Complementing traditional economic indicators with social and environmental factors in this manner would improve macro-economic policy-making by integrating social and environmental values into decision-making, and allowing governments to benchmark progress toward or away from their sustainable development objectives.

There has been some progress over the past decade. A 1992 OECD survey of market-based instruments found some 169 instruments in use across 23 countries. Most common among these were product taxes (e.g. on packaging and fertilizers) and deposit–refund systems (e.g. on glass bottles and aluminum cans) (Pearce and Barbier 2000: 170-73). Since 1992, the rationale of economic instruments appears to have been broadly accepted, at least in theory; but governments have a hard time integrating such tools into existing legislative contexts (Pearce and Barbier 2000: 209). The increased cost to a consumer or to a company of such an instrument is immediate and obvious, but the savings to society are not so immediate or obvious. So such changes are resisted.

Thus, overall progress in appropriately costing resource use and pollution and adjusting national accounts has been slow. UNEP (1999: 206) reported in its *Global Environmental Outlook 2000* that 'the Earth Summit placed great stress on economic incentives as a means of making production and consumption patterns more sustainable, but despite pleas for more use of market-oriented instruments, increase in the use of such instruments has been limited'.

Full-cost pricing and full-cost accounting have not been widely adopted, and environmental and social values remain largely excluded from the most fundamental of market tools—the pricing mechanism (see Figure 5). The result is that markets are still essentially failing to reflect the true cost of production and consumption. One salient consequence of this failure to price natural resources accurately is that vital environmental commons such as fresh water, ocean fisheries, and the atmosphere continue to suffer from overuse, depletion, and escalating concentrations of carbon dioxide.

Another problem is that in this competitive world a company that might want to embark on such a full-cost pricing journey cannot do so unilaterally. The goal must be to encourage whole market segments to change so that supportive companies are not doomed to unfair competitive disadvantage.

Lack of progress is partly a result of the theoretical difficulties inherent in valuing natural resources, services, and sinks. Attaching a value to nature is both complex and controversial and, although efforts are under way to develop frameworks for the internalization of external costs, these have yet to be harmonized and widely adopted. As argued a decade ago in *Changing Course* (Schmidheiny 1992: 16), however:

*Companies barely internalize the financial implications of
environmental policies and measures*

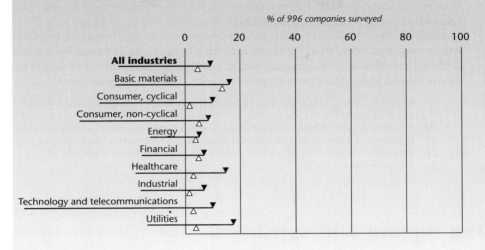

% of 996 companies surveyed

▼ *Environmental profit and loss
   accounting to some degree*

△ *Environmental accounting influences
   product pricing to some degree*

Source: sam

● Only 101 companies conduct a systematic
  financial analysis of their environmental
  policies and measures

● 39 state that their 'environmental accounting'
  influences certain product pricing measures

Figure 5 **ADOPTION OF ENVIRONMENTAL ACCOUNTING**

the lack of accuracy in determining the actual and future costs of pollution
should not allow us to conclude that no price can be established at all. As
individuals set prices for privately owned goods, society must establish
through political processes prices for the use of goods held in common:
waters, atmosphere, and so on. This work must be based both on the best
available scientific evidence and on people's preferences and choices.

Simon Upton, former New Zealand environment minister and now chairman of
the OECD Roundtable on Sustainable Development, calls on his fellow politicians to
find more political will for the issue. He states that 'governments have to stop
pretending that they can exhort people to make changes when the prices people pay
tell them otherwise' (Upton 2001: 13). The European Environment Agency (EEA 2001:
12) acknowledges this, admitting that a 'fair and efficient pricing' policy for the
European Union (EU) 'is far from being achieved; road and aviation in particular, the
modes with the highest external costs per transport unit, thus receive an implicit
subsidy from society'. To deal with this, the Commission of the European Commu-

nities (CEC 2001: 13) intends to propose in 2002 a framework for transport charges 'to ensure that by 2005, prices for different modes of transport, including air, reflect their costs to society'. This is a move in the right direction, which, combined with tax reform, subsidy shifts, and the enforcement of effective property rights, will help ensure that markets begin to reflect ecological truths.

In the South, meanwhile, where little primary research is being conducted on full-cost pricing, South African utility Eskom is filling the gap through an extensive study of how consideration of externalities might improve decision-making on corporate environmental expenditure. Says Thulani Gcabashe, Eskom chief executive:

> It isn't possible to simply use the numbers or ranking that have been developed elsewhere in the world, due to our unique environmental endowments and socio-economic framework. Research has [therefore] been initiated in Eskom to try and establish a robust methodology to examine impacts of externalities of various options for meeting future electricity demands (Eskom 2000).

Tax reform and subsidies

Tax shift is another phrase that is frightening to most business people, because we tend to focus on the word 'tax' and forget the word 'shift'; and it is true that governments have a track record of adding taxes in one area without the 'shift' of decreasing taxes in another area. We are worried that environmental taxes, sloppily devised and applied, could hurt our nations' economic competitiveness. But our appropriate caution ought to be balanced by an appropriate outrage against a system that taxes—and thus discourages—things that all citizens want, such as jobs, while failing to tax—and thus discourage—things that we do not want, such as pollution and waste. Environment-related taxes can be applied to resources and inputs, imports and exports, or to waste and polluting emissions (UNEP 1999: 206).

Acceptance of the logic of a tax shift does seem to be gaining ground. Led by Scandinavia, Europe has been among the early adopters. Energy taxes have been introduced in Denmark, Finland, Norway, Sweden, and the Netherlands, and France, Britain, Germany, Italy, and Switzerland have similar policies in the pipeline (Holliday and Pepper 2001: 34). Under an energy products tax directive the EU intends to develop 'ambitious environmental targets for energy taxation aiming at the full internalization of external costs' (CEC 2001: 10).

'Green taxes' can be extremely effective market instruments. Sweden's 1991 sulfur tax, for example, led to a drop in the sulfur content of fuels to 50% below legal requirements and stimulated power plants to invest in abatement technology, and Norway's carbon tax, also levied in 1991, lowered emissions from power plants by 21% (OECD 2001c). Significantly, no reductions in competitiveness appear to have occurred as a result of the taxes, although this may be accounted for by the often sizeable exemptions applied to energy-intensive industries (OECD 2001c).

This experience reminds us of Harvard Business School Professor Michael Porter's argument that countries that apply high environmental standards also experience high rates of competitiveness (Porter and van der Linde 1995b). This is borne out by Germany and Japan, both of which have instituted substantial energy taxes, as witnessed in their high respective rates of taxation applied to regular unleaded gasoline. Far from injuring competitiveness, the tax has resulted in higher energy productivity while lowering CO_2 intensity. The German economy grew by 1.1% per annum between 1990 and 1994, whereas energy consumption actually decreased by 1.5% per annum. In China, in contrast, where energy is subsidized, energy productivity (as measured by GDP per kilogram of energy used) is almost ten times lower (Pearce and Barbier 2000: 174).

More leadership could be shown by governments in so-called 'ecological tax reform'. In 1997 an early US state-level attempt at such a tax shift was made by a group called Minnesotans for an Energy-Efficient Economy (ME3). Their proposal was to tax carbon emissions, with a net offsetting reduction of existing property taxes. Extensive economic modeling showed that the tax would help squeeze waste and inefficiency out of industrial processes and improve competitiveness while lowering taxes on property. However, the proposal failed to garner enough political support, largely because of fears over competitiveness. ME3 concluded that such a sweeping structural shift in the tax system would require a stronger strategy for engaging important constituencies (WRI 2001). The collapse of the ME3 initiative highlights a fundamental problem facing policy-makers: how to raise support for unilateral action. Says Eugenio Clariond, president of Mexico's Grupo IMSA:

> Since *Changing Course*, we've been talking to governments about a tax shift from 'goods' to 'bads'. The problem is that although these ideas are good, it's very hard for one country to apply them in a vacuum. It's always seen as promoting an uneven playing field.

Along with revenue neutrality, any tax instrument should be pre-announced and introduced gradually, giving market players time to plan, and exemptions should be phased out gradually, with compensatory measures where necessary. Last, tax reform should involve extensive stakeholder consultation (Ribeiro 1997). If properly designed, tax reform can be a powerful tool for steering the economy in the right direction (Box 4).

In Chapter 1 we explained how subsidies disrupt international trade and work against sustainable progress by penalizing developing countries. As we noted, subsidies are not necessarily perverse and harmful but, when poorly designed, without clear sunset clauses, they can end up perpetually propping up uncompetitive companies and processes, harming markets and the environment nationally as well as internationally.

UK economists David Pearce and Edward Barbier point out that the worst perverse subsidies occur in developed countries. They note, 'it is interesting that advanced countries often criticize the poorer economies for bad management of their economies, when the rich countries persist in some of the worst forms of mismanagement through subsidization' (Pearce and Barbier 2000: 153).

There have been some notable successes in removing subsidies at the national level, of which New Zealand's elimination of agricultural support is perhaps the most renowned. Russia, Eastern Europe, China, and India have all reduced their subsidies for fossil fuel; Brazil has eliminated subsidies for ranching; and the USA, Mexico,

- **Fiscal neutrality.** If environmental taxes are established, other taxes should be reduced to prevent over-taxation.

- **Credit for early action.** Companies that take voluntary early action in environmental impact reduction should not be put at a competitive disadvantage by subsequent regulatory action.

- **Border tax adjustment.** Trade in goods and services should not be unduly affected by the tax policies of specific nations.

- **Transition mechanisms.** Temporary mechanisms are required during changes in market structure in order to avoid negative social, economic, and environmental consequences.

- **Adequate phase-in time.** A transition period should be allowed for to avoid undue impacts on infrastructure industries with long lead-time investment obligations.

Box 4 **DESIGN CRITERIA FOR ENVIRONMENTAL TAXATION**
Source: Holliday and Pepper 2001: 34

Australia, and South Africa have all gone some way toward removing subsidies in the water sector. Indonesia, Bangladesh, and Hungary, meanwhile, have achieved sizeable savings in government spending through removing pesticide, fertilizer, and irrigation subsidies (Panayotou 1998: 69-70).

The days may also be numbered for distorting subsidies on the world's fisheries, since Australia, Iceland, New Zealand, Norway, Peru, the Philippines, and the USA, which take some 25% of the world's marine fish catch, have called for the WTO to oversee reform of the sector's subsidy regimes. It is a move welcomed by Ross Tocker, general manager of operations at Sealord Group, the largest fishing quota holder in New Zealand, who has urged the eradication of incentives for vessel overcapitalization (Tocker 2001), and by Volker Kuntszch, buying director of Frozen Fish International, owned by Unilever. Says Kuntszch (2001: 6):

> We've set ourselves the goal of buying all our fish from sustainable sources by 2005, [but] this goal will be difficult given fish stock declines. I'm concerned that some policy-makers and other stakeholders remain unaware of the fish stock crisis—and I strongly question the value of subsidies for this sector.

Subsidies may be of some help toward sustainable development, though that is a controversial notion. As Pearce and Barbier (2000: 156) have observed, 'investing in new and clean technology is risky. Subsidy payments could greatly assist the reduction of those risks, stimulating further output of renewable/nuclear energy and further environmental benefits.' In the USA the senate of the State of Michigan passed a package of bills in 2001 aimed at helping low-income families install energy-efficient appliances. In Germany, parliament agreed to increase subsidies to solar, thermal, biogas, and geothermal energy in 2002 from the equivalent of $135 million to $180 million (Reuters 2001: 422).

Property rights and market creation

Many natural resources are undervalued in our market system, and many ecosystems services are provided for free. As markets depend primarily on price signals to function correctly, these resources are frequently wasted or overused, since their depletion or dysfunction are market externalities, and consumers rarely value what they use for free (Holliday and Pepper 2001: 35).

Economists Pearce and Barbier (2000: 166) have identified four different types of property right: private ownership, state ownership, common ownership, and open access (in which access to the resource is open and free to all). Of these, the first is most likely to favor sound resource stewardship, since private owners will seek not to despoil their asset. The last, on the other hand, is most likely to increase the risk of rapid resource exploitation, since individual users have an incentive to extract as much personal value as possible over as short a time as possible in competing with other users, even at the cost of depleting the resource. Establishing and enforcing effective property rights is therefore a vital step in the creation of a properly valued market for environmental goods and services, argue Pearce and Barbier. An appropriate and effective system of ownership 'will lead to greater incentives to conserve natural resources at the local level' (2000: 169).

This theory is borne out by experience in the fishing industry, where lack of defined property rights has been widely blamed for extensive over-fishing of the marine commons. Both in the US North Pacific and in New Zealand's fisheries, the problem of fish stock depletion has been tackled through the use of tradable quotas, or property rights. Under New Zealand's quota management system (QMS), introduced in 1986, the government decides each year what quantity or total allowable catch (TAC) of all quota species may be caught by commercial and non-commercial fishers. Commercial operators such as Sealord, which is the largest quota holder in New Zealand, each receive an individual transferable quota (ITQ), which they can fish, sell or lease to other operators. This approach, says the company, 'is actively supported by the New Zealand fishing industry . . . [It] gives the industry security of access, coupled with flexibility, and encourages seafood companies to look after their assets' (Sealord 2001).

According to Ross Tocker (2001: 6-7), general manager of operations at Sealord Group, the New Zealand property-rights quota system has helped establish sustainability as a key corporate objective, resulting in voluntary industry initiatives, such as a code of practice to avoid catching fur seals:

> Allocating property rights ensures that sustainability becomes a priority for the owner of the right—namely, the company—as well as for government. If there's no property right, then individual businesses simply compete for fish with other companies.

Property rights are just the first step in creating a market for natural resources. As we argue in Chapter 9, creating an effective market requires the clear definition of objectives, performance measurements, establishment of an exchange, capping and trading. It needs effective monitoring, penalties and enforcement for non-compliance, and should include performance objectives to reduce free-riders. Above all, it requires good governance, which is discussed below.

Democracy and governance

To work efficiently, markets need rules and enforcement mechanisms and they need organizations and institutions promoting market transactions. Chief among these are an effective governance framework, transparent and unbiased legal and judicial systems, an efficient financial regulatory system, and a social safety net (World Bank 2002: 1). To work sustainably, they need, in addition, cohesion, inclusivity, and long-term vision. Without accountable government and effective institutions, sustainable development is impossible.

Governance is the exercise of administrative, economic, and political authority over a nation's, or a company's, affairs. According to the OECD (2001b: 246), it requires, along with the rule of law, 'predictable, open and transparent policy-making, a professional bureaucracy, an executive arm accountable for its actions and strong civil society participation in public affairs'. Sustainable development needs strong political leadership. It means committing to a long-term vision, a new approach to policy-making and negotiating difficult trade-offs between conflicting interests. And, beyond 'putting one's own house in order', it means becoming a responsible partner in a globalized world (CEC 2001).

Harvard University's Theodore Panayotou (2000) is firm about the link between good environmental stewardship, wealth creation and improved governance:

> As long as property rights remain ill-defined and insecure, as long as polluting inputs and extractive industries are being subsidized, as long as polluters free-ride on the environment and users of public services free-ride on the treasury, and as long as the dynamics of private sector and the spirit of civil society are bureaucratically constrained from making their full contributions, current trends cannot be reversed and the gap between economic and environmental performance will continue to grow.

He adds that:

> only a policy paradigm shift can put the developing world on the fast track to environmental recovery that parallels its fast track of economic growth. The new policy paradigm involves less government bureaucracy, an enhanced role for the private sector and civil society, and the aggressive pursuit of untapped win–win policy reforms and high-return investment opportunities that would result in both environmental and economic gains.

In societies where these elements are ineffective or lacking, progress toward sustainable development and participation in global markets will be hindered. 'This is a barrier we impose upon ourselves,' says Eugenio Clariond of Grupo IMSA in Mexico, 'It's a consequence of our own mismanagement. We have very inefficient bureaucracy; there's corruption and red tape. To incorporate a corporation in Mexico takes over 75 days—in the US it takes two! These things harm our productivity.'

According to the World Bank, good governance and strong institutions are also key to solving poverty and its related development challenges. In its 2001 *World Development Report*, governance and institutional capacity issues predominate (World Bank 2001a). Drawing on the work of Peruvian development economist Hernando de Soto, the World Bank found that the economies that are most likely to develop and become competitive are those that promote the open flow of information, that ensure good protection for property rights of rich and poor and that provide widespread access to judicial systems. 'Efficient formal and informal institutions . . . are crucial for turning subsistence farmers, petty traders and other would-be money-makers into a boon for the general economy', comments *The Economist* (2001d); 'if it is too expensive and time-consuming, for example, to open a bank account, the poor will stuff their savings under the mattress'.

De Soto (2000) has argued that a great deal of poverty is avoidable, given some basic institutional improvements. Even the very poor have assets, de Soto maintains, but many of these fall outside the legal property system and therefore cannot be leveraged to produce additional wealth. The result is so-called 'dead capital'. By providing simple and accessible institutions to the poor, such as deeds for their homes, the 'extralegal' economic activity that currently dominates developing-world economies can be legitimized and harnessed for wider societal wealth creation. Growth, in other words, follows respect for the property rights of the poor, given the right institutional framework.

Future governance challenges will include achieving greater policy coherence across the economic, social, and environmental domains, particularly as increased crossover between policies, greater international interdependence, and growing complexity of issues heighten the need for consistency and integration in policy-making (WWF 2001a).

Human rights

The ideas and rhetoric of human rights, along with the notion of respect for human rights as a fundamental precondition for sustainable development, have gained a great deal of prominence in recent years. It has come to be accepted by many in business that we have a role to play in their pursuit and enforcement, exerting our influence to ensure that human rights are observed in the countries in which we operate.

Others in business, however, feel that using corporate power and influence to pressure national governments and guide their behavior is wrong and that companies have no business 'meddling' in politics to pressure governments on human rights issues. Whichever view you take, the fact is that companies are best at respecting human rights within the sphere of their own operations and are less successful trying to force governments to do likewise.

Rio Tinto has expressed support for the UN Secretary General's Global Compact, which encourages industry to adhere to nine principles of best practice in the areas of human rights and environmental and labor standards. Says Sir Robert Wilson (2001), company chairman:

> The Global Compact fits together well with a wide range of Rio Tinto initiatives in the fields of corporate social responsibility and sustainable development. For example, our statement of business practice, *The Way We Work*, includes policies in all the areas covered by the Global Compact.

Rio Tinto's aim in this area is to contribute to the development of best practice. With the help of outside experts, the company has developed detailed guidance on implementing its human rights policy. The guidance covers four areas: communities, employees, security, and 'difficult issues'—setting out procedures and a checklist of questions for the manager. Rio Tinto is realistic about its power to influence governments over human rights issues. Wilson (2001) notes that 'We focus on what we can manage and what we can strongly influence, recognizing that we don't have a mandate for global diplomacy.'

Shell in 1997 revised its business principles, and a key change was accepting a duty to speak out for fundamental human rights while noting that fulfilling its responsibilities as a corporate citizen should not mean trying to dictate Western cultural norms (Watts 2000). This more active advocacy role acknowledges the influence that companies can exert in countries where they have a presence, but it also has at its heart the notion that universal recognition of the ideal of human rights should not be used to undermine human diversity.

Bribery and corruption

Tolerance or encouragement of corruption is a serious policy flaw which impedes sustainability through the market and subverts free and open trade.

As well as rendering the market inefficient by raising the cost of business transactions, corruption has a negative impact on the corporate bottom line. In 1999, *The Economist* estimated that bribes made to Indonesian bureaucrats totaled some 20% of business costs in that country (BSR 2001). A World Bank survey in Uganda, meanwhile, found companies were paying an average of 6% of their turnover in bribes (Jafferji 2001). Fighting corruption is therefore in companies' self-interest. In a corrupt environment, where contracts may be awarded not on merit but on the size of the kickback, competitive advantage based on efficiency and innovation is undermined. Bribery corrodes the rule of law and undermines democratic institutions, hampering development by diverting funds away from local communities and the poor and by eroding public services. Paradoxically, corruption can lead to even greater bureaucracy and red tape as officials seek further opportunities to raise illicit revenue and governments create more bureaucracy to limit corruption. The degree of corruption can range from the petty—often among civil servants, motivated by low salaries—to the grand, whereby fraud and extortion become so entrenched the entire state system becomes a 'kleptocracy'.

The growing global market has moved corruption toward the top of the global political agenda. By standing firm against corruption, companies can begin to cut unnecessary costs, minimize bureaucracy, and, usually, become more competitive. Taking a strong ethical stance on graft also helps iron out any ethic of corruption among employees, and being seen to be clean often carries with it tangible benefits to brand and image. General Electric holds that campaigning against bribery actually spurs competitive advantage. The company now uses its compliance program and ethics handbook as a sales tool with customers—and can point to contracts won in

Latin America as a direct result of its integrity policy (see BSR 2001). Honeywell Inc. has also benefited commercially from its anti-corruption strategy. In one instance, the company was asked for a bribe in connection with a major Asian airport contract. In keeping with its anti-corruption policy, Honeywell opted not to bid. Shortly afterwards, a corruption scandal broke over the project. When it was revealed that 11 other bidding companies had paid bribes, they were disqualified; Honeywell was awarded the contract.

Business can therefore play a valuable role in tackling the supply side of corruption. Where companies' involvement in corruption is concerned, many argue that verifiable voluntary codes of conduct could go a long way in stamping out corruption and bribery. Shell, for example, has a 'no-bribes' policy in its general business principles and has procedures to detect violations and, like others such as DuPont and Aracruz Celulose, it has pledged to report on its performance. DuPont has a strong policy and audit process, and a number of people have been fired over non-compliance with the ethics policy. But, says Shell's Robin Aram, vice president of external relations and policy development, 'the world is full of bribery and corruption, so we don't pretend this is easy to deal with' (in Jafferji 2001).

In Figure 6 we illustrate the extent of adoption of codes of conduct in the companies surveyed.

Others therefore claim that binding regulation is the only sure way to tackle this deep-seated problem. Alan Larson, undersecretary for business affairs at the US State Department, agrees that bribery should be banned, but he would sweeten the regulatory pill to companies by adding incentives for good behavior, such as granting export credit guarantees (in Dale 2001). Other effective moves might include determined action by financial institutions to make strict auditing and reporting a condition for access to grants and loans, mobilizing transparency to help root out the problem at source (IISD 1998a). Eskom Chairman Reuel Khoza is a firm supporter of this strategy. Action on corruption could be linked to debt relief for the South, he argues, and access to funds should involve conditions. He states that 'the north needs to make common cause with the south on this issue. But for every penny of debt relief granted, financial institutions must say "we'll be watching the spending of every dollar".'

International moves are already afoot to make corruption and bribery a punishable offense. The OECD Convention on Combating Corruption and Bribery went into effect in January 1999. By September 2000 it had been signed by all 29 OECD members and by five non-members (Argentina, Brazil, Bulgaria, Chile, and the Slovak Republic; see OECD 2000a). The convention opens the way for enforcement and prosecution of those who engage in corruption by requiring signatory countries to 'establish the criminal offense of bribing a foreign public official, and to have in place adequate sanctions and reliable means for detecting and enforcing the offense' (OECD 2000a).

Recognizing that criminalizing acts of corruption is insufficient to tackle the problem as a whole, the OECD also attacked the 'supply' aspect of bribery through a new chapter in its 2000 revision of its 1976 Guidelines for Multinational Enterprises (OECD 2000b). The OECD 1998 Council Recommendation on Improving Ethical Conduct in Public Service, the OECD Public Management Committee (PUMA) and the Financial Action Task Force on Money Laundering, meanwhile, will be mobilized to deal with

Half of the companies surveyed have a code of conduct valid for all employees

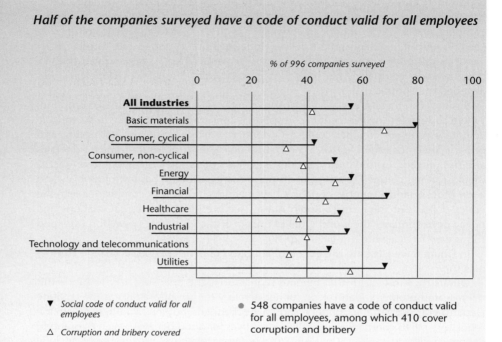

% of 996 companies surveyed

▼ Social code of conduct valid for all employees

△ Corruption and bribery covered

● 548 companies have a code of conduct valid for all employees, among which 410 cover corruption and bribery

Source: sam⟨⟩

Figure 6 **ADOPTION OF CODES OF CONDUCT**

the demand side, together with various technical cooperation efforts to help build governance capacity in developing economies.

Partnerships between public and private sectors and between regions will be essential to ensure smooth coordination of anti-corruption strategies. The OECD is already working with non-OECD countries in the fight against corruption. Initiatives are under way to help tackle the problem in Central and Eastern Europe and the former Soviet Union, and the OECD's Development Assistance Committee (DAC) is addressing the issue in developing countries.

Ultimately, though, the solution to corruption lies in greater corporate and governmental accountability. According to the World Bank (2002: 109), 'lack of information breeds corruption'. Tellingly, the World Bank reports a clear association between indicators of press freedom and the absence of corruption. Meanwhile, Transparency International, a Berlin-based NGO, is calling for governments to report their performance on corruption; for both the supply and demand sides of the corruption equation, greater transparency is at the heart of the solution.

Transparency and accountability

A fundamental precondition for well-functioning markets is the free and open flow of information; and a fundamental condition for a well-functioning society is consultation and inclusion. Although recent years have seen a groundswell of initiatives aimed at increasing governmental and corporate accountability, there is still much to do both in these sectors and in ensuring that the organizations claiming to represent civil society, many of them just as 'multinational' as large corporations, are also transparent and accountable.

Progress is also needed in ensuring that the institutions underpinning the emerging architecture of global governance are seen to be transparent and inclusive. Indeed, among the chief reproaches of the anti-globalization movement to the WTO has been its lack of transparency, citizen consultation and participation and the fact that many key decisions are taken in closed arenas beyond the public purview.

The broad trend is toward greater openness and inclusion. In 1998, 35 countries signed the UN Economic Commission for Europe (UNECE) Convention on Access to Information, Public Participation in Decision-making and Access to Justice in Environmental Matters—known as the Aarhus Convention (Box 5). This Convention sets rules for public disclosure by government and corporations of environmental and other

---

The Aarhus Convention on Access to Information, Public Participation in Decision-making and Access to Justice in Environmental Matters was adopted in 1998 and came into force on 30 October 2001. As of January 2002, its status of participation comprises 17 ratifications, approvals, acceptances, or accessions and 31 signatories among the European member countries of the UNECE—the United Nations Economic Commission for Europe (Europe and North America).

It rests on three main pillars: the right of individuals and corporations to demand information; the early inclusion of the public in decisions that will have an environmental impact; and the right of the public to appeal in case of denied environmental information.

The Convention has two task forces:

- Task Force on Electronic Tools

- Task Force on Access to Justice

and three working groups:

- Working Group on Compliance and Rules of Procedure

- Working Group on Genetically Modified Organisms

- Working Group on Pollutant Release and Transfer Registers

The GMO working group focuses, for example, on trying to fill in gaps that exist in the international or regional frameworks regulating GMO-related product information (such as the Cartagena Protocol on Biosafety, the Codex Alimentarius Commission, Directive 2001/18/EC and so on).

Box 5 **THE AARHUS CONVENTION**

Source: UNECE 2001

information and establishes a framework for civil participation in environmental decision-making. It also establishes a framework for judicial remedy for non-compliance with the convention (Petkova and Veit 2000).

Economist Joseph Stieglitz in his Nobel-winning work showed that market failures are often caused by imperfect information—one-sided, too costly, or simply impossible to obtain (Sweeting 1998). This inequality of information can lead the market to function inefficiently: for example, by allowing a low-quality product to displace a higher-quality equivalent. Most importantly, Stieglitz claims, it can undermine confidence in the market. Governments therefore have a central role to play in setting the framework for greater market transparency, a move that would help ensure both that markets operate to their maximum efficiency and that they allocate resources more fairly (Shorrock 2001).

Companies, too, need to improve their levels of transparency, on financial matters as well as social and environmental issues. A salutary tale on the importance of openness is provided by US energy giant Enron, a sector leader whose lack of transparency was largely responsible for its loss of market credibility and its eventual bankruptcy. It has taken over a century to establish relatively clear rules for financial accountability in the corporate world; even so, experiences such as that of Enron highlight the need for ongoing evolution toward greater transparency in this area.

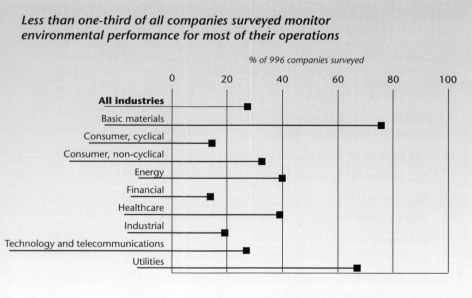

Less than one-third of all companies surveyed monitor environmental performance for most of their operations

% of 996 companies surveyed

- 282 companies monitor environmental performance for all units generating more than 90% of their total revenues

Source: sam

Figure 7 **MONITORING OF ENVIRONMENTAL PERFORMANCE**

Accountability for environmental and social issues is far less developed. For example, a 1998 study by the US Environmental Protection Agency (EPA) found that 74% of publicly traded companies had failed to disclose adequately environmental legal proceedings in their Securities and Exchange Commission-mandated 10-K registration requirements (Sutherland 2001). Guidelines—such as the EU's recent issuing of a voluntary recommendation to clarify existing EU accounting rules and improve the transparency, quality, and comparability of corporate environmental data—go some way toward filling that gap, but full corporate environmental disclosure is still a minority sport (Figures 1 and 7).

Although many leading corporations now produce voluntary corporate environmental reports (CERs) and accounts of their corporate social responsibility, this practice is still reserved to a small minority of the business community. Moreover, there is still some degree of apparent dissonance between what companies state in their CERs and what they lobby for behind closed doors. Such discrepancies undermine public trust in business and can be damaging to both brand and image. Shell's Robin Aram maintains that, proprietary competitive matters apart, the appearance of secrecy in business dealings is a risky strategy for companies: 'If you have what appears to be a secret club, people will assume secret things are happening. That's not in our interest' (in Cowe 2000). Transparency and consistency, argues Aram, are the overriding requirements: 'What you say should actually be true . . . then you should assume that what you say in private will appear on the front page of the newspapers. If that would create embarrassment, it's probably not such a good idea.'

Voluntary codes of conduct on disclosure can help plug the transparency gap. The WBCSD's sustainable development reporting project, for example, has identified 27 separate elements which it includes in a so-called 'inventory' of good reporting practices. These range from top management commitment and corporate profile issues to the impacts of the core business and the reporting process itself. At the root of it, however, transparency and accountability—whether corporate or governmental—are merely the reverse side of the governance coin: if institutions are well governed, accountability, and the transparency that this embodies, will follow.

CASE STUDY 6

Business Council for Sustainable Development–Gulf of Mexico

Mississippi forests

Prior to European settlement, approximately 10 million ha of bottomland hardwood forests existed in the Lower Mississippi Alluvial Valley (LMAV) from Southern Illinois and Missouri to Louisiana and Mississippi. Today, approximately 1.6 million ha of this ecosystem remain, mostly in private ownership.

The reduction in forest cover reflects the region's history of logging and of converting forests to farms. Cotton, soybeans, and other commodity crops are successfully produced in the region, but large areas are marginal for farming because of frequent flooding by the Mississippi River. Subsidized soybeans are the primary crop grown on these flood-prone lands.

Agricultural run-off pollutes waterways in the LMAV and helps cause the low-oxygen zone in the Gulf of Mexico at the mouth of the Mississippi River. Forest loss has also diminished regional biodiversity and wildlife populations. In addition to environmental challenges, the LMAV faces economic hardship, with over 30% of the population of 32 counties living below the US poverty line.

Replanting forests can help to address these challenges. Studies show that, on marginal land, mixed hardwood forests are likely to be more economically viable than soybeans. However, farmers have to wait about 15 years before making a profit if they convert their land from commodity farming to forests. To cope with this issue, Business Council for Sustainable Development–Gulf of Mexico (BCSD–GM) developed the LMAV Afforestation Project with support and encouragement from the Triangle-Pacific Corporation, the Westvaco Corporation (now MeadWestvaco), the Temple-Inland Company and AgForest Partners. The project aims to assist farmers in bridging the revenue gap and establishing mixed hardwood forests that could be sustainably managed over the long term for economic returns and a wide range of environmental benefits. The BCSD–GM hopes to establish forests on 28,000 ha of marginal farmland in the LMAV by 2005. By 2020, the BCSD–GM hopes that the project can increase beyond these 28,000 ha to make a substantial contribution to the restoration of one million or more acres of bottomland hardwood forests.

By establishing the forests described above, the project should raise and diversify farm incomes, address a wide range of environmental challenges, and, simultaneously:

- Reduce and then eliminate reliance on direct-subsidy support for commodity row crops

- Provide the economic support necessary to bridge the revenue gap between row-crop agriculture and sustainable forestry

- Respect and leverage the rights of private property holders in the region

- Take advantage of developing markets for certified, sustainably produced forest products and carbon sequestration credits to build long-term economic support for LMAV forests

The BCSD–GM works with state offices of the US Department of Agriculture to modify enrollment criteria for the Conservation Reserve Program (CRP). CRP offers contracts to farmers to put their land under conservation practices (e.g. trees or grass) for a specified term (e.g. 15 years) in exchange for market-driven rental payments. Standard CRP enrollment criteria permit the planting of narrow riverside buffer strips. In contrast, the enrollment criteria advocated by BCSD–GM allow farmers to enroll any flood-prone lands in the floodplain of the river that are adjacent to a waterway and subject to scour or deposition.

Illinois was the first state to make changes to its CRP enrollment criteria to promoted establishing forests at the scale advocated by BCSD–GM. To date, Illinois, Missouri, and Mississippi have made some or all of the changes advocated. Arkansas and Louisiana are in the process of making similar changes. By the spring of 2002, over 1,335 ha should be planted in bottomland hardwoods, and 32 landowners should be in line for forest-based revenue. The first cottonwoods should be harvested from these lands in 2015.

CASE STUDY 7
Dow *SafeChem*

Owing to their cleaning efficiency, chlorinated solvents are used in a variety of industries, including pharmaceuticals, plastics, dry-cleaning, and metalworking. They are also used for the production of everyday items such as the Swiss army knife. In some cases, especially high-technology applications, chlorinated solvents are irreplaceable.

However, in the mid-1980s new information about the potential hazards associated with the use of these solvents became available. Thus regulatory authorities had some difficult decisions to make. Some countries chose to heavily restrict the use of these solvents. Invariably, this led to the development of substitutes, but many of these substitutes were untested products that were not necessarily safer. However, the three main chlorinated solvents that were on the market had been subjected to extensive health studies and toxicological reviews. Consequently, their health profiles were well known, and effective safety procedures could be adopted. Germany chose not to ban the use of chlorinated solvents but rather to require that their use take place in a closed-loop system.

Convinced of the advantages offered by these products, the Dow Chemical Company remained in the chlorinated solvents business. The company was also confident that managing the risks would provide a better, safer option than turning to insufficiently tested alternatives with unknown risks—following the principles of 'Responsible Care'. Dow began exploring new business models that would provide users with an environmentally and economically sound product in a safe and reliable manner. In 1992 Dow Deutschland Inc. and RCN (Recycling Chemie Niederrhein) founded a joint venture to offer chlorinated solvents in a closed-loop delivery system accompanied by a support service.

The new system offered not only the safe delivery and take-back of solvents but also assistance to customers in the use of these solvents in closed-loop equipment.

The company was called SafeChem Umweltservice GmbH and in 1998 became a fully owned subsidiary of Dow Deutschland Inc.

Today SafeChem markets the Safe-Tainer® (a trademark of the Dow Chemical Company and its subsidiaries) system across Europe. The system centers on two specially designed double-skinned containers (one for fresh solvent and one for used solvent) and each has an integrated drum for the solvent. This is intended to give protection against accidental damage, discharge, and spillage. The offering, however, comprises far more than just safe containers: the Safe-Tainer® system is an entirely new business model, the success of which is founded on two considerations: ecological and economic sustainability.

With the implementation of closed-loop systems, solvent consumption has dropped considerably as a result of the reduction in emissions. The solvent remains for extended periods (up to one year and more) in the closed cleaning equipment. The goal of this approach is to use the solvent for as long as possible in a recycling loop at the customer's site prior to external recycling.

SafeChem is a service-focused business, selling minimum volumes of solvents and maximum support services to allow the customers to achieve the desired goal. SafeChem and Dow offer this service platform in Germany, Switzerland, Austria, Italy, Spain, France, the United Kingdom, Sweden, the Benelux countries, and Portugal.

It is thanks to the legislative development favoring the use of chlorinated solvents in closed loops, rather then their prohibition, that the idea of SafeChem as service and solution provider has proved such a significant success in Europe.

Eco-efficiency

"Eco-efficiency catches at a glance the balance business strives toward: sound ecology and profitable operations."

Björn Stigson, president, WBCSD

The basic business contribution to sustainable development, one we have worked on for a decade, is *eco-efficiency*, a term we invented in 1992. The WBCSD defines eco-efficiency as being:

> achieved by the delivery of competitively priced goods and services that satisfy human needs and bring quality of life, while progressively reducing ecological impacts and resource intensity throughout the life cycle, to a level at least in line with the Earth's estimated carrying capacity (WBCSD 2000b).

This is a management strategy that combines environmental and economic performance. It enables more efficient production processes and the creation of better products and services while reducing resource use, waste, and pollution along the entire value chain. It creates more value with less impact by de-linking goods and services from the use of nature. It can open up significant business opportunities. As an energy conservation tool, it can be helpful in limiting climate change.

Eco-efficiency helps wealthier countries to grow more qualitatively than quantitatively—providing more service, function, and value, not transforming more materials into energy and waste. Eco-efficiency also helps developing countries to continue to grow quantitatively while saving resources.

We have identified four aspects of eco-efficiency that make it an indispensable strategic element in today's knowledge-based economy:

● *Dematerialization.* This involves companies developing ways of substituting knowledge flows for material flows. Another route to dematerialization is product customization: less waste is created when resources a consumer does not want are not produced.

- *Production loop closure.* The biological designs of nature provide a role model for sustainability. The goal is to work continuously toward closed-loop production systems and zero-waste factories wherein every output is returned to natural systems as a nutrient or becomes an input in the manufacture of another product.

- *Service extension.* We are moving from a supply-driven economy to a demand-driven economy. Companies are rethinking how they can satisfy demand and are developing customized responses to client needs. Consumers are increasingly gaining access to product services by leasing goods, particularly durable goods, rather than buying them outright.

- *Functional extension.* Companies are manufacturing 'smarter' products with new and enhanced functionality and are selling services to enhance the products' functional value.

The WBCSD has developed a framework that can be used to measure and report progress toward eco-efficiency in a consistent manner. Although the framework provides a common set of definitions, principles, and indicators, it is flexible enough to be widely used and interpreted to fit the individual needs of companies across the business spectrum.

Setting the frame

Eco-efficiency works in companies that try it; that is the good news. The more troubling news is that eco-efficiency is not yet being tried on a scale that truly makes a difference in the way most business is conducted today or at a pace that will significantly stem the tide of damage to the natural environment as populations grow and poor nations develop.

Stepping up efforts in eco-efficiency will require a new contract among society, government, and business. Under such a contract, corporate leaders would pledge to invest in eco-efficient innovation—that is, to achieve radical rather than incremental environmental improvement over the long term, to work to reduce global inequalities, and to be responsible employers and community members (DeSimone and Popoff 1997).

Governments would agree to establish a framework of regulations, economic instruments, and information disclosure to encourage long-term progress and penalize free-riders if this were to be done without damaging competition. Members of society must be willing to pay the 'real costs' for goods and services, as discussed in Chapter 2.

The European Environment Agency (EEA), established by the European Union in 1990 to serve as the hub of the European Environmental Information and Observation Network (EIONET), has adopted eco-efficiency ratio indicators for countries, asking for an absolute and relative 'de-linking of growth of welfare from the use of nature'. It intends to measure and compare economic sectors and countries with each other according to their eco-efficiency status and improvements. The OECD environment ministries in 1996 observed that 'a strategy to improve eco-efficiency might enable industry, governments, households to decouple pollutant release and resource use from economic activity'. The OECD has recommended the use of eco-efficiency ratios as macro-level indicators (WBCSD 2000b).

The OECD identified innovation as the key driver for improving eco-efficiency and said that it was best stimulated by strong competition, high-factor prizes, regulatory incentives, an effective process of disseminating 'best practice' and the presence of a good climate for innovation. What is needed now are radical improvements, better product design and further adoption of eco-efficient principles by small and medium-sized enterprises (SMEs), which constitute the majority of industry in most countries. This calls for greater leadership by business, governments, and civil society, further refining of targets and metrics, and continuous improvement. It will also mean over-coming barriers to further expansion of eco-efficiency, including the absence of the right market signals and an insufficient regulatory framework.

Despite these obstacles, eco-efficiency has gained enough momentum to redefine the way many leading companies conduct their everyday business and view the world around them. For these companies, dematerialization, closed production loops, ser-vice extension, and functional extension have become ways of doing business more profitably. The move from a supply-driven to a demand-driven economy is also prompting companies to rethink how they can satisfy demand by creating cus-tomized responses to client needs or manufacturing products with new and enhanced functionality.

The aim of eco-efficiency is to dematerialize. The Factor 10 Club, a group of leading international figures in environment and development, have argued that a process of dematerialization requiring a tenfold increase in the average resource productivity of the industrial countries is essential in the long term (F10C 1997). Their interim target for the short to medium term is a Factor 4 improvement (von Weiz-säcker *et al.* 1998).

A journey, not a destination

As quoted above, the WBCSD defines eco-efficiency as being

> achieved by the delivery of competitively priced goods and services that satisfy human needs and bring quality of life, while progressively reducing ecological impacts and resource intensity throughout the life cycle, to a level at least in line with the Earth's estimated carrying capacity (WBCSD 2000b).

The OECD has called eco-efficiency 'the efficiency with which ecological resources are used to meet human needs' and defines it as a ratio of an output (the value of products and services produced by a firm, sector, or economy as a whole) divided by the input (the sum of environmental pressures generated by the firm, the sector, or the economy) (OECD 1998b). The EEA defines it as 'more welfare from less nature' and says it comes through decoupling resource use and pollutant release from economic development. However defined, scaling up eco-efficiency will mean changing those attitudes that limit the full understanding and potential of the concept. Eco-efficiency is not limited simply to making incremental efficiency improvements in existing practices and habits. Rather, it should stimulate creativity and innovation in the search for new ways of doing things. Furthermore, it is not limited to areas within a company's boundaries, such as manufacturing and plant management, but is just as valid for the entire supply and production value chains.

Eco-efficiency's flexibility makes it useful to all companies and through changing times. Customer needs change, and so does our understanding of the environment and the extent of eco-capacity. New risks emerge, such as climate change, and existing ones become better characterized. The continuing pressure of economic and population growth mean that some challenges—such as availability of clean water— CASE STUDY 8 General Motors page 96 become increasingly serious. That is all the more reason to focus on eco-efficiency as a journey rather than as a destination, a process rather than a panacea. No company today or in the foreseeable future can truly say it is eco-efficient. What leading firms can say is that they are practising eco-efficiency by having a mind-set to constantly create more from less (DeSimone and Popoff 1997).

Some limitations

Many people who criticize the concept of eco-efficiency do not understand it. William McDonough and Michael Braungart, specialists in architecture and design chemistry, wrote in *The Atlantic Monthly* in 1998 that the concept was 'fatally limited'. They claimed that eco-efficiency 'tells us to restrict industry and curtail growth—to try to limit the creativity and productiveness of humankind'. In fact—and this upsets some environmentalists—eco-efficiency sets no limits to growth and no inherent restrictions on industry. It seeks more efficient growth and in doing so calls for a great deal of 'creativity and productiveness' on the part of humankind. As far as we can ascertain, McDonough and Braungart's (1998) only proposed solution to the perceived problems with eco-efficiency was to change the term to *eco-effectiveness*!

Eco-efficiency is also criticized for not achieving all the goals of sustainable development, as it lacks stated limits and a social side. However, it was never intended to wrap up the whole concept for business; it was meant to give business a business-like way into sustainable development. It is a helpful tool that allows companies to do better business while playing their part in the environmental side of sustainable development. Most of the companies that have embraced eco-efficiency have gone on to explore the social aspects of sustainable development.

By itself, eco-efficiency cannot cope with the harmful effects of business on the environment. Economic growth is required to create jobs and opportunities for growing populations and to help people pull themselves out of poverty. One can imagine a world in which companies are increasing their eco-efficiency by 5% a year while industrial output is increasing by 10% a year—and the planet is not becoming a cleaner place to live.

Strategies for eco-efficiency

For many companies, the main harmful effects on the environment with which they are associated actually occur outside their fences—either upstream in the raw material generation and supplier processing phases, or downstream in the product use or disposal phases. In light of this, the WBCSD has identified seven elements that businesses can use to improve their eco-efficiency (Lehni 2000):

- Reduce material intensity

- Reduce energy intensity

- Reduce dispersion of toxic substances

- Enhance recyclability

- Maximize use of renewables

- Extend product durability

- Increase service intensity

These seven elements may be thought of as being concerned with three broad objectives:

- Reducing the consumption of resources, including minimizing the use of energy, materials, water, and land, enhancing recyclability and product durability and closing material loops

- Reducing the impact on nature, including minimizing air emissions, water discharges, waste disposal, and the dispersion of toxic substances as well as fostering the sustainable use of renewable resources

- Increasing product or service value; this means providing more benefits to customers through improving the functionality and flexibility of products as well as providing additional services (such as maintenance, upgrading, and exchange services)

Emerging opportunities

In addition to a move from selling services rather than selling products, three other areas provide opportunities for achieving eco-efficiency. First, companies can re-engineer their processes to reduce the consumption of resources, reduce pollution, and avoid risk while at the same time saving costs. Experience shows that there are many possibilities, some straightforward, some less obvious. Ultimately, the whole workforce must be involved in identifying opportunities and in making the changes necessary to seize them. Process changes may also be related to delivery or to supplier operations as well as to distribution, customer use, or disposal (Lehni 2000).

CASE STUDY 9
Grupo Minetti
page 96

Second, by cooperating with other companies, many businesses have found creative ways to 'revalorize their by-products', which is jargon for selling their waste products to companies that can use it as feedstock. In the chemical industry, for example, some by-products have even become a real cash-generating result of a production process. Zero-waste targets and by-product synergies lead to more effective use of resources and create an additional cash benefit. They are eco-efficient because they allow the creation of more value with fewer resources and less waste.

Product designers and procurement managers play a key role in a company. Their influence is not only crucial to product functionality and price but also has a big effect on costs and the environmental impact of production, product maintenance, and disposal. This suggests the third area for eco-efficiency opportunities: companies can redesign their products. Products designed to ecological design rules are sometimes cheaper to produce and use. They tend to be smaller and simpler. They may include a smaller variety of materials and are easier to disassemble for recycling. Often, too, they offer higher functionality and better service and are easier to upgrade. Because they can provide a higher value for their users, while the negative influence on the environment related to their use is minimized, they are eco-efficient products.

Often, dematerialization can be achieved through *design for environment* (DfE), which occurs at the level of product, process, service, and function design and implementation and represents the integration of environmental considerations into the entire fabric of economic activity. Also called 'eco-design', the basic idea is to include environmental factors at the beginning of the design process. Some of the strategies include developing completely new concepts, selecting low-impact materials, reducing material usage, optimizing production techniques and the distribution system, reducing impacts during use, and optimizing the lifetime of a product as well as the end-of-life system.

Another important tool for eco-efficiency is *life-cycle assessment* (LCA), in which all environmental impacts (such as energy and resource consumption, pollution, and impacts on biodiversity) are determined from 'cradle to grave' or for any part of the process. For a product or device, this implies that the impacts of mining, production of raw materials, production process, product use, and final disposal (including re-use or recycling) are taken into account.

CASE STUDY 10
Norsk Hydro
page 97

A number of companies are developing closed-loop production systems and zero-waste factories in which every output is returned to natural systems as a nutrient, such as compost, or becomes an input for manufacturing another product. This approach revalorizes by-products to gain the maximum value from materials throughout the product life-cycle.

Companies can use closed-loop manufacturing to create new products and processes that can totally prevent waste. This, plus more efficient production processes, can cut companies' long-term material use by more than 90% in most sectors. For example, a DuPont agricultural products team from LaPorte, Texas, reduced its toxic emissions by 99% through closed-loop recycling, off-site reclamation, selling former wastes as products and substituting raw materials. Overall savings included $2.5 million of capital and more than $3 million in annual operating costs. In California, waste-water from a Unilever tomato-processing plant is used as a soil conditioner to allow crop production on a site never previously farmed (UNEP 1999).

Companies are also using eco-efficiency information to develop their product portfolio mix. BASF, the world's largest chemical company, based in Ludwigshafen, Germany, has been using eco-efficiency since 1996 as a way to have the right products at the right time, and the concept is now part of the corporate culture. It began, says Walter Seufert, president of BASF's environment, safety and energy division:

CASE STUDY 11
BASF
page 98

> as a means of survival—to improve our product portfolio over others. We do not want to invest in a product that a customer will not want to use in five or ten years because of ecological or economic problems (*CMR* 2001).

The use of this approach also helps improve the image of the company. According to Seufert, 'when we adjust our portfolio by focusing on the most environmentally sound products, it makes sense . . . Customers, as well as the community, are recognizing that.'

This sense of needing to weigh more than the economic considerations in business decisions also prompted the company to form a Sustainability Council in 2001, consisting of board members and seven division presidents, each of whom is given responsibilities in the three areas: economy, ecology, and society. The move is aimed at better coordinating all of BASF's activities in eco-efficiency and sustainability areas—'to give it a greater push and to be faster and more successful', says Seufert (*CMR* 2001).

Eco-efficiency can lead to innovative partnerships. For example, the Retec Group is a US-based environmental services company that helps industrial companies perform reclamation or re-use of polluted sites. One of its customers is BP, which has formed an alliance with ThermoRetec. A set of metrics jointly established by BP and ThermoRetec in early 2001 gives different weights to factors such as safety, environmental performance, and keeping the project on budget. Under this system, safety and environmental performance are weighted higher than coming in under budget. This means, in effect, that 'if they win, we win and if they lose, we lose', says the Retec Group CEO Michael Knupp:

> So it's more important for us to pay attention to safety and health and environment than our budget because our absolute profit margin is tied to environment and safety. Also, under these alliances, it doesn't matter who caused an accident; everybody suffers. That makes you work more cohesively as a team. I have found this type of partnership to be a very effective control mechanism on behalf of the customer to make us do the right thing. It has nothing to do with regulations and everything to do with economics. We don't live in fear of OSHA [Occupational, Safety and Health Authority], we live in fear of the BP inspector.

The use of more daylight and low-energy light fittings, building management systems, a cheap and innovative cooling system, and natural gas and co-generation systems are innovations that differentiate the shopping centers of Sonae, based in Maia, Portugal, from competitors. Also, over 50% of the wood it uses in its wood-panel business consists of wood waste and by-products. In some factories, the amount of recycled wood constitutes up to 75% of wood used. In a waste-recycling innovation, waste at one large shopping center is deposited at collection points linked to a network of underground pipes. The waste is then removed by suction through the network to two underground collection centers. Here, it is hermetically stored for later transport and treatment. Collection points exist for each type of waste, allowing selective collection for recycling. Since the system is almost totally underground, there is no urban blight and no need for rubbish trucks or visible rubbish containers. At the same shopping center, air-conditioning is achieved by continuous watering of a glass skylight 110 m long. This lowers the ambient temperature while creating a crowd-pleasing visual effect as sunlight backlights the water flowing across the glass.

Measuring and reporting on eco-efficiency

CASE STUDY 12
Warehouse
Group
page 98

Companies choose to measure their eco-efficiency performance for many different reasons. These include tracking and documenting performance and progress, identifying and prioritizing opportunities for improvement, and identifying cost savings and other benefits related to eco-efficiency. A company may also want to demonstrate why improvement is limited in certain areas or will not be possible to the degree expected by certain stakeholders.

Eco-efficiency indicators also help managers take decisions on a product or business portfolio. They can provide managers with the information on how to make a business portfolio more eco-efficient or more sustainable overall—and usually more profitable as well. Monitoring and reporting eco-efficiency publicly is a way to communicate a key element of the corporation's progress on sustainable development to external audiences, including investors, insurers, consumers, and other interest groups (Verfaillie and Bidwell 2000).

Essentially, progress in eco-efficiency can be achieved by providing more value per unit of environmental influence or unit of resource consumed. Using this basic equation, companies can calculate eco-efficiency in a number of ways. The choice of indicators will depend on the needs of individual decision-makers. A plant manager may wish to focus on the number of products shipped per kilojoule of energy consumed during manufacturing. A financial analyst may instead focus on the economic value of products sold per kilojoule. Value and environmental influence can also be measured for different entities, such as production lines, manufacturing sites, or entire corporations as well as for single products, market segments, or entire economies (Verfaillie and Bidwell 2000).

The WBCSD has developed a framework for measuring eco-efficiency that can be used to measure and report progress toward eco-efficiency in a consistent manner. Although the framework provides a common set of definitions, principles, and indicators, it is flexible enough to be widely used and interpreted to fit individual needs of companies across the business spectrum.

'The old maxim "only what gets measured gets done" is as true in this case as anywhere else,' says Markus Lehni, director of Global Sustainability Services at management consultancy Deloitte & Touche; 'setting targets and measuring progress is very important, both internally and externally. With good metrics, we can better demonstrate how these things are connected environmentally and economically.' However, Lehni points out that the numbers themselves are not sufficient to make the eco-efficiency case, stating that 'these figures need interpretation, comparisons with

CASE STUDY 13
CH2M HILL and
Nike
page 99

other companies in the same sector, and benchmarks. All of this creates credibility among investors and stakeholders.'

Eco-efficiency in developing countries

It is sometimes claimed that eco-efficiency will not work in poor economies because preventing pollution is too costly and requires legal enforcement and substantial financial help. But, given that the concept is about producing more with less (as well CASE STUDY 14
Cemento de El
Salvador
page 100 as decreasing pollution), then poor countries need eco-efficiency more than do wealthy countries, especially poor countries where feedstocks such as oil are expensive and some natural resources, such as wood and water, are already in short supply. In fact, improving the efficiency of operations may be the only way in which many developing-world companies can compete in the global market.

Yao Sheng Chen, chairman of the Taiwan Prosperity Chemical Corp. and Taiwan Cement Group, says that eco-efficiency in Taiwan has not progressed as far as he would like, for several reasons:

> There is a lack of commitment from senior management of most businesses; thus the top-down process of integrating eco-efficiency into daily business operations is not functioning well. Most businesses are still emphasizing environmental, health, and safety issues rather than social issues, on improving processes rather than on product or service issues, on direct operational rather than on supply chain or whole life-cycle management, on minimal standards of compliance rather than leadership.

He adds:

> Since the concept of eco-efficiency was introduced to the local business circle and to the government only in the last three to four years, with the formation of the Business Council for Sustainable Development in Taiwan, we need time to implement eco-efficiency. We have started to ask our member companies to do environmental accounting and reporting on environmental and social performance. We are also going to introduce modern management tools to local businesses by inviting experts to conduct seminars or workshops. We are also building partnerships with important government offices such as the Environmental Protection Agency and the Industrial Development Bureau to promote eco-efficiency.

However, a number of case studies show that eco-efficiency does work in developing countries and countries in transition. In water-stressed southern Africa, the energy company Eskom has developed unique systems to reduce water consumption in electricity generation, including the use of dry cooling systems at power stations and the implementation of effective environmental management systems that emphasize improved water management and consumption.

Beximco Textiles, a division of Beximco, Bangladesh's leading industrial conglomerate, integrated high environmental standards from the outset. The company benchmarks itself against World Bank pollution guidelines and was awarded the Öko-Tex certificate for hazard-free production in 1999, now regarded as a basic requirement for entry into key markets such as Germany (Robins 2000). According to Syed Naved Hussain, CEO of Beximco Textiles:

> At Beximco, we feel strongly that innovation—not merely low-cost production—is key to success. The costs of compliance with high environmental standards represent a small expense in the overall cost structure of most textile products. Rather than trying to reduce these, a strong focus on innovation gives a much better return. Innovation leads companies not only to reduce environmental compliance costs, but also to reduce use of energy and raw materials by eliminating waste and increasing productivity. And it leads to more value-added products—which usually fetch a much higher price without a proportional increase in cost.

The Brazilian timber and cellulose company, Aracruz Celulose, has put eco-efficiency to use in improving the productivity of its plantations while simultaneously protecting biodiversity. The company has doubled the productivity of its fast-growing eucalyptus plantations, getting more cellulose out of each hectare. Chairman Erling Lorentzen recognizes that the sustainability of forestry operations in the area depends greatly on the company's ability to eliminate the use of native forest for timber and cellulose. Brazilian timber companies that can demonstrate they are not destroying rainforest gain a competitive edge in a market that is starting to reward environmentally responsible companies. According to Lorentzen, 'if more of the world's forest products came from well-managed plantations, you would need far less forest acreage for timber and cellulose production. The more you can use high-growth, planted forest, the more we save native forests.'

Julio Moura, CEO of the holding company GrupoNueva, which is headquartered in Costa Rica and groups together companies involved in water systems, construction material, and forestry and agricultural products, has been overseeing the production of the new group's first sustainability reports. He feels that companies in Latin America will take up sustainability if and when they see other sustainability-driven companies making money:

> We have many good cases; many of our companies are doing a very good job already. But we still need to show a sustainably good financial performance, which is very difficult in Latin America because of the political volatility and because of the competitive environment. You can only succeed by showing a good example. Others will follow us if the financial rewards are attractive and interesting. That is our big, big challenge.

Reaching small and medium-sized enterprises

Multinational companies have the staff and the cash flow to explore and reap the benefits of eco-efficiency. Many of those heading up SMEs feel they do not have the time or cash for anything but survival. It is an understandable feeling, but it is a little like a fisherman who has got so many fish to clean he does not have time to sharpen his knife. In some places, big companies have been helping small companies reap the benefits of the concept; the BCSDs of Colombia and Brazil have programs to do this.

CASE STUDY 15
Fundación
Entorno
page 100

Yao Sheng Chen, chairman of the Taiwan Prosperity Chemical Corp. and Taiwan Cement Group, says that:

> we can support SMEs' adoption of eco-efficiency in two main ways. First is the reinforcement of the supply chain management. The larger companies can play a very important role in encouraging their SME suppliers to practise eco-efficiency. Second is the support by the government, including training, financing, and incentives.

In Latin America, as trade barriers have fallen, companies must be much more competitive to survive. This is particularly true for the SMEs, which represent 90% of industrial companies in Latin America. These firms produce less than half of all industrial output and a disproportionately high amount of pollution because they are under-regulated and lack the high visibility of bigger companies.

A recent report to the Inter-American Development Bank (IADB 2001) on environmental investment strategy argued that:

> with some notable exceptions, firm eco-efficiency practices in the region lag behind those of their OECD competitors by at least five to ten years. Latin American firms compete in a global context where eco-efficiency is integral to leading firms' business strategies. But they also operate within a distinctively Latin American context defined by pressing social needs, fundamental environmental and public health problems, arcane regulations and limited regulatory enforcement, macroeconomic policies that favor environmentally unfriendly practices, and limited environmental infrastructure.

The challenges for small and large firms in Latin America, say IADB, are to compete in a global market where eco-efficiency helps their competitors, while taking into account local circumstances, and to capitalize on local and international markets for environmental products.

Where cost savings do not make the case, then SME investment in eco-efficiency depends on the strength of government institutions and market demand. Often, the latter is non-existent. Enterprises in the region lack the local demand for, information about, or sources of finance for cleaner products. However, these challenges can create opportunities: to benefit from other countries' experiences, the acquisition of 'leapfrog' technology, the chance to avoid costly mistakes, and an opportunity to develop an approach to environmental management that addresses Latin America's needs and capabilities.

Creating local markets

There are some encouraging signs that companies are beginning to seize these opportunities when the right incentives are in place. In Bogotá, city environment authorities have been helping SMEs for the past six years to finance a transformation to more eco-efficient practices and have paid for training, so that 20% of the SMEs in Bogotá have adopted some kind of eco-efficiency project.

At present, there is little market for eco-efficiency, and governments are realizing that they must help to create that market. Strengthening government institutions and business associations, creating regulations, making the certification process and environmental management systems more widely available, providing education and training, and setting up more demonstration projects will help create the market. For instance, the cost of becoming certified by an accredited certification authority such as the International Organization for Standardization (ISO) is prohibitive for most SMEs. In many cases, the barrier is more of a management problem than a technical problem. Environmental problems tend to be generated by a lack of good management in all areas, so such problems cannot be fixed by a technical change here or there.

Eco-efficiency solutions must be adapted to local conditions, both culturally and economically. This means that working on best practices and good housekeeping often yields greater success than a large technology transfer or the implementation of an 'environmental management system' (EMS). María Emilia Correa, vice president of Social and Environmental Responsibility for GrupoNueva, says that in Latin America, as elsewhere:

> one of the most important drivers of change is people inside companies. Unfortunately, in Latin America, universities are not teaching this kind of thinking; so young people who may be enthusiastic about environmental issues while at university are not provided the tools to express that creativity and ingenuity once they are out in the business world.

As a former director of the Colombian Business Council for Sustainable Development, Correa says she has seen some progress in acceptance of environmental issues as part of a company's responsibilities, along with occupational health and safety, for example, but that it is far from enough. She points out that 'if it is better, and more profitable, to do things responsibly, people will do things responsibly. But without the right framework and structures in place, the motivation will be lacking.'

Correa adds that the 'informality' of many SMEs is another significant barrier to further adoption of eco-efficiency:

> Because there is generally little pressure from authorities or civil society, many small or medium-sized businesses practise business in an informal way. They don't pay taxes; they obtain water or energy illegally; and they don't pay social security or minimum wages. And that way they can start out with a lower cost structure than a competitor who is determined to do things legally. This is why it is so important to set the right framework so that others don't get a free ride.

A number of steps have been identified for improving SME eco-efficiency. These include working with supply chains, neighbor companies, or NGOs to create environmental improvement and generate information that allows SMEs to demonstrate improvements to the market (i.e. through ISO 14001 [ISO 1996]). Eventually, industry and government must generate home-country demand by fostering environmental technologies that anticipate market demands and requirements. Another measure is to engage the community and workers. In OECD countries, the availability of public information concerning firms' environmental performance, coupled with local-community activism, has been a major driver of improved performance. The same model can be applied in Latin America and other developing and emerging economies (IADB 2001).

Additionally, finance institutions and insurers can require improved environmental performance and make assistance available. A Mexican SME found a major source of savings in reducing its social security payments when it was reclassified as a non-hazardous workplace. Also, companies will be more likely to improve performance if they can meet realistic regulations and be publicly recognized for their efforts. The necessary infrastructure is another overriding concern. If firms are to segregate and manage hazardous waste, for example, there must be a place to dispose of, recycle, or treat the waste. Additional steps on the road to eco-efficiency for SMEs include more training and assistance, greater access to information, and the development of low-cost, effective certification systems (IADB 2001).

Stepping up the pace

Ten years after Rio, as we look at where eco-efficiency is now and what companies that are implementing it have learned, the overall message is that eco-efficiency works and builds value for customers and stakeholders. The challenge is to move away from a compliance-focused, crisis-avoidance mentality to seeing good environmental and social performance as the essential foundation for the market and public reputation. Also, a stronger argument for eco-efficiency needs to be made to service organizations, the individual environmental impacts of which are often relatively minor but account for a large proportion of economic activity in developed economies. Stepping up the pace will mean strengthening the link between eco-efficiency and shareholder value and devising new accounting techniques to enable organizations to assess eco-efficiency in a way that makes sense to the financial community.

Companies that are leading the way to eco-efficiency recognize business's responsibility to provide leadership in embracing eco-efficiency challenges. Business is uniquely placed to understand fundamental customer needs and how these can be delivered through much more eco-efficient services and products that create step CASE STUDY 16
TEPCO
page 101 improvements in environmental performance. Business is also in a position to create the core technologies that are critical to sustainable development and to transfer ideas and technologies around the world. Finally, business can use its marketing skills to inform those consumers who may sometimes be unaware of the urgency and requirements of sustainable production and consumption. Progressive companies are aiming to make markets eco-efficient: for example, by offering less resource-intensive service solutions instead of bulky products, by entering into alliances with stakeholder groups, or by providing the information consumers need to help them buy more responsibly.

CASE STUDY 8

General Motors de México *water conservation*

General Motors de México's Ramos Arizpe Automotive Complex (RAAC) is located in an arid region of north-east Mexico, where the only source of water is a small, semi-confined aquifer with a relatively high salt content (0.2%).

Expansion of the complex increased the demand for high-quality water. However, since 1986, water levels in the area had been decreasing, water access fees had been increasing, well-water withdrawal limits had been tightened and limits had been issued on waste-stream concentrations. RAAC saw that a change in its approach to water management was required. The company's challenge was to secure water for production without depleting the aquifer (also a source of local drinking water), to desalinate the well-water supply and to establish a recycle and re-use process for the industrial and sanitary waste-water.

The program began with an intensive effort to find water-saving opportunities as well as to find leaks and repair them. Then efforts were begun to reduce water consumption, to suppress pollution from industrial and sanitary waste-water discharge, and to re-use treated effluents.

To help reduce its consumption from the aquifer, the facility used a variety of physical, chemical, and biological waste-water treatment processes to recover and re-use 70% of its industrial waste-water. RAAC used simple techniques such as solar evaporation ponds and high-technology methods such as micro-filtration and membrane filtration to tailor its water conservation and recovery program and to make it as efficient and cost-effective as possible.

As a result, RAAC has reduced annual well-water withdrawal from 1,470,000 m^3 in 1986 to 700,000 m^3 in 2000. It has cut the average amount of well-water needed to produce a vehicle from 32 m^3 to 2.2 m^3. These reductions occurred at the same time as a sevenfold increase in production in terms of cars produced and a 50% increase in production in terms of engines; in addition, these improvements also coincided with the opening of a new transmission plant manufacturing 171,000 units in 2000.

CASE STUDY 9

Grupo Minetti *cement kiln technology in the disposal of industrial wastes*

The Argentine company Ecoblend, part of the Minetti group of cement companies, was created in 1994 to select, collect, transport, and dispose of industrial waste. The company has developed a technology to use this refuse as a fuel in cement kilns.

This alternative fuel process has several benefits. It conserves fossil fuels such as gas or diesel, it saves companies the chore of disposing of some of their own waste, and it removes waste from the environment, with no leftover material such as ash, which is often the case with other technologies.

The process also contributes to the reduction of carbon dioxide, sulfur, and nitrogen oxide emissions. The use of the waste products in cement kilns avoids emissions that would be generated through incineration.

Since 1997 the use of industrial refuse as an alternative fuel in cement kilns in Argentina has saved 49,350 m³ of fossil fuels, and a total of 122,500 tonnes of industrial waste has been saved from landfill.

CASE STUDY 10

Norsk Hydro *aluminum recycling*

Norsk Hydro has been in the aluminum business since 1948. For decades, demand for aluminum has grown faster than that for other competing metals. The transport sector, for example, is one of the main end-users, with the highest growth rate in use. In 2001 Norsk Hydro produced over 1.5 million tonnes of aluminum.

However, producing primary aluminum is not the most energy-efficient way to meet this growing demand. Norsk Hydro began exploring eco-efficiency during the late 1980s, and this initial review of operations produced some cost and resource efficiency gains. However, the real benefits came when the company adopted a 'life-cycle assessment' (LCA) approach, evaluating production and potential eco-efficiency opportunities from a value-chain and systems perspective. As a result, the company began to develop its recycling and remelting concept for aluminum. In particular, LCA revealed that the recycling of aluminum saves up to 95% of the energy used for primary production. The unique recycling characteristics of aluminum are such that quality does not deteriorate in subsequent recycling cycles.

During the 1990s, the company substantially increased its remelting capacity to increase the amount of recycled aluminum provided. In 1992, remelted aluminum accounted for 180,000 tonnes, but primary aluminum levels were much higher, at 610,000 tonnes. By 2001, primary levels had grown by 30% as a result of the increase in demand, to approximately 800,000 tonnes. However, the recycled and remelted content grew by more than 400% in the same period, to 750,000 tonnes.

The company uses systems thinking to design the recycling operations and implement the best commercial, economic, technical, and ecological solutions. This includes designing a company network of remelters capable of producing products from recycled material to ensure associated costs are minimized and efficiencies are gained. For example, this network provides efficient logistical operations, with minimum transportation and reduced costs in the loop to ensure that overall life-cycle impacts are minimized. The network also functions as a platform for sharing best practice.

The Norsk Hydro technology uses largely standard remelting equipment but, through the balance of scrap and metal treatment, high-quality products are obtained. Remelting operations have been developed in Norway, Germany, Luxembourg, the United Kingdom, Italy, France, Portugal, Spain, and the USA, and the objective is to increase them further still.

CASE STUDY 11

BASF *an eco-efficiency tool*

BASF has developed a tool for measuring the eco-efficiency of important products and processes and integrating the results in strategic business decisions. The eco-efficiency method, developed by BASF and Roland Berger & Partner, is a strategic life-cycle tool that makes it possible to compare economic and ecological advantages and disadvantages of various products and processes.

The two values—environmental burden and total costs—are plotted on a two-axis graph, known as the eco-efficiency portfolio, which makes it easy to determine the product's environmental efficiency. When assessing environmental impacts, six categories are examined:

- Consumption of raw materials

- Consumption of energy

- Emissions to air and water emissions and waste disposal

- Potential toxicity of materials

- Potential risks

- Land use

BASF used this tool to determine the cheapest and most environmentally friendly way to transport some 25,000 tonnes of styrene from Moerdijk to Arnheim (the Netherlands). To determine the best approach, BASF drew up an eco-efficiency analysis.

Rail transport over 115 km required tank cars with a loading capacity of 60 tonnes, whereas a tanker truck on the 114 km road route could carry 33 tonnes. A costs-only analysis gave road haulage a slight advantage. However, considerations such as energy consumption, emissions, and health risks to workers showed rail to be far better. For example, a truck would need about 50,000 liters of diesel over the course of a year. As the railways are electrified, the rail journey consumes in total about 20% less primary energy. Thus, since 2000, BASF has transported styrene by rail between these two sites, resulting in a significant reduction in pollution.

The results of eco-efficiency analysis have helped the company to improve products and processes by demonstrating exactly where the improvement would benefit the environment most and what its financial consequences would be. The system also allows BASF to define and monitor research and development targets.

CASE STUDY 12

The Warehouse Group
new software for energy efficiency

The Warehouse Group has 75 stores and 32 Warehouse Stationery stores in New Zealand with a total retail area of 300,000 m². It is run from a head office on Auckland's North Shore, with two distribution centers, one on the North Island and one on the South Island. The company recently purchased 117 stores in Australia; and although the rate of new store openings in New Zealand is slowing the floor area of existing stores is being expanded—with a five-year goal to increase retail space 50% to 450,000 m^2.

Working behind the scenes is a small team that has been saving the company a lot of money—the Energy Management Team. The Warehouse has designed a software program that automatically controls lighting, heating, and air-conditioning. This smart computer system allows the entire retail chain to be operated from one central office. The sheer size of the operation creates enormous opportunities for standardization and economies of scale.

Over seven years, the air-conditioned volume of the Warehouse stores increased dramatically but was not matched by a commensurate rise in power usage. In fact, the average power consumption dropped from an original 200 kWh per m^2 to 100 kWh per m^2.

Colored screen displays give three-dimensional representations of the stores, their floor plans and the configuration and status of the lighting, heating, ventilation, air-conditioning, and other energy-using equipment, providing a user-friendly interface for staff. Energy consumption, measured every half-hour, in each store is available on a secure website run by a metered supplier. The stores have no light switches: all is controlled by the system, which responds to the lighting levels and time of day.

Another aspect of energy management is the provision of reports and benchmarks that are e-mailed to store managers, allowing them to see how their store is performing against the others, or against historical data, and whether there are any 'exceptions'—if the equipment is not operating properly. If there are any significant changes in actual costs or energy use compared with budgets, corrective action can be taken immediately. This reduces energy waste and contributes to the cost savings achieved.

CASE STUDY 13
CH2M HILL and Nike
eco-efficiency through supply-chain metrics

Since 1997 CH2M HILL has been working with Nike to define environmental impacts and find ways toward cleaner production systems and reductions in the amount of raw materials used.

As part of Nike's Sustainability Initiative, CH2M HILL has worked with Nike's large and diverse supply chain on issues such as the reduction of solid waste and hazardous chemicals, sustainable product design and manufacturing, as well as product life-cycle activities. As Nike's supply chain includes over 750 direct contractors, this presents a huge opportunity to improve both the natural and the human environment. For example, CH2M HILL has worked directly with over 250 vendors in more than 20 countries to preserve and conserve water and to reduce the environmental impacts of waste-water discharge in production operations.

A key element of this work has been the collection, validation, and reporting of key environmental metrics. The work has included developing a database, issuing reporting forms to factories, collecting quarterly data from factories, validating data, and generating quarterly corporate environmental reports. Under the metrics program, CH2M HILL established a baseline for solid waste produced in 45 footwear factories in Asia. The goal is to document and report reductions in the production of solid waste in the facilities as well as increases in the amount of recycled solid wastes. Engineers evaluate the most efficient production processes and provide on-site data validation.

An important part of this extensive program was also working with the individual factories and Nike production experts to develop best practice in the form of case histories. CH2M HILL supported efforts to transfer the technology and share lessons learned among factories. These efforts not only enhance local, regional, and global systems but also provide models for improving environmental and economic performance to other public and private institutions in the countries concerned.

CASE STUDY 14
Cemento de El Salvador *furnaces and forests*

Cemento de El Salvador SA de CV (CESSA), established in the late 1940s, is the sole cement-producing company in El Salvador, with a production of 1.175 million tonnes in 2001 and employing more than 515 people in its integrated operations and services. Since 1993 CESSA has been using an eco-efficiency initiative to save energy and improve environmental impacts. The focus of this effort has been the installation of a new production line based on dry furnaces. Previously, three of CESSA's furnaces had been of the wet rotary type, very inefficient in fuel use. A dry furnace uses much less energy. Also, by using this new technology, installed in 1997, CESSA has reduced its electricity consumption and emissions of CO_2 and nitrous oxide particulates.

CESSA is also reforesting an average of 4 ha per year, each hectare of forest offsetting four tonnes of CO_2 emissions. Many of the reforested areas were former mining pits, abandoned roads or simply land that had been deforested. This effort demonstrates the industry's compatibility with the environment to help achieve sustainable development.

CASE STUDY 15
Fundación Entorno *eco-efficiency kit*

In 1999 the Spanish business council, Fundación Entorno, launched a pilot project to demonstrate the viability of products, processes, and services developed through eco-efficiency concepts. As a result of this work undertaken with 12 Spanish companies, the software tool Eco-Efficiency Toolkit 1.0 was developed to help companies improve and quantify their eco-efficiency. It has three modules with the following functions:

- *Eco-design module:* for planning material consumption, transport, use and disposal of any product, using life-cycle assessment principles and 'rucksack' impact assessment

● *Base module:* for analyzing the material balance throughout each process and for detecting inefficiencies

● *Eco-efficiency module:* for compiling data to show environmental costs and helping to design improvements

The electrical engineering and electronics company Siemens AG used this toolkit for its Barcelona factory, which makes train, subway, and streetcar engines. Siemens conducted an analysis of processes and products developed in-house to determine which of these required further improvements, focusing particularly on processes that used a lot of energy. The study helped the company select alternative technologies that have simplified construction, cut energy consumption by 45%, extended the working lives of key machinery, and saved €8,803.70 ($7,847).

One of Spain's largest consulting groups, TYPSA Group, working mainly in civil engineering, the environment, and architecture, used Eco-Efficiency Toolkit 1.0 to analyze a water-purification plant for a project in a developing country. The kit helped the group to identify and introduce eco-efficiency improvements in each activity throughout the process and assign environmental costs. Energy consumption was improved by 66% and the cost of the final product improved by 85%—demonstrating the benefits of eco-efficiency in developing countries.

At the beginning of 2001, Fundación Entorno launched a program for small and medium-sized enterprises. Six conferences were held in Spain's main industrial regions in order to disseminate the eco-efficiency concept and to present eco-efficiency initiatives. As a result, Eco-Efficiency Toolkit 1.0 has now been sent to more than 800 companies, and 55 firms are participating in the initiative.

CASE STUDY 16
Tokyo Electric Power Company
eco-efficient energy

The Tokyo Electric Power Company (TEPCO) supplies electricity to the Tokyo metropolitan area. It sees global warming as a pressing energy issue, and the company has implemented various carbon dioxide (CO_2) emission-reduction measures both on the supply side and on the demand side.

In March 2001, TEPCO set a target to reduce CO_2 emissions by approximately 20% (from 1990 levels) to about 0.31 kg CO_2 per kWh in 2010, using a host of different measures based on a diverse and complementary energy mix. 'We are making every effort to guarantee a stable supply of high-quality electricity, including the promotion of an optimal mix of energy sources by balancing hydroelectric, thermal, and nuclear power, and also renewables as supplemental sources', says TEPCO President Nobuya Minami; 'Nuclear power, which does not emit CO_2 or pollutants during generation, plays an important role in countering such environmental issues as global warming.'

The company is undertaking a range of measures on the supply side, including the expanded use of non-fossil energy sources, creating an optimal configuration centered on nuclear power and the diffusion of renewable energy sources. The optimal use of its nuclear power has alone accounted for 92 million tonnes of the total 134 million tonnes of CO_2 emissions cut during 2000.

TEPCO also works to improve the efficiency of thermal power generation and to reduce transmission and distribution loss rates. These improvements, coupled with hydroelectric production, save fuel costs and valuable resources while cutting CO_2 emissions. In fact, these efforts reduced CO_2 emissions in 2000 by the equivalent of about 14.6 million tonnes compared with 1990 levels.

On the demand side, TEPCO promotes and supports customers' energy conservation efforts to enhance overall energy efficiency. In October 2000, based on its surveys of consumer willingness to pay for renewable energy, TEPCO launched its Green Power Fund to further promote renewable energy.

The fund supports the promotion of renewable energy through donations from individual customers. It is run by the Greater-Kanto Industrial Advancement Center (GIAC), a non-profit organization, to ensure its transparent management.

Participants in the fund make minimum donations of ¥500 (around $4) per month and receive a certificate of contribution. TEPCO makes its own financial contributions by matching the donations from the program's participants. As of October 2001 the fund had 14,719 contributors. The donations are used to promote wind and solar power generation. For corporate customers, TEPCO has established another mechanism to promote renewable energies. As of April 2001, 20 companies participated in contributing funding for 25.5 GWh from wind power generation for 15 years.

Corporate social responsibility

> **As a company, we are part of this society; we have a certain privilege; we are educated; we have access to resources, and we have been entrusted with those resources, so we have also responsibility to do something good, to make the community around us prosper.**
>
> *Julio Moura, CEO of GrupoNueva, Costa Rica*

After working with stakeholders around the world, the WBCSD defined corporate social responsibility (CSR) as 'the commitment of business to contribute to sustainable economic development, working with employees, their families, the local community and society at large to improve their quality of life'. Thus environmental concerns are part of a company's CSR (Holme and Watts 2000).

CSR is a fundamental concept—like liberty or equality—that is always being redefined to serve changing needs and times. The social responsibilities of a food company are different from those of a transport company. Companies' social responsibilities will be viewed very differently in a decade's time as by then society's expectations will have changed. Therefore, our CSR work offers companies a guide on how to approach their responsibilities rather than a list of what to do. We believe that companies should first determine what they really stand for, their vision and values, their 'corporate magnetic north'. Then they should integrate corporate social concerns into the business strategy. They should:

- Focus on individuals, since CSR reaches out to all stakeholders but will be judged by its implications for individual employees, managers, and citizens

- Determine a corporate legacy by instilling an ethic of education and learning and by instituting processes to foster this ethic

- Put employees first as the best assets and ambassadors of the business

- Know their neighbors, both in terms of their communities and in terms of their culture
- Establish a system for keeping CSR debates and dialogues transparent and continuous
- Form smart partnerships, not for publicity or cover but to realize CSR goals
- Measure and account for what they do
- Report externally, but in ways that reach all stakeholders, not just those on their mailing list or on the Internet

There remain many questions that must be answered by ongoing debate among all sectors. What are the respective roles of government and the private sector in providing social, educational, and health services? How far along the supply chain does a company's responsibility extend? How should it adapt to local cultures? How far into the future should a company plan? What is the distinctive corporate contribution to the poverty–sustainable livelihood problem? All of these issues are works in progress.

Despite areas for ongoing debate, we remain convinced that, as we advised business in 2000, 'a coherent CSR strategy, based on integrity, sound values and a long-term approach, offers clear business benefits to companies and a positive contribution to the well-being of society'.

Pros and cons

CSR is a fad, is intellectually wrong, is bad for business and is bad for the planet, argues David Henderson, a British academic economist formerly head of the Economics and Statistics Department at OECD (Henderson 2001). We business people are always reassured to see how little most economists know about the realities of running a business. If they knew any more, we would have to take them seriously. Nevertheless, Henderson's arguments probably reflect the views of those corporate bosses who have thought little about their company's wider responsibilities to society. So, in refuting Henderson in this chapter, we have the opportunity to preach to the unconverted, using ideas the unconverted might appreciate.

In *Misguided Virtue: False Notions of Corporate Social Responsibility* Henderson concludes that 'CSR has caught on'. This we find surprising, as we see only a minority of companies even mentioning it, much less trying to practise it. But Henderson finds that it 'has been endorsed by a substantial and growing number of businesses, especially multinational enterprises' (Henderson 2001), as well as by academics, NGOs, investment institutions, international agencies, including the OECD, and many governments.

According to Henderson, 'many advocates of CSR show a lack of understanding of the rationale of a market economy and the role of profits within it'. To explain the rationale of a market economy, he quotes Milton Friedman:

> Few trends could so thoroughly undermine the very foundations of our free society as the acceptance by corporate officials of a social responsibility other than to make as much money for their stockholders as possible. This is a fundamentally subversive doctrine (Friedman 1962, in Henderson 2001).

First, Friedman wrote this in 1962, four decades ago, well before today's surge in globalization, deregulation, privatization, and a virtually instant and extreme corporate transparency changed the norms of doing business in a market economy. We would argue that a growing number of firms are adopting CSR not because they do not know how the market works but because they know all too well how it works in this century as opposed to 40 years ago.

Second, and very much related to this, is the argument that dominates this chapter: to an accelerating degree, corporate officials cannot maximize returns to shareholders over the long term *without* engaging in, and being seen to engage in, CSR. Henderson argues that good corporate citizenship is expensive to corporations and that society ultimately pays. We argue that corporate irresponsibility is more expensive to corporations and to society.

Henderson argues that CSR leads to what he calls 'global salvationism'—a desire to save a failing planet through moral stances and actions. In our experience, this does not seem to be evident in debates within the WBCSD, where members clearly avoid the appearance of pretending to 'save the world'.

Henderson also argues that CSR leads companies to demand common international standards on issues such as labor practices and pollution. In contrast, we find that, because each company's situation is unique, business people approach international standards with great care. The WBCSD reports on CSR and on how companies can best find their own approaches to CSR make it clear that there can be no 'one-size-fits-all' approach (Holme and Watts 2000). Companies have been cautious about signing up to global guidelines such as the UN's 'Global Compact', even though its nine statements covering human rights, labor, and the environment are very broad and universal. Companies—and their lawyers—are wary of the possible legal implications.

We would point out that we embrace CSR for the purposes of competition. Being better at CSR than one's competitors is going to become more and more advantageous as the century advances and as society's expectations of business continue to change. This, we feel, is the main point that Henderson seems to fail to understand and appears to be the single misunderstanding on which most of his other assumptions are based.

Henderson also maintains that by acknowledging that business could do better in terms of social and environmental impacts it is playing into the hands of anti-business NGOs. He criticises what he sees as the 'studiously uncritical politeness' of business toward NGOs (Henderson 2001). We believe, however, that, in the main, the approach of business to NGOs has been what can be described as civilized. We have always maintained, and maintain throughout this book, that it is more effective—not to mention right and proper—to engage with critics rather than to ignore them and hope they go away. Thus there is much in this book about stakeholder dialogues and partnerships and about how companies engaging in those activities have benefited from them.

Economists allegedly worry constantly over the question: 'That may be true in reality, but does it work in theory?' Henderson's arguments seem practical at first glance, but we suggest they are very much dependent on outdated theories of how capitalism works. In the rest of this chapter we consider CSR and the issues surrounding it, basing our discussion firmly on 21st-century realities.

Beyond environment to social concerns

We described in Part 1 of this book how during the 1990s companies turned toward the social side of sustainable development. In fact, today, environmental concerns tend to get put under the umbrella term 'corporate social responsibility', covering all areas of good corporate citizenship. 'Among many large companies today it is widely recognized that a company needs a business model that integrates ethics and social responsibility as well as concern for the environment. That's a big change since Rio', observes Lise Kingo, senior vice president of stakeholder relations at the Danish pharmaceutical and biotech company Novo Nordisk:

> Back then, we all equated sustainable development with the environment. There wasn't any understanding that sustainable development was also about people. Ten years ago, no one in industry talked about the human and social elements of sustainable development.

Of course, business has always had a vested interest in contributing to society, in one form or another. According to Wilson (2001) of Rio Tinto:

> Debate about corporate social responsibility may be of recent origin but caring, responsible management is certainly not . . . In many companies there has long been recognition that there is more to business than simply short-term profit. Indeed, in complex and sensitive businesses, such as those in the extractive industries, the creation of long-term shareholder wealth is incompatible with a purely near-term profit focus.

CASE STUDY 17
Severn Trent
page 115

The concept of CSR can be traced to the development of corporations in the 19th century. Their owners and leaders often saw a broader role for themselves in society and participated in development or nation building by helping to finance the construction of houses, schools, libraries, museums, and universities.

The late 1950s saw the rise of consumer power as a force to influence corporate behavior, joined in the early 1970s by environmental concerns and the growth of single-issue pressure groups. During the 1970s and 1980s, corporate reputation, issues management, and community relations became ever more closely linked. The increase in shareholder activism in the 1980s, intended to pressure companies to improve labor or environmental standards, also contributed to companies aligning social investment more closely with business strategy.

With increasing market globalization during the 1990s it became clear that business had a broader social responsibility or citizenship role. The 1990s also marked a radical rethink of the respective roles of the state and business in society. Governments are privatizing more of what they used to do, so that business plays a greater role in the provision of crucial services such as water, electricity, telecommunications, and energy. Companies operating in these areas must be extremely sensitive to the social issues connected to them. Such companies must be in business for more than short-term gains. Also, as governments privatize, deregulate, and reduce corporate tax burdens, then companies are certainly seen by the general public to be becoming more powerful. So companies must be seen to be acting in keeping with their new powers and new responsibilities. As television and the Internet make the dissemination of information both easy and instantaneous, companies are being scrutinized as never before. Critics of business are better informed, and consumers and customers are better educated and more aware of their rights and their potential power to influence corporate behavior.

Companies are also experiencing demands for change from within, largely driven by a generational shift, with younger managers more keenly aware of a need to align their personal and corporate value systems with those of the consensus in the broader society. As a result, companies are under constant pressure from both outside and within to be more open, more accountable for a wide range of actions, and to report publicly on their performance in social and environmental arenas.

CSR has moved beyond a simple equation of profitability plus compliance plus philanthropy to becoming more about understanding the societies in which business operates. Top executives are finding themselves dealing with a wide spectrum of issues, including greater accountability, human rights abuses, corporate governance codes, workplace ethics, stakeholder consultation and management, and sustainability strategies. In a changing global arena, the social aspects of business are taking on a more business-focused meaning—whether in the form of ethical trade, social accountability, community investment, or good labor practice.

CSR is not just a rich-country trend; it is global. In 1999 in Argentina, Brazil, Thailand, Ghana, and the Philippines the WBCSD held a series of dialogues on CSR, attended by more than 200 African, Asian, and Latin American business people, opinion leaders, and representatives from labor, media, government, religious groups, and environmentally and socially minded NGOs. We found that in Argentina, for example, CSR as a business concept has appeared only fairly recently. However, its profile is increasing as a result of greater media attention to the issue and growing public demand for company reports and greater transparency on social and environmental issues, following the controversial privatizations of many state-run companies in the 1970s and 1980s. In parts of the developing world where media coverage is weak and/or government-controlled, companies do not feel as compelled to adopt CSR strategies.

It is the subsidiaries of multinational companies, under scrutiny wherever they operate, that are most likely to lead in CSR in developing countries, though there are notable exceptions of domestic companies taking a lead. Multinationals have found that it is easier to work to one global operating standard than to develop different standards for different countries. And that global standard is more likely to contain a CSR strategy.

A growing number of business leaders in Latin America are recognizing the value of some of the intangible benefits of CSR, such as improved image, a sounder 'license to operate', increased credibility and consumer and employee loyalty and trust.

CASE STUDY 18
Terranova
page 116

Julio Moura, CEO of GrupoNueva, a Latin American manufacturing conglomerate based in San José, Costa Rica, states:

> I think the concept of 'license to operate' is a very compelling argument for Latin America . . . As I see it, there is a strong moral argument to sustainable development. As a company, we are part of this society; we have a certain privilege; we are educated; we have access to resources, and we have been entrusted with those resources, so we have also responsibility to do something good, to make the community around us prosper.
>
> If your neighborhood is not sustainable, if you have criminality, if you have poverty, if you have revolt, if you have hatred, if you have illness, if you have poorly educated people, if people emigrate to the big city because they don't find interesting work—then your community is not sustainable, so your business will not be sustainable. Ultimately, this is true for a whole nation and it is also true for the world. If society is not healthy, then the market will not be healthy, and, ultimately, the economy and business will not be healthy.

CASE STUDY 19
Companhia
Vale do Rio
Doce
page 117
Brazil is becoming a center of corporate citizenship, and much of the credit goes to Oded Grajew, former toy manufacturer and founder and president of the ETHOS Institute of Social and Business Responsibility. Grajew's toy business led him into issues of children's rights, and he led other business people with him. Believing that their personal commitment to social issues should also be their companies' commitment, they created in 1998 the ETHOS Institute, the slogan of which is 'Your business ethics in peace with your personal ethics'.

ETHOS helps member companies improve their ethics, strengthen human resource policies and integrate with the community. Based in São Paulo, ETHOS has over 300 member companies. Grajew notes that 'until a couple of years ago, CSR was synonymous with philanthropy in Brazil. We are changing this concept. We are bringing the issue to the business pages of the newspapers.'

An ETHOS survey showed that 31% of Brazilians think that the social responsibility of a company affects the way consumers shop. However, 'the consumer movement is young in Brazil', maintains Maneto de Oliveira, executive director of ETHOS, who says that ETHOS strives to direct consumer buying power toward appreciating and rewarding companies that are socially responsible. The main goal of ETHOS is to plant CSR in the heart of the corporate world: 'ETHOS is an international reference for CSR', says the executive of a local advertising agency, 'and Brazilian companies are getting more and more interested in the issue; they see the market opportunity to do the right thing'.

Usiminas, the Brazilian steel company, has long considered CSR the right thing to do. Since its founding in 1962 the company has contributed significantly to improving the social, educational, and environmental aspects of the communities in which it is located. It has invested $370 million in equipment and processes to reduce the negative impacts of its industrial activities, and involved over 100,000 people in educational programs. Usiminas was the first steelmaker in Brazil and the second in the world to comply with ISO 14001. The company has built 28 schools, runs a professional training center serving 1,500 people and has built, maintains, and runs a hospital in the region in which it operates. Beyond meeting basic health and education needs, the company has built 20 sports and leisure clubs and invested $7.91 million in supporting local cultural projects.

In Brazil, where state funds are scarce and unequally distributed, large companies have long played a role in promoting regional development, says Rinaldo Soares, president of Usiminas. Such efforts are not merely altruistic, he adds:

CASE STUDY 20
Holcim
page 118

> The investments we make in improving the social structure naturally sup-
> port the growth of our business through the development of skilled and
> educated workers. Being considered a good neighbor also means we have
> greater acceptance for our operations in the region.

Pressure of events

It often requires a crisis or extreme public pressure—usually both at once—to make companies take the CSR lesson to heart. In the past decade, we have seen an increase in public protests about corporate activities, whether over the manufacture of sportswear in Asian sweatshops, oil company operations in countries ruled by authoritarian governments, or the price of drugs for people with HIV (human immunodeficiency virus) and AIDS (acquired immunodeficiency syndrome) in Africa.

Crises can bring breakthroughs in corporate behavior. Companies often make the most progress in CSR when hit by negative public pressure. Executives at Shell have acknowledged in many company reports and interviews that there was a huge loss of morale and a significant downturn in recruitment when Shell, in the mid-1990s, was accused of not doing enough to prevent human rights abuses in Nigeria. At the same time it faced intense public opposition to its plans to dispose of the Brent Spar oil platform in the North Atlantic. However, once Shell had made its commitment to CSR, through greater transparency and engagement with external stakeholders, job applications poured in. This new wave of employees believes that Shell's use of a sustainable development strategy, including CSR, helps it to predict future risks and succeed in a turbulent world.

Companies have also found themselves under pressure to make sure their global supply chains were meeting sufficient CSR standards. Supply chains have become the target of intense public pressure as consumer concerns and media coverage reinforce one another over poor labor standards associated with well-known consumer brands such as Nike and Reebok. A company can no longer use the argument that it is the supplier, and not the company itself, that is responsible for labor abuses.

CASE STUDY 21
adidas–
Salomon
page 118

Global outsourcing has allowed companies to order products from manufacturers overseas without owning or being involved in the operation of those factories. With many large companies centralizing and downsizing, their managers often do not know what subcontractors are doing. The public has essentially told them that it is their duty to know and to stop abuses.

The price of not being accountable can be quite high, and not only to reputation. Claims of serious human rights abuses can lead to significant financial liabilities. The Coca-Cola Company paid out a record $19.25 million in November 2000 to settle a racial discrimination lawsuit brought by black employees who claimed that Coca-Cola discriminated against them in pay, promotions, and evaluations (*New York Times* 2000).

Pressure from employees

Increasingly, employees are demanding that the companies they work for commit to and act on socially responsible values. In a research study sponsored by the Council on Foundations, Walker Information interviewed a representative sample of employees from a cross-section of US employers. It found that a company's corporate responsibility activities have a positive effect on the satisfaction and loyalty of average employees. In particular, a company's support of employee volunteerism is a key driver in influencing employees' feelings about their job. Also, employees who perceive their companies as having good corporate social performance view their companies more positively and are therefore more committed to them (Zadek and Weiser 2000). According to Lise Kingo of Novo Nordisk:

CASE STUDY 22
Western Power
page 120

> A commitment to corporate social responsibility helps us attract and retain the most talented people. We know it particularly means a lot for young people to work for a company they can feel proud of and a company that reflects their own personal values. People today want to work for a decent company.

Indeed, the 1999 Business Ethics Study found that 'employees are more likely truly loyal when they believe their workplace has ethical practices. In contrast, employees with negative views of workplace ethics are more likely to feel trapped or be at risk of defecting' (Walker Information 1999).

With inspired leadership from top company management, employees may find that their personal values are being aligned with corporate values, which increases their commitment to their employers. An example of management and employees working together is the street children project of Volkswagen

CASE STUDY 24
Volkswagen
page 122

Pressure from consumers

A growing number of customers are starting to consider companies' CSR profiles before making purchasing decisions. According to the Chronicle of Philanthropy, Harris Interactive interviewed 2,594 adults in the USA and found that nearly 80% took corporate citizenship into account when purchasing products and almost 70% considered corporate citizenship when making investments (in BSRRC 2001).

In December 2000 and January 2001, the research and polling firm Environics International surveyed 20,000 people in 20 countries to obtain results representative of 65% of the world's population. Of those asked, only 42% said they trusted companies to operate in the best interests of society (Environics International 2001).

In a poll of European consumers in 2000 by MORI, the London market research firm, 70% of consumers said that a company's commitment to CSR is important when buying a product or a service (in CSRE 2001).

Doing it

CASE STUDY 23
BC Hydro
page 121

Many companies are acting on perceived gaps in their social performance. To guide them, the WBCSD has published two reports on how companies can, and why they should, develop their own CSR strategies. The authors, Richard Holme, special adviser to the chairman of Rio Tinto, and Phil Watts, concluded that 'a coherent CSR strategy, based on integrity, sound values, and a long-term approach, offers clear business benefits to companies and a positive contribution to the well-being of society' (Holme and Watts 2000). But there are a lot of ways to do it. Below we outline a few examples.

The retailer Reebok found that by incorporating internationally recognized human rights standards into its business practices it achieved improved worker morale, a better working environment, and higher-quality products. Other textile manufacturers such as Nike and Gap are finding that actively engaging with NGOs to develop fair labor initiatives such as the Clean Clothes Campaign in Europe and the Apparel Industry Partnership in the USA helps protect their reputations.

Retailers are putting pressure on their suppliers to improve labor practices; these suppliers in turn impose the same standards on their own suppliers. This has been the case for the Pou Chen Group, a Taiwan-based producer of athletic footwear and leisure shoes that counts among its clients Nike, adidas, Reebok, and many other leading brands. The Group employs about 220,000 workers and has factories in Taiwan, China, Vietnam, Indonesia, and the USA. Given the growing pressure on suppliers to maintain high labor standards, Chi-Jui Tsai, chairman of Pou Chen Group, says:

> We have adopted the strict policies established by our customers. This in turn has set a good example for the industry. In fact, some of the brands with which we work have adopted our CSR policies as their standard and have introduced our CSR practice to their subcontractors.

A number of companies, including BP, Shell, Rio Tinto, and Novo Nordisk, have incorporated elements of the UN Declaration of Human Rights (UNDHR) into their core business principles, an example of companies aligning themselves with basic human norms. In order to make this commitment meaningful to managers of operations in remote areas, mining company Rio Tinto developed, with the help of outside experts, detailed guidance on implementing the company's human rights policy, especially in complex local situations. The guidance covers areas such as communities, employees, security, and other difficult issues, setting out procedures and a checklist of questions for the manager.

Novo Nordisk has incorporated the UNDHR into its core business principles in a variety of ways. The company has found that the most effective way to make human rights concerns 'operational' is by adding specific human rights goals to the balanced business scorecard used by managers to evaluate business performance. In 2002 the company added non-discrimination and the right to health as elements of the scorecard, to which managers' bonuses are tied. These targets supplement health and safety requirements that will continue being a focus area. Each year the company intends to introduce other human rights concerns to business operations where they are relevant. Furthermore, the company is training its team of facilitators—employees charged with ensuring the implementation of company values—as well as managers about how basic human rights should be observed in day-to-day business operations. Novo Nordisk also has two human rights lawyers employed by its stakeholder relations department, one of the few companies in the world to hire such expertise.

Canada's Placer Dome, faced with tension between the company's exploration groups and indigenous populations in opening a gold mine in Venezuela, developed an innovative project to benefit indigenous populations and local miners. Working with consultants, Placer Dome helped miners, who had no legal rights to the area, form an association. The company also dedicated a portion of the planned mining area to artisanal mining and funded technical support to help these miners adopt more environmentally sound mining practices. Placer Dome also invested in a new access road and helped the association establish a food store and an education fund (Streeter 1999).

A strong community relations program involving ongoing community consultation, dialogue, and a community development program helped Shell Prospecting and Development in Peru identify and address a potentially significant community issue. Shell had been using hovercraft to transport supplies along rivers. Local indigenous populations objected to the hovercrafts because they were noisy, physically frightening, and were believed to carry demons. Through a culturally sensitive public consultation program, the company was able to address these concerns by making changes in hovercraft design to reduce noise; adding red boats to precede the hovercraft in order to forewarn community members; instituting stops so community members could inspect for demons; and stopping hovercraft usage on Sundays, a day with a large volume of competing river traffic (IFC 2001). The consultation program helped the company identify the issue early and avoid potential delays and breakdowns in community relations.

A community development program can also help with socially responsible settlement. When Tata Steel was planning a new steel plant at Gopalpur in western India it first turned to the Tata Steel Rural Development Society (TSRDS), the company's community development program. The company wanted to establish good communication links with community members to prepare for resettlements that would accompany the new plant. They relied on the TSRDS staff—experts in community consultation and relations—and over the next four months this group built up a fully fledged community resettlement and rehabilitation team (IFC 2001).

Benefits and opportunities

Companies find that good community relations can help raise awareness of unforeseen issues or problems, avoid unnecessary conflicts and hostility, create a better working environment for employees from outside the area, recruit employees from within the area, and build business links with people and companies in the area.

Three key benefits of CSR are brand value and reputation, improvements in human capital, and revenue generation, particularly in large and as yet undeveloped markets. In analyzing shareholder value associated with a company's demonstrations of social responsibility, SustainAbility concluded that companies that flaunt or ignore human rights run a real, demonstrable risk of seeing their share price drop as a direct result. Whereas community initiatives have a weak, yet positive, impact on shareholder value, bad community management can destroy reputation and seriously endanger financial performance (SustainAbility/UNEP 2001).

A commitment to social responsibility can build the competence and vitality of a company and guide it along a path of knowledge and innovation-based success. Positive links between social and financial performance are emerging, particularly in light of the growing relevance of intangible assets, such as reputation, brands, and knowledge networks. According to Adrian Henriques (1999), former head of CSR at the New Economics Foundation:

> The rewards, for those who aspire to such world-class performance, come from improved reputation, improved staff loyalty, motivation and retention, and from lower transaction costs. But, perhaps above all, they come from an improved quality of management through working more closely with all the players in the business environment.

Another reward is the respect of one's peers. In 2000 some 720 business executives from around the world were asked in the *Financial Times* (2000b) survey of 'The World's Most Respected Companies' to rate the importance of social responsibility. Some 70% of the executives felt CSR was 'very important', and 28% considered it 'important'. A total of 50% of fund managers thought social responsibility was 'very important' for companies, and 38% considered it 'important'. Clearly, even the mainstream investment community, previously reluctant to acknowledge the shareholder value of CSR, is slowly coming around.

However, a company's investment in CSR will pay off financially only when the investment is focused and connected to its core business strategy. A long-term commitment to CSR can also pay off in times of crisis when consumers are more willing to give the benefit of the doubt to a company with a long history of exemplary behavior.

Unanswered questions

Leading companies are making up their own versions of CSR as they go along, and this is as it should be, for companies must guarantee a good fit with their own market realities.

CASE STUDY 26
Statoil
page 123

There are many unanswered questions. What are the respective, and most effective, roles for government and the private sector in providing social, educational, and health services? How far along the supply chain does a company's responsibility extend? How should it adapt to local cultures? How far into the future should a company plan? What is the distinctive corporate contribution to the poverty–sustainable livelihood problem?

The mining company Anglo American has been wrestling with its role in providing social, educational, and health services in some of the countries in which its operations are based. For instance in South Africa, with its large number of people who are HIV-positive and who have developed AIDS, the company believes that its CSR requires it to act in the face of this disaster. It has established policies to encourage voluntary testing of all head office and underground staff and has put wellness programs in place. A voluntary HIV/AIDS prevalence study was conducted in the Anglo American Johannesburg head office to act as a benchmark for programs to prevent the further spread of the disease and promote the wellness program. Anglo American is also using a number of mechanisms to build family awareness of HIV/AIDS and extend support to rural communities. It has used theatre performances, videos, in-house electronic mail, and other communication tools to spread the message.

CASE STUDY 25
Eskom
page 122

Many companies with a commitment to CSR are being challenged by critics because of their presence in countries with allegedly corrupt and repressive regimes. How does a company maintain high corporate standards of behavior in parts of the world where the rule of law is weak? What should companies do in such a case? Is it better to operate in such a place and try to improve things or to stay out and not be seen to be helping to financially empower a corrupt regime? Anglo American CEO Julian Ogilvie Thompson maintains that some countries are simply not acceptable places for a company to operate if it is prevented from observing its own high ethical standards:

> If the rule of law is weak and hopeless and you don't think it's going to get better, you probably don't go in [to that country] . . . If you're already there, it's very difficult. Do we pull out? In which case the situation of the local people will be even worse; it won't be better. A company can try to influence local civil-society organizations; it can make representations to the government, based on the power of its investments in the country, but, in the end, we have no sanctions on governments.

According to Sir Robert Wilson of Rio Tinto:

> If we were a major influence in a country and had a lot of contacts with the government, we would use that influence to try to change the direction of the government. But if we are realistic, there is no point in telling a government leader how to behave; such actions are likely to be counterproductive, to be honest. No government in the world likes to be told how to behave by foreign visitors. Certainly, if our immediate host communities were victims of human rights breaches, we would take action. But if such events happened in areas more remote, there is a question of whether we have sufficient influence.

A solid business case

Despite the challenges, many companies are convinced that CSR will be a guiding vision for the future for companies that wish to maintain their license to operate in an increasingly globalized—and critical—world. 'A good business should be both competitively successful and a force for good', says BP in its statement of business policies, *What We Stand For: Our Business Policies*, published in 1998.

World Bank president James D. Wolfensohn made the following comment to a group of senior executives at a workshop on the financial sector sponsored by the bank in October 2001:

> Corporate sustainability today includes recognition of the leadership role that the private sector must take in ensuring social progress, improved equity, higher living standards and stewardship for the environment. Corporate responsibility is not philanthropy—it is good business.

Wilson of Rio Tinto comments:

> Corporate social responsibility [is] not something invented yesterday. To many, it was simply known as good corporate citizenship and was founded in treating employees, customers, and suppliers with respect and integrity and taking all due care to minimize harm to the environment. Put like that, would any company choose *not* to be responsible? . . . A handful of cowboys, perhaps.

He goes on to say:

> But if CSR is to mean anything, it has to go beyond bland generalities, and to many companies social responsibility is now taken to cover a much wider field. Delivery, though, is of the essence, and successful delivery, like genius, consists of an infinite capacity for taking pains. The danger is that, like politics, the promises are large, but delivery is flawed and partial. [Business needs to] minimize that damage. As practical managers, our aim is simple. We want to turn our policies into practice; and to keep learning so that we can improve both.

CASE STUDY 17

Severn Trent *Cromford Venture Center*

As an environmental services company, Severn Trent is a leading provider of water, waste management, and utility services. The Group, which includes Severn Trent Water, Biffa Waste Services, and Severn Trent Services, employs more than 14,000 people, of whom 9,000 are based in the United Kingdom.

Severn Trent became involved with the Cromford Venture Centre in Derbyshire, UK, following a visit in 1995. The visit highlighted economically depressed areas that had recently been affected by the national downturn in manufacturing. Included in the visit was a tour of a secondary school, where it was apparent that pupils needed help to raise their self-esteem, confidence, and aspirations.

The Venture Center was founded on the belief that young people respond positively to opportunities for self-development if those opportunities are offered in surroundings that provide stimulus and the challenge of new activities and experiences. The company could see that the Center would be the ideal catalyst to help disadvantaged young people improve their prospects. Severn Trent believes in encouraging young people to continue in education so that they see employment as both attainable and desirable.

Thus Severn Trent decided to build a strong relationship with the Center, making an effort to understand its objectives and needs and to involve Severn Trent employees as fully as possible at every opportunity. In 1995/96, with capital funding from the Group and help in kind from others, a derelict grain mill was transformed into a new Venture Center for disadvantaged young people. In 1996/97, further funding from Severn Trent enabled groups to begin attending the Venture Center.

Severn Trent has a network of senior and middle managers who champion and support the Group-wide Employee Volunteering Program. Employees from a variety of companies within the Group have volunteered their own time to the Venture Center in various guises, including fundraising. In 2001, the Group's employees gave over 460 hours of their personal time to the Venture Center. Employees from across the Group have worked together on projects that have included gardening, creosoting, repairing flood-damaged bedrooms, pond clearing, and the construction of an astroturf play area. Fifteen employees took part in a sponsored hike through the Peak District to raise much-needed funds.

At the beginning of 2001, Severn Trent and the Venture Center celebrated their sixth year of partnership. The success of this long-term commitment has been made possible by the belief that successful partnerships entail more than financial contributions. The policy has been to respond effectively to the differing needs of the project. These needs are identified by feedback gained from visiting groups. For example, IT facilities were provided in 1999 after groups suggested that this would be a valuable resource at the Venture Center.

The Venture Center is now able to provide residential facilities, and some 880 young people have visited it as a result of financial support by Severn Trent. In addition, over 4,000 disadvantaged young people have benefited from the Center's facilities.

The strong and committed relationship between the company and the Severn Trent/Cromford Venture Center has been crucial to the project's effectiveness and the provision of residential places to thousands of young people, who have been given the opportunity to help themselves—a vital element of everyone's progress in life.

CASE STUDY 18
Terranova
San Isidro development and training center

Terranova, a GrupoNueva forestry products company, has created a development and training center to offer training in various trades to adults in the community of Cabrero, in the south of Chile. Cabrero has 15,000 inhabitants, and 15,000 more people live in the nearby countryside. This is a low-income community; many adults could not finish their school studies and need training in order to find a job or improve their earnings. Courses were selected according to community needs, and the center stays in close touch with the municipal government to make sure that training fits investment plans in the area.

Classes at the center started on 30 April 2001 in four trades; by the end of the year that number had doubled. Each class has some 15 students, with an average basic schooling of six years each. The training is complemented with courses in math, personal development, speech, sustainable development, safety, and environmental education, in order to help them upgrade their basic schooling. The courses follow an incremental modular system: every quarter, students receive a certificate of attendance at the different levels, so, if they find a job, they can come back after a while and take the other modules.

Half the students are women, and the schedule has been planned to allow men and women to attend. Mothers can take the course during the day while children are at school, and all working people can attend courses at night.

This project promotes voluntary work from professional people in the community. Terranova is pleased that 17 of the 20 volunteer teachers working at this center are Terranova employees from all levels of the company: from management to those involved with forest operations. This requires personal sacrifice and great commitment from the volunteers because they leave work to teach at night and often do not get home until midnight.

Courses are practically free, and the company provides the infrastructure for the center, including four workshop areas, a library, and a 50-seat auditorium.

CASE STUDY 19

Companhia Vale do Rio Doce
Education on Rails

Companhia Vale do Rio Doce (CVRD) is a diversified mining and logistics company that owns and operates two railroads and has holdings in three others. One of these, the Carajás Railroad, extends over 900 km through the states of Pará and Maranhão, Brazil. It transports over 800,000 passengers per year and is one of the most important means of integration of a region that has one of the highest population growth rates in Brazil. Travel time between each of the main passenger stations is between 4 and 16 hours. Additionally, passengers arrive at the stations up to 2 hours before train departures.

CVRD supports educational projects, and this railway system was identified as a unique opportunity to offer education programs to a large number of people. The company developed the *Education on Rails* program with the Futura Channel, a private education television station. By transforming the railway stations and passenger cars into 'live' education environments, a variety of programs are being offered to the public. Themes such as citizenship, basic and medium-level teaching, science and technology, the environment, health, basic sanitation, arts, and folklore are provided to the users of the Carajás Railroad. Television is the basic medium.

Two hours before the train departs, in the five main passenger stations the *Estação do Conhecimento* (Knowledge Station) begins. Once the train departs, the *Teletrem* (Teletrain) offers special programming from the Futura Channel on TV monitors in each car. The passengers are offered a series of educational and general-interest programs for children and adults. In addition, some of the old passenger cars have been transformed into classrooms. Here, many adults are completing their basic and medium-level education through distance-learning courses.

The Education on Rails program is in its infancy, having been introduced in 2000. However, passengers have enjoyed the courses. Surveys found that those dealing with health matters and practical information were the most popular. In addition, vandalism and littering in cars has decreased.

CASE STUDY 20

Holcim *the youth center*

Holcim's Colombian subsidiary, Cementos Boyacá, has developed a project to help improve the living standards of rural communities within the area of influence of the cement-manufacturing facility in Nobsa. The project provides secondary education and agricultural training to children of local farmers and promotes environmental awareness and improvements.

The project started in August 1998 amid the enthusiastic participation of the entire Cementos Boyacá. At a cost of approximately $220,000, a center with a total floor space of 1,500 m^2 was constructed in a record time of 83 days. On 19 December 1998 the dream came true. About 90 girls and boys, selected with the agreement of their parents, attended the center, coming from farming and mining communities in which Cementos Boyacá is active.

The center's aim is to educate and train the youth of the region so that they are not forced to leave it. They need to learn to use their country's resources in a sustainable manner, contributing to sustainable development and the wellbeing of their families and the region, by becoming leaders and entrepreneurs. To achieve these objectives, the project has two focuses: education and farming.

The children live at the center from Monday to Friday. During the mornings they are taught educational basics; in the afternoons they learn agricultural skills and arts and crafts. At all times, emphasis is given to strengthening cultural values and promoting love of their rural heritage in the hope of developing leaders who will feel responsible for the development of their region.

The center includes a farm with laying hens, cattle, pigs, rabbits, 5,000 m^2 of fruit orchards, and a worm culture project for making humus. The pupils receive their agricultural training at the farm and learn how to grow and cultivate all the produce they need to turn their homes into self-supporting farms.

CASE STUDY 21

adidas–Salomon *supply chain management*

Using an external supply chain has allowed adidas–Salomon to keep costs down and remain competitive. However, this cost-saving approach is not without its risks: the company has less control over workplace conditions at suppliers' factories than at company-owned sites.

The company believes that outsourcing supply should not mean outsourcing moral responsibility. Thus adidas–Salomon has designed and implemented a comprehensive supply-chain management strategy. This is based on the company's standards of engagement (SOEs) and is meant to source the cheapest *acceptable* supplies and not the cheapest *possible*, this level of acceptability being based on the values of the company itself. Therefore, contractors, subcontractors, suppliers, and others are expected to conduct themselves in line with the companies' SOEs.

Outsourcing raises a broad range of issues and concerns for the company. Employment standards must be evaluated and dealt with throughout the supply chain to ensure fairness and compliance with labor laws, taking into account concerns over child labor, discrimination, wages and benefits, working hours, freedom of association, and disciplinary practices. Health and safety issues, such as the provision of a safe and clean working environment, environmental requirements, and community involvement, also need to be considered.

The supply chain of adidas–Salomon is large and complex. The company relies on about 570 factories around the world. In Asia alone, suppliers operate in 18 different countries. To cover this broad area, there is an SOE team of 30 people, largely based in the countries where suppliers are based—Asia (China, Hong Kong, Indonesia, Malaysia, Singapore, Taiwan, Thailand, and Vietnam), Europe (Germany and Turkey), and the USA. These individuals know the labor laws and safety regulations in the countries for which they are responsible and are often able to interview workers in their own languages.

Before any supply relationship is formed, an internal audit is conducted to ensure working conditions are acceptable. Each business partner signs an agreement that commits it to comply with the SOE and to take responsibility for the performance of its subcontractors in terms of workplace conditions.

The strategy is based on a long-term vision of self-governance for suppliers, as adidas does not wish to be forever in the position of looking over the shoulders of its suppliers. Therefore, training forms an important part of the process, more so than monitoring, as it goes beyond a policing role to one that will have a long-term impact. In 2000, an estimated 150 SOE training courses were held for suppliers, supervisors, and managers. In 2001, 200 training sessions had been provided to business partners before the end of the year; and 200 such sessions was the target for 2002. The monitoring process is continuous, as suppliers are audited at least once annually—more regularly if serious problems are detected. In 2000, 799 audits were conducted at different levels in the supply chain. This involved interviewing managers and workers (on-site and off-site), a review of documentation, and facility inspections.

Based on this process, an action plan is compiled and presented to managers. This outlines problems and consequential action points, with clearly defined responsibilities and time-lines agreed with the site managers. Where serious problems are detected, a follow-up visit may be conducted within one to three months. If the factory is not willing to make improvements, business may be withdrawn. This course of action is a last resort; the company prefers to stay in partnership and to work from the inside to help encourage factory improvements.

In 2000, adidas–Salomon implemented, for the first time, a system of scoring suppliers' performance. This has provided an initial overview of the supply chain and the main issues and problem areas on a country-by-country basis.

These processes and strategies are new and need refining. In 2000, the scoring system was presented in detail within the annual social and environment report. New improved and extended systems are expected from 2001/2002 that will allow the company to produce even more detailed reports about progress in these important areas of social and environmental impact for a firm managing large and complex supply chains.

CASE STUDY 22

Western Power *the Greening Challenge*

Western Power, Western Australia's electric utility corporation, was looking for innovative means of involving the company and the community in helping to resolve Western Australia's worst environmental problem: salinity and land degradation. What emerged was the Greening Challenge—Australia's biggest-ever, volunteer-based, revegetation project. Launched in 1996, the Challenge was designed to engage Western Power people and their family, friends, and the community in an annual tree-planting venture to plant one million trees by 2000.

The timing of the Western Power Greening Challenge was a godsend for the Landcare groups and farmers in the Hotham River catchment area. Landcare, a not-for-profit company addressing land care issues in Australia, had already proposed reforestation projects on behalf of the farmers to Australia's National Landcare Program and the West Australian State Revegetation Scheme, but these had been unsuccessful because of lack of funds. So, when Western Power stepped in with its project, the farmers and the Landcare officers were ready, with detailed plans already on paper.

Western Power agreed to fund accommodation, transport, seedlings, fencing materials, and catering for volunteers. The strategy promoted a synergy between the skills and commitment of Landcare, state government agricultural officers, and Western Power, with the energy and goodwill of community volunteers.

The million-tree target was met in 1999, a year ahead of schedule. In fact, more than 2,500 volunteers planted 2.51 million native tree and shrub seedlings on degraded land between 1996 and 2000. This sparked a new project—the Hotham–Williams Western Power Greening Challenge, stretching the original targets to an additional 3 million seedlings by 2002. With the support of the Natural Heritage Trust, the new Challenge provided a rare opportunity for anyone—farmers, Landcare workers, city people, and local communities—to help reduce salinity and land degradation. As in 1996, organizers were overwhelmed by the response, with more than 2,000 volunteers and only 900 spaces to fill!

There has been a 70% return rate of Western Power staff to these annual planting programs; even staff that have retired or left the organization still return to plant seedlings each year. The program has become a somewhat unexpected family affair. Children make up 20% of the volunteers, and they appear to make every effort to do their bit for the environment. Staff relationships have improved. Many groups have formed teams, and most look forward to this event as a social highlight of the year. In addition, Western Power and the Greening Challenge have received four major awards for environmental excellence in business.

Many additional benefits have been realized. In particular, there has been an increase in the exchange of skills on managing large volunteer groups and raised awareness of the potential for volunteers that can work at the community level. Recognition of how Western Power, Landcare, and Agriculture Western Australia can interact with community groups on large-scale sustainability issues make this a model for other similar partnerships.

CASE STUDY 23
BC Hydro *aboriginal relations programs*

BC Hydro, one of the largest electric utilities in Canada, is a Crown corporation owned by the province of British Columbia, home to 197 First Nation bands (North American aboriginal groups). BC Hydro has facilities on at least 168 of these bands' reserve lands. Consequently, building sustainable, mutually beneficial relationships with aboriginal peoples is critical for BC Hydro.

In 1993 BC Hydro developed a comprehensive approach to managing aboriginal issues. Addressing the past, building for the future, and effectively managing its aboriginal relations initiatives are key elements. The main components of the relationship-building strategy are facilitating participation in resource management and development decisions, fostering economic development, supporting education for aboriginal peoples, and contributing to community projects and events.

To increase economic development opportunities for First Nations, BC Hydro negotiates contracts for work on reserve lands and assists aboriginal-owned businesses in improving their tendering practices. Start-up and expansion grants to aboriginal-owned businesses are provided and in some cases joint ventures are explored. BC Hydro has also developed an Aboriginal Business Directory that is used throughout the corporation and is available to government and private-sector companies as a source for products and services.

Within BC Hydro education is a key component of the strategy. Cross-cultural training programs address historical facts, court decisions, and cultural issues. More than 4,700 BC Hydro employees have taken at least one half-day, cross-cultural, training course. Those who frequently interact with First Nations have taken more rigorous training. BC Hydro's cross-cultural training, which has also been delivered to more than 100 external organizations, received the 1999 Province of British Columbia Multiculturalism Award. Aboriginal education is also a priority, with education scholarships, aboriginal language, and culture preservation programs, and stay-in-school programs forming a part of the strategy.

The biggest challenges faced by BC Hydro in this field flow from the prevailing legal and political uncertainty both as to the outcomes of treaty negotiations and the nature and extent of aboriginal rights and titles. BC Hydro addresses these uncertainties by seeking 'interest-based' rather than 'rights-based' solutions to problems and by providing input into the treaty process. Open dialogue with First Nations is a key component of the strategy for managing this uncertainty.

In soliciting feedback on its aboriginal relations strategy from First Nations, BC Hydro heard that the company's principles, which guide its relationship-building activities, are the right ones. The findings also revealed that although relationships have improved over the past ten years much work still needs to be done. Consulting with aboriginal communities in the early stages of a project, cooperating with aboriginal peoples and educational institutions to develop initiatives and programs, encouraging aboriginal peoples to take advantage of any economic, social, or other opportunities from BC Hydro projects, and developing employment equity programs were goals First Nations identified as most important in contributing to improved relationships. Those who thought that relations with BC Hydro were still poor cited a lack of respect toward aboriginal peoples and insufficient communication as the main reasons.

Perhaps the most critical lesson that BC Hydro has learned in this area is that problems cannot be solved overnight or with simple, one-size-fits-all solutions. First Nations share the need for better business relationships, and they work with BC Hydro when they see that the company's commitment is real and sustained.

CASE STUDY 24

Volkswagen *street children project*

Volkswagen, which produces and distributes passenger cars and small trucks world-wide, employed 324,402 people in 2000; it was from this workforce that the company's successful street children project, One Hour For The Future, has grown.

The project, begun in September 1999 in partnership with the children's rights organization *Terre des hommes*, aims to supply continuous, long-term financial support to street children projects run by local institutions and initiatives near Volkswagen sites around the world (Mexico, Brazil, South Africa, and Germany). The project wanted to encourage every employee at Volkswagen's German factories to donate the equivalent of one hour's wage every year.

In mid-1999 a letter was sent to every employee in Germany asking him or her to donate one hour's wage out of the November 1999 paycheck. The rate of participation was extremely high, and factories outside Germany joined the initiative. The campaign was repeated in 2000, and employees were encouraged to make donations on a regular basis to guarantee long-term support for the projects. In the meantime, many suppliers and business partners of Volkswagen began to make regular donations, as did many retired employees and various clubs and action groups involving Volkswagen employees. By the beginning of 2001, over $1.9 million had been donated.

CASE STUDY 25

Eskom *HIV/AIDS program*

Since the start of the AIDS epidemic, some 83% of all AIDS-related deaths have occurred in Africa. In South Africa, there are estimated to be 4.7 million people with AIDS or who are HIV-positive.

As an organization conducting its businesses mainly in South Africa, Eskom, South Africa's electric utility, sees the containment and management of HIV/AIDS as a strategic priority. New infections among employees are projected to cost Eskom 4–6 times the annual salary of the infected individual. Annual costs of existing HIV infections during the period 2006–10 are estimated to average 7% of the payroll.

To address this issue, Eskom's employees, suppliers, and customers have all become part of Eskom's HIV/AIDS strategy. This began with an information management and self-awareness program to maintain a strategic focus on the prevalence of HIV/AIDS in the business and increase the level of awareness among employees.

Following this, high-risk areas and situations for contracting HIV were identified and are being addressed by business units. A communication strategy was developed and education and training are undertaken to try to give all employees the skills, knowledge, and information to deal effectively with HIV/AIDS. In addition, care and support programs provide support to HIV-positive employees. The program ensures that Eskom's policies and practices do not discriminate against HIV-positive people.

A budget of 125 South African Rand ($12) per employee was spent on HIV/AIDS projects and activities in 2000 (excluding the salaries of employees working full-time on the HIV/AIDS program). Partnerships were established with national and international institutions and organizations working in this field. This includes a search for an HIV/AIDS vaccine, to which Eskom contributed $2.8 million over five years to a partnership with the South African Department of Health, the Medical Research Council, and the Institute for Virology.

In addition, Eskom shared its experience with and assisted more than 20 companies in the country to help them start their own programs. Eskom was instrumental in establishing the South African Business Coalition against HIV/AIDS (SABCOHA) and chairs the Southern African Power Pool Workgroup on HIV/AIDS. Eskom is currently involved in a major HIV/AIDS research project with Horizons (a US organization) in KwaZulu-Natal. The focus of the research is on stigma, prevention, care, and support.

Eskom's HIV/AIDS program was presented to the 12th World Aids Conference and was commended as a good model for a workplace program. Further, the program has received two international awards, for Business Excellence by the Global Business Council, and from the United Nations AIDS Program. The HIV/AIDS program was also nominated for a South African award and has three best series documents that are distributed worldwide.

CASE STUDY 26

Statoil *educating judges*

In 1999 Statoil Venezuela (a subsidiary of the Norwegian company Statoil) partnered with the local UNDP office, the local chapter of Amnesty International, and the branch of the Venezuelan judiciary responsible for training and administration, the Consejo de la Judicatura. There began an effort to create a better judicial system by increasing judges' abilities to handle human rights cases.

Judicial and constitutional reforms undertaken in 2000 and 2001 place a greater emphasis on human rights. Now, people accused of crimes will no longer be considered guilty until proven innocent but rather innocent until proven guilty. The reformed judicial system is accompanied by new legislation with a stronger human rights focus and a new penal code.

When approached by Statoil, the local UNDP office first suggested that Statoil get involved in a traditional social development project. However, on learning about Statoil's wish to support human rights, UNDP suggested that Statoil participate in the training and awareness-raising program for judges already being planned with the judiciary and Amnesty International. The project uses interactive training sessions conducted by Amnesty International in cooperation with the judiciary. The first phase, 'training of trainers' (24 specially selected judges), was completed in December 1999. In the second phase, which was initiated after some delay at the end of 2001, the training will be carried on by those who originally received it, to judges in the states of Zulia and Anzuategui.

Statoil contributed financially, maintaining a low profile—monitoring rather than trying to control things. The company had several reasons for getting involved and has since realized several benefits from participating. It felt that it was ethically right to show that it believed in human rights: 'We can't stand passively by when these rights are breached or international law is ignored in countries where we have operations', says Staffan Riben, president of Statoil Venezuela.

The project offers Statoil a reputational dividend and a chance to promote corporate values without overstepping its role as a commercial entity in society. As the company seeks to build up a culture based on high ethical standards, such examples help to demonstrate that Statoil is committed to its basic moral values. The company believes in the power of its presence to positively influence social conditions.

Statoil has sought to integrate respect for human rights into its statement of values, and this venture is part of a broader effort to build a culture centered on these values. Other measures include the development of an internal human rights training program in cooperation with Amnesty International Norway.

The project seems to be working for all partners, whose roles are well defined and appropriate to each—a secret of the project's apparent success. The judiciary has maintained its responsibility for training judges. However, it has answered to the pressure from civil society and has invited other partners to support its efforts and thereby accelerate them.

UNDP found that the Venezuelan project 'represents a best-practice case study' that could serve as a model for corporate engagement in human rights and be replicated in other countries. The project was therefore presented at a workshop in the presence of some 50 representatives of various UN organizations, NGOs, and companies, highlighting the importance of learning from concrete experiences when developing a general approach to corporate engagement in human rights.

Learning
to change

> **"Responding effectively to change and then using our achievements to initiate change in the market demands that we encourage innovation not only in products and services, but also in all aspects of management.""**
>
> *M. Shosaku Yasui, CEO and chairman of Teijin Corporation, Japan*

Movement toward corporate concern for the 'triple bottom line'—financial, social, and environmental performance—requires radical change throughout the corporation. It is not 'either/or'. The new paradigm is 'and also'. A sustainable business excels on the traditional scorecard of return on financial assets and shareholder and customer value creation. It also embraces community and stakeholder success. It holds its natural and cultural environments to be as precious as its technology portfolio and its employees' skills.

Several decades of business lessons from 'total quality management', 're-engineering', 'managing uncertainty' and 'six sigma' boil down to managing three critical areas in any business transformation:

- Purpose and results (why and what)

- Principles and processes (how)

- Leadership (who)

These three areas form a dynamic interplay that can lead to unified learning and success or to corporate disconnection and failure. The goal is unification of vision from shop floor to boardroom. This requires new systems of rewards. It requires hard looks at corporate basics such as the product portfolio and relations with suppliers and customers. Unified vision is maintained by approaches like public reporting of announced goals, accountability, corporate transparency, and stakeholder dialogues.

Sustainable development broadens corporate vision. Concern for stakeholder wellbeing, reputation enhancement, and environmental care are added to purpose and results. Processes start accounting for future costs and externalities in decision models; this stimulates resource efficiency improvements and funding of innovation. Leadership learns to think several moves ahead in terms of social and environmental value while also uncompromisingly focusing on the economic and market realities of today. It empowers innovation and encourages continuous skills development of the people involved. It also seeks new forms of dialogue and partnership with stakeholders.

Making change happen

There is no one way to integrate sustainable development as a strategic objective into a company. Much depends on corporate culture and institutional structure, on current performance, and on the credibility with key stakeholders.

Working in the three areas critical to business transformation listed above—purpose and results, leadership and empowerment, and principles and processes—those who have already begun transforming their organizations tend to agree that the sustainability learning curve is mainly about vision, leadership, employee empowerment, stakeholder engagement, and new performance indicators. Changes required will not all be sweeping and radical; implementation will tend to use management tools and systems already in place. The business of being the customers' preferred supplier and the investors' favorite equity goes on. The sustainability transformation is about enhancing the company's success, value, and resilience for the long term.

Vision and leadership

Designing this enhanced company is the role of corporate leadership. The required leaders need many qualities, but the one that counts is a deep sense of what is important to the success of their organizations. Therefore as leaders we must personally attend to the articulation of corporate purpose and vision. We must stimulate this shared drive toward a highly desirable future.

This vision forms the framework within which corporate transformation takes place and gives the process direction. Its very quality of being shared also means that vision formation does not require that we retreat to inspired isolation. Pasquale Pistorio, president and CEO of Italian silicon chip producer STMicroelectronics, underwent a conversion of sorts instigated through conversations with his son (see page 127). Dialogue with employees, particularly the young generation of future leaders, advice from stakeholders, and feedback from customers and investors are essential sources that enrich the vision. This does not make the vision an exercise of design by committees or management consultants.

Pasquale Pistorio *eco-evangelist*

It is not often that a heated discussion at the family dinner table can prompt the eco-transformation of a man and his company. However, Pasquale Pistorio, CEO of STMicroelectronics, can point to his eldest son and the arrival of his first grand-child as the main impetus behind his commitment to sustainable development.

Until the 1990s, Pasquale Pistorio was a typical executive, moving his way up the corporate ladder. After a 17-year stint at Motorola, the native Sicilian returned to Italy in 1980 to head the electronics group SGS. In 1987 the company merged with France's Thomson Semiconductors and in 1998 changed its name from SGS-Thompson Microelectronics to STMicroelectronics, now the world's third-largest semiconductor company, based in Geneva, Switzerland.

As CEO in the late 1980s Pistorio thought that by delivering a healthy financial return to his shareholders he was doing all that was required to fulfill his duty as chief executive. Then his son Carmello, newly a father himself, started to challenge his father, pushing him to acknowledge that responsible corporate leaders had a higher duty than simply to make money. Fired by his son's passion, Pistorio began to develop an environmental consciousness.

> Over time Carmello challenged several values, or, should I say, the lack of values of the industrial society I represented. He said that, if I were serious about making the company's economic model benefit human-ity, rather than to destroy humanity, the company might have to con-sider a commitment to sustainable environmental development (in Kador 2000).

In the 1990s Pistorio came up with a shortlist of objectives that would define his company; at the top of the list was a determination to achieve environmental responsibility and sustainable development. The STMicroelectronics decalogue consists of ten commandments that put the company's environmental vision into concrete form. Says Pistorio:

> I accept a moral responsibility towards protecting the environment. The wealth of a corporation can only be amplified if we upgrade the wealth of the society in which we operate . . . I want our employees to under-stand that this kind of commitment is not only good for themselves, their children and their grandchildren, but it is also good for the com-pany's bottom line.

CASE STUDY 27
Interface
page 142

Drafting such a framework always requires that we express our personal convictions. Change must first be sown in the minds and attitudes of senior executives, allowing them to project their sense of a positive legacy. This is where sustainable development broadens traditional corporate vision. Many excellent visions drive corporations to outstanding profits, market expansion, innovation, and quality. In a sustainable business, our vision and purposes go beyond those traditional success indicators. They address the role we play in society and our contribution to society's needs and success. But it is not an either/or choice. It is about outstanding business performance *and also* outstanding contribution to a better society.

A sustainable business excels on the traditional scorecard of return on financial assets and shareholder and customer value creation. It also embraces community and stakeholder success. The ability to envision a roadmap for transformation of a company is becoming all the more important as a leadership quality in the light of changing societal expectations about the role of the corporation.

'In the next society', observes Peter Drucker (2001), professor of social science and management at Claremont Graduate University, California, 'the biggest challenge for the large company—especially for the multinational—may be its social legitimacy: its values, its missions, its vision.' Success in such a society requires curiosity and the art of detecting the silent signals of profound changes beyond our normal scope or planning horizons. As we look back, the signals of ozone depletion, acid rain, and water pollutants were there long before general scientific concern and popular outcry. This lack of foresight meant that solutions were found and mandated in a climate of near crisis. The polluters were faced, in a short period, with the internalization of costs that significantly depressed their financial performance.

It is a lesson M. Shosaku Yasui, CEO and chairman of Japanese chemical company Teijin Corporation, has taken to heart:

> The task for executives in the twenty-first century is to find ways to enhance economic activity while minimizing its impact on the environment. The key to all these challenges—and to increasing capital efficiency, ensuring the effective use of management resources, and ensuring a successful future—is, of course, wisdom (Teijin 2001: 16).

A sustainability vision does not dismiss important signals because they are not reflected in current market surveys and the trade press. It does not assume that the corporation can get away from the diffuse financial consequences of climate change, water scarcity, failed economies and democracies, and mounting poverty even in remote regions that it would not consider as markets (WBCSD *et al.* 2002). Insurance and security costs can climb at the mercy of an accident. A sustainability vision on the contrary will look at the opportunity to be prepared with solutions and to contribute to the elimination of the potential destructive consequences. This is a courageous step within business as it breaks ranks with the prevailing paradigm based on the more visible and published trends.

In short there are really only two dimensions that transform an outstanding business vision into an outstanding *sustainable* business vision—a deeper anticipation of the silent currents that move the world and a commitment to make a lasting contribution to society.

Chad Holliday *action for change*

" I always link the 'sustainability virus' with leadership because I contracted the virus through the example of two leaders who helped put sustainability on the map of modern global business. In the early 1990s Stephan Schmidheiny was trying to ensure business input at the Rio Summit and generate support for forming the organization that would become the World Business Council for Sustainable Development. One of the leading CEOs he wanted to involve in the effort was DuPont's Ed Woolard, who had already established his environmental bona fide through a series of ground-breaking speeches and commitments he began making soon after becoming DuPont's chairman in 1989.

It seems, however, that Stephan just couldn't get on Ed's calendar to make his pitch. One day Stephan called Ed and tried one more time to arrange a meeting. Busy as he was, Ed said, okay, if you can be in my office tomorrow afternoon, we can talk. Stephan agreed to be there the next day. What Ed did not know was that Stephan was in Europe when he made that commitment. He dropped everything, got on a plane, and made it to Ed's office in Wilmington less than 24 hours later. Ed was so impressed with Stephan's fierce dedication to the idea of sustainability that he agreed to support his efforts, and DuPont became a founding member of the WBCSD. I was so impressed with Ed's commitment to this idea and to the genuine leadership he exerted toward sustainability goals within DuPont that I caught the 'virus' long before I became CEO.

But it's one thing to believe in sustainability yourself and it's another thing to lead others in that direction. I don't spend a lot of time talking about vision; I focus on leadership reality. To me, leadership reality is vision, grounded. Sustainability is such a grand and noble vision that people can subscribe to it and then go about business as usual, never making it a reality. At DuPont we've grounded the vision of sustainability in the reality of real activity and performance measures that tell us whether or not we're moving in that direction.

The biggest challenge any leader faces is what will be the first step—what *action* will you take? Plans are worthless without action steps. I think that for industry overall the WBCSD represents a first step toward sustainability. That's why case histories have been such a prominent part of our publications and presentations. Another key to successful leadership is diversity of thinking. I worked to bring more diverse thought into the WBCSD just as I have at DuPont. The perspectives of developing countries, for example, are critical if sustainability is to have global impact.

Finally, a leader has to communicate. The message has to be simple. It has to be visual. And it has to be repeated over and over again. Few employees in industry today are inspired by philosophical concepts. They need a clear message that they can act on. At one stage in our sustainability journey at DuPont we created the message that 'The Goal Is Zero'. We meant zero accidents, wastes, and emissions. In plants and offices all around the world, we started seeing green and white signs that say 'The Goal Is Zero'. Everyone in the company today understands why that's important. It speaks volumes about our commitment. Everyone can devise action steps to help get us there. There is no mistaking failure to achieve it, and there is no ambiguity when we succeed.

The critical challenge of sustainability remains communicating the idea through simple messages that people can visualize and then devising concrete actions that companies can apply and individuals can execute in the normal course of their jobs. "

As this requires taking a broader and deeper look at the business environment, business leaders are often criticized for their short-sightedness or their blind submission to the tyranny of the capital market and the rhythm of the Wall Street closing bell. This again is not an either/or dilemma but a test of the leaders' ability to set and keep a worthwhile vision and also deliver operational and financial performance day after day. It is a little like racing a sailboat around the world. One needs a vision of victory, a vision of the race as a whole, and a vision of one's master plan that will work itself out over weeks at sea. But victory will depend as much, and usually more, on day-to-day split-second decisions under extreme conditions.

In their book, *Built to Last: Successful Habits of Visionary Companies* (1993: ch. 3), management consultant James C. Collins and Professor Jerry I. Porras make a long-term comparison of 18 leading companies with their closest market rivals. The study identifies the key management principles that helped the leaders to create, as a cluster, six times more shareholder return than the rival cluster. First is the dedication to define core values and a sense of purpose greater than profitability alone. They also conclude that the hallmark of highly successful and visionary companies is the ability to escape the 'tyranny of the OR' by using the 'genius of AND' (Collins and Porras 1994: 43-44). This is exactly our learning from integrating sustainable development into company strategy.

Sharing the vision: employee empowerment

There are no easy levers for directing complex organizations in a fast-moving, changeable and challenging world. Decisions are rarely simple, time presses, conditions change, information is limited, understanding incomplete, choices unclear, and outcomes uncertain. So how do we effectively communicate—and share—the vision and the resulting changes throughout a business while operating on such shifting sands?

CASE STUDY 28
Swiss Re
page 144

Sir Robert Wilson, executive chairman of Rio Tinto, suggests that:

> effective implementation throughout a geographically and culturally diverse organization requires leadership and sustained commitment from the top. These are necessary conditions for success.

They are not, however, sufficient:

CASE STUDY 29
Rio Tinto
page 145

> Corporate values only really take root in an organization if they are shared values—as distinct from policy edicts imposed from on high. They must be embedded in corporate culture, not painted on like a coat of varnish (Wilson 2001).

Wilson says that if you want the commitment of the management cadre to a revised set of business principles, it must be co-owned. 'You can't have it delivered by someone who says, "This is it, guys, this is how we work." ' For this reason, Rio Tinto's statement of business principles, *The Way We Work*, did not rely solely on CEO vision but sought to draw directly on the personal experience of management and was worded in a way all could understand. As a consequence, says Wilson, most of them identify with the finished product. 'The principles have been genuinely embraced by the large majority of our management and have served us well as a guide to action'. However, getting wide agreement to *The Way We Work* required 18 months of interaction and discussion.

DuPont talks internally about the concept of 'felt leadership'; it is not enough for a policy to be written and posted on the walls; everybody in the organization must feel it. This means that it is considered in decisions, it is referred to at management reviews, and tough decisions are made to support the vision.

Leaders must clearly establish the importance and urgency of the vision. Employees must also sense no hesitation about implementation. Most institutional change is really personal change, and personal change does not happen when people are simply told what to do. They can be told, but they then must opt in. Get enough people to opt in, and you have created the critical mass necessary for deep, abiding change.

Leaders must set an example and 'walk the talk', serving as models and providing enough resources, education, direct challenges, encouragement, and follow-up to their employees. They must also be seen in public debates as promoters of their vision and ambassadors of their corporation's performance. The public profile must be managed wisely with a fine balance. The vast majority of employees and business observers expect the leaders to care first for the financial sustainability of the business. It is thus unwise to make the conference rounds on, say, sustainability indicators when the financial performance indicators are blinking red.

However, it also sets back progress to drop all reference to long-term sustainability during times of economic downturn. This is a time when employees will be looking hard to see if the sustainability vision is nothing more than a fad for flush times. Again, it is not an either/or choice but a consistent balancing act.

One clear signal is the amount of education and training that is designed and provided to support the implementation. Employees fully appreciate the dimension of this investment in training materials, time, travel, and executive participation. Danish biotech company Novo Nordisk uses participation in task groups and committees as a way of educating its staff. Says Lise Kingo of Novo Nordisk:

> We tend to involve many employees in learning activities but also in activities where we want to improve our knowledge on a certain topic. For instance, a way of involving people in bioethics was by forming task groups and committees and having education activities.

The company also assembles Novo Nordisk environmental managers from all over the world once a year to discuss strategies, targets, and goals.

Business education and executive training programs are also valuable ways to raise awareness and nurture buy-in from managers. Many companies use their own in-house universities for this purpose. The ABB Academy, for example, now includes sessions on sustainability in its management programs. However, few mainstream business schools have incorporated innovative sustainability thinking into their curricula. Says Stuart Hart of the Kenan-Flagler Business School at the University of North Carolina, 'no major business school in the world has yet adopted this key emerging global challenge as a core platform' (in Coleman 2001).

CASE STUDY 30
Companhia
Siderúrgica de
Tubarão
page 146

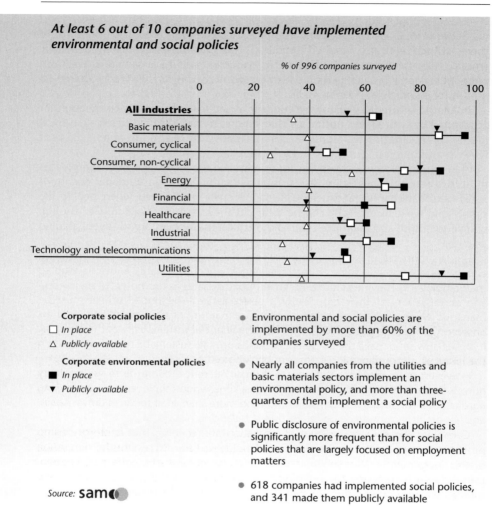

Figure 8 **ADOPTION OF ENVIRONMENTAL AND SOCIAL POLICIES**

Leaders also need to challenge their organizations and people to rise above the various 'paradoxes' of sustainable development. We have described various companies setting 'zero' waste and emission targets. Meeting such targets is probably impossible—but who knows how close a company can get? We have written of the triple bottom line whereby companies take social and environmental results as seriously as financial results. Is this really possible when business pages tend to report only financial results? Perhaps if enough companies engage in triple-bottom-ine thinking and reporting, business pages will report their reporting.

First, paradoxes are the sources of great innovations. Moving heavier-than-air machines through the air, moving frail human organisms through the vacuum of space and sending signals into space to bounce them to another place on Earth: all were at one point apparently impossible. Second, creating a sustainability-driven corporation requires a conspiracy approach: we know this sounds crazy, but we are all in it together, so let's confound the doubters and make it work.

According to the Teijin Corporation's M. Shosaku Yasui, change must infiltrate not only individual values and attitudes but all aspects of management:

> To ensure Teijin remains a key global player, we must effect changes in individual mentality and corporate structure aimed at building the ability to effect change from within. Responding effectively to change and then using our achievements to initiate change in the market demands that we encourage innovation not only in products and services, but also in all aspects of management (Teijin 2001: 16).

US consumer products company Johnson & Johnson offers a compelling example of a firm that is actively nurturing a questioning culture. 'We encourage our people to question everything we do to make us more innovative', claim Johnson & Johnson chairman and CEO Ralph Larsen and vice chairman Robert Wilson:

> We want an organization made up of inquisitive people, for we are seeking innovation—constant improvements in the ways people do their jobs—in all areas of the business. Conducting 'business as usual' does not belong in an inquisitive culture (Johnson & Johnson 2000).

For Johnson & Johnson, this means decentralizing power and decision-making down to individual business units. 'With our well-known aversion to bureaucracy we simply have to have confidence in our operating units to develop their own business plans against their own target markets . . . and then deliver on their promises', say Larsen and Wilson.

Corporate rewards systems must be reorganized to recognize and reinforce desired performance and the innovative spirit. Most bonus and awards systems favor tangible breakthroughs. The sustainability transformation is a process where the early achievements may not be as obvious as a sales breakthrough or production record, yet early sustainability achievements must be recognized if you want employees to share the vision seriously.

'Human nature is the greatest barrier', says Grupo IMSA's Eugenio Clariond. 'People dislike change; it's not intrinsic, especially as you get older, and there are often competing priorities'. Good leadership therefore involves sending the right signals to employees, to reinforce the sustainability message and provide the incentive to change and innovate.

Establishing clear lines of responsibility and defining progress milestones that are tied to remuneration and bonuses is a sure way to overcome implementation barriers, according to Clariond. At Grupo IMSA sustainability performance is included as a defining component of employees' bonuses, together with profitability and worker satisfaction.

Costa Rica's GrupoNueva also links progress in meeting sustainable development goals with remuneration. According to CEO Julio Moura, objectives are periodically set in financial performance, health, safety, environment, eco-efficiency, and CSR, against which performance will be assessed. People are asked to submit a strategic plan, including each of these aspects in their planning and budget and are assessed, annually, against those objectives. 'These elements should be part of the bonus, otherwise the loop is not closed', stresses Moura.

The same principles can be applied to the supply chain and to service contractors, where, as a corporate customer, companies can insist on high social and environmental standards as a condition for doing business. Faster than good words and advice, a determination to align the choice of business partners with the vision and corresponding performance expectations will transform the business playing field.

Management systems

CASE STUDY 31
Sony
page 147

Adopting the sustainability paradigm may require a tweaking, or even a radical reorganization, of a corporation's management systems to formalize the values, the expectations, the performance reporting, and recognition. In the wake of the quality movement, many companies were quick to recognize that waste, emissions, and environmental impacts were symptoms of an unproductive system. They adapted the experience from the quality excellence framework to this new challenge and initiated environmental management systems (see Figure 9).

Nestlé is among those companies that have found the EMS to be a powerful driver of environmental improvement. Implementation of the Nestlé Environmental Management System (NEMS), set up in 1996, is mandatory throughout the company. Nestlé draws on company policy, international commitments, and local environmental considerations to implement well-defined programs for improvement, setting targets and tracking performance against these. The company describes its systematic approach to environmental management as a 'spiral for continuous improvement'. To ensure success, environmental officers are appointed at different levels of the organization, from corporate headquarters to factory floor.

'This cascade of environmental responsibility at all levels of the organization remains the cornerstone of NEMS success', Nestlé (2000) reports. Key elements of NEMS include efficient monitoring and auditing, periodic reporting, and ongoing evaluation of progress. Since 1995 the company has reported significant progress in reducing resource consumption and waste generation, as well as improvements in manufacturing efficiency and capacity utilization. NEMS has also led to increased awareness by personnel.

Complete sectors, especially the chemical industry, designed systems that would respond to all companies' needs and also integrate stakeholder communications and reviews. US chemical company Dow Corning, for example, has set up a product stewardship code to make health, safety, and environment an integral part of designing, manufacturing, marketing, distributing, using, recycling, and disposing of products (Dow Corning 2000). The company has also signed up to the chemical industry's Responsible Care program. Says Gary Anderson, CEO, president and chairman:

> We're committed to building a sustainable future and focusing today for both short- and long-term success. With Responsible Care as the framework

Every second company surveyed has adopted an environmental management system but only one in four has extended it to cover all operations

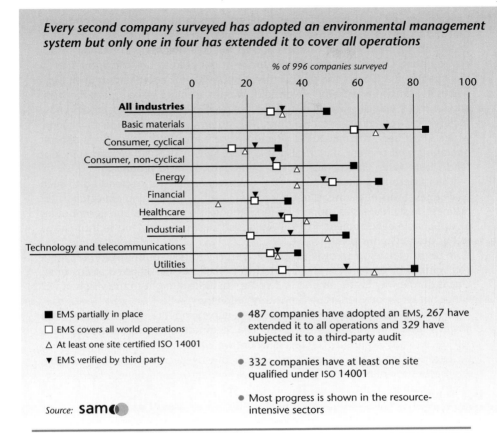

EMS partially in place
□ EMS covers all world operations
△ At least one site certified ISO 14001
▼ EMS verified by third party

Source: **sam**

● 487 companies have adopted an EMS, 267 have extended it to all operations and 329 have subjected it to a third-party audit

● 332 companies have at least one site qualified under ISO 14001

● Most progress is shown in the resource-intensive sectors

Figure 9 **ADOPTION OF ENVIRONMENTAL MANAGEMENT SYSTEMS (EMSs)**

we use to manage environmental, health and safety at Dow Corning, and the strong bond to our corporate vision and values, today's actions will, no doubt, have [an] overriding long-term positive impact (Dow Corning 2000).

Spanish forestry-timber company ENCE has also found EMS to be an effective tool for improving environmental performance. It has implemented an EMS, which it calls SIGMA, to assure management quality in environmental matters. This consists of an environmental training plan for workers, audits, a procedural handbook and environmental certification, and an annual environmental statement. As a result of ENCE's efforts, its Huelva and Pontevedra pulp mills were the first in Spain to achieve ISO 14001 certification. As part of its environmental renovation program the group has invested heavily in technological and environmental improvements to its mills, which are now among the cleanest in Europe and produce low-environmental-impact pulp (ENCE 2001).

Philip Watts *valuing change*

❝I always wanted to do a good job in Shell and was proud of being in a company that did its job properly. Then two experiences forced me to think much more deeply about the nature of business and its role in society and in relation to our environment. One of these was the outrage at our plan to sink the Brent Spar in the Atlantic in 1995. As the person then responsible for coordinating Shell businesses in Europe I was deeply involved. It was an absolute wake-up call for Shell, and for me. It was clear we were right off the pace in terms of understanding how society's expectations were changing. The other was the situation in Nigeria, where I had been the managing director in the early 1990s. It is a very difficult operating environment. But it also is a place where people—lacking sufficient food, clean water, and medical facilities—desperately need progress.

Then I became leader of our central units responsible for responding to such challenges. I was at the heart of the process looking at changing expectations of business, in such areas as support for fundamental human rights and contributing to sustainable development. In 1998 we added clear commitments in those areas to our business principles.

In terms of leading an organization, it is crucial to have both a vision of where you want to be and a clear idea of what can practically be achieved at any time. One is on the way to the other. But if you try to jump straight to the vision, it will either not work, or your vision is not very visionary.

We faced this problem when we were enhancing our health, safety, and environment processes. So we expressed a 'commitment' and then adopted a 'policy' for carrying it out. The first is where we want to be: for example, having no fatal accidents. But we can't just ordain this by decree. We need workable approaches for pursuing it. The policies are mandatory and have a compulsory internal assurance process. But for societal expectations we realized we also need an external assurance process, through our new *Shell Report*.

Why do I value sustainable development as a leader? Quite simply because it is good business. The need to balance economic, social, and environmental considerations makes it a very powerful concept. It provides common ground for discussion. Businesses sometimes think only about economic considerations. NGOs sometimes think only about the environment, or only about social issues. Sustainable development forces us all to confront the reality of integrating those considerations and making hard choices.

Business has a particular capacity to make a difference. Increasingly, other institutions—governments, the UN under Kofi Annan, thoughtful NGOs—realize that business is part of the solution, not the problem.

Being a leader is all about being up-front. People shouldn't lose sight of you. They should know what you stand for and see that you mean it. I am severely practical about sustainable development. It is not philanthropy or window dressing. It is about doing our business in a way that meets the expectations of our customers, our shareholders, our neighbors and—not least—ourselves.

We have our own values. That's very important for people in Shell, particularly young people joining us. They want to feel they are part of an organization with values, principles, standards . . . which does a good job.❞

The fact that ISO managed to design and ratify through its thorough government and stakeholder consultation process the extensive suite of ISO 14000 standards in only eight years (from 1991 to 1999) speaks for the maturity and value of EMSs. We must declare an interest: the early BCSD helped to conceptualise the ISO 14000 series around the time of the Rio '92 Summit. Such approaches offer a systematic approach to identifying areas for improvement, setting firm goals and targets, then tracking progress toward these and reporting on performance, all within the policy framework set by the vision. According to ABB, six years of experience in applying ISO 14001 have demonstrated beyond doubt that a formal EMS, correctly implemented, has tangible positive effects on an organization's environmental performance.

Management systems such as EMSs are not only useful in tracking progress on achieving sustainable development targets but also, critically, can provide the concrete performance data that backs up the business case for sustainability. Success stories identified through such management systems provide tangible evidence that sustainability pays and that EMSs are a valuable tool in reinforcing the need for change (see Box 6).

UNEP and UK consultancy SustainAbility Ltd have identified 12 key steps for helping companies integrate sustainability into mainstream business operations by establishing links between business success and sustainability performance. The 12 steps are as follows:

1. Get cracking!

2. Communicate the importance of the business case across the organization

3. Join key business case initiatives

4. Build an understanding of how performance in different sustainable development dimensions could potentially affect various measures of business success

5. Account for the environmental and social implications of decision-making

6. Inventory tangible evidence of real events with potential business case impacts

7. Harmonize your business case project into the mainstream business, using common language and systems

8. Find useful sparring partners across your organization, particularly if you are not in a line function

9. Disclose the headline results of your analysis externally

10. Engage the attention and interest of investors and of the financial analysts that track your company

11. Keep the business case evolving

12. Lobby for policy changes that will make your business case stronger

Box 6 **12 STEPS TO MAKING THE BUSINESS CASE FOR SUSTAINABILITY**

Source: SustainAbility/UNEP 2001

Stakeholder engagement and performance indicators

ASE STUDY 32
Suncor
page 148

Another factor of corporate change is dialogue with external stakeholders. We cover relationships with stakeholders in Chapter 6, but it should be noted here that simply being open and transparent to those outside the company—from confirmed customers to confirmed critics—stimulates and adds meaning to corporate change.

Danish biotech company Novo Nordisk has been a pioneer in this respect. For ten years the company has held dialogue with a wide range of NGOs, meeting regularly several times a year to discuss major themes currently on the agenda. Such dialogue, says Lise Kingo, 'is about building trust, about building respect, and about building a relationship, but not necessarily building up an agreement'.

The process, says Kingo, is more important than getting a tangible result—a fact that is sometimes hard for business people to accept. An indirect result of dialogue is that certain issues have not been allowed to grow into problems. Moreover, the trust Novo has thus built up with various NGOs has led to some interesting partnerships, notably its collaboration with the Danish Nature Preservation Society, PROGENUS, to produce school materials on genetic engineering. The project won plaudits for its innovative approach in uniting partners with diverging views on the subject. 'We don't want to create one particular position,' says Kingo, 'we want to create debate on the pros and cons of genetic engineering. The fact that we are partners not in agreement has encouraged more acceptance and respect for the project.'

This approach develops the company's sensitivity to the weak signals of unmet social needs or simmering fears. It helps to anticipate solutions and develop them ahead of potential competitors. Dialogue also hedges against damages in reputation. Maintaining brand credibility and a license to do business is a matter of choices, made long before a potential crisis, in the context of an ever more complex set of expectations. Says Ewald Kist, chairman of ING Group:

> as a responsible corporate citizen, ING also has to address the concerns of non-governmental organizations. NGOs are increasingly vocal about the negative impact of globalization, such as damage to the environment, human rights abuses and unfair labor conditions. They expect companies like ING to address these issues in their policies and practices. We acknowledge these societal demands and pay attention to the interests of all our stakeholders. We aim to have an open dialogue with them (ING Group 2000).

To ensure that the company is addressing the concerns of its stakeholders, ING has developed a strong set of company values and business principles and since 1995 has published annual environmental performance reports to recount progress in meeting these. The principles, Kist claims:

> provide our employees with a solid framework of values and rules that cover environmental and social issues. In the coming years, we will continue to embed these principles in our business policies and activities . . . This will become even more important as we are transforming towards a common, global, ING brand . . . We have to 'walk our talk' and live up to our commitment to be a socially responsible financial services provider (ING Group 2000).

Stephan Schmidheiny *vision and deliverables*

66 After the 1992 Earth Summit, I was moving out of owning companies, except in Latin America, where I was beginning to try to bring together my 40 companies, with 30 production plants, in 15 countries, into one holding company called GrupoNueva.

I was excited about putting my big new company on a sustainable, eco-efficient footing, so I explained it all at a meeting of my key executives. They were supportive, excited; they came up afterwards and told me so.

Of course, nothing happened. The strongest force on Earth is inertia, defined by some cynics not in physics terms but as 'people's resistance to change'. It was not my people's fault; I had done absolutely nothing a leader must do to cause change except to describe a vision—and this is only the first step.

That vision should be bold, far-reaching, and almost impossible to achieve; if it is not bold and nearly impossible, it is probably not worth doing and will not capture your people's interest. Then the leader must break the vision down into 'bite-sized chunks' of objectives, action plans, and measurable results. There will be many trade-offs between performing successfully over the short term and at the same time building the basis for a different future. There is no one right answer to this conundrum; it will always mean walking a tightrope between short- and long-term views and expectations.

The biggest challenge is to convince people that they need to change. Do not try to *sell* them the vision. Who would buy a vision? It is too distant, abstract, and inconvenient. Show the concrete objectives and their relevance to your people's daily work. Do not get lost in the analytical arguments about the need to change. Often a vision cannot be argued totally rationally, and the resulting debates become endless. Name the deliverables and declare them compulsory for all planning purposes. And of course make the deliverables count in remuneration packages, bonuses, and job assessments.

Once I stopped preaching to my colleagues at GrupoNueva and did all the above, things began to change. The many corporate sites, with their different backgrounds, cultures, and experiences, complicated things at first. But then a spirit of competition between sites kicked in and sped things up. We produced for the first time in 2002 independently audited 'sustainability reports' for all areas of the business, which cover water systems, sewerage and irrigation systems, construction materials, pine plantations and wood products, and special agricultural products such as macadamia nuts and teak. We are reporting financial, social, and environmental results. We are also developing corporate social responsibility (CSR) programs.

I had been afraid that I was forcing a very expensive, personal vision on a company that could not benefit by it financially. Is there a 'market' for sustainable development in Latin America? Then we hired a consultant to advise us on how to deal with a powerful competitor in a key market. We were advised that the competitor had a reputation for being cold and aloof, both to customers and society in general. We were perfectly positioned to play our CSR card against them—without having devised it for competitive purposes.

So colleagues that had tended to regard me as the 'idealistic owner' now see me as a sound corporate strategist.

Which brings me to my final rule of corporate change—Rule Number One: it is better to be lucky than smart. 99

The ING example demonstrates how external accountability—in this case to NGOs—can be harnessed as a powerful driver for internal change. The need to be seen to be 'walking the talk' ensures continuous improvement.

But stakeholders will tire of all this dialogue if they do not see tangible, measurable change. Likewise, managers and employees need a scorecard that tells them that progress is made and resources therefore applied efficiently. Reporting is an inseparable part of implementing the vision.

There is a right order in which to approach the implementation challenge, says Rio Tinto's Sir Robert Wilson (2001):

> From a company's perspective, reporting and verification are *not* the next step after pronouncement of a policy. After policy development comes implementation; next, comes training where it is required and then internal reporting systems. External reporting and verification [are] the final step for those of us in the world of converting words into action.

The number of companies implementing environmental and social reporting is growing, but even in 2000 those acting only represented a small fraction of the business world (see Figure 1, page 23). There is a lively debate about the selection of meaningful performance indicators, particularly for social and ethical performance now being held in forums such as the Global Reporting Initiative (GRI). However, the business voice has been rather muted in this debate. Yet this question of indicators should be tied to the more fundamental question of understanding value creation.

CASE STUDY 33
Global
Reporting
Initiative
page 163

Throughout the 1990s the attention of the financial world was drawn to the decreasing correlation between the stock market value of a corporation and its traditional financial parameters such as earnings and book value. Even discounting for cycles of investors' exuberance and gloom, the market values of successful companies are significantly more than the sum of their financial assets. For example, several of the 20 sustainability leaders of the Dow Jones Sustainability Index (see pages 30-31) were worth 5–15 times their book value in 2000. These multiples differed from one company to another and also changed notably from 1997 to 2000 (see Table 2).

This large surplus of value is the investors' estimate of future cash flows derived from assets that the company does not report in the balance sheet because of their intangible nature. Alan C. Shapiro, professor of Finance and Business Economics at the Marshall School of Business, University of Southern California, writes:

> Intangible assets are excluded from the balance sheet because of the difficulty in objectively valuing them. Yet such assets—in the form of management skill, reputation, strategic positioning, and patents and copyrights—are usually the most important assets for successful firms (Shapiro 1991: 704).

Braden Allenby, environment, health, and safety vice president for AT&T, agrees:

> Rather than depending on traditional inputs like capital, labor, and natural resources, much of tomorrow's value-added will come from 'knowledge-based' operations. Mobilizing the process of corporate transformation around valuing and retaining such intangible assets will be crucial.

That very importance has triggered many initiatives to improve the current system of measuring and disclosing corporate performance. It may take time, but, because of

Company name	2000	1999	1998	1997
Bristol-Myers Squibb	14.98	14	16.72	12.39
British Telecommunications	3.75	3.39	3	1.81
Dofasco	0.82	1.24	0.93	1.13
Dow Chemical	2.7	3.58	2.7	3
Granada	0.43	n/a	n/a	n/a
ING Groep	3.32	1.68	1.7	1.49
Intel Corp.	5.41	8.52	8.86	5.98
Ito-Yokado Co.	3.92	4.36	4.55	3.77
3M	7.31	6.21	4.82	5.6
Procter & Gamble	7.02	11.46	11.69	9.36
Royal Dutch Petroleum	3.84	4.22	3.22	3.25
Severn Trent Water	0.76	1.17	1.57	0.96
Skanska	2.26	2.2	1.89	2.52
Sony	7.33	2.74	2.96	2.46
Swiss Reinsurance	2.51	1.94	4.69	3.1
UBS	2.51	2.95	3.07	3.11
Unilever	5.79	5.94	8.59	3.12
Volkswagen	2.64	2.43	3.1	3.19
BASF	2.13	2.3	1.58	1.72
Henkel	2.74	2.78	3.89	2.9

n/a = not available

Table 2 **THE MARKET VALUE DIVIDED BY THE BOOK VALUE FOR THE 20 LEADING COMPANIES IN THE DOW JONES SUSTAINABILITY INDEX**

Source: Bloomberg LP, New York, www.bloomberg.com

the financial stakes, these initiatives will not go away until they have reached a consensus on additional performance indicators that will monitor intangibles as reliably as return on capital, inventory turnover, or return on sales monitor core assets performance. The US Securities and Exchange Commission, the European Union, and the OECD are studying improvements in corporate disclosure. Pension funds, banks, and insurance companies encourage a host of financial analysts to research and evaluate indicators that enable them to maximize the value–risk balance of their shares portfolios by looking at innovation, knowledge, and the more fuzzy areas of reputation, sustainability, and ethics. The apparent overnight collapses of such firms as Enron and Swissair will accelerate the overhaul and tightening of disclosure standards.

NGOs dedicated to environmental and social progress have been quick to leverage this concern from the other side of the argument. Corporations, they argue, shift environmental and social consequences outside the boundaries of the balance sheet. The current accounting conventions encourage them to externalize such costs with impunity. Adequate performance indicators and transparency would at least let the investors appreciate the risk of the intangible liabilities they acquire with their share portfolio. They would either shun the company's shares or exercise their ownership prerogative by putting pressure on management to change in the direction precisely desired and recommended by the NGOs.

There is no way back. The competition for indicators that value intangibles is on, and will bring results—like it or not. This has not escaped forward-looking companies who have started to share their own experience with indicators by disclosing them in an attempt to both learn and shape the effort. When management is dedicated to increasing the value of the firm and creating value for its shareholders, it must also come to grips with its set of meaningful progress indicators. It is in the interest of a simple and reliable disclosure system that those with the operational experience actively contribute to its design.

CASE STUDY 27

Interface *a learning experience*

Interface Inc. is a large manufacturer of carpet tiles and upholstery fabrics for commercial interiors. However, Interface's core vision is not about carpet or fabrics per se; it is about becoming a leading example of a sustainable and restorative enterprise by 2020 across five dimensions: people, place (the planet), product, process, and profits. As a company with 27 factories, sales offices in 110 countries, annual sales of $1.3 billion, over 7,000 employees, and a supply chain heavily dependent on petrochemicals, that is a substantial challenge.

Founder and chairman Ray Anderson presented this challenge to the organization in 1994. As a result, Interface has undergone considerable transformation in its effort to reorient the entire organization. Some positive results were achieved in the beginning. Through its waste elimination drive, the company has saved $165 million over five years, paying for all of its sustainability work and delivering 27% of the group's operating income over the period. Over and above that, since 1994 Interface has reduced its 'carbon intensity'—its total supply-chain virgin petrochemical material and energy use in raw kilograms per dollar of revenue—by some 31%. However, Interface recognized that sustainability means far more than that.

The company developed a shift in strategic orientation based on a seven-step sustainability framework, using the systems thinking of 'The Natural Step'. These steps include:

- Elimination of waste (not just physical waste, but the whole concept of waste)

- Elimination of harmful emissions

- Use of only renewable energy

- Adoption of closed-loop processes

- Use of resource-efficient transportation

- Energizing people (all stakeholders) around the vision

- Redesign of commerce so that a service is sold that allows the company to retain ownership of its products and to maximize resource productivity

Throughout the business, all employees were trained in the principles of systems thinking. They were required to examine the impact of their work and how they could work more sustainably in their business area. The feedback on this training has been very positive, and a great deal of progress has been made as a result. However, there were three areas where Interface could have improved the process.

The first is the need to establish a positive environment for inspired employees, fresh from their training courses, to return to. The company found that employees became passionate as their understanding of sustainability grew, and they need an outlet for action. Although there were many areas of good supportive management across the business, there were also too many areas where local managers were not prepared well enough to facilitate motivated employees wanting to make a difference. Issues of management and leadership explain why some of the expected progress did not happen in certain areas.

Second, people engage in different ways with sustainability issues, and learning programs need to provide the space to explore these differences. Programs need to be flexible enough to go into detail on a 'hot' issue such as climate change, while the next question may well be about equity of resource use. To keep people motivated, programs need to maintain this flexibility.

Third, follow-up was not quick enough; it takes much more than two days for people really to understand sustainability. Sustainability issues need to be revisited again and again, as employees begin to understand how it impacts their daily lives. It is a big commitment to revisit these issues on an ongoing basis, but the company recognized that it was vital for employees continually to 'buy in'.

Interface has also learned the importance of making sustainability a 'whole-company' approach. Those who 'got it' quickest were inevitably those working in either the manufacturing or the research areas of the business—people used to talking about the environment, systems, and material substitution. A high number of the company's early wins came on the manufacturing side: green-energy purchase, waste elimination, and recycling. However, it took longer to achieve the 'buy-in' of the sales and marketing teams, with the result that 'whole-company' issues such as strategic product development planning and communicating sustainability externally took longer to be integrated.

For Interface this has been a comprehensive sustainability learning approach for the company; a great deal has been learned along the way and the process has benefited from mistakes and successes. The company is now very aware that sustainability needs to *become* 'business as usual' for everyone across the business, and these experiences have made a solid contribution to successful change. The company is now well on the course to achieving its 2020 vision.

CASE STUDY 28
Swiss Re *building sustainability know-how*

Many firms are faced with changing business landscapes that present a range of new risks and new opportunities. This is certainly true for insurance companies; many such firms have been confronted with an increase in major losses as a result of natural catastrophes worldwide, as well as changing regulations and other political, social, and environmental forces.

The challenge for the reinsurance firm Swiss Re has been to develop new reinsurance solutions and expand its environmentally oriented risk management. Such challenges are helping the firm realize that sustainability is an essential part of corporate strategy that benefits the interests of all stakeholders.

Managing environmental liability risks tests the firm's 'knowledge content' in that such risks demand very specialized know-how relating to legislation, risk assessment, and insurance solutions. However, Swiss Re's more than 9,000 employees in 70 countries worldwide give the company the power to identify developments in the areas of environment, society, and technology that may present many new business opportunities.

The development of knowledge capacities and capabilities requires effective systems for collecting and disseminating information and building solid knowledge networks within the firm. Information must be converted into know-how to enable Swiss Re to evaluate the current risk landscape and its future development with stakeholders. Several structures have been put in place to facilitate knowledge transfer: the Environmental Impairment Liability (EIL) Center of Competence, the Knowledge Management Initiative and the group-wide Environmental Management Project.

The EIL Center has helped Swiss Re to develop insurance products in response to the growing demand for environmental liability solutions. Swiss Re employs a range of tools to make client managers, underwriters, and claims managers aware of the relevant environmental risks and the approaches to be taken. Yearly internal workshops are held to provide a knowledge-sharing forum. Also, several training modules have been formulated and numerous internal manuals and periodic publications have been produced.

Needing to optimize know-how on sustainability in a decentralized organization, Swiss Re launched its Knowledge Management Initiative in 1997. This initiative helped build group-wide knowledge networks devoted to subjects of strategic importance. Swiss Re now has eight such networks, including the group-wide Environmental Risk and Underwriting (ERU) network. These networks ensure that know-how is shared and that the risk dialogue progresses. They bring together pools of experience within the Swiss Re group that work to assemble knowledge as well as help in the creation of new knowledge. Much of this exchange is conducted electronically across the group. All Swiss Re staff can access the list of experts on the network platforms or search for a specialist by specific themes or fields of interest.

The ERU network sees itself as a central point of contact for all questions concerning environmental risks and the underwriting associated with them. It is intended to support and to accelerate the process of recognizing risks at an early stage, to maintain instruments for assessing environmental risks and to develop innovative products. The network currently includes around 70 experts in environmental risk.

Such initiatives help Swiss Re develop new reinsurance solutions to meet changing demands. This innovative capability, coupled with effective risk-management solutions, helps Swiss Re to position itself in society as a leading reinsurance company.

CASE STUDY 29

Rio Tinto *Borax*

Rio Tinto's borate mining subsidiary, Borax, ships about one million tonnes of refined borates a year from its mining and refining operations in Borax, California. Borates are key ingredients in many industrial processes, including the manufacture of glass, ceramics, fiberglass insulation, detergents, fertilizers, and wood preservatives.

In 2000 Borax launched a sustainable development project to better understand, measure, and maximize the contribution that it could make toward sustainable development. The project was designed as both a learning experience for the Borax company and as a learning model for Rio Tinto, as Borax embraces the entire spectrum of Rio Tinto activities, operating with large and small businesses in diverse geographic regions, environments, and communities.

The project's objectives were twofold. First, the company needed to determine how it could build policies and programs better to weave sustainability practices into the full spectrum of the business. Second, it wanted to examine how its participation in, and contribution to, sustainable development would provide business advantages and opportunities for Borax.

Sustainable development issues required new thinking and new measurements and a holistic framework for the integrated project. Environment, health, and safety (EH&S) had held an important place within the company's mission, and environmental improvements were already being examined and implemented. However, this project brought these and some new issues under one heading and sought to convey sustainable development as an opportunity for the whole company.

The new challenge was to develop a framework to help Borax employees identify these opportunities and see how what they are doing could contribute to a bigger picture of sustainable development.

A multidisciplinary group was formed from areas such as operations, communications, technical areas, and EH&S. The team developed a set of principles along with five primary objectives to support the mission:

- To protect the safety and health of employees, neighboring communities, and the public

- To enhance the human potential and wellbeing of communities and employees

- To maximize efficient utilization of resources while maximizing environmental impacts of operations

- To optimize the economic contribution to society

- To expand how products contribute to sustainable development

The group constructed indicators, metrics, and goals to judge performance to date and set priorities for the coming year. Community leaders, state regulatory officials, and environmental NGOs made up the external review panel. Borax reported its 2000 performance and 2001 objectives in its 2000 social and environmental report, distributing more than 5,000 copies to employees and stakeholders around the world.

Strong leadership has been essential to gaining support by employees, especially across multiple sites. Such a framework must be integrated into decision-making processes, and employees must be motivated and made accountable for their actions. Experience thus far indicates that greater benefit will come from involving external groups earlier in the reporting process, as this will enable the company to better incorporate more substantive input.

Borax is recognizing the necessity of reconsidering some existing strategies. For example, mine development plans must be reconfigured based on community impacts and concerns; strategies to process lower-grade but abundant ore reserves may be reconsidered in light of how the longevity of the operation affects the community; and decisions about capital investment will need to be weighed in light of all three pillars of sustainability.

'As we've rolled out new projects, talked about sustainable development more and undertaken this project work, people have begun to get excited', reports Dr Elaine Dorward-King, global executive for environment, health, and safety. The benefits have not been just about improved efficiency in areas such as emission reductions and cleaner production work. The work has led to improved products and real value-added components as a result of opportunities identified.

CASE STUDY 30

Companhia Siderúrgica de Tubarão
employee education programs

Sometimes a company's learning to change begins with employee education. Companhia Siderúrgica de Tubarão (CST) is a large steel plant supplying semi-finished products to the world steel industry. Located in south-east Brazil, the company has been operating for 18 years and has 3,500 employees.

Since its 1992 privatization, CST has developed a $2 billion program for technological update, production increase, and operational and environment improvements. It carries ISO 9001 and ISO 14001 certificates and focuses on the continuous improvement of product quality as well as community relationship and environment control.

Education programs play a key role in the company's environmental improvement efforts. CST seeks to enhance employee learning opportunities as well as providing education tools and opportunities to other groups.

The focus on employee education sparked in 1993 the school unit project, aimed at improving employees' educational levels. Research had found that 1,200 employees had not completed high school, and many had not completed primary school. CST decided to establish on the company premises a school with a places for 2,100 students studying in three different shifts. The school has been closing in on its objective of bringing every employee up to high-school level by 2002.

Aside from basic subjects taught by 20 qualified teachers, the classes also discuss corporate issues and projects. One topic was 'CST in the world scenario', in which the students discussed the history of the company while learning of its different markets and its relations with the rest of the world.

The environment educational program is meant to translate the company's environment policy to employees and to foster changes in their behavior. This program enables them to learn, understand, and participate in all the company's environmental policies. From May 2000 contractors' employees have been part of the program through the 'Interacting with Partners' module. Since the program's implementation in June 1996, 7,235 employees and partners have qualified, accomplishing 39,000 hours of qualification in environment education.

Given the widely differing levels of education among the employees, 'company learning' has required a complex, multi-level education program. Building capabilities among CST employees and those of business partners, both generally and in specific areas such as environmental studies, required the company to develop an educational program covering everything from reading and writing to thorny technical issues.

CASE STUDY 31
Sony *Green Management 2005*

Sony manufactures audio, video, communications, and IT products for the global consumer and professional markets. Sony's top management has made environmental preservation a 'key long-term management challenge' for the company. To meet this challenge, Sony has developed environmental action programs, the most recent of which, Green Management 2005, determines targets and programs to measure and motivate change and innovation within the Sony group.

Employees are encouraged to incorporate environmental perspectives into their own job assignments in areas ranging from R&D, procurement, product design, site and production management, through to marketing, distribution, repair service, and customer service.

Green Management 2005 comprises 16 chapters, each containing detailed and concrete goals to be accomplished by fiscal year 2005. For example, with regard to resources, the following targets have been announced

- Replace all packaging materials with environmentally sensitive materials (e.g. recycled materials)

- 20% reduction of product weight or number of parts

- 20% increase in recycled materials used, by product weight

- 30% reduction of total waste generation at business sites

Sony will also expand water-saving efforts and will reduce CO_2 emissions. Under Green Management 2005, Sony aims to achieve the intermediate target of '1.5 times eco-efficiency by 2005' and the ultimate goal of 'double eco-efficiency by 2010'.

Meeting such goals basically comes down to actions by individual business units and employees. So staff education takes a high priority, with environmental management workshops focusing on issues such as product development and design. Sony also provides company-wide, awareness-raising initiatives such as a touring education exhibition, newsletters and promotional posters, and Internet and intranet environmental information pages.

Under the action programs, business units are encouraged to pursue local strategies. However, Sony also focuses on diffusion of innovation to foster an organization-wide transformation. This allows units to innovate in ways best suited to local markets and legislative requirements, while at the same time fostering a culture of knowledge-sharing across business units. Regional and global communications are fostered through Sony's environmental conservation committees (ECCs). There are also specialized task forces and global committees created to ensure that regional communications are maintained on general, cross-cutting topics and specialized issues. An annual conference is conducted to facilitate information exchange and solution-sharing, and a series of other interim events and communication tools enable ongoing dialogue and capacity-building.

Sony has succeeded in obtaining ISO 14001 certification at all manufacturing sites, eliminated 95% or more of the waste generated at 35 sites (against fiscal year 2000 figures), introduced products with lead-free solder and halogen-free printed wiring boards and has reduced and replaced much packaging.

The worldwide implementation of EMSs at manufacturing facilities has helped Sony to identify most of the production processes that should and could be improved. However, years of product optimization and fine-tuning have left little room for further material savings, so more improvements depend on new technological innovations.

A number of recent innovations from Sony show how new approaches make such targets possible. In August 2001 Sony Europe announced its most environmentally sound television, the KV29FX66. This set is constructed using lead-free solder, a halogen-free flame-retardant cabinet, recycled paper for packaging (with no expanded polystyrene) and instruction manuals, and a standby power consumption of only 0.3 watts. With these environmental features, KV29FX66 is setting the environmental standards for all Sony TVs in the future.

Several lessons have been learned through this change process. Most important, clearly stated targets make progress evaluation possible. These indicators have enabled managers to monitor performance and report on improvements as well as on problems. The support of Sony's stakeholders, such as consumers, environmental organizations, politicians, and global suppliers is critical to the success of environmentally conscious products. Without stakeholder dialogue it is much more difficult to set and meet targets that are relevant and to communicate environmental benefits to consumers.

CASE STUDY 32

Suncor *valuing diversity*

Suncor Energy Inc. is a growing Canadian-based integrated energy company. During the past decade, Suncor has transformed itself from an unprofitable traditional oil and gas company to a highly profitable growth enterprise with the ambition of becoming a successful 'sustainable energy company'.

This move toward becoming a sustainable energy company has meant enormous changes in attitude, management decision-making, business strategy, stakeholder relationships, and employee engagement. The goal would take leadership, collaborative efforts, long-range planning, and a dedicated management framework. Therefore, in 1998, Suncor developed a management system to ensure that economic, environmental, and social performance was being addressed.

One of the major objectives of Suncor's new management framework was to increase the communication, consultation, and collaboration with the company's stakeholders, so issues and concerns could be more clearly understood and resolved. This was a new approach for Suncor; the company had historically taken an approach of informing stakeholders often after decisions had been made rather than at the planning stages of business opportunities.

This approach to relationship-building stems from a belief that supplying energy in a manner that meets the economic, environmental, and social expectations of stakeholders creates a solid foundation for increasing shareholder value over the long term. Essentially, Suncor's ability to operate and grow the business depends on the company's ability to derive value through, and learn from, a diversity of collaborations and inputs.

Once identified, stakeholders are involved by receiving timely information through news releases, mailings, advertising, websites, community newsletters, and public meetings; through meeting and working with Suncor executives to resolve issues and concerns; and by being provided with opportunities for shared decision-making through partnerships, alliances, and multi-stakeholder forums.

Suncor has found that these discussions often lead to better ideas, reduced risk, the resolution of outstanding issues, increased savings, and significant improvements in decision-making and the development of sounder solutions. Suncor credits many of its key successes to stakeholder engagement. Relationships have been built and trust has been improved between Suncor and aboriginal communities and other environmental and social interest groups and individuals. This has also enhanced Suncor's societal 'license to operate' and grow its business, particularly in the Athabasca Oil Sands region in northern Alberta.

A powerful example of this multi-stakeholder collaboration approach is the Cumulative Environmental Management Association (CEMA), a voluntary process co-founded by Suncor that began as a result of the rapid development of natural resources and the cumulative impacts on the Athabasca region. CEMA has emerged as an independent not-for-profit organization, operating with significant buy-in, transparency, and credibility from the community while addressing the important issues of cumulative effects.

In addition to successfully introducing stakeholder involvement in the decision-making process more broadly, CEMA has established a series of technical and research working groups that address the management of nitrogen oxides (NO_x) and sulfur dioxide (SO_2), trace metals and air contamination, sustainable ecosystems, water, and traditional ecological knowledge. These groups feed back into the overall objectives of CEMA.

By increasing the diversity of membership (within associations or issue-specific groups), environmental, social, and economic interests are addressed in a consultative manner. Based on past successes, Suncor has come to believe that a powerful way to operationalize sustainable development is by valuing diversity and bringing the interests of all to the table, in a fair, equitable, and cohesive way.

From dialogue to partnership

"On the ground, NGOs are capable of helping us to get in touch with the local inhabitants and play the role of local mediator. A large company can often engender a feeling of distrust, even if our intentions are good. The NGO can help to create a climate of trust between the local people and the company."

Gérard Mestrallet, chairman and CEO, Suez, France

The WBCSD and most of its members have demonstrated in their own work the business value of stakeholder dialogues. Corporate stakeholders range through employees, shareholders, communities, NGOs, consumers, partners, suppliers, governments, and society at large. Dialogue with these allows us to learn and to spread that learning throughout the company. This learning decreases uncertainty, misunderstanding, risk, and liability; increases public acceptance of corporate activity; and increases predictability of regulators.

Business has much experience with stakeholder dialogue, but still too little with the next step: practical partnerships composed of players in different sectors. Not only do such partnerships combine skills and provide access to constituencies that one partner may not have, but also they enhance the credibility of the results—results that might be less effective and believable if they come only from business, civil society, or government.

CASE STUDY 33
Global
Reporting
Initiative
page 163

Progress toward sustainable development requires many more—and more complex—partnerships. Smart companies are recognizing that the most effective way to leverage change in our interdependent world is through common endeavor with others and by learning from the experience. We can manage cooperatively what we cannot manage individually. This is the essence of a very old, very powerful idea called community. The whole is more than the sum of its parts.

A history of conflict

For most of modern history, business looked mainly to government for indications of whether it was acting within the expectations of society. Then from the beginning of the 1960s the groups now known variously as non-governmental organizations (NGOs), civil-society organizations (CSOs), private volunteer organizations (PVOs), citizens' groups, not-for-profit organizations, and non-profit organizations increased in strength, reach, and political savvy.

Up until the early 1990s it was largely a bipolar world: government and non-government. Business was caught in limbo between, certain that it was non-government but also fairly clear that it did not belong to the world of the NGOs. Slowly, as business began to occupy places at UN summits and other international gatherings, the world turned tri-polar: government, civil society, and business.

We find this a somewhat unsatisfactory situation, because we tend to view business as inseparable from 'civil society'—providing opportunities, innovation, and wealth for progress. Besides, the divides are not neat. Greenpeace, a transnational operation, has developed and marketed a refrigerator. Many companies are involved in extensive social projects (see Chapter 4). In addition, much important rule-making occurs these days without government involvement (see the discussion on forestry certification on pages 178-79). In a sense, then, this chapter is about how the three sectors can work together to get done things that are in the interest of all. But first we need to look back at progress toward the possibilities of these partnerships.

Environmental NGOs grew up to take on what they saw as the environmental crimes of companies and the environmental neglect of these crimes by governments. In 1962, Rachel Carson's book *Silent Spring* launched the contemporary environmental movement with an exposé on the harmful effects of pesticides on people and their natural environments. The chemical industry responded mainly by attacking environmentalists and denying the threat. The large amounts of the insecticide DDT (dichlorodiphenyltrichloroethane) found in birds' eggs and the sharp decline in the populations of some hawks proved to much of the public that the environmentalists were more trustworthy than the companies.

The environmental movement grew in the late 1960s and early 1970s, with the newly formed Friends of the Earth (FOE) harassing Rio Tinto until it abandoned its proposal for a huge copper mine in the Welsh National Park of Snowdonia. Other high-profile campaigns included FOE-UK's dump of 1,500 non-returnable bottles on the doorstep of the drinks manufacturer Schweppes; the first Greenpeace International anti-nuclear demonstrations off the Muroroa Atoll and its first anti-whaling missions, which set out from Canada with a crowd of 23,000 seeing the activists off. These events were a new form of protest, peaceful yet confrontational, and global in scale (Murphy and Bendell 1997). There were now multinational NGOs to confront multinational corporations.

For much of the 1960s to the 1980s, business response to such attacks was largely defensive. Then, the late 1980s saw the popularization of environmental issues and a heightened profile for them on the international political agenda. In many Western countries, membership of environmental organizations rose substantially, outstripping membership of political parties. With this new popularity, environmental groups became better funded and more powerful. While some of these groups began to shift toward looking for solutions and working with business to achieve those ends, others maintained strategies based on protest and confrontation.

'The emergence of NGOs acting as civil regulators of corporations through public campaigning and other forms of pressure is one of the notable features of the last decade', writes Simon Zadek in *The Civil Corporation: The New Economy of Corporate Citizenship*. 'More than any other body of institutions, NGOs have driven the process of popular education and political and economic mobilization around social and environmental issues' (Zadek 2001). Yet, even at the time of the highly publicized protests of the mid-to-late 1990s, environmental groups and companies had begun talking to one another. Some leading NGOs were adopting an increasingly pragmatic view of the role of environmental campaigns in bringing about societal change. During the late 1980s and early 1990s a flood of environmentalists left campaigning groups to work as consultants, seeing potential in moving beyond protest toward practical action. The recent case of Lord Peter Melchett's move from Greenpeace to the leading public relations firm Burson-Marsteller illustrates that the trend is continuing. Dr Claude Martin, secretary general of the World Wide Fund for Nature International (WWF), heralded this attitude when he said, 'The time for protest alone is over—if, indeed, it ever existed. Conservationists today must develop practical solutions to environmental issues.'

Not every NGO has been willing to work with business. Dr Daniel Vasella, CEO of the Swiss pharmaceutical company Novartis, divides organizations into those that want a dialogue with his drug company—such as the famine-relief group Oxfam—and those, such as many animal-rights activists, that do not: 'Don't try to convert the inconvertible,' he counsels; 'Talk to the "decent people" who respect different points of view' (in Elliott 2001).

From the other side, Charles Secrett, executive director of FOE-UK, concedes that some activists believe just talking to corporations is a sell-out and that only violent revolution will change the world (in Elliott 2001). But the violent approaches of the more radical NGOs can also play into the hands of those groups willing to work with business. 'The more stridency and hostility on the part of activist groups, particularly the anti-globalization forces, the more interest we see on behalf of business to work with the groups which take a more moderate approach', says Glenn Prickett, executive director of the Center for Environmental Leadership in Business at Conservation International (CI), a US-based NGO.

A transition to dialogue

Dialogue is about communication among stakeholders in ways that take serious account of expressed views. It does not mean that a company need involve other stakeholders in every decision or that every stakeholder request will be met. It means that input is acknowledged and thoughtfully considered; it is about giving other stakeholders a voice, listening to what they have to say and being prepared to act or react accordingly (WBCSD 2001i).

The purpose of stakeholder dialogue is to enable serious discussion that ultimately leads to real change. Stakeholder dialogue is important in any movement toward sustainable development because it enables people to recognize differences and common views; it acknowledges and values different needs and interests and therefore the need for trade-offs. It uncovers and encourages synergy, new ideas, and collaborative partnerships and it enables joint ownership of difficult decisions. Participation in such dialogue is illustrated in Figure 10.

The move toward dialogue between former sparring partners began with some caution and skepticism. Yet business and NGOs—and governments too, which soon joined discussions to enable a tri-sector approach—each found significant reasons for wanting to talk rather than battle.

Many companies have realized that there is nothing to be gained and much to be lost by ignoring NGOs. Many have experienced first-hand just how sophisticated NGOs have become in their campaigning activities and just how fast they can summon worldwide support for a campaign through use of the Internet. Lord Browne (2001), group chief executive of BP, observes:

> We have to accept that attention and even the fire because if we're going to succeed we have to be capable of listening, of understanding what is happening in society and capable of arguing our case with anyone at any time. And we have to welcome the engagement because so much of what we want to achieve cannot be delivered by any organization working on its own. If globalization marks the end of sovereignty for national governments, it should equally end any sense of splendid isolation which exists in the corporate world.

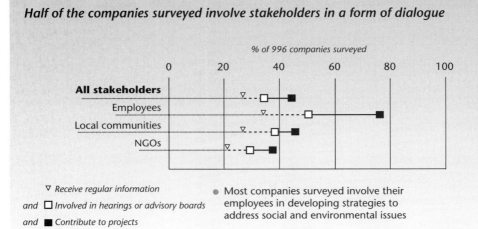

Half of the companies surveyed involve stakeholders in a form of dialogue

% of 996 companies surveyed

▽ *Receive regular information*
and ☐ *Involved in hearings or advisory boards*
and ■ *Contribute to projects*

Source: **sam**

● Most companies surveyed involve their employees in developing strategies to address social and environmental issues

● Half of them also involve local communities but fewer involve NGOs

Figure 10 **PARTICIPATION IN STAKEHOLDER DIALOGUE**

The move toward dialogue, and later toward partnership, has been driven largely by a desire to manage corporate reputation—a critical asset. It is built around intangibles such as trust, reliability, quality, consistency, credibility, relationships, and transparency. It is also built around tangibles, such as investment in people, diversity, and the environment (SustainAbility *et al.* 2001). All of these can be affected either positively or negatively by the ways in which a company engages in dialogue or partnership. Yet few companies actively engage in stakeholder dialogue (see Figure 11).

However, that is the liability-reduction side of the equation. The opportunity side involves listening to and better understanding the needs of society as ways to improve business offerings and create competitive advantage (Grosser and Walker 2000). Companies that can successfully compete for the attention and positive engagement of those shaping the agenda politically have a strategic advantage. They have new forms of market intelligence. They can test out new concepts or business models for potential problems before investing to the point where they are virtually locked in. In addition, they can build strategic alliances with some NGOs and other partners to begin shaping political agendas and markets in such a way that these agendas and markets support and reward companies investing in more sustainable technologies, products, and services (Elkington 2001).

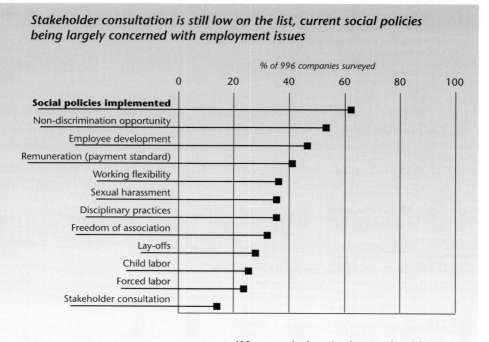

Stakeholder consultation is still low on the list, current social policies being largely concerned with employment issues

Figure 11 **IMPLEMENTATION AND CONTENT OF SOCIAL POLICIES**

It is natural that companies and NGOs be motivated to engage with each other as they are both accustomed to working 'on the ground' and 'in the field', says Gérard Mestrallet, chairman and CEO of the French energy, water, waste services, and communications company Suez. This affords many opportunities for contact and for achieving a concrete dialogue and partnership:

> On the ground, NGOs are capable of helping us to get in touch with the local inhabitants and play the role of local mediator. A large company can often engender a feeling of distrust, even if our intentions are good. The NGO can help to create a climate of trust between the local people and the company.

Successful dialogues and partnerships help to build trust with important stakeholders—one of the key benefits of such collaborations. According to Peter Brabeck-Letmathe (1999), CEO of Nestlé:

> The rapid pace of social, political and technological change has clearly increased the consumer's longing for reliability and authenticity . . . What this means for corporations is quite clear: presence and visibility are vital in order to build up that capital of trust. Trust is created slowly. It stems from consistency between word and deed, from carefully argued positions and from the willingness to adapt and learn. Trust also comes from the courage to say things clearly and straightforwardly, even if that risks provoking negative reactions in some quarters. And trust comes from admissions of fallibility, to openly say it if things have gone wrong.

Many NGOs recognize that they cannot ignore the market if they want to find and deliver solutions to complex environmental and social problems. These organizations may believe that the private sector and the market cause many of those very same problems, but a number of them realize that for that very reason these institutions are part of the solution. According to Jane Nelson of the International Business Leaders Forum and author of several books on partnership:

> NGOs are more operations-oriented and solutions-oriented and much more nuanced in the way they work with business today. They are engaging around specific problems with a solutions orientation, while still maintaining an advocacy position on other issues.

Nelson believes there is greater respect shown for the value that business brings to the table: 'Greenpeace and Oxfam, for example, were totally aggressive at one point and then recognized that you can't completely ignore the market. The market is powerful; business is powerful, and you need to engage to find solutions.'

Some campaigners recognize that facts rather than dogma influence governments and that they are more likely to achieve victories with a pragmatic approach. Many have also become disillusioned with government as a provider of solutions. And many want to move beyond 'campaigning against' to advocating solutions. Even groups such as Greenpeace, still best known perhaps for boycotts and direct action, will work with companies to achieve their aims. In 1992 they helped to launch a hydrocarbon called Greenfreeze that could replace an ozone-damaging coolant in refrigerators. Those efforts resulted in 70,000 orders.

Conservation International (CI) has long recognized that business is part of the equation in efforts to conserve biodiversity, says Glenn Prickett, executive director of CI's Center for Environmental Leadership in Business:

> We work with developing countries where economic development is a key priority. This means we must work with governments and the private sector to find ways to preserve biodiversity without sacrificing economic growth. That led us to working with business almost from the beginning.

He goes on to say:

> I think many NGOs are recognizing that business plays a more influential role than it did in the past as the result of economic liberalization. Business can often have more of an impact on a community and ecosystem than government can, and put more investment into solutions. It's a pragmatic recognition on the part of NGOs that you have to deal with the people who have the power, the influence, and the resources. Business also has recognized that what it does in faraway places can immediately be scrutinized by public pressure groups. So smart businesses realize they have to focus on projects that deliver value to the community and environment as well as the company.

NGOs are also finding that in many cases it is more efficient to work with businesses than with governments, because companies can act faster; they do not have to go through the lengthy process of creating laws and legislation.

Governments, too, have a vested interest in collaboration with companies. Governments are spending less time on command-and-control regulations and more on forms of cooperation with industry to produce workable, incentive-based solutions. They are finding that historically intractable social and environmental problems, such as poverty, disease, and threats to biodiversity, can only be solved through partnership.

In the words of Simon Upton, chairman of the OECD Roundtable on Sustainable Development, 'The only way forward in resolving complex sustainability problems is to partner across national and international boundaries, engaging both the public and the private sector' (in Holliday and Pepper 2001: 21).

A move to partnership

In recent years it has become apparent that dialogue, although helpful and important, is not enough to effect real change. Companies, NGOs, and governments need to move beyond dialogue to partnership (Bendell 2000).

Partnerships actively encourage innovative approaches to social and environmental problems as well as business challenges and opportunities. It opens people's minds to the possibility of breaking down historical barriers and forming working relationships between key organizations spread across different parts of the local, national, and international community. Dialogue is often the first step, but partnerships are able to mobilize a wider range of resources, enhance innovation, and increase access to different types of skill. Partnerships can therefore succeed where companies, NGOs, or governments working alone have previously failed.

According to Suez CEO Gérard Mestrallet, the partnership approach worked well for his company in Argentina precisely because various sectors came together to provide specific competences and to play unique roles:

> Because the NGOs are independent, in general local community residents don't suspect them of having ulterior motives. That makes it easier to set up a dialogue—and later, a partnership. We each bring different resources to the table. The private sector offers managerial, technical, and, frequently, financial competence, while the government maintains a balance between the different partners by setting up a regulatory framework. Public–private partnerships can only work if each part plays a specific role based on its own competences.

Partnerships are contributing in areas such as conservation, health provision in developing countries, and supplies of safe water to some of the world's poorest neighborhoods.

CASE STUDY 34
Suez and
CH2M HILL
page 164

BC Hydro, one of the largest electric utilities in Canada, developed Water Use Planning (WUP) as a joint initiative between the company and the provincial and federal governments in consultation with the First Nations indigenous group and the public. In an effort to find a sustainable balance between competing uses of water, the WUP process offered a collaborative approach to incorporating traditional ecological knowledge into Western decision-making and to enhanced cross-cultural learning (WBCSD 2001a).

In 2000 the Ford Motor Company and CI established the Center for Environmental Leadership in Business, a $25 million, five-year investment by Ford. The Center works with business worldwide in creating solutions to critical environmental problems, particularly in three areas: biodiversity, water, and climate change. A Ford manufacturing plant in Sonora, Mexico, is being used to develop replicable business practices and policies that conserve water resources, enhance water quality, and protect watersheds in critical ecosystems.

The world's biggest mining companies, members of WBCSD's Global Mining Initiative, have formed a partnership with the International Institute for Environment and Development (IIED) in London to explore how the industry could contribute to the global transition to sustainable development.

The RMC Group, one of the world's largest producers of heavy building materials, donated 370 ha of wetlands at the edge of the Everglades and Biscayne Bay to Florida International University (FIU). As a result, FIU will be offering one of the first study programs in the world to focus specifically on wetland restoration. Further donations are planned up to 2022, when a total of 702 ha will be handed over to the university.

A number of pharmaceutical companies, including Aventis, Novartis, GlaxoSmithKline, and Pfizer are partnering with the World Health Organization (WHO) to help reduce diseases such as malaria, tuberculosis, HIV and AIDS, and African sleeping sickness. Aventis, for instance, has committed $25 million over five years to assist in combating sleeping sickness through drug donations, disease management and control, and R&D. Novartis is supplying at cost to developing countries a new treatment for drug-resistant malaria. Credit Suisse is also collaborating with WHO, making the first corporate financial pledge to a new Global Fund to Fight AIDS, Tuberculosis, and

CASE STUDY 35
Aventis
page 166

Malaria proposed by the United Nations and G8 countries (United Kingdom, France, Germany, Japan, USA, Italy, Canada, and Russia). As of January 2002 the fund had pledges of $1.7 billion.

CASE STUDY 36
Global
Compact
page 167
In 1999, UN secretary general Kofi Annan announced the creation of the Global Compact, in which business is encouraged to embrace a set of nine principles, based on UN conventions and declarations, in their own operations, and to support complementary public policy initiatives. At this writing, over 400 corporations have joined the Compact, including BP, DuPont, Ford, Rio Tinto, Shell, and Unilever, as well as the emerging corporate leaders of the South, such as the Brazilian communications corporation Globo, the Indian conglomerate Tata, and the South African utility company Eskom. Also joining in this unprecedented partnership were traditional and newfound partners of business such as the International Confederation of Free Trade Unions, Human Rights Watch, and the WWF.

Overcoming challenges

Business partnerships with governments and NGOs are an important tool to help ensure that corporate goals converge with social obligations in the developing world, but they do require overcoming significant challenges. As Jane Nelson and Simon Zadek point out in their book, *Partnership Alchemy: New Social Partnerships in Europe* (2000), key challenges include:

- *Bridging diversity.* Ignorance and/or mistrust between different constituencies must be overcome. Beyond this are the many practical and cultural obstacles to overcome in building cooperation among groups with different characteristics, structures, methodologies, time-scales, expectations, and languages.

- *Attracting and sustaining participant involvement.* There are many problems with engaging and sustaining the interests of different participants in a long-term and meaningful way. Managing expectations is critical. Many participants enter partnerships with unrealistic expectations of the time-frame and time-related costs, for example. Most partnerships require more management time (for building trust, overcoming culture clashes, undertaking consultations, etc.) and take longer to show results than expected at the outset.

- *Addressing power.* Few partnerships gather groups of equal power. For example, community groups sometimes do not get sufficient recognition by other partners and are excluded from meaningful participation in the partnership process. Often greater authority is given to the participant(s) who bring the most financial resources to the partnership, despite the fact that money is only one type of resource. Mutuality of interests and activities is hard to attain where participating organizations have different levels of economic and/or political strengths.

● *Assessing value-added.* Partnership-building can be extremely costly in terms of both time and money. It is therefore essential that these additional costs are demonstrably worthwhile. It is not, however, always easy to assess the value added of a partnership over and above what would have been achieved without the participants pooling their resources and competences.

To put all of this in business terms, companies need to enter a partnership with a non-business entity in the same spirit they would bring to a business partnership with a customer or supplier. For the partnership to be successful each partner needs to be clear on his or her needs and to have those needs met.

Some NGOs, usually those that have not worked with business, feel that companies entering partnerships are in it merely for the good publicity it may bring. In some cases they have accused companies of working with them while undermining environmental or social regulations. They also feel they risk alienating grass-roots supporters if they are seen to be too close to business (Houlder 2001a). We should point out here that, when companies do enter such engagement solely for publicity, the publicity they get is usually bad, and such partnerships tend to break down with much mutual mud-slinging. But even the most sincere engagement will not satisfy everyone or deal with every situation. Mutual advantage is not always attainable. There will be occasions when there are unbridgeable differences of opinions that are not susceptible to compromise.

Ways and means

The WBCSD's considerable work with multi-stakeholder engagement has led us to conclude that partnerships for progress are built on the following foundations: common goals, empathy, open feedback, flexibility, ability to compromise, and sharing rewards (Holliday and Pepper 2001). It is essential to establish each partner's individual goals and aims and to design the partnership to ensure that these goals are met. This includes understanding the resources, skills, and capacities required and concluding an agreement on the legal and organizational structure. If partners' activities are not in line with these defined aims from the beginning, it will be difficult to guarantee the partners' continued involvement in the project. For business, partnerships are more attractive when the activities help the business meet its contractual obligations, spotlight new market opportunities, or help manage risks and expectations related to a specific site or contract. Thus it is important to co-evolve the process and agree shared priorities.

CASE STUDY 37
Severn Trent
page 169

Empathy and understanding for the other partner is also a vital ingredient. In some cases, the values of each partner mesh immediately and it becomes much easier to see a situation from another perspective. However, the most dynamic results often come when partners that seemed unlikely at first find an ability to listen to and understand each other. This requires the early recognition of dissenting opinion and the readiness to work together.

Openness in presenting feedback and transparency in all activities goes a long way toward ensuring the success of a partnership. In most partnerships, there is rarely a defined mechanism for ensuring accountability. This dilemma can be resolved through critical monitoring by a range of external observers: for example, by business associations, NGO networks, activist groups, and local authorities as well as governmental and UN agencies. Other experts have suggested that a code of conduct could provide a useful framework for NGO–business partnerships.

Benefits

All participants can gain considerably by observing these critical success factors. The tangible business benefits include: better management of risk and stakeholders' expectations, development of new markets and innovative products and services, legal and contract compliance, and business process and productivity. Partnerships are also a useful learning and informational tool for companies and their boards, enabling them to benefit from outside views and enabling stakeholders to improve their knowledge of and trust in the company.

CASE STUDY 38
Nestlé
page 170

A number of studies have shown that a relationship with an NGO can bolster a company's credibility. Outside the USA, NGOs are deemed far more trustworthy than business on environmental, health, and social issues, according to a study in 2001 by Edelman PR Worldwide (in Houlder 2001a).

CASE STUDY 39
Rio Tinto
page 171

NGOs can benefit from and be stretched by partnerships with business. The need for additional technology and resources, a greater cross-fertilization of ideas to address complex problems, more and stronger advocacy for their mission, and practical help in delivering services prompt these groups to reach out to other players.

Yolanda Kakabadse, president of IUCN–the World Conservation Union, sees multiple benefits. Local communities benefit by being presented with economic alternatives and new processes to manage their natural resources. NGOs working as a link between local communities and the business sector benefit from the capacity to multiply their projects and processes. The business sector makes good business out of a new pattern of working, and even the financial and banking sectors are benefiting.

IUCN's Business and Biodiversity Initiative strives to make capitalism work for conservation by promoting: (1) biodiversity plans for business, (2) business plans and financial strategies for protected areas and sustainable landscapes, and (3) investments in biodiversity benefiting businesses. A number of active partnerships with the corporate sector have been established under the initiative.

For instance, under the initiative IUCN is partnering with the International Finance Corporation, the Global Environment Facility, and others to develop Kijani, a new venture to promote biodiversity benefiting businesses in Africa, generate ongoing financial returns and conserve the integrity of nature. Kijani encourages the sustainable and equitable use of natural resources, strengthens rural economies, creates access to new markets and job opportunities, and alleviates poverty (see www.kijani.com). According to Kakabadse:

> Globally, the biodiversity sector is overworked and under-funded. If we—IUCN and its members—are to succeed in our mission, we must become more business-like. We need to harness capitalist tools for the purpose of biodiversity conservation and sustainable development.

Throughout 2001, the WBCSD Sustainable Mobility Project conducted eight stakeholder dialogues in eight cities on four continents. All the member companies co-hosted one or more of the dialogues. The eight dialogues brought together 500 people from 39 countries, with roughly one-third of the participants each coming from business, politics, and academia or civil society.

The project is aiming to develop a vision of Sustainable Mobility 2030 and provide possible pathways to fulfill it. Member companies include BP, DaimlerChrysler, Ford, General Motors, Honda, Michelin, Nissan, Norsk Hydro, Renault, Shell, Toyota, and Volkswagen.

The members realized early on that they would need to consult different sectors of society from all parts of the world. For a vision to be viable and shared, people's needs would have to be both the point of departure and the destination.

All eight dialogues shared a pattern. The first step was to identify the local or regional issues of concern to the participants; the second step was to capture what sustainable mobility might encompass; the third step was to specify which sectors would need to do what in order to achieve it.

The dialogue provided input to the *Mobility 2001 Report* (CRA *et al.* 2001), a comprehensive study of patterns of mobility at the end of the 20th century. It was produced by a team of researchers from MIT and Charles River Associates, commissioned by the WBCSD and identified a series of challenges that, if dealt with, would go a long way in attaining sustainable mobility.

The challenges have been divided into three groups, classified by how close to the core business of the member companies they seem to be and hence to what extent the member companies can themselves make a substantial difference:

- Challenges that our stakeholders expect companies to take a major role in because of their special expertise and/or the impacts of our products:
  - Adapt the personal-use motor vehicle to the future needs and requirements of the developed and developing worlds (e.g. in terms of capacity, performance, emissions, fuel use, safety, materials requirements, waste, ownership structure)
  - Drastically reduce carbon emissions from the transportation sector, which may require phasing carbon out, having a transition period to move from petroleum-based fuels to a portfolio of other energy sources
- Challenges to sustainable mobility that cannot be credibly addressed without the significant involvement of other sectors:
  - Provide accessibility for those not having access to personal motor vehicles, including those in the developed and the developing worlds; provide a reasonable alternative for those who do have access to personal motor vehicles (i.e. 'reinvent' the relationship between public transport and the private car)
  - Resolve the competition for resources and access to infrastructure between personal and freight transportation in the urbanized areas of the developed and developing worlds
  - Anticipate congestion in inter-city transportation and develop a portfolio of mobility options for people and freight
- Overarching challenges (i.e. challenges that transcend any one mode or region):
  - Reinvent the process of planning, developing, financing, and managing mobility infrastructure.
  - Improve institutional capability to identify, build consensus about how to solve, and implement approaches that promote sustainable mobility
  - Ensure that our transportation systems continue to play their essential role in economic development and, through the mobility they provide, serve essential human need and enhance the quality of life

Box 7 **MOBILITY: DIALOGUE FOR CHANGE**

In 1997, the WBCSD partnered with IUCN to produce *Business and Biodiversity: A Guide for the Private Sector*, which outlined opportunities and responsibilities of companies in this area. In cooperation with IUCN and the Earthwatch Europe, an updated report was released in the third quarter of 2002. *Business and Biodiversity: The Handbook for Corporate Action* provides information on the business case for biodiversity, as well as current biodiversity issues for business, corporate biodiversity strategies, and key biodiversity resources.

The power of joint effort

Powerful synergies can emerge from partnerships that fuse the complementary capabilities of business, NGOs, and, in some cases, governments, parts of governments, and governmental institutions.

Partnerships among the sectors require new approaches to governance in light of the shifting balance between the state, business, and civil society. Governance used to be principally about what governments do. Today, the concept is increasingly about balancing the roles, responsibilities, accountabilities, and capabilities of different levels of governments and different actors or sectors in society. Governance can be defined as the framework through which political, economic, social, and administrative authority is exercised at local, national, and international levels. In today's world, this framework consists of a wide variety of mechanisms, processes, institutions, and relationships (including partnerships) through which individual citizens, groups, and organizations can express their interests, exercise their rights and responsibilities, and mediate their differences (PWBLF 2002).

A successful approach to partnership governance requires transparency, representation, and accountability both within the partnership and externally. This requires determining the rights and responsibilities of each partner, the most appropriate means of decision-making, how the intended beneficiaries will participate in the decision-making, and who is accountable for the partnerships' behavior (e.g. regarding its use of resources). Ultimately, who is responsible for the partnership's success or failure (Nelson and Zadek 2000)?

The partnership trend will continue to gather momentum, with an increasing number of such alliances demonstrating their value and moving beyond the experimental stage. The first wave of partnerships is helping to spread good practice and share what works more widely with other potential partners. This inspires innovation and helps to make the process of partnership-building part of policy frameworks. Working together in this way is the very essence of community.

CASE STUDY 40
TEPCO
page 172

CASE STUDY 33
The Global Reporting Initiative

Many organizations worldwide, primarily corporations, are producing voluntary environmental and social reports, and a small but growing number are moving toward sustainability reports. However, in contrast to financial reporting, there has been an absence until recently of a generally accepted reporting framework. As environmental and sustainability reporting has increased, so too has the diversity of reporting methods.

The Global Reporting Initiative (GRI) was established in 1997 to tackle this issue. Convened by the Coalition for Environmentally Responsible Economies (CERES), in partnership with UNEP, the GRI is seeking common ground on which to build a consistent reporting framework. Specifically, the mission of the GRI is to develop and disseminate globally applicable reporting guidelines for voluntary use by organizations reporting on the economic, environmental, and social dimensions of their activities, products, and services.

Sustainability reporting enables NGOs, investors, corporations, governments, labor, and other stakeholders to gauge the progress of organizations in the implementation of voluntary initiatives and other practices supportive of sustainable development. A common reporting framework, such as GRI's *Sustainability Reporting Guidelines*, provides the basis for benchmarking and a process for identifying opportunities for internal management improvements. Achieving this commonality was not a straightforward procedure. The key was an open and broadly inclusive process that brought together a large and diverse group of stakeholders interested in transparency. As a result, an array of different interests, understandings, and objectives were brought to the table. 'The process of building the *Sustainability Reporting Guidelines* is equally as important as the product', says GRI director Allen White:

> If any interested stakeholder group were left out of the *Guidelines* development process, the *Guidelines'* credibility, usability, and quality would be seriously threatened. We work very hard to bring all stakeholders to the table, and to help form unique and dynamic working relationships between parties that may not have had previous exposure to one another.

A broad array of stakeholders interested in sustainability reporting came together to fashion the March 1999 exposure draft *Sustainability Reporting Guidelines*. A total of 21 companies, representing diverse countries and multiple industry sectors, tested and provided comments on the draft *Guidelines*. At the same time, hundreds of additional comments were provided by external stakeholders, representing perspectives from human rights, accountancy, government, business and labor organizations, and from multilateral, international, environmental, and religious organizations.

As a result of the breadth and depth of this consultative process, the June 2000 *Guidelines* represented a major step toward a generally accepted, global framework for sustainability reporting at the organizational level. A second revision process was launched in 2001, involving the work of 120 experts organized into 10 working groups focused on revising and improving the sustainability performance indicators. Input from 31 companies and a network of more than 2,500 stakeholders from 60 countries aided the working groups. A revision team spent the first half of 2001 consolidating all of this input and strengthening the other sections of the *Guidelines*. The result of this global effort is contained in the 2001 version of the *Guidelines*, the most comprehensive and credible set of sustainability performance disclosure standards ever produced.

Other essential aspects of the GRI process include accessibility and transparency. In terms of accessibility, GRI had to go much further than merely inviting stakeholders to meetings. Sponsorships were provided for participants from developing nations to attend events. Dozens of regional and national briefings have been held. Strong partnerships have been formed across the globe. A transparent structure has been maintained from the start. All governance and working documents have been made openly available for review on the GRI website (www.globalreporting.org) and are available on request via mail. The *Guidelines* have been translated into eight languages so far, and GRI produces a regular news update to keep its 2,500-plus network informed.

In 2002, GRI became an independent, permanent institution. A unique feature of the new organization is the Stakeholder Council. It is the formal stakeholder policy forum within the GRI structure, where stakeholders are equal partners in charting the future of the organization. It is an active multi-stakeholder body for debating and deliberating key strategic and policy issues facing GRI. The Stakeholder Council membership is balanced across constituencies and geographic regions.

GRI will continue to strive to be a transparent and inclusive organization that is truly global, multi-stakeholder, and independent and which operates with the highest level of integrity.

CASE STUDY 34

Suez and CH2M HILL
partnerships for the provision of water

Fresh water is becoming scarce in many regions; globally, 1.2 billion people lack access to clean drinking water. Governments are increasingly unable to provide good-quality, reasonably priced water to their citizens. The private sector is able to offer some solutions, and this presents business with new opportunities in developing markets. However, such opportunities are best realized through collaborative efforts drawing on local experience and capabilities, coupled with local government and local community support and cooperation. The cases presented here describe two different approaches to water partnerships.

Suez

Ondeo Services, the French water services company of Suez serving 115 million people, has established a program based on public–private partnerships called 'Water for All'. Forty-six and a half million people from Buenos Aires, Casablanca, Córdoba, Djakarta, La Paz–El Alto, Manaus, Manila, Santa Fe, Santiago, and the Eastern Cape and northern provinces of South Africa have gained access to water through this program—8.7 million of them poor.

The partnerships involved local communities, neighborhood organizations, NGOs, and local governments, and they take advantage of each institution's different capacities. The company provides the design and supervision during the implementation phase of the project. Local institutions and municipalities provide logistical support and construction materials. Communities provide work and participation; in some cases, NGOs provide social training to the company and coordinate and organize projects. Environments of cooperation and coordination were fostered to ensure the long-term sustainability of the systems, promoting an attitude of ownership in the communities and making them guardians of the system for generations to come.

In Buenos Aires, the consortium in which Ondeo Services was involved, Aguas Argentinas, set up a program that enabled 800,000 people to be connected to the drinking-water system and 120,000 people to the sanitation system. In La Paz–El Alto, Bolivia, Aguas de Illimani managed to raise the global coverage for a drinking-water supply to 96% of the population (compared with 68% three years before) and for waste-water services to 63% (compared with 50% three years before). In South Africa, the partnership known as Build, Operate, Train and Transfer (BOTT), launched in 1997, is based on the principle that sustainable management can be achieved only by involving national and local authorities at every stage in the development and management of services. It is the first known example of large-scale involvement of the private sector in the water supply and sanitation of rural areas in developing countries. The program, implemented by Water and Sanitation of South Africa, reaches 2.2 million people.

CH2M HILL

In the Ukraine, the company CH2M HILL found that citizen involvement was central to meeting the challenge of providing fresh water at an affordable price. As the old infrastructure in the region deteriorated, a new approach was required to make the transition from a centralized model to a customer-focused process in which consumers pay for services that were formerly heavily subsidized by the government. It was an approach that involved members of the local community in planning and funding new water systems. This was a radical concept in a newly independent nation facing complex economic and political changes.

The project was led by CH2M HILL, which for more than 50 years used technology to deliver clean water to people while protecting natural systems throughout the world. In addition to the basic equipment to analyze systems, CH2M HILL provided Ukrainian water utilities with on-site training on how to involve the public in planning and decision-making. The program delivers information through technical workshops on topics including water distribution, energy use, and public participation. At the heart of the project in each participating city are the activities of a joint advisory work group that promotes public involvement. The work groups consist of people with a wide range of backgrounds and interests.

Virtually the entire project is carried out by local Ukrainians. As a result, even with the end of CH2M HILL's involvement, the concept of engaging people in decisions on infrastructure planning and funding will remain in place to ensure that the achievements are sustainable. In the final analysis, the project does much more than improve the delivery of water to meet basic needs; it helps to create a human infrastructure that empowers people by involving them in their own future.

CASE STUDY 35
Aventis *partnerships for health*

Life sciences company Aventis focuses on the discovery and development of products such as prescription drugs, vaccines, and therapeutic proteins through its business units Aventis Pharma and Aventis Pasteur.

Aventis's products are increasingly becoming essential tools in dealing with the many emerging and re-emerging epidemics that threaten people the world over. However, in places where many of these epidemics are prevalent, the fight requires more than products. A lack of clinics and skilled personnel, insufficient supply chains, missing health insurance systems, and in some cases political unrest and violence make provision of health products complex.

However, there are institutions such as the World Health Organization (WHO) that have the capabilities and regional knowledge required, and it makes sense for companies such as Aventis to share competences with such bodies. Thus Aventis teamed up with WHO and other groups to ensure that the products needed to tackle such epidemics reach those in need. Partnerships include the Global Alliance for Vaccines and Immunization (GAVI), the Global Polio Eradication Initiative, and the recently formed partnership to tackle African sleeping sickness.

Concerned about the disparity between the quantity and types of vaccines supplied in developed countries and those made available in developing countries, Aventis has become a partner in GAVI, which includes others in the vaccine industry, WHO, the United Nations Children's Fund (UNICEF), the World Bank, governments of developing countries, and many OECD governments. The alliance was founded on the belief that protecting the health of children through immunization is a fundamental cornerstone for economic development and global security. Its goals are to improve access to sustainable immunization services, expand the use of safe, cost-effective vaccines where needed, accelerate the development and introduction of new vaccines and technologies, accelerate R&D efforts for vaccines needed primarily in developing countries, and make immunization coverage a centerpiece of international development efforts.

Jacques Berger, Aventis Pasteur's senior vice president for corporate public policy, states:

> For Aventis Pasteur, industry participation in the alliance is necessary to help ensure supply for these markets—and to make vaccines available to the 40 million to 70 million children born each year who would otherwise not have access to this preventive intervention.

He points out that the vaccine industry is the only one that supplies large volumes of products to the poorest segment of the population at highly discounted prices. 'This private–public alliance is a model for other basic-needs markets', he adds.

Aventis is also a partner in the Global Polio Eradication Initiative, launched in 1988 by WHO, Rotary International, the US Center for Disease Control, and UNICEF, with the goal of eliminating polio worldwide. Aventis Pasteur has launched a website (www.polio-vaccine.com) devoted to polio eradication. The trilingual site (in French, English, and Spanish) provides current information about the disease. Between 2000 and 2002 Aventis Pasteur will be donating 50 million doses of oral polio vaccine to Angola, Liberia, Sierra Leone, Somalia, and Southern Sudan. Since 1997 Aventis Pasteur has donated nearly 90 million doses of oral polio vaccine to African countries.

'As the largest historical producer of polio vaccines, we have an obligation to contribute to the final assault on polio,' says Jean-Jacques Bertrand, chairman and CEO of Aventis Pasteur; 'Today, when now more than ever polio eradication is within our reach, we believe that we must sustain this momentum and intensify our fight.'

There is a dramatic resurgence of African trypanosomiasis, more commonly known as sleeping sickness, in sub-Saharan Africa. The disease is spreading in some of the poorest Central African communities, threatening more than 60 million people in 36 countries. It has become one of the greatest causes of mortality, ahead of AIDS-related deaths in some provinces.

Aventis and WHO, working with medical humanitarian organization Médecins sans Frontières (MSF), designed a large-scale program to combat the disease. 'This partnership is an example of a public–private partnership wanting to find viable solutions for life-threatening diseases', says Richard J. Markham, CEO of Aventis Pharma.

Aventis Pharma has committed $25 million to support WHO's activities in the field of African trypanosomiasis over a five-year period. This is not a simple donation of products but rather a structured partnership that involves three related efforts to tackle the epidemic. Key pharmaceuticals will be provided to WHO, to be distributed by MSF. Aventis will also finance the acceleration of disease surveillance, control activities, and support new research. For any undertaking to be successful, it is necessary to address the integrated considerations of drug manufacturing and provision, as well as the ongoing treatment and needs of patients.

Aventis could not have tackled such programs alone. The company lacks the experience of working with patients in such affected areas; neither does it possess the capabilities to conduct the necessary surveillance and control of activities. The administration of drugs in some cases is also very demanding on the provider. For example, those affected by sleeping sickness require treatment four times a day, at six-hour intervals, for one month. WHO, however, possesses the capacity and experience and knows the affected regions, but it does not possess the capacity to manufacture the treatment drugs. Clearly, then, partnerships that bring together these necessary skills, experience, and capacities are required.

CASE STUDY 36
The Global Compact

In January 1999 UN secretary general Kofi Annan challenged world business leaders to take part in the collaborative venture that was to become known as the Global Compact. Then, in July 2000, senior executives from some 50 major corporations and the leaders of labor, human rights, environmental, and development organizations were brought together to launch the operational phase of the Compact. The objectives of this collaboration include mutual understanding and a growth in the ideas and practices of corporate citizenship.

The Compact encompasses nine principles, drawn from the Universal Declaration of Human Rights, the International Labor Organization's Fundamental Principles on Rights at Work, and the Rio Principles on Environment and Development. These principles cover topics on human rights, labor, and environment:

- *Principle 1:* support and respect the protection of international human rights within their sphere of influence

- *Principle 2:* make sure their own corporation is not complicit in human rights abuses

- *Principle 3:* freedom of association and the effective recognition the right to collective bargaining

- *Principle 4:* the elimination of all forms of forced and compulsory labor

- *Principle 5:* the effective abolition of child labor

- *Principle 6:* the elimination of discrimination in respect of employment and occupation

- *Principle 7:* support a precautionary approach to environmental challenges

- *Principle 8:* undertake initiatives to promote greater environmental responsibility

- *Principle 9:* encourage the development and diffusion of environmentally friendly technologies

Those companies that support the Global Compact commit themselves to act on these principles in their own corporate domains, to integrate these principles into corporate strategy, and to demonstrate this integration in practice.

This is not an effort to draw up a code of conduct but rather to develop common understandings. To enable companies to integrate the principles into their actions, a platform for institutional learning is essential. In bringing a diversity of actors to the table and designing a space for learning by sharing the Compact promotes good practice based on common understanding.

The Compact brings together these actors to work in four core areas:

- *Dialogue:* to craft cooperative solutions to the challenges of globalization

- *Learning:* to stimulate a culture of change and to identify and disseminate good business practices

- *Outreach:* to make the Compact truly global

- *Partnership projects:* to advance UN goals, especially developmental goals

The dialogue process got under way with the Compact's first policy dialogue examining the role and responsibilities of business operating in zones of violent conflict. This was explored in September 2001, engaging some 60 participants representing the private sector and governmental and non-governmental organizations.

Participating companies are expected to post on the Global Compact website (www.unglobalcompact.org) at least once a year concrete steps they have taken to act on any one of the nine principles in their own corporate domains as well as the lessons learned from doing so. As part of the pilot phase of the learning forum, a review of case studies was conducted in October 2001 to analyze and share key themes that emerged from the comparative review of the submissions.

The Compact invites participants, on an optional basis, to work with the UN and its agencies in partnership projects. The objective of these partnerships is to advance broad UN goals such as poverty eradication. Companies can work with any UN agency or in some cases with the Compact's labor and civil-society partners.

To advance business understanding and action, the Compact will remain an innovative, open-ended, and network-based experiment. It is this open process of engagement and system of partnering that will enable a critical mass from industry to have maximum impact.

CASE STUDY 37

Severn Trent *water for St Petersburg*

Recent water studies in Russia have found urban problems such as poorly maintained infrastructure, frequent service interruptions, high consumption compared with that in other countries, deteriorating treated water and waste-water quality, and substantial wastage.

Over-ambitious quality targets lead to inflated cost estimates for compliance, and inappropriate action priorities lead to ineffective investment strategies and waste of resources. Although there is a move toward full cost recovery, capital repairs, and new investment, expenditures currently depend on municipal subsidies and are generally insufficient to maintain the current infrastructure.

To address these problems, the City of St Petersburg, through its State Unitary Enterprise Vodokanal (VK), plans to modernize the water supply and waste-water facilities within the city and in the surrounding suburban areas. The enterprise serves approximately 4.7 million people, about 90% of whom live in the city. The main objectives of the modernization program are to comply with European drinking-water supply standards and the Convention on the Protection of the Marine Environment of the Baltic Sea Area recommendations for effluent discharges to the Gulf of Finland. The European Bank for Reconstruction and Development, the Nordic Investment Bank, and the bilateral funding agencies of the governments of the United Kingdom, Finland, France, Germany, Sweden, and Denmark have committed to providing financial support to VK through a combination of loans and technical assistance grants.

A diverse team of partner organizations enables VK to use various types of technical and financial assistance. Consultants from six European countries completed medium-term and long-term investment planning studies in 1997. The Corporate Development Support Project (CDSP), which commenced in mid-1998 and is funded by the governments of the United Kingdom, Finland, Sweden, and Denmark, helps VK to plan and carry out institutional reforms to achieve sustainable financial viability and efficient management. CDSP has also enabled VK to develop and adopt a strategic planning approach to service delivery, optimize the use of all resources (financial, human, and technical) and therefore to accelerate improvements in the level of services needed by customers.

The CDSP set-up combines the resources of the funding partners and the know-how of UK, Swedish, Finnish, and Danish water companies and consultants within a single project. The UK partners—Severn Trent Water International (STWI) and Mott MacDonald—provided overall project management and were responsible for five of the ten institutional strengthening components. These included developing strategy for corporate development and change management, strengthening the customer billing and collection system, strengthening the financial management systems, and reporting and improving the legislative base for rationalization and observance of environmental norms.

Early in the project it was recognized that the management of complex environmental issues required a systematic approach. The development and implementation of an environmental management system (EMS), consistent with overall corporate development plan management practices, was therefore added to the scope of the environmental component.

By working very closely with VK counterparts, STWI consultants were able to adapt the EMS model used in Severn Trent to meet the cultural and organizational needs of VK in a structured and systematic way and avoid an overly bureaucratic system. Over the course of 18 months, the EMS progressed through several stages: review of environmental impacts of VK's activities, development of an environmental policy, development of the environmental management structure, development of the environmental management system, and establishment of a pilot to test the EMS in an operational division.

The different contractual arrangements for the various teams have demanded exceptional flexibility and willingness to cooperate in drawing the whole toward the common goal of assisting VK in its management reform process. The use of corporate planning techniques is new to Russian water utilities, but, in St Petersburg, the CDSP has become the catalyst for a process of change toward a more commercially orientated enterprise. By working together in St Petersburg, Russian and Western European specialists have developed solutions to technical and management problems that will also help other water utilities in Russia and in countries in the Commonwealth of Independent States (CIS). The Russian federal authorities are showing strong interest in the project and are planning to disseminate results from St Petersburg to other urban water utilities.

CASE STUDY 38

Nestlé *partners for a green supply chain*

Nestlé Philippines Inc. (NPI) is the third-largest Nestlé company in the group region of Asia, Oceania, and Africa. Nestlé products have been in the Philippines for over a hundred years, finding their way from the trading houses in London and Paris. Today NPI, operating six factories supplying the needs of the local market and exports, has a diversified operation and an extensive supply chain in the Philippines.

Nestlé has a long and clearly established commitment to environmental protection throughout the supply chain. However, the company felt that this commitment could not be truly realized until its business partners developed similar commitments. Therefore, in August 2000, NPI gathered 42 of its key upstream business partners' CEOs and general managers to launch the Greening of the Supply Chain (GSC) initiative. The aim was to establish a dynamic venue through which NPI and its partners could interact, exchange information, share best practice, and raise concerns to help improve each other's environmental performance.

The first stage of the GSC initiative involved educating business partners about environmental management tools and the benefits of improved environmental performance. Workshops, focusing on environmental management systems (EMSs), were expanded in collaboration with the US–Asia Environmental Partnership. This was supported through seminars at business partners' sites to extend the training to their key personnel. Following the education and information phase, initial environmental reviews (IERs) are conducted to evaluate the environmental impacts of site activities.

To sustain the initiative, an environment forum is organized every three months. These events provide updates on regulations and technical issues as well as allowing partners to present status reports and share learning. Best-practice examples are a strong feature of this forum, which also encourages discussion of any challenges and stumbling blocks encountered. This is a particularly important aspect of the program as it strengthens partnerships among all participants.

As a result, many partners have begun to really understand and appreciate the business sense of this environmental commitment and practice and they have realized many improvements and success stories. Nestlé hopes that these partners will build relationships within their own supply chains to achieve similar benefits. For NPI and its suppliers, the initiative improved performance and improved relationships.

CASE STUDY 39

Rio Tinto *the Earthwatch partnership*

What do an international mining company and international NGO devoted to raising money for and awareness of scientific conservation projects have in common? The three-year partnership between Rio Tinto and Earthwatch, formalized in 1999 and recently renewed, is based on the principle that sound scientific data is critical for effective conservation. It is also based on the idea that Rio Tinto as a company supports conservation efforts and wants this effort to permeate employee thinking.

The projects supported through the partnership address biodiversity conservation and ecosystem management and are selected from Earthwatch's global portfolio of field research. At the core of the partnership is the Rio Tinto Earthwatch Global Employee Fellowship Programme. Since 1999, 71 employees have participated in Earthwatch projects in Australia, Europe, Asia, and South America.

As participants on these field research projects, employees join a team of volunteers working as field assistants for 10–14 days. Their tasks vary, depending on the project, and are often physically challenging in unfamiliar environments. The cost of funding a Fellowship is £3,000–£4,500 ($4,300–$6,400), excluding travel.

In the hundreds of applications for fellowships received each year, the main reasons given by employees for applying have been to increase their environmental awareness, to increase cultural awareness, to act as an ambassador for Rio Tinto, and to take advantage of the opportunity to contribute to international projects.

The Employee Fellowship Programme has contributed to cross-cultural understanding and has helped to reinforce awareness among employees of Rio Tinto's commitment to responsible environmental management. On their return, fellows report that the experience has changed their perspective of environmental issues. Not only have they learned new approaches to teamwork but also they have gained insights into the complexities of finding sustainable solutions to environmental issues and of the interface between social and cultural issues and environmental conservation.

They report that the experience has helped develop them as environmental champions within Rio Tinto and encouraged them to take action locally. Collins Chidimuro, a trainee environmental officer from Zimbabwe, reported:

> The project exposed me to international practice in terms of conservation and environmental management. From the project, I learned that industrial activity should be carried out in an environmentally friendly way. I would like to see a situation in my country where all operations (be it mining, agriculture, sport, or recreation) are working towards being in harmony with the ecology they find themselves in.

The partnership between Rio Tinto and Earthwatch has provided Earthwatch with long-term substantial support for its scientific research, public education, and conservation projects. Since this partnership began, Earthwatch has been able to develop similar fellowship programs with five other major companies, including British American Tobacco and KPMG. For Rio Tinto the partnership has proved itself to be a powerful model for corporate engagement in environmental conservation and sustainable development.

CASE STUDY 40

Tokyo Electric Power Company
Office Neighborhood Association promotes recycling

Although offices in Japan's urban areas are discharging an increasing amount of waste paper, it rarely pays to collect and recycle the small amounts produced by individual offices. The Tokyo Electric Power Company (TEPCO), which supplies electricity to the Tokyo metropolitan area, thought it had an answer. In August 1991 TEPCO created an Office Neighborhood Association (ONA) to promote the efficient and economic recycling of waste paper.

The program does not rely on a single agency to gather in the waste paper from offices, but more on the collective action of the staff of the small offices to hand it over to centralized points. In its very first year of operations, the association had 30 member companies, 38 establishments, and one collection agency; it collected 100 tonnes per month. At the end of 2000 it had 163 member companies, 287 establishments, and 46 supporting waste-paper collectors; it was bringing in nearly 720 tonnes per month.

The Office Neighborhood Association is now selling ONA brand paper products, made fully of office waste paper, so as to expand the waste-paper recycling drive. ONA brand papers include toilet rolls, tissue, and paper towels. To support this effort, TEPCO is promoting the wider use of recycled paper, mainly trying to change people's perceptions about the whiteness of copying paper. ONA activities have now been replicated in other parts of Japan, greatly increasing the amount of recycled paper on the market.

TEPCO's experience highlights the effectiveness of collective action in overcoming barriers to schemes that contribute to social, environmental, and economic benefit. Where action by individual companies may not pay off, cooperation by companies can make such activities economically feasible.

7
Informing and providing consumer choice

> **❝**In my experience very few consumers come out and say, 'I want products that help the environment.' But if we listen hard, we might hear them say, 'I want to do more with less. I want my life to be more simple. I don't want to waste.' Those words have strong eco-efficiency undertones—and give us the incentive to keep delivering more value with less resource.**❞**
>
> Joe Mallof, president of Asia and Pacific
> consumer products at SC Johnson, USA

If business believes in a free market where people have choices, business should accept responsibility for informing consumers about the social and environmental effects of those choices. Since consumers want that information to be provided, it can build market share and customer loyalty. It can build brands. It benefits the consumer, who is able to shop around and compare products, and it benefits those producers who have the best products and practices.

Sustainable development is about ensuring a better quality of life for everyone, now and for generations to come. For freedom of choice to effectively enhance quality of life while protecting the environment and promoting social equity, consumers need information and price signals to make intelligent decisions. Experience shows that consumers may not necessarily choose the 'greenest' or most socially beneficial option—despite what they indicate on surveys. Consumers want performance, value, safety, and reliability, ahead of environment, social concerns, and aesthetics. The solution is to create the right value–cost ratio, including all information consumers consider relevant to their purchases. Providing all of this information—at the right level of detail—is a challenge, though the Internet and other new communication technologies offer possible ways forward.

Business and other stakeholders can apply the influence of the media and promote sustainability messages and a new vision of the 'good life', but nothing can be

CASE STUDY 41
Ontario Power
Generation,
BC Hydro, and
Eskom
page 184

achieved if the message is not consistent with an offering of goods and services that deliver the promise. There is no point in advertising eco-efficient living without the readiness to deliver eco-efficient products and services and push up their market share.

Informed, responsible, and knowledgeable consumer choice can help achieve sustainability through the market via a triple-win situation: by improving quality of life for consumers, by reducing environmental and social impacts, and by increasing the market share of sustainability-minded companies.

The 'green' or ethical consumer

We are consuming at an unprecedented rate. According to the UNDP Human Development Report of 1998, private and public consumption expenditures reached $24 trillion that year, twice the level of 1975 and six times that of 1950 (UNDP 1998). Our consumption patterns are disproportionately distributed, and the gap between the world's richest and poorest consumers is widening. The 30 member countries of the OECD represent about 20% of the world's population, but they account for 80% of global GDP and 80% of world trade. Per capita private consumption in the OECD has been increasing over the past 20 years and is expected to do so over the next 20 years (Flisi 2001a).

Against this background of escalating consumption, a growing consumer movement emerged in Europe and North America in the late 1980s, aimed not only at environmental issues but also increasingly, in the 1990s, at social concerns. Consumers were growing impatient with the snail's pace of legislation to deliver significant environmental improvements. Consumers started boycotting products they found lacking in environmental or social standards, from refrigerators with ozone-destroying coolants to shoes made under unfair labor standards. They started asking difficult questions of retailers and manufacturers, triggering real market changes. Some producers took the cue, removing lead from gasoline, phosphates from detergent, mercury from batteries, and chlorine from pulp and paper processing. Prodded by consumers, many supermarket chains began introducing their own brands of 'green' or organic products, such as unbleached paper, to satisfy niche market demand.

Some issues, driven by NGO campaigns and taken up by the media, have become hot topics around which consumers are rallying. Examples include child labor and environmental degradation. Consumers are demanding assurances that goods are safe, are produced in conditions that do not deny workers their rights and that do not degrade the environment in their production, consumption, or disposal (Zadek *et al.* 1998).

Just how many green or ethical consumers are there? The answer varies widely. One of the most comprehensive studies of ethical consumer behavior was undertaken by The Co-operative Bank in the United Kingdom. The study found that 60% of consumers have looked for products with ethical qualities, although only 5% do so consistently (Cowe and Williams 2000). It would seem that, all else being equal, superior environmental performance boosts sales, but only a small segment of consumers are willing to pay more for such products. These findings are in contrast to those of Environics International Ltd, a research group that tracks consumers' environmental views. It found that 25% of consumers worldwide can be considered 'green' in actions as well as attitudes (in Flisi 2001a).

Some 50% of baby-boomers in the USA now say they are thinking of slowing down the pace of their lives; 40% say they would rather be bored than busy and stressed out. A year ago only 25% of respondents agreed with that sentiment. J. Walker Smith, president of Yankelovich market research, says the terrorist attacks on the USA on 11 September 2001 accelerated several trends. Consumers are rejecting 'radical' materialism and individualism in favor of 'old values': family, community, integrity, balance, authenticity, and security (in Brooks 2002).

Real answers doubtless lie between extremes. Many people may buy the occasional organic vegetable, but they do not become self-motivated green consumers in every purchase they make. There is a limited trade-off that consumers are prepared to make in the real world. Although they might be willing, at least in theory, to let their principles guide their purchasing, most consumers are just not prepared to give up the products they know and the price and performance standards they have come to expect. Education and information, a clear explanation of the issues, and relevant product solutions will go a long way in helping consumers to consume differently in action, not just in theory.

Selling to the new consumer

Although the green and/or social consumer movement may still be in its early stages, companies are noting the increase in customers' interest in the environmental, social, and ethical performance of companies and their products. As a result, some companies are taking steps to ensure that their purchasing and manufacturing practices reflect the environmental sensitivities of their customers and that their products incorporate the environmental attributes customers seek.

At consumer products company Procter & Gamble (P&G), boosting the sustainability of the company's products means taking a life-cycle view. It involves enhancing the degree to which the products improve people's lives both in performance and in terms of criteria such as safety, meeting legal requirements, wise use of resources, minimizing waste, and responding to the interests of people involved in their production, consumption, and eventual disposal. Peter Hindle, director of external relations worldwide of P&G, supports the idea of 'STM'—'sustainability through the market':

> This title derives from the recognition that business operates through the buying and selling of goods and services. Consumption and production are two sides of the market—demand and supply . . . We do not see that people will stop consuming; we do believe that people need to consume differently (in van Dijk 1998).

Acknowledging that the socially aware are a growing niche in the marketplace, and that people are becoming more concerned about letting their money speak for them,

Working Assets, a long-distance telephone services company in the USA, directs 1% of its customers' phone charges to non-profit organizations such as Greenpeace, Rocky Mountain Institute, the Natural Resources Defense Council, and American Rivers (Ottman 1998).

SC Johnson, one of the world's leading providers of cleaning, maintenance, and storage products for home and industry, adopted a new marketing approach in which the environmental benefits communicated on a product label relate to the consumer on a personal level. For example, a product with fewer volatile organic compounds (VOCs) in its formulation and therefore reduced fumes will be more comfortable for the consumer as well as reducing air pollution caused by VOCs (Alston and Prince Roberts 1999). Redefining the environment in this way broadens the appeal of such products beyond the small market niche previously targeted by environmental marketers to encompass mainstream consumers, the vast majority of whom care deeply about the health and safety of themselves, their families, and their communities.

This view is echoed by Jacquelyn A. Ottman, author of *Green Marketing: Opportunity for Innovation* (1998), who says, 'Consumers are prepared to give up their prejudice that green products cost more (or don't work as well, or whatever), at the moment that other benefits are linked to environmental soundness' (Ottman 2000). CASE STUDY 42 BP *page 187* Understanding the importance of linking other values to the environmental value of products has guided Philips Electronics, headquartered in Eindhoven, the Netherlands. Philips researchers found that linking such environmental attributes as energy reduction, materials reduction, and toxic substance reduction with various material (lower-cost), immaterial (convenience), and emotional (quality-of-life, feel-good) benefits desired by consumers raises consumer purchase interest to 60% or above, a figure that includes consumers who may be negatively predisposed to making purchases based on environmental issues (Ottman 2000).

Allianz, the global financial services company, introduced in 2001 an 'eco-package' into its real estate insurance as a way to reward eco-minded building owners. For example, when the owner of a commercial property decides to rebuild the premises after a fire, the cost of using more expensive insulated glass units for the windows is covered by the eco-package. By the same token, it is possible to use the compensation for damage caused to a roof during a storm to partially finance a solar energy installation on the roof. Previously, insurance policies guaranteed compensation only for returning the building to its original condition. Measures taken to modernize the building, which often improve energy efficiency in the process, were never considered when assessing the amount of claim to be paid. Allianz decided to give its customers a choice to make a more ecologically sustainable decision (Allianz 2001).

Getting the information across

If business wants people to consume differently, it has to help them understand the environmental or social impacts of their purchasing decisions. Companies are doing this in a number of ways. There has been a boom in environmental auditing, as retailers CASE STUDY 43 Detergent makers *page 187*

CASE STUDY 44
Deloitte Touche
Tohmatsu
page 189 and manufacturers realized they knew little about the impacts caused through their supply chains. Life-cycle assessment was embraced by many companies, often in pursuit of eco-labels.

Green consumerism has also been decisive in the growing number of firms publishing environmental or sustainability reports. SC Johnson, for example, is using sustainability reporting to inform consumer choice. Its reports try to provide relevant data while also being readable, digestible, and pertinent to all regions and stakeholders worldwide. Use of electronic compact disks (CDs) allows the company to provide a great deal of information without the need for paper, and web-based reporting extends the reach of the information.

Judging a product by its label

Eco-labeling, based on the use of labels or symbols to designate preferred products, is increasingly being used in the marketing of timber, foods, fish, and other products. Certified products can lead to higher prices and expanded market share as well as to satisfy consumers' concerns about the safety or environmental impact of such products. Eco-labeling from environmental NGOs can also help overcome a potential credibility gap between business and consumers.

CASE STUDY 45
Thailand BCSD
page 190 Today, eco-labeling schemes are being used worldwide to inform consumers about products ranging from paper products and paints to household appliances and construction materials. The EU is even looking into creating an eco-label for hotels, which would be the first government label in a service-industry sector. Such a label would overcome the confusing variation in environmental performance schemes for hotels; Germany alone has 40 such schemes.

The first eco-label program was the German Blue Angel, which began in 1978 and now covers 4,885 products in 79 product groups from 944 manufacturers. Others include the US Green Seal Program, the EU Eco-label, Swedish Environmental Choice, Taiwan's Green Mark, Zimbabwe's Environment 2000 Foundation, Canadian Environmental Choice, the Korea Environmental Labeling Association, Japanese Eco Mark, Environmental Choice New Zealand, Thailand Green Label, and the Nordic Swan.

One of the better-known examples of eco-labeling involves the standards established by the Forest Stewardship Council (FSC). Composed of representatives from environmental organizations, the timber trade, the forestry profession, indigenous groups, and forest product certification organizations from around the world, the FSC uses an independent certification system to evaluate environmental performance against a set of environmental, social, and economic standards. According to Gill Parker, Council Administrator of Pan European Forestry Certification (PEFC), as of December 2001 over 25 million hectares of productive forest land were certified worldwide in accordance with FSC standards. Some 600 companies, including Home Depot and IKEA, have joined global forest and trade networks that commit to buying certified wood (FSC/WWF 2001).

The FSC scheme led to the creation of other certification schemes—namely, the PEFC and the Sustainable Forestry Initiative (SFI). The FSC scheme, the PEFC, and the

SFI are the three major certification systems, although there are 35 in total. The PEFC Council was launched in 1999 as a voluntary private-sector initiative. The scheme aims to provide assurance to customers of woodland owners that the products they buy come from independently certified forests managed according to the PEFC criteria (as defined by the resolutions of the 1993 Helsinki and 1998 Lisbon ministerial conferences on the Protection of Forests in Europe). Timber products from these forests will be identifiable through the PEFC logo, and customers buying these products will be making a positive choice for sustainable forest management.

Adopted by the American Forest and Paper Association (AF&PA) in October 1994 and officially launched in 1995, the SFI program is a standard of environmental principles, objectives, and performance measures that integrates the perpetual growing and harvesting of trees with the protection of wildlife, plants, soil and water quality, and a wide range of other conservation goals. An independent external review panel, comprising representatives from the environmental, professional, conservation, academic, and public sectors, reviews the program and advises AF&PA on its progress. A total of 16 member companies have been expelled from the association for failure to uphold the standard set for the SFI program. Current members include the timber company Georgia-Pacific, the International Paper Company, and leading civil-society groups, such as Conservation International and The Nature Conservancy.

Naturally, there is competition among these certification schemes, and the International Mutual Recognition Framework for Forest Certification is an attempt to get all the eight regional intergovernmental certification processes (Pan European, Montreal, Tarapoto, International Tropical Timber Organization, Lepaterique, Dry Zone Africa, North Africa and Near East, and African Timber Organization) to agree on high-quality standards. Since a critical mass of at least 200 million ha is necessary to enable certified forest products to actually be available for customers, the WBCSD supports the scheme.

CASE STUDY 46
Forestry
certification
page 191

There is still a long way to go in terms of certifying tropical forests, according to Gill Parker, Pan European Forest Certification Council administrator: today only 2.4% of world forests are certified, representing 99 million ha (approximately 41.5 million ha have been certified through the PEFC, 25 million ha through the FSC, 15.5 million ha through the SFI, 11 million ha through the ATFS [American Tree Farm System] and 6 million ha through the CSA [Canadian Standards Association]). Some 96% of those certified forests are in developed countries (59% in Europe, 37% in North America); only 4% are in developing countries.

Fish have also been a subject of eco-labeling. The Marine Stewardship Council (MSC) was founded in 1996 as a joint initiative between the food and home products company Unilever and the WWF. Since 1999 the MSC has been autonomous. It is committed to the long-term viability of the global fish supply and health of maritime systems. So far, six fisheries have been certified to the MSC standard and several more are expected to join.

In 2001, the restaurant chain *fish!* became the first restaurant in the world to use the MSC label on its menus. Unilever also has the label on some of its frozen fish products—a step toward its goal to buy all its fish from sustainable sources by 2005 (WWF 2001b).

Eco-labeling is not a perfect tool. For instance, eco-label schemes are not comprehensive, often choosing one environmental feature out of many as the basis for awarding the label. Some schemes only scratch the surface of the immensely complex interactions between a product and the environment. The lack of harmonization of global standards leads to criticism that eco-labels pose a barrier to trade. Applying for a label can be costly and time-consuming, particularly for companies that have to seek eco-labels from many national programs with different qualifying requirements. In addition, eco-labels require that consumers understand what the labels imply and that there be an open dialogue between experts designing the criteria for the labels and the manufacturer.

Despite these difficulties, eco-labels can increase sales. Flourishing programs in the Far East and Northern Europe suggest that eco-labeling does work, especially with promotion at point-of-sale. A UK in-store advertising campaign for Reckitt & Colman's Down to Earth washing powder carrying the European eco-label's flower logo, for example, resulted in a 50% increase in sales. Likewise, Arthur Weissman, president and CEO of Green Seal, reports that a Korean company using Green Seal heavily in its advertising realized a 15% sales increase over six months (in Bradbury 1998).

In recent years a new phenomenon has arisen: the advent of social labels—words and symbols on a product that seek to influence the economic decisions of one set of stakeholders by providing an assurance about the social and ethical impact of a business process on another set of stakeholders. The Ethical Trade Initiative, like similar efforts such as the FairTrade Foundation and the Clean Clothes Campaign, aims to ensure that the conditions within production chains meet basic standards and to eradicate the more exploitative forms of labor such as child and bonded labor and sweatshops. Labeling criteria are generally based on conventions of the International Labor Organization (Zadek *et al.* 1998).

These efforts are finding a receptive audience, as consumers increasingly want to buy goods produced under conditions of fair labor practice. Yet consumers are confused about which products are more 'ethical' than others and in what ways. Companies are not clear how best to move 'ethical consumerism' from its current negative focus to one that embraces 'positive choice'. Civil-society institutions are reluctant to endorse products and companies without being absolutely sure that agreed standards are being met. Governments and international institutions are unsure as to what interventions are feasible, let alone effective (Zadek *et al.* 1998).

Despite these difficulties, social labeling is increasingly being used or considered as a tool for more effectively communicating to people about 'ethical trade'. Labeling can provide information and can act as an incentive to improve the social and environmental impact of trade.

The role of advertising

Marketing and advertising can be potent ways to shift purchasing behavior toward offerings in line with consumer habits that enhance rather than hinder sustainability. Through advertising and marketing, business helps to set trends that influence consumer demand. 'The major force will not be to reduce consumption', says the advertising agency Ogilvy & Mather (in SustainAbility 1995):

> This would probably be a futile exercise. Of far greater importance is to change the nature of consumption towards more environmentally friendly products that can prosper within a strategy of sustainable development. In this, advertising has a major role to play.

The growing power of advertising to sell not only products but also values and lifestyles was among the chief findings of a report by Consumers International in 1997: 'Gone are the days when the main function of advertising was providing information to consumers . . . advertising sells not only goods but a lifestyle and an identity.' UNEP's Division of Technology, Industry, and Economics has established an international expert committee on advertising and sustainable consumption. The committee has some 65 members, including advertising agencies, major corporate advertisers, and representatives of NGOs and UNEP.

Advertising agencies bring an important set of skills to the table, says UNEP's Bas de Leeuw, stating that 'Governments should be using sophisticated methods of communicating with their public—not just eco-labeling. You need to add emotion to the information.' Eco-labeling might tell you where a tomato was grown or how energy-efficient a light bulb is, but it does not persuade the consumer that an organic tomato tastes good or that an eco-friendly bulb emits a warm, inviting light (Flisi 2001b).

Some argue that the advertising industry has an obligation to try to influence patterns of consumption along a more sustainable path, as it is often accused of contributing to the problem of over-consumption. Some advertising agencies decline responsibility for promoting over-consumption, saying that they have to respond to their clients and that advertisements reveal and amplify underlying cultural trends but do not create them. Other advertising agencies claim that they want to be part of the solution, not by discouraging consumption so much as encouraging a more refined view of it (Flisi 2001b).

The value of brands

Building a relationship with consumers also depends on branding. Successful branding in the future will more forcefully tap into social changes. One indication of this shift in brand thinking is the multi-million-dollar rebranding of the former British Petroleum Group. The company has now begun to describe their familiar acronym, BP, as standing for Beyond Petroleum. Furthermore, they have adopted a sun icon known as the Helios mark as their new logo. They see this as allowing them to reach sustainability-minded consumers, who can now access special web pages on the BP website (www.bp.com) dedicated to conservation, climate change, environmental reports, Earth Day, and BP Solar (the world's largest solar energy company; see Heal 2001).

The attempt by companies to imbue their brands with a social component, a 'life-style' statement, is giving consumers a lever to influence the behavior of these companies. Brands are a conduit through which influence flows between companies and consumers, but most often it is consumers that dictate to companies rather than the other way around. This has been illustrated in recent years by the failure of such high-profile product launches as 'New Coke', the disastrous effect on Hoover of a badly designed sales promotion in Britain a few years ago and the boycotts of genetically modified foods by Europe's consumers (Heal 2001).

Brands of the future will have to stand not only for product quality and a desirable image but will also have to signal something wholesome about the company behind the brand. According to Wally Olins, a corporate-identity consultant and co-founder of the consultancy Wolff Olins, 'The next big thing in brands is social responsibility. It will be clever to say there is nothing different about our product or price, but we behave well' (in Heal 2001).

Niall FitzGerald, CEO and chairman of Unilever plc, concurs:

> What is interesting today is that consumers' expectations of consistency extend well beyond the quality of the ingredients they expect to find in a branded product, or the customer service standards they expect to find from a branded service. Increasingly consumers expect the values of a brand to be reflected in every aspect of the business behind the brand (FitzGerald 2001a).

Retail leads the way

Retailers are well positioned to influence more sustainable consumer choice. Retailers act as a medium for the demands of the customers upstream to their suppliers and delivering new products and services downstream to these customers. Retailers quickly pick up the trends that lie behind millions of separate consumer decisions each day, and in this context could serve as an educator, providing information and analysis to help customers make better choices.

The growth of the use of packaging is one of most notable signs of the consumer society. Consumer goods packaging contains much useful information, protects the product from damage and spoilage and helps protect the retailer from shoplifting, but most packaging has been designed with little thought to eco-efficiency or circular systems. Thus retailers are under pressure to minimize packaging waste, and governments are imposing regulations on packaging. Consumers can return some packaging to retailers, who in turn can pass it on to the manufacturers, and so on up the chain to the packaging producer. Some stores are trying to reflect a product's full environmental costs in the prices they charge.

Retailers in Europe are increasingly focusing on supply-chain management to satisfy legal requirements, such as those on food safety, and to ensure quality. They need to be able to trace the source of products and the processes involved in their production. As the gatekeepers between consumers and producers, retailers therefore play a critical role in shaping production processes as well as consumption patterns.

Retailers, for instance, through point-of-sale promotions, play an important role in determining whether eco-labeled products make it off the shelves.

Retailers Sainsbury's, Safeway, Tesco, and Birdseye (Unilever) have committed themselves to explore sustainable fish supplies, and Budgens Stores Ltd, MIGROS Cooperatives, Albert Fisher plc, and Shaw's Supermarkets Inc. have all signed the MSC's sustainable fish initiative. In addition, more supermarkets than before are carrying organic products, with a quadrupling of the market predicted by 2002 in the UK alone (Spencer-Cooke *et al.* 1999). Sainsbury's, a leading UK retailer, carries only FSC-endorsed timber products and offers guidance to suppliers on sourcing raw materials and products from the wild. More organic products have appeared on Sainsbury's shelves in response to growing consumer concerns about food safety and animal welfare (Johansen *et al.* 1998).

In their effort to enable consumer choice, wholesalers and retailers need to insist on open and continuous information from manufacturers on production processes with respect to energy consumption, use of raw materials, and pollution. Some retailers are already buying mainly from manufacturers who demonstrate a commitment to sustainable development. New supplier codes are being drawn up, setting out process and product requirements to help manufacturers minimize impacts throughout the product life-cycle.

Stimulating market demand is particularly important in the energy sector, which is characterized by a host of technically viable and environmentally preferable technologies, and the Green Power Market Development Group hopes to create greater market demand for some of these technologies. This group of 11 companies, including DuPont, GM, IBM, Interface, Johnson & Johnson, Pitney Bowes, and Kinko's, has formed a partnership with the World Resources Institute and Business for Social Responsibility to help stimulate the market over the next decade. Together, these companies account for about 7% of industrial energy use in the USA (SustainAbility/UNEP 2001).

Winning consumers' trust

Questionable green-marketing or social-marketing activities tend to backfire. Consumers' environmental or social concerns cannot be exploited simply by communicating superficial product changes and regulatory compliance. Increasingly, what companies stand for is just as important as what they sell. According to Robert Walker, chief executive of environmental services company Severn Trent:

> To meet the goal of sustainability, we must move away from a throwaway society to one that is better able to recover resources and use them more productively. We have a key role to play, using our expertise to help our customers meet their environmental responsibilities (Severn Trent 2001).

Unilever's Niall FitzGerald notes that educating and informing consumers is really about engaging them in a different way of consuming:

> To those of us in business, it may seem obvious that our [products] will benefit consumers in real, practical ways. But we have to win people's trust by engaging in a frank dialogue—or else we may never get the opportunity to deliver [our products]. No product can ever succeed if it is marketed against the will of consumers—and by the same token, public acceptance of such products will only be achieved on the basis of mutual trust. For a company that prides itself on 'understanding', our challenge is to apply ever deeper consumer insights into products people trust and want to buy (FitzGerald 2000a).

Individuals will change their consumption practices when they realize that they can gain added value from sustainable behavior in terms of financial benefits, quality of life, and security. Business can be the bridge to a new way of consuming for the 21st century. Informed, responsible, and knowledgeable consumer choice helps achieve sustainability through the market via a triple-win situation: by improving quality of life for consumers, by reducing environmental and social impacts, and by increasing the market share of sustainability-minded companies.

CASE STUDY 41
Ontario Power Generation, BC Hydro, and Eskom *energy options*

Environmentally preferable electricity choices are now available to many people in many countries. However, customers are not always as enthusiastic as energy companies feel they should be. Costs can be prohibitive and there may not be enough information available on the benefits and availability of such products. (Members of the WBCSD engaged in power generation are running a working group on the most sustainable ways of getting energy to people and companies.)

To create new markets for new products and to develop customer loyalty many energy companies are offering customers incentive schemes to encourage them to conserve energy and to consider new energy options. Such programs provide market-based choices for all consumers, including industrial customers, enabling them to purchase power from alternative sources such as solar, wind and geothermal generation, hydropower, and energy generated by various forms of biomass systems.

Ontario Power Generation (OPG) and BC Hydro in Canada have designed programs to expand green power options and encourage new customer behavior in Canada. In South Africa, Eskom is also bringing new options to new markets through various demand-side management programs. One of Eskom's biggest current programs is the Efficient Lighting Initiative.

Ontario Power Generation

OPG strategy is to lead the development of green power in Ontario. The company has created a new operating division, OPG-Evergreen Energy, which is to invest $32 million by 2005 to expand OPG's capacity in wind, solar, biomass, and small hydroelectric power. This strategy will allow OPG to align its sustainable energy development objectives with new commercial opportunities in the emerging competitive market for green power and services. These opportunities, however, present many challenges.

Green power is a relatively unknown commodity to Ontario's consumers, and customer interest remains untested. OPG has recognized the need for consumer education on the benefits of green power and has developed information material to support its green power offerings. Green power is also showcased through a computer information kiosk and website link in the lobby of OPG's corporate office. The various technologies that contribute to the company's green power generation mix are also profiled. OPG's installation of North America's largest wind turbine has proved to be an effective 'billboard' for green power. Last, OPG actively supports the adoption of green power certification systems to provide consumers with clear and accurate information on green power products.

OPG expects that consumers who share its commitment to sustainable development and climate change management will embrace opportunities to buy green power. At the same time, OPG recognizes that green power will have to compete with conventional power on availability and price. OPG is structuring green power offerings to balance affordability and availability with customer preferences for some of the more expensive sources such as wind and solar.

Looking to the future, customer demand for green power will grow as more reliable and affordable sources become available and as its environmental benefits are better understood. In support of cost-effective green energy options for the future, OPG is investing significantly in R&D and in companies with promising alternative energy technologies.

BC Hydro

BC Hydro e.points (energy points) is a new initiative that rewards commercial customers for fast-tracking electricity-saving measures in their key facilities. In addition to rewarding energy-conservation activities (e.g. training that promotes employee awareness and change regarding turning off lights and equipment), the program rewards customers for capital investment in 'upgrades'—products or technology (e.g. compact fluorescent lighting) that become permanent fixtures and deliver sustainable electricity savings. Electricity savings over a 12-month tracking period result in an e.points award. The dollar value of e.points can then be redeemed against additional electricity-efficiency upgrades.

The e.points program was launched in July 2001 to encourage BC Hydro's largest 366 commercial customers to achieve significant electricity savings within their accounts. These customers represent more than 75% of BC Hydro's commercial revenue. The flow-on benefits of this conservation effort for BC Hydro include a reduction in greenhouse gas (GHG) emissions, deferral of new sources of electricity generation, revenue enhancement through electricity export sales, and the creation of customer loyalty.

An aggressive marketing and communications campaign was developed to support an 11-week customer enrollment period from 3 July to 15 September 2001.

Additional support for the program is provided through an exclusive website (www. bchydro. com).

BC Hydro hoped to have most of its large commercial customers enroll during the first year. In fact, forecasts for the first year have already been exceeded. As of 29 October 2001, 447 customers with an electricity base load of 3,778 GWh were enrolled. Savings for the first year looked to be approximately 185 GWh, which represents $8.5 million in electricity savings, equivalent to 97,500 tonnes in avoided GHG emissions.

The e.points program is a highly structured, low-risk, customer-focused, energy-efficiency marketing campaign that is 'shelf-ready'. If the e.points program is successful, there will be a compelling argument to encourage energy conservation by offering the program to other commercial, industrial, and residential customers (e.g. rebranding e.points as 'e.points at home' for residential customers).

Eskom

Eskom and the Global Environment Facility have helped set up the South African Efficient Lighting Initiative (ELI), a 20-year program aimed at transforming the local market to use more energy-efficient lighting technologies in all sectors of the market. The ELI is aimed at reducing electricity demand, increasing efficiency, and reducing emissions. The two set up a joint-venture company, Bonesa, to implement the ELI program, which was officially launched at the end of July 2000.

ELI is intended to promote technologies such as the compact fluorescent lamp (CFL): essentially, light 'bulbs' that use less electricity, last longer, but produce the same amount of light as a regular bulb.

The initiative consists of several programs. The Public Education Program, the biggest, is designed to increase awareness about energy-efficient lighting, includes a broad range of marketing and public relations activities and feeds directly into programs in different income segments as well as the Commercial, Industrial, and Institutional Program activities. One of the major objectives of the program is to get energy efficiency included in the curriculum not only of schools but also of all places of learning.

The Schools Program is being offered to teach school pupils the benefits of energy-efficient lighting. Bonesa will seek to increase the awareness of students and faculties of energy-efficient lighting by providing participating institutions with technical information on lighting and by providing teaching and study aid materials to lecturers and students. The Commercial, Industrial, and Institutional Program is intended to urge these three sectors toward greater use of energy-efficient lighting technologies. Bonesa will make CFLs available to newly electrified homes and to new home-owners under South Africa's Reconstruction and Development Program.

Eskom has learned that research is needed before and after such efforts for continuous feedback to the programs, and interaction with stakeholders is critical. Bonesa is attempting to promote a concept fundamentally new to many South Africans. Most of the programs do not have South African (or other developing-country) experience to draw from, and international experience has tended not to be that useful. The learning curve has been very steep but is flattening out. Bonesa is learning how to break through barriers and to profit by experience.

CASE STUDY 42

BP *local choice; global atmosphere*

BP is offering customers in Australia a new choice: a new, cleaner product and a supporting offset program to reward purchases. BP Ultimate is the new fuel available in service stations, and BP Global Choice has been designed to provide an offset scheme for emissions.

BP Ultimate is a powerful, high-octane unleaded fuel that according to BP is environmentally cleaner than any other gas on the Australian market. It can be used in all vehicles, from the family sedan to high-performance sports cars, as well as any older vehicles still using leaded fuel. It is a high-density fuel; therefore the user benefits from more energy per liter.

BP Ultimate is highly refined and so produces low emissions. With low levels of sulfur, benzene, and aromatics, BP Ultimate helps contribute to cleaner, healthier air. The fuel has been available in BP service stations throughout Perth, Australia, and at selected sites in other states, and was being rolled out in more service stations across Australia.

For those customers who choose this fuel, emissions produced are offset under the BP Global Choice program, designed to help reduce Australia's greenhouse gas (GHG) emissions. When drivers fill up with BP Ultimate, BP Australia will offset the GHG emissions by investing a percentage of the purchase price in independently verified and government-certified GHG reduction projects. These include renewable energy (clean energy from solar, wind, tidal, hydro sources), GHG capture (turning methane gas from landfills into electricity), planting new forests (to absorb CO_2 from the atmosphere), and innovative technology (providing cleaner technology solutions).

If sales exceed expectations or projects fail to provide the expected reduction in GHGs, BP will invest in additional projects. However, the pump price will not be increased to cover the costs of the program, as BP Ultimate is a premium-quality fuel currently costing around six cents more than other unleaded gas because of the increased refining costs.

CASE STUDY 43

Detergent makers *Washright*

Members of the International Association of the Soap, Detergent, and Maintenance Products Industry (AISE), which now represents more than 1,200 companies in Europe, covering approximately 90% of the market, are encouraging consumers to use their products more efficiently. In fact, they want customers to help them reduce the environmental impact of soaps and detergents by using the products correctly.

A life-cycle assessment (LCA) conducted by the AISE LCA Task Force shows that much of the environmental impact of household laundry detergents is caused during the use phase. The task force also found that consumers control around 70% of total energy use, 90% of air emissions, and 60% of solid waste attributable to product impact across the entire product life-cycle. Thus the way the consumer uses products has a big effect on the environmental impact of those products.

The AISE suggested providing consumers with product information, particularly about their use. This suggestion led to a multimedia awareness-raising and education campaign called Washright. A European media campaign and a product labeling scheme, supported by a Washright logo and website (www.washright.com), conveyed washing messages. A media plan, developed by AISE and followed in each country by the relevant national industry associations, included a series of 15-second television advertisements, 5-second message inserts at the end of supporting companies' advertisements, and use of the Washright logo in all participating laundry detergent brands' advertisements.

All companies supporting the initiative may display the logo, thus indicating to consumers their commitment to the program of reducing the environmental impact of household laundry detergents. Such packaging visuals have, since 1998, started to include a 'short reminder panel' that provides helpful hints and explanations as to why such actions reduce environmental impact.

The Washright website also provides information on the AISE and the Code of Good Environmental Practice as well as the full range of short reminder panels with relevant information. As of March 2000 more than 90% of the European market had committed to the Code, representing more than 150 companies (including multinationals and their subsidiaries). Since the implementation of the Washright campaign, consumer communication material has been developed by AISE and placed on billions of laundry detergent packages throughout Europe; there are estimated to be in excess of 500 million packages carrying the Washright visuals sold across Europe each year.

The campaign has four key messages:

- *Reduce packaging waste:* retain permanent or refillable packaging and buy refill packs where available

- *Avoid under-filling the machine:* washing more clothes in one wash reduces water and energy use

- *Measure according to soil level and water hardness:* the amount of detergent used should relate to the hardness of the water in your area and the soil level of the laundry

- *Use the lowest recommended temperature:* most of today's washing detergents work well at low temperatures, so using very hot water is not usually necessary and wastes energy

The effort is not aimed only at consumers' use of soap. Under the AISE Code, Unilever has adopted cleaner manufacturing processes and developed product innovations to meet the targets of the Code and support the Washright initiative. For example, improvement to the Persil brand manufacturing processes has resulted in reduced emissions, recycling of waste-streams, and more energy-efficient processes. Unilever has been constantly looking at new ways of reducing the environmental impacts of Persil products through developing products that work better at lower temperatures, monitoring ingredients and their impacts, and continually identifying areas for further improvement.

CASE STUDY 44
Deloitte Touche Tohmatsu
helping consumers choose

Consumers are beginning to think about the entire life-cycle of the products they buy. Many want to know where the products come from and how they, or their parts and materials, are going to be disposed of or recycled. They want certainty that what they buy has been produced in accordance with international norms and human rights standards, international labor standards, and internationally acknowledged principles for the protection of the environment.

Some corporations, particularly those close to the consumer, are working on meeting this demand for information, by, for example, developing ethical guidelines for their operations at home and abroad and for the manufacturing of their products. At the same time, governments are developing initiatives to monitor and report to the public on company behavior. Many of the initiatives overlap and there is no consensus about the best way to collect and report on the data available. 'This is where the accounting profession is playing an increasingly active part', says Preben Sørensen, global leader of Deloitte & Touche's environment and sustainability services:

> Both the accounting profession itself and many public bodies consider ethical assurance services a natural extension of the existing assurance-related services traditionally offered by accounting firms, and companies like Deloitte & Touche are heavily involved in developing tools to help corporations and governmental bodies report on ethical issues.

In Denmark, Deloitte & Touche has been working with Danish Consumer Information (DCI), a public body informing consumers about a variety of issues relating to products and services in the market. DCI has developed an 'ethical database' to allow companies to provide consumers with information over the Internet about company products and services. This is increasingly important in a world where image and brand are key competitive devices. Participation is voluntary and offers the company an opportunity to demonstrate its commitment to corporate social responsibility (CSR).

'Rather than seeing the ethical database as a threat to their image, companies consider it an opportunity to promote their work with CSR and to link this work to their brands', says Jens Schierbeck, director for CSR at Deloitte & Touche, Denmark. The long-term vision is to place terminals in every shop to enable the consumer to obtain information about a product and a manufacturer before deciding to buy the product.

'Ideally, the information provided should exceed the legal requirements for the provision of social/ethical information,' says Mette Reissmann of DCI, 'and we have been working with Deloitte & Touche on developing a large range of questions that participating companies must answer.' For the 30 companies participating in the pilot phase, the database offers profiling, branding, and risk management on national and international markets. The consumer, in turn, is given assurance about the reliability of the data provided through frequent random sampling performed by a third-party auditor.

CASE STUDY 45

Thailand Business Council for Sustainable Development

Green Label Scheme

Thailand Business Council for Sustainable Development (TBCSD), established in 1993, consists of representatives from 32 leading business organizations and operates as a non-profit group to promote sustainable development. The TBCSD initiated a Green Label scheme soon after it was established. This provides an environmental certification for products that are shown to have minimum detrimental impact on the environment compared with other products serving the same functions. The TBCSD provides financial support and policy advice, and the Thai Environment Institute and the Thai Industrial Standards Institute lead project management and criteria development.

The Green Label scheme is intended to:

- Provide reliable information and to guide customers in their choice of products

- Create an opportunity for consumers to make an environmentally conscious decision, thus creating market incentives for manufacturers to develop and supply more environmentally sound products

- Reduce environmental impacts that may occur during manufacturing, use, consumption, and disposal of products

The scheme came from the idea that consumers have the power to purchase products that do not damage the environment. Selection of a product should be weighed against its impact on the environment as well as its price, performance, and other attributes. A demand for environmentally sound products would persuade business to develop these products to fulfill consumers' needs.

The Thai Green Label applies to products and services but excludes food, drink, and pharmaceuticals. Products or services that meet the Thai Green Label criteria can carry the Thai Green Label. Participation in the scheme is voluntary, and it is open to domestic and foreign suppliers.

At last count, the Thai Green Label had established criteria for 32 product categories, and a study was under way for developing criteria for 4 new categories: fertilizers, personal cars, wood-substitute construction materials, and refillable containers. In the project's first six years, more than 200 products have received the Green Label award.

CASE STUDY 46
Forestry certification
the need for mutual recognition

In response to public concern about the destruction of the world's forests, a multitude of forestry certification schemes and guidelines have emerged to assure customers that the wood products they buy come from well-managed forests. In 1993, as a collaborative effort between WWF, Greenpeace, and several other groups, the Forest Stewardship Council (FSC) was founded. Certification from the council is given to products that come from forests that have been independently certified as meeting the FSC Principles and Criteria of Forest Stewardship. The FSC received considerable support from many environmental groups. However, by 1999 only 16 million hectares had been certified, representing only 0.5% of the world's forests; 75% of this was concentrated in three countries: Sweden, Poland, and the USA.

During the 1990s, other national and regional forest certification systems emerged. One of the first of these was the Canadian Standards Association (CSA) Sustainable Forestry Management Standard, approved in 1996. In the USA, the Sustainable Forestry Initiative (SFI) emerged in 1998 as an industry-wide effort following the CSA. In Europe, the Pan European Forest Certification (PEFC) was launched in 1999, offering an alternative to FSC certification for the European market. Each of these schemes differs in the standards underpinning it, the manner in which certification can be presented, and the degree to which it recognizes other international, national, or regional standards.

These schemes, in offering varying approaches, have met with success in several countries. However, every scheme has been criticized for certain weaknesses and no one scheme presents commonly accepted international standards suitable for all countries and parties involved in the process. The abundance of schemes creates confusion in the marketplace, weakening the value of all sustainable forestry certification schemes. Retailers also suffer, because by signing on to any single certification body they are restricted to the limited supply available under that scheme. However, by supporting numerous schemes, they risk confusing customers.

The current situation suggests that no single scheme is likely to gain a monopoly. Thus the International Forest Industry Roundtable (IFIR) has been developing a working plan for a framework of mutual recognition for credible forestry certification schemes. The Mutual Recognition framework is intended to provide a critical mass of credibly certified wood products by recognizing that different certification systems could provide substantially equivalent standards of sustainable forest management. Mutual Recognition is a reciprocal arrangement whereby forestry standards bodies collectively agree to recognize the scope, design, process, and output of all critical components of the other programs, provided each provides a high level of forest values.

The many different certification systems can, in combination, supply large quantities of wood products from sustainably managed forests. So a Mutual Recognition framework would enable products from the different schemes to meet expanding market demand for certified wood products. Retailers would not be restricted to one scheme and they would not be forced to bombard customers with a plethora of logos and certification criteria.

Mutual Recognition has been criticized as providing a 'lowest common denominator' approach to certification. Its advocates deny this charge and claim that any system seeking mutual recognition must meet a very high level of performance. Further, the schemes must effectively drive change within the industry by providing an effective, clearly understandable system that creates customer pull. One objective of Mutual Recognition is to provide a critical mass of products from certified forests, thus assuring that sustainable forestry practices become more widespread and that 'good wood' products are available everywhere to meet growing demands. Advocates argue that Mutual Recognition would reward the best performers, encourage industry-wide improvements and help root out destructive practices such as illegal logging.

To support the effort to make sustainable forestry schemes more understandable, Sustainable Forestry and Certification Watch has designed the website www. mutualrecognition.org to bring together information on Mutual Recognition among forest certification systems.

Innovation

For us, innovation is the best way to make a contribution to changing consumer habits—not by persuading the customer to consume less but to consume differently.

Belmiro de Azevedo, CEO, Sonae, Portugal

Recent history suggests that those living in wealthier countries do not intend to consume and waste less. Given that the other 80% of the planet's people appear to seek to emulate those consumption habits, the only hope for sustainability is to change forms of consumption. To do so, we must innovate. We must produce much more energy, but with lower carbon intensity; more wood and paper, but from planted forests rather than virgin forests; more food, but not in ways that spread deserts and waste water. Sustainable consumption is not necessarily about consuming less but consuming differently: consuming efficiently. It is about more quality and knowledge and less quantity and waste.

Human creativity is one resource that is not being depleted; it must not be misdirected. We need the right framework conditions to guide innovation in eco-efficient directions. To preserve their freedom to innovate, corporations will have to include in their development processes an evaluation of a broader set of impacts, including the social, environmental, and economic impacts of their innovations, thereby keeping themselves aligned with public expectations. In the past, firms tended to innovate in 'black boxes', springing results on consumers. The world is now too transparent for this to be a viable tactic. Also, many of today's innovations come packed with moral, ethical, environmental, and social controversy, as innovations occur in human, animal, and plant reproduction, the production of food, and the maintenance of health. Such innovations require discussion.

Business has much to gain from transparency, except in cases where commercial confidentiality must be preserved. Thus innovation will be carried out in 'goldfish bowls'. It will be stimulated by stakeholder dialogues and new partnerships. It will be best accepted coming from companies that have made their values clear and have a solid reputation for acting on them.

Recent developments in areas such as waste recycling, nanotechnology, information technology, biotechnology, and alternative energy could contribute markedly to sustainability. Sustainable solutions are not only about technical innovation; economic, social, and institutional innovation are as important. Innovation can enable our global economy to depend more on the progress of technology than on the exploitation of nature. Innovation can enable companies to create wealth in ways that reflect the changing concerns and values of our world. In essence, the key test to determine if innovations will meet with success in the market must be: 'does it really improve overall quality of life?'

Sustainable development demands innovation

Innovation is critical for the ongoing success of any enterprise. Institutions that do not innovate disappear—and not only businesses. Innovation spans the realm of possibilities for business: products themselves, the technologies deployed to extract, refine, or manufacture, and the mechanisms that deliver these products and services ever more efficiently and effectively to the marketplace. New technologies constantly appear at scales that range from minor modifications to existing facilities, to new applications for existing knowledge, to breakthrough approaches based on completely new science (WBCSD 2001j).

CASE STUDY 47
Gerling
page 210

Technologies, however, are discovered, developed, and marketed in an environment that consists not only of markets, supply chains, and distribution networks but also of a number of disturbing social and environmental trends throughout the world: threatened ecosystems, increased CO_2 levels in the atmosphere, depleted fisheries, an increasing gap between the rich and the poor, and growing concerns over the impacts of globalization. Can innovation and technology be part of the solution to reversing these negative trends and, if so, how can companies innovate in ways that have a positive impact and generate the most value (WBCSD et al. 2002)?

CASE STUDY 48
DuPont
page 211

There is growing acceptance that to move toward sustainability there must be changes in the ways in which business operates and in the products and services it provides. There also must be changes in the choices people make in the market, in how they use products and services and how they deal with waste. However, people must believe that these changes will improve their own lives and the lives of their children. Thus the challenge for business is to provide the service and functional component of our consumer society, but to innovate new ways of doing so with markedly lower reliance on materials, energy, labor, and waste. The marketplace continues to demand quality, convenience, and content. Successful businesses will find the ways of providing them, but not at the expense of the health of the planet. According to Claude Fussler, a director at the WBCSD:

> Business faces two choices: keep on with business as usual, make the best use of assets and react to new trends as they become irresistible; or anticipate the changes and embrace a strategy of innovation and entrepreneurship to outsmart competitors stuck in the business-as-usual mindset (Fussler with James 1996).

The new economy is driving the way innovation is being applied in business today. Whereas the old economy was based on rules, science, R&D, and intellectual property, the new economy is being formed with the addition of communications, the involvement of interested parties, and a growing drive for more universal equity. It is being driven by the tremendous advances made in information technology and the natural sciences, especially biology (WBCSD 2000c).

The old economy was and still is driven mainly by and based on the physical production and distribution of goods. Increasing production and consumption of these goods leads to growing consumption of limited raw material resources and increasing burdens on the environment as a result of pollution and waste. The old economy involves the mass industrial production of mass products. Growth in this sector is slow and linear because the innovative potential of many companies in this sector is oriented toward end-game strategies that do not add value, and the resulting growth tends to be tied to growth of the economy in general.

A transformation process is under way, especially among major corporate groups. They are shifting their focus toward the new economy and are selling, spinning off, or outsourcing functions and businesses that were once considered to be at the core of the enterprise. In the pharmaceutical and biotech industry, new methods in R&D are accelerating the quest for new drugs, vaccines, and diagnostics. Chemical companies such as Dow, DuPont, and Aventis are now focusing their strategy on knowledge-based and science-based solutions.

CASE STUDY 49
Cargill Dow
page 212

Other industrial sectors are also undergoing this type of innovation-enhancing transformation. In the energy industry, for instance, there is a move toward a new diversity in micro-power solutions rather than the mega schemes (nuclear power plants, dams) favored in the past. The trend started with new technologies such as the highly flexible gas turbine. Now major companies are responding. Swiss–Swedish power engineering company, ABB, for example, is refocusing its entire business away from mega to micro business, with a growing focus on wind turbines and fuel cells. These technologies are ideally suited to support remote and rural communities that tend to get bypassed by national power grids, both in developed economies and, particularly, in emerging economies. Furthermore, 'distributed power generation'—electricity generated from small sources usually close to users—is expected to create $1 billion in business annually for ABB by 2005, rising to $2.5 billion by 2010 (Holliday and Pepper 2001: 13). 'Companies are transforming their understanding of scale, from "bigger is better"—which in practical terms means the capability to marry highly distributed small-scale operations and a few world-scale capabilities', says Jörgen Centerman, president and CEO of ABB (in Holliday and Pepper 2001: 11).

CASE STUDY 50
Conoco
page 213

Christian Kornevall, senior vice president for sustainability affairs at ABB notes that motors consume 65% of all energy used in industry. ABB's business is motors, so 'if we can make them more efficiently, we can save a lot of energy', he says. 'Businesses that buy them will have a payback in a few years' time. Innovation leads to higher efficiency for society and a competitive edge for us' (in Flisi 2001c).

Under its new Sony Environmental Vision, launched in 2000, Sony is applying that same innovation to environment-related business models. For example, Sony has developed a new technology for recycling polystyrene foam from packaging and in April 2001 launched this as a business at a supermarket in Kochi prefecture in Japan for recycling food packaging. In addition, Sony has initiated a product take-back and recycling system for Sony products in the state of Minnesota in cooperation with the state and with recycling and collection companies.

The transition to digital technologies is also boosting innovation in the direction of improved functionality of products. For example, Sony has now introduced the new Network Walkman and has developed a music distribution business based on a state-of-the-art network technology.

Redefining how we make and sell things

Anyone who does not believe that there has been a major change in the ways in which innovation must be done need only look at US life-sciences company Monsanto and its efforts to sell its new genetically modified (GM) seeds in the late 1990s. Monsanto had reason to believe that its innovation would be embraced by consumers. After all, it had the blessing of government authorities, and sales of GM seeds to farmers were soaring. However, it did not realize that it was asking consumers to try a new type of product, with some perceived risks, while offering those consumers no perceived benefits. It was playing by old-economy rules, where government makes the rules of engagement between business and civil society. In the new economy, civil society plays an informal but increasingly influential guiding role. Companies that do not seriously engage with critics can find their innovations abruptly rejected. By misjudging the level of public concern over GM foods in Europe, Monsanto's reputation was so badly damaged that the valuation of the biotechnology section of the company collapsed. By February 2000, the value that the financial markets placed on Monsanto's $5 billion-per-year agricultural business unit was less than zero (Stipp 2000). 'Monsanto believed that if it influenced government, it could have its way. That's old paradigm thinking. It doesn't work anymore', notes Paul Gilding, executive director of the Sydney-based consultancy Ecos Corp. (in Frankel 2000).

In October 1999 Monsanto's then CEO Robert Shapiro acknowledged the need to find common ground with biotechnology's opponents. He told the Greenpeace Business Conference in London that, until then, Monsanto had 'irritated and antagonized more people than we have persuaded' (in Lehrman 1999). The company promised that year it would not develop the controversial 'Terminator Technology' that would make sterile the grain of its GM crops and therefore unusable as seeds, forcing farmers to buy new GM seeds every year (Lehrman 1999). In late 1999 Monsanto merged with the US–Swedish pharmaceutical company Pharmacia-UpJohn, which then spun off Monsanto's agricultural business into a separate, publicly held company.

Monsanto seems to have taken aboard its hard-earned lesson. Its new CEO, Henrik Verfaillie, has started a stakeholder dialogue with a number of NGOs. He says they have done this 'so we would have the benefit, as we develop these technologies, of different perspectives that we would not see' (in Buerkle 2001). Monsanto pledged in 2000 that it would not put animal or human genes into seeds and would share technology with developing countries, as it has already done with a disease-resistant rice seed (Buerkle 2001).

Business risk can be reduced by the introduction of more robust means of stakeholder input throughout the business development process. In this way, innovation can be challenged before capitalization is complete. This includes not just more effective market research but also external reviews prior to commercialization and at key stages in the development process. The whole process is fed by a keen desire to understand and integrate external issues very early, even into basic research.

Market acceptance is easier when a company does not deal in basic consumer goods such as foods and can make claim to sustainable development considerations. Taiheiyo Cement Corporation in Japan has developed 'eco-cement' using incinerated waste ash. This helps in dealing with the problems of coping with 24 million tonnes of industrial waste produced by the Japanese cement industry annually and the limited landfill sites in this densely populated country. The process contributes to energy conservation and CO_2 reduction, maximizing the use of alternative fuels, and reduces raw material use during cement production (Buerkle 2001).

Sonae, based in Maia, Portugal, is innovating in ways to change forms of consumption in all its business operations, from wood products and decorative laminates to communication, information technology, leisure, and tourism. For example, in its retail business, the company has involved about 300,000 schoolchildren, approximately 23,000 teachers, and about 2,000 schools in a broad consumer education program. The program, Buy, Weigh, and Measure, is intended to help young people make more informed choices about what they buy and how they dispose of waste. In addition, the company distributes purchasing guides for domestic appliances on how to make better use of the equipment and save water and energy. According to Sonae CEO Belmiro de Azevedo:

> For us, innovation is the best way to make a contribution to changing consumer habits—not by persuading the customer to consume less but to consume differently. At Sonae, we are not fundamentalists. We understand that as far as sustainable development is concerned, there are no radical changes. It is a process that involves cultural changes and changes in people's minds which normally happen by a process of evolution and not revolution.

Sony is innovating to reduce the environmental impacts of its products in the 'user phase'. In the European home, consumer electronics devour 36 TWh (terawatt-hours) of electricity, a figure forecast to grow to 62 TWh by 2010. Sony's SDM-N50 liquid-crystal display (LCD) incorporates a set of features that reduces the energy consumption of the product using it. Sony is also developing technologies and services that contribute to the extension of product lifetime (Holliday and Pepper 2001: 12).

OPP Quimica, part of the Odebrecht Group, one of the largest private corporations in Brazil, produces vinyl resins, caustic soda, chlorine, and other products. It finds that innovation provides a competitive edge in South America's challenging market. 'If we don't continually improve our products and processes, our competitors will do it, and we'll be left behind', says CEO Alvaro Cunha:

44% of our sales are from products we developed in the past five years. For example, a new catalytic process we developed for our polypropylene slurry plant practically eliminated residues, reduced effluent by more than 80% and also lowered our production costs. Each one of these innovations focused on increasing our client's eco-efficiency by providing them with products that boost their productivity.

Information and communication technologies can also play a unique role to help drive sustainable consumption through the use of innovation. Commercial products and services such as mobile phone pre-payment cards, Internet cafés and Internet through television, and mobile phones are rapidly addressing the need for mass-market access to information and communication technology.

New ways to fuel and connect the economy

The automobile offers people personal freedom and mobility, with side-effects such as smog, traffic jams, junkyards, and greenhouse gas (GHG) emissions. As a result, the industry is exploring technologies that radically improve efficiency, reduce auto-motive material content, and eliminate tailpipe emissions. Designers of fuel cells, ultralight bodies, and radical new drive-trains can potentially revolutionize all aspects of the automobile, from manufacturing to after-market services and disposal (Hart and Milstein 1999).

Petroleum-based fuels, which provide more than 96% of transportation energy, are key culprits in GHG emissions. Among alternative fuels being tested are natural gas, electric power, ethanol, methanol, and hydrogen, used in such applications as fuel-cell vehicles, which turn hydrogen and air directly into electricity, emitting only a harmless water-vapor exhaust. Hydrogen is seen as the best long-term prospect, since it can be produced from a variety of new and renewable energy forms. While the technological capacity exists to convert from petroleum-based fuels to alternative energy, meeting the infrastructure costs and creating a market for something new presents greater challenges.

Some leading auto-makers are supporting the move to a hydrogen economy. DaimlerChrysler plans to launch its own fuel-cell technology, first in buses, then in cars, but it does not expect mass production that could contribute significantly to sustainable mobility before 2010 (Mitchell 2001).

Under the auspices of the WBCSD, 11 leading companies—BP, DaimlerChrysler, Ford, General Motors, Michelin Group, Honda, Norsk Hydro, Renault, Shell, Toyota Motor Corporation, and Volkswagen—embarked in 2001 on a $10 million sustainable mobility project. The three-year initiative aims to evaluate the global effects of the land, sea, and air transport industries and to develop a vision of sustainable mobility and pathways for achieving it.

CASE STUDY 51
Toyota
page 213

Information and communication technology (ICT) has come to define the new economy and is a prime contributor to innovation. Investments in ICT, one of the key sectors in the knowledge-based economy, grew twice as fast as GDP between 1987 and 1995, and represented 4% of GDP in OECD countries in 1997 (OECD 2001d).

These communication technologies are spreading and spawning more quickly than anyone ever imagined and are beginning to close what some refer to as 'the digital divide' between rich and poor people and regions. In 1998, according to UNDP, only 12% of Internet users were in non-OECD (i.e. less-developed) countries. By 2000, this proportion had almost doubled, to 21%. The Internet is helping developing countries adopt outside technology faster, and sometimes to develop their own. Indian scientists who have produced a prototype of a battery-powered device called the Simputer, short for 'simple computer', used free, open-source software, which they could not have downloaded without the Internet. From Internet link-ups that allow fishermen in the Bay of Bengal to get weather forecasts from the US Navy's public website to medical research being disseminated cheaply to doctors in Bangladesh, ICT is speeding the pace of development (*Economist* 2001i).

In many Northern countries, companies view e-mail, telecommuting, teleconferencing, and Internet transactions as ways to dramatically reduce overall levels of material and energy consumption. AT&T has been a pioneer in telecommuting and providing office space for workers who spend a lot of time outside the office with customers. Company-wide, AT&T's telework program now includes some 36,000 workers (or more than half of AT&T's US-based managers) who work at home part of the time. AT&T studies have found that employees see telework as a way to have more control over their lives, enhancing productivity and work satisfaction. It estimates its program saves 80,000 tonnes of CO_2 a year in reduced transportation-related emissions (Romm 1999).

Setting a framework

New technologies are key to decoupling economic growth from long-term environmental degradation, but there is no guarantee that innovations will appear when and where they are most needed or at a price that reflects environmental and social externalities associated with their deployment. As we argue in Chapters 2 and 9, governments need to create a policy environment that provides the right signals to innovators and users of technology processes, both domestically and internationally, to fund basic research and to support initiatives in an appropriate manner.

Though we shall probably get into trouble with the US car companies that are WBCSD members, we cannot resist pointing out one framework condition that the Ford Motor Company has publicly worried about: although other consumer choice factors are involved, cheap gas in the USA encourages the purchase of gas-hungry sport utility vehicles (SUVs), resulting in a lot of carbon emissions. In its 2000 corporate citizenship report, *Connecting with Society*, Ford admitted that its SUVs were unsustainable, an admission that sparked widespread media coverage (FMC 2000). SUVs are permitted higher emissions than cars as they are regulated as trucks. At the very least, it is difficult to see how low fuel prices are stimulating innovation toward a more sustainable society.

These issues reflect choices, or framework conditions, made by society. Ford is going beyond the requirements of society in that, in the USA and Europe, the company has implemented emission reductions ahead of regulatory schedules. In the USA, Ford voluntarily upgraded its SUVs and F-series pickup trucks to meet low-emission vehicle standards from one to five years ahead of schedule. Ford also has certified one of its 2001 minivans to the even cleaner Ultra Low Emission Vehicle standards (FMC 2001). In late July 2000, Ford announced a program to improve the average fuel efficiency of its US SUV fleet by 25% over the next five years. We offer this example to show how a company can move beyond the current set of market and regulatory conditions toward a more sustainable path.

In its report, *Policies to Enhance Sustainable Development*, published in June 2001, the OECD (2001e) recommends the following framework conditions for linking science and technology to the goal of sustainable development:

- Provide permanent incentives to innovate and diffuse technologies that support sustainable development objectives by expanding use of market-based approaches in environmental policy. When market-based instruments are not appropriate, use performance standards in preference to measures that prescribe and support specific technologies.

- Support long-term basic research through funding and efforts to build capacity (e.g. development of centers of excellence). Increase research on ecosystems, the value of the services they provide, the long-term impact of human activity on the environment, and the employment effects of new technologies.

- Address unintended environmental and social consequences of technology by separating technology-promotion responsibilities within government from those on health, safety, and environmental protection.

- Support applied research activities when they are clearly in the public interest (e.g. protection of public health and environment) and unlikely to be provided by the public sector by:
  - Cooperating with the private sector to develop and diffuse new technologies
  - Facilitating public–private and inter-firm collaboration with the innovators of cleaner technologies and practices
  - Seeking out opportunities for greater international collaboration on research, especially on issues critical for sustainable development
  - Allowing competition among technologies that can meet the same policy objective and equal access to 'learning opportunities' (e.g. protected niche markets and similar schemes) by foreign as well as domestic investors

A critical foundation for success includes, at a minimum, some combination of unshackled communications systems, sustained support for R&D in both the public and the private sectors, education policies and investments that can help nurture a sufficiently strong skills base to meet local needs, and sufficient regulatory capacity to sustain and manage all these activities. Domestic initiatives need to be supported by far-sighted global initiatives and institutions that help provide resources and lend support for capacity-building in developing countries and that pay more attention to neglected areas, from treating tropical disease to helping developing countries better participate in and benefit from global intellectual property regimes.

CASE STUDY 52
DaimlerChrysler
page 215

Regulation, properly conceived, can in fact promote innovation, resource productivity, and competitiveness, according to Harvard professor Michael Porter (Porter and van der Linde 1995b). This requires governments to focus on outcomes, not technologies, and to avoid prescribing one particular remediation technology. Yet regulations should be strict enough to promote real innovation, says Porter, and should take advantage of market incentives. It is important that the regulatory process is stable and predictable and that industry participates in setting standards from the beginning.

Safe use of new technologies is best ensured by a systematic approach to risk assessment and management. This calls for clear regulatory policies and procedures— not just writing legislation, but implementing, enforcing, and monitoring its provisions. For the introduction of genetically modified crops, the UN recommends in its *Human Development Report 2001* that every country create a biosafety system with clear and coherent guidelines, skilled personnel to guide decision-making, an adequate review process and mechanisms for feedback from farmers and consumers (UNDP 2001). This will be a tall order for many poorer countries.

Innovating in a goldfish bowl

Companies have traditionally been given broad license by society to introduce new products and services. The marketplace has generally been the arbiter of success, supported by regulations to protect the general welfare of society. To preserve the opportunities inherent in this fairly free market system, corporations will have to include the evaluation of a broader set of impacts in their product development processes, including the social, environmental, and economic impacts of their innovations, thereby keeping themselves aligned with public expectations.

A number of companies such as Dow, DuPont, and BASF have introduced systematic processes to examine innovations to see if they reduce environmental and/or social impacts throughout the value chain. According to Jürgen Dormann, when chairman of the board of Aventis SA:

> As a business enterprise, we cannot simply introduce new technologies and innovations and expect that they will be accepted by society. In a society where information flows quickly around the world, businesses need to be connected to their stakeholders and understand how to work both internally and externally to maximize the value of their innovations while reducing the risks and concerns about the use of the technology (Dormann 2000).

Facing dilemmas head-on through open, transparent dialogue among all stakeholders is the only way to ensure that technology will be seen as part of the solution and not part of the problem. Taking a cue from Monsanto's hard-earned lesson,

DuPont formed in 1999 a global biotechnology advisory group for the purpose of guiding the company's actions and helping to create positions on important issues and challenges in the development, testing, and commercialization of new products based on biotechnology. The panel audits the company's progress and reports on a regular basis.

Our 2001 WBCSD report, *Innovation and Technology* (Stevens and Rittenhouse 2001), argued that the changing landscape for business means that the current generation, unlike previous generations, often questions whether technology will continue to solve its problems. Although innovation and creativity are still highly valued, many wonder whether new technologies will bring greater risks than benefits. Society is seizing a more active role in determining the acceptability of new innovations and technologies. Society is questioning the balance between the risks and benefits of new technologies and the value of international conventions on trade or on intellectual property rights. Meanwhile, despite good news on Internet access, the gap between those with access to many new technologies and those without is widening (Stevens and Rittenhouse 2001).

Every technological advance brings benefits and risks, some of which are not easy to predict. Biotechnology, in particular, seems to have served as a lightning rod for public anxieties over new technologies. While biotechnology is being applied in many industrial sectors, its main applications today—and the most controversial—are in the fields of agriculture and pharmaceuticals (UNDP 2001). Over the past decade, scientists' ability to alter the traits of living organisms by directly changing the genetic make-up of those organisms has moved out of the laboratory and into mainstream use. Already many US farmers have found benefits in growing corn, soybeans, and cotton plants that have been genetically modified to be more resistant to pests or certain herbicides. But these developments have ignited a heated debate about the safety, environmental impact, economic effects, and ethics of this new technology. NGOs have challenged business by insisting that sustainable agriculture will best be achieved by leaving control of agriculture in the hands of the farmers (PIFB 2001).

Proponents argue that agricultural biotechnology has the potential to improve the nutritional value of foods, reduce crop losses to pests and drought, slow soil erosion, reduce the use of chemical pesticides, and increase food security in the developing world. They believe biotechnology could enable animals and fish to grow faster and be more disease-resistant, produce trees that grow quickly or with improved pulp and paper characteristics, or alter ornamental trees and grasses to require less care and be more stress- and disease-resistant. While many of these applications are still vague promises, it is clear that the current generation of genetically modified crops is but the first of many possible applications of biotechnology to agriculture. Today's relatively simple gene manipulations are likely to yield to more complex applications as scientific knowledge grows (PIFB 2001).

The OECD Task Force on Biotechnology for Sustainable Industrial Development has declared that 'biotechnology should be on every industrial agenda', and that 'significant environmental benefits can be realized'. It also noted that 'there is an urgent need to reconcile economic, environmental, and societal requirements in a sustainable development framework' (OECD 2001f).

Financing innovation

Public funding plays an important role in financing the development of new technology, but on its own it is never enough. In all advanced countries, public and private research complement each other. Taxpayers' dollars paid for the basic research that underpinned the Internet, but it took private companies to enable users to access the Web. Public laboratories helped sequence the human genome, but it will be profit-driven pharmaceutical firms that turn genomic data into drugs and treatments. In the same way, private equity or venture capital funds will help pave the way for innovative technology that contributes to sustainable development.

SAM Sustainable Asset Management of Zurich is one of the leaders in the field of private equity directed at sustainability. In 2000 and 2001 it launched two private equity funds in the areas of emerging energy, resource productivity, and healthy nutrition because it believes that these sectors will benefit from sustainability trends and that the returns will be attractive. The first fund, SAM Sustainability Private Equity LP, closed at $54 million in October 2001; the second fund, SAM Private Equity Energy Fund LP, closed in December 2001 at $69 million. The launch of the energy fund was based on 'very strong demand from energy companies wishing to gain access to European emerging energy technologies through a venture capital fund', says Gina Domanig, head of private equity at SAM.

The companies in which the funds were invested are:

- Evergreen Solar, a Boston-based developer and manufacturer of photo-voltaic modules

- CellTech Inc., also based in Boston, working on the development of novel solid-oxide fuel-cell technologies

- PowerZyme Inc. of Princeton, New Jersey, developing a proton-exchange membrane (PEM) fuel cell

- ZOXY AG, a German company, based near Stuttgart, that developed a zinc oxide cell that can be both mechanically and electrically recharged

- Oxford Natural Products plc, based near Oxford, England, a phyto-pharma-ceutical company

- AgraQuest Inc. of Davis, California, developing, manufacturing, and market-ing natural pesticide products for farm, home, and public pest management

CASE STUDY 53
Swiss Re
page 215

Channeling private equity into technological innovation geared toward sustain-ability is 'clearly a growing market', says Domanig:

> I believe it is driven by several factors including increased investor interest and asset allocation in sustainability, and industrial strategic interest coincid-ing with sustainability thrusts (e.g. emerging energy). Private funding is a necessary spur to technological development: relative to public financing entities, venture capitalists are much more demanding. For example, we tend to press the companies for commercialization milestones and closely monitor and support their progress, which requires very close working relationships with the portfolio companies.

In the USA, people with good ideas have usually been able to find the cash to put them into practice. In many developing countries, however, science is almost entirely state-funded. In the Philippines, for example, public spending on R&D accounts for 98% of total such spending. In the developing countries that have caught up fastest, private investment has played a crucial role. As capital flows more freely across borders, developing-world entrepreneurs can increasingly tap into the savings of rich countries, and some developing countries are copying aspects of Western capital markets. Gina Domanig analyzes the striking transformation in South Korea: in the 1970s only a fifth of Korean R&D was privately financed; now the proportion is four-fifths. The Asian economic crisis of 1997 prompted a further shake-up. Before then, most private R&D was done within huge conglomerates, or *chaebol*, that were financed by bank loans. Lenders assumed that the government would never let the biggest *chaebol* fail and so let them over-borrow. Small firms, meanwhile, found it almost impossible to raise money.

In 1997 South Korea nearly defaulted. The most indebted *chaebol* went bankrupt and were broken up. Those that were left realized they had to change. They cut their workforces and their debts and started outsourcing more high-technology work to small companies. At the same time, the government rushed to stimulate high-technology start-ups. Hefty tax breaks and subsidies for venture capital created a new market, and venture capital investments shot up from $1 million in 1995 to $65 million in 2000. *Chaebol* employees left what they had always assumed were jobs for life to design and market computer games. New firms scurried to list on Kosdaq, the Korean Nasdaq, whose market capitalism soared from $7 billion in March 1999 to $113 billion a year later, before Kosdaq slumped at the same time as Nasdaq.

Industrialized and developing countries will continue to take advantage of private capital wherever and whenever possible to further their drive toward greater techno-logical innovation. Backed by funds that put a priority on healthy returns for the investor *and* the planet, sustainability-linked innovation should have a rosy future.

Developing-world perspective

The voice of the South has sometimes been lost in the furious battles in the North over technological innovations. For example, public opposition to agricultural biotechnology in industrial countries could rob developing countries of the fruits of genetic research that are vital to their survival.

Southern farmers need crops that resist drought, salt, and pests and that have high nutritional levels. Southern scientists need help with setting up safety and testing regimes, and they need access to germplasm so that they can breed crops for local farming conditions. The race by corporations, encouraged by governments, to lock rights to germplasm away as much as possible makes it hard for developing nations to get the benefits of genetic modification and other crop innovation. Biotechnology multinationals could do more to pass along those IPRs (intellectual property rights) that they are not using to developing nations that need the technology. In fact, the Rockefeller Foundation is working with several biotechnology companies to get their

IPRs affordably into the hands of poor Southern farmers. The fierce debate over GM crops is also making Northern public-sector laboratories shy about developing these technologies as public goods.

Another approach is the decentralization of innovation into cooperative efforts with scientists from developing countries themselves. The Center for the Application of Molecular Biology to International Agriculture (CAMBIA), in Canberra, Australia, has drawn together 40 researchers from around the world and is providing on a not-for-profit basis tools that enable the development of food crops with features of value in challenging agricultural regimes.

Developing countries have distinct concerns about and interests in the biotechnological revolution. Some have feared that biotechnology could displace their traditional products: for example, by using tissue culture to make low-cost laboratory-grown substitutes for such things as gum arabic and vanilla. Others have wanted to use new tools to raise productivity, reduce chronic malnutrition, and convert their abundant bio-resources into value-added products.

A number of Southern voices are calling for a chance to deliver their own opinions on agricultural biotechnology. They include international food and crop genetics expert M.S. Swaminathan of India:

> We have uncommon opportunities today to enlist technology as an ally in the movement for economic and gender equity. Recent advances in biotechnology and space and information technologies are helping to initiate an evergreen revolution capable of enabling small farm families to achieve sustainable advances in productivity and profitability per unit of land, time, labor, and capital. The new genetics, involving molecular mapping and modification, is a powerful tool for fostering ecofarming as well as for enhancing the productivity of rainfed and saline soils. Genes have been transferred by scientists in India from *Amaranthus* to the potato for improving protein quality and from mangroves to annual crops for imparting tolerance to salinity. Mapping based on geographic information systems and progress in short- and medium-term weather forecasting, coupled with advanced markets and pricing information, are helping farmers strike a proper balance between land use and ecological, meteorological, and marketing factors (UNDP 2001: 75).

The *Human Development Report 2001* (UNDP 2001) quotes Nigeria's minister of agriculture and rural development, Adamu Bello:

> Agricultural biotechnology, whereby seeds are enhanced to instill herbicide tolerance or provide resistance to insects and disease, holds great promise for Africa . . . We don't want to be denied this technology because of a misguided notion that we don't understand the dangers or the future consequence.

The evidence that technology helps development is strong. The decline in mortality rates that took more than 150 years in the now-developed world took only 40 years in the developing world, in large part part because of the use of antibiotics and vaccines. Technological innovations in plant breeding, fertilizers, and pesticides have doubled the world's cereal output in a mere 40 years, compared with the 1,000 years it took English wheat yields to quadruple. More recently, the development of oral rehydration packets, a simple solution of sugar and salt that increases the absorption of liquids, has cut the cost of treating diarrhea and has saved millions of lives (*Economist* 2001a).

We discussed in Chapter 1 the difficulties that developing countries have with IPR regimes. In terms of innovation, there are home-grown and international examples of the South benefiting from IPRs. In India, the Honey Bee network, run by the Society for Research and Initiatives for Sustainable Technology and Institutions (SRISTI), aims to share people's knowledge while making sure they do not become any poorer by sharing. The group tries to ensure that when people's knowledge is documented they will not remain anonymous, that there will be cross-pollination through local language databases accessible to them, and that they will share in any wealth generated through added value or otherwise. During the past 12 years, the Honey Bee network, under the auspices of SRISTI, has documented more than 12,000 innovations, including small devices, herbal pesticides, veterinary medicines, new plant vaccines, agronomic practices, and other products. These have been based either on traditional knowledge or contemporary research, primarily from India, but also from all parts of the world (Gupta 2001).

In an attempt to share intellectual resources between the developed and developing world, ten leading pharmaceutical companies, the Wellcome Trust (a private charity), and several academic centers formed the SNP Consortium in April 1999. The goal is to create and make publicly available a high-quality map of single nucleotide polymorphisms (SNPs) of the human genome. SNPs are places in the genetic code where individual variations take place. These variations hold the clue to genetic predispositions for various diseases and thus are extremely important in the attempt to find new cures. By making the SNP map publicly available, the pace of discovery should be faster than if any company tried to hoard the information for itself.

The WBCSD is sponsoring a broad dialogue involving global experts from business and the public sector to determine new approaches to the protection of intellectual property in the biotechnology sector. This study focuses on the disparities between developed and developing countries in current IPR regimes.

In April 2000 Monsanto announced that it had come up with a working draft of the genetic structure of rice—the first time a crop genome had been described in such detail. Instead of keeping this commercial asset to themselves, executives said they had decided to make the data, a key tool in the drive to develop high-yielding rice varieties, freely available. Scientists roundly applauded the move as unprecedented. The offer did not come cheap. Monsanto will not reveal how much it spent establishing the 'working draft' of the rice genome, but researchers estimate the cost at between $20 million and $50 million. The decision was likely triggered by growing public concern about who 'owns' crucial genetic information, as well as Monsanto's own troubled corporate experience (*Financial Times* 2000a).

Technology is a cross-fertilizer that enables firms to work within diverse partnerships. For example, some telecommunications companies have recognized the benefit of avoiding prohibitively expensive land-lines. Through satellite and radio systems, they are reaching previously unserved rural areas with telecommunications comparable to those found in urban areas. Such wireless systems help to erase differences among regions and nations in access to information, allowing for rural economic development that reduces pressures on urban areas.

Establishing research partnerships between institutions in rich and poor countries is only one of the many areas in which dialogue and partnership are needed to further innovation. It is important to extend the principles of transparency and learning, corporate social responsibility, and eco-efficiency throughout the innovation process.

In April 2002, the sixth Conference of the Parties to the Convention on Biological Diversity adopted the first-ever international guidelines on access to genetic resources and benefit-sharing. Also known as the 'Bonn Guidelines', these aim to facilitate access to genetic resources on mutually agreed terms and on the basis of the country of origin's prior informed consent. The guidelines provide guidance to the parties to support these provisions, including encouraging the disclosure of origin of the genetic resources and associated traditional knowledge, in application for intellectual property rights. Foreign companies, collectors, researchers, and other users of genetic resources must share the benefits with countries of origin and local communities through profits, royalties, scientific collaboration, and training.

Making technology work for sustainable development

In the recent past, technology was viewed as the source of environmental degradation. The challenge is to make new technologies a means by which we can decouple economic growth from environmental degradation (OECD 2001d). Ensuring that new technologies contribute to environmental sustainability requires not only technological innovation but also economic, social, and institutional innovation. New thinking and a receptive public are needed to unleash the ability to learn and in effect use technology to create new resources. For example, it will require more than the invention of new engines to transform car transport. Hydrogen fuel-cell vehicles will CASE STUDY 54 DaimlerChrysler Shell, and Norsk Hydro page 216 not and cannot be widely accepted without major changes in the fuel infrastructure.

Developing countries need the kind of political, social, and economic arrangements that foster innovation if they are to start coming up with inventions of their own. Governments can remove obstacles and push things in the right direction, but, when they start making detailed plans, they tend to come unstuck. Public investment in basic science is useful, for those countries that can afford it, but public investment in developing high-technology products is usually wasteful. Many of the things that governments can do to promote technology are worth doing anyway, from maintaining peace and stability, to improving education, to creating open systems of trade and investment, a sound infrastructure, a sensible approach to intellectual property rights, and a flexible financial system.

However, governments can also spur innovation by working in new ways with companies and other organizations. A new product introduced by Procter & Gamble was conceived in association with leading health authorities and illustrates both a technological product innovation and an institutional innovation from the groups involved. NutriDelight combats the problem of 'hidden hunger' (a popular term for micronutrient deficiency) in developing countries. The product contains GrowthPlus, a patented source of iron, vitamin A, and iodine. Test results from an independent clinical study have shown that the nutrients in NutriDelight help children grow and boost mental alertness and performance. Based on these results, Procter & Gamble formed a strategic alliance with UNICEF and several local government institutions to distribute and test-market NutriDelight in the Philippines (Flisi 2001c).

'Technical innovation alone is not enough to guarantee sustainable solutions', says Alvaro Cunha, CEO of OPP Quimica, a manufacturing company in Brazil:

> Our social structure is in continuous change, particularly in developing countries such as Brazil. Civil society's demands on our environmental and social impact motivates the way in which we innovate. We believe that institutional innovation is the most important kind of innovation. Everything depends on it.

The need for institutions, economics, and social structure to support innovation is underlined in *The Global Competitiveness Report 2000*, which argues that

> Our tests based on the growth experience of the 1990s suggest that sustained high rates of economic growth depend on the ability of a national economy to upgrade technology, either through innovation at home or through the rapid and extensive adoption of technologies developed abroad (Porter *et al.* 2000).

When their institutional, economic, and social capacities are strong, countries are far more able to ensure that technological change becomes a positive force for development. Societies ultimately face choices in the timing and extent of embracing technological change. Given the importance of getting it right and the risks of getting it wrong, countries need to build national policies and need international support, to create the capacity that will enable them to embrace new opportunities.

Toward a better quality of life

The ultimate test to determine if innovations will meet success in the market must become: 'Does it really improve overall quality of life?' If the consuming public more and more asks this question of itself, and finds satisfying answers in what it finds in the marketplace, then society will be on a more sustainable path.

Judging one's quality of life is a very personal thing. Many factors are involved (e.g. food, shelter, clothing, freedom, economic stability, health, safety, security, education, relationships in both one's family and the wider community, sense of purpose, free time, etc.) and individuals need to be able to choose how they balance these factors for themselves. Priorities change constantly.

Business provides many of the products and services individuals draw on to satisfy their personal choices for their own lives. In this way, it plays a significant role in shaping the ways in which people are able to satisfy their personal desires and their quality of life. This means that companies must understand the effects that their products and services have on the quality of life of those who use them or whose lives are affected by them, and this must be done within ever-changing societal contexts.

In 1999 the WBCSD completed a biotechnology scenario project. The project described three potential futures. Under only one scenario—the Biotrust World, where companies joined with NGOs, patient-rights groups, and other stakeholders to create a common agenda on which to build trust among all stakeholders—were the products based on biotechnology successfully introduced. The scenario clearly illustrated that new technologies will turn into sustainable business assets only if they are acceptable to society at large. Eight keys to success emerged:

- Transparency
- Ongoing stakeholder involvement
- Ground rules for risk–benefit analysis
- A global system of safety standards
- Benefits for developing countries as well as for developed countries
- Data protection
- Guidelines for patenting and licensing
- Responsibility for externality costs and other liability issues

The challenge for companies is to find new ways to align innovation with public expectations and to provide a management framework that is based on discussing, deciding, and then delivering sustainable value. Enterprising companies understand that this depends on understanding the evolving nature of society and redefining the relationships they want to build with customers, employees, and suppliers, with governments and with the public at large. Dealing well with these responsibilities takes time, vision, leadership, and courage. According to Robert Craig (2001), vice president of services and best practices, customer fulfillment, at Shell Chemicals, 'Only the adaptable and visionary will survive. The ones that survive and prosper will be those that are more adaptable, more effective, use technology better, and are more customer-focused.'

CASE STUDY 47
Gerling *drinking water on Milos*

The Gerling Sustainable Development Project GmbH (GSDP) is a project development company of the Gerling Group, based in Cologne, Germany. GSDP was established to make sustainable development principles operational: that is, to develop and implement practicable, business-oriented solutions. GSDP helps the Gerling Group to develop new markets while at the same time developing new, sustainable solutions to 21st-century problems.

The Greek island of Milos has some 5,000 permanent inhabitants, and about 85,000 tourists visit the island in the summer months. Water demands and the number of tourists increase annually. The economy of the island is highly dependent both on tourism and on extractive industries. GSDP sought ways to improve water supplies on the island. It chose, as the most sustainable solution, to desalinate sea water and cool the resulting fresh water with an innovative geothermal energy-driven desalination plant.

The project group also worked with the municipality of Milos and the regional government offering technical and administrative assistance to ensure effective integration of the water-supply facility into the grid. GSDP plans to install heating and cooling systems as well as hot water; cooling was previously provided by conventional, fossil fuel-based, electrical systems, which released CO_2 and polluted indoor air.

To guarantee an effective operation and management of the plant on its completion, GSDP founded a privately based company—Milos SA—to take over the planning, construction, owning, and operating of the installations. Currently, people pay an average of $356 per m³ for bottled water. Milos SA will produce the desalinized water at not more than $1.8 per m³. Therefore the total cost for water on Milos will be considerably reduced and the saved money can be used for other purposes.

These innovations should bring several benefits to Milos. Water could be used for irrigation. Groundwater levels should be able to recover, making it harder for sea water to intrude. Water bottles should no longer be needed, easing the island's garbage problems. Appropriate water will be available for such things as watering flowers and filling swimming pools. Household and industrial equipment involving water will be using cleaner water, and thus less money will be needed for maintenance. There should be more jobs and a generally improved quality of life all around.

The Milos project is innovative and very attractive from a technological perspective. Only a small proportion of the geothermal utilization schemes applied on a worldwide scale to date are combining different technologies in an energy-efficient and cost-effective way.

GSDP plans to replicate the project on at least four other islands in the region. These projects will begin by producing drinking water and then move on to producing cleaner energy. The new projects should benefit from the experience and contacts gained on Milos. Several areas in the Mediterranean, and elsewhere, lack fresh water but have geothermal energy possibilities and could make use of the innovative technology that is being developed and tested within the GSDP project.

CASE STUDY 48
DuPont *'zero' targets driving innovation*

Founded in 1802, DuPont is a science company, delivering science-based solutions from operations in 70 countries with 83,000 employees. In its 200-year history the company has undergone several transformations, evolving from an explosives company to a chemical company and now to a science company.

The DuPont mission is to achieve 'sustainable growth', defined as creating shareholder and societal value while reducing the 'ecological footprint' throughout the value chain. Paul Tebo, vice president for safety, health, and environment has been a driving force behind implementing sustainable growth within DuPont. Tebo has been spreading the vision to DuPont businesses worldwide, setting challenging targets based on elimination of all injuries, illnesses, incidents, waste, and emissions throughout the value chain. In short, 'The Goal Is Zero'. The critical aspect of the goal is that businesses must still grow while driving toward 'zero'.

'The Goal Is Zero' thinking impacts on each of DuPont's core strategies, from improving productivity, to increasing knowledge intensity, and, finally, to delivering new products through integrated science. The mission of sustainable growth is creating alignment between business strategies and societal expectations and the 'goal of zero' is driving new innovations within the company.

Innovations include progress on reducing waste and emissions at DuPont sites. A global team developed new technology for the manufacture of Terathane® brand PTMEG, a key raw material for Lycra®. The innovation increased yields, resulting in additional revenues of $4 million while eliminating 2 million kilograms of waste per year.

Another team developed and implemented methods to reduce approximately 3 million pounds of annual releases of HFC-23 through process optimization. The innovation saved $20 million in capital investment and reduced GHG emissions on a CO_2-equivalent basis by 18 billion kilograms. In Asturias, Spain, the Sontora® business determined that second-quality material could be used productively rather than be disposed of as waste. With the assistance of DuPont and some local organizations, a group of unemployed women formed Novatex SA to take the second-quality Sontora® and produce one-time use products for medical and laboratory applications. Novatex is now a stable business with 13 direct and stable jobs for women who previously had difficulties being hired into the local economy, and material that was formerly a waste is now a valuable product.

The real benefit to growth has been in those 'goal of zero' innovations that have gone beyond DuPont sites to include customer impacts. A packaging and industrial polymers team in Europe created a peelable lid system for a packaging application to eliminate solvent emissions from lacquer coatings. This innovative product reduces packaging material and improves taste and odor impartation. As a result of this effort, DuPont has gained a 10% share of the lid market and has reduced more than 1,000 tonnes of methyl acetate solvents per year in Europe. A DuPont of Canada team instituted a new business model with Ford Canada. Instead of selling liters of paint, DuPont sold the painting of cars. Over the four-year term of the program, Ford's emissions were reduced by 50%. A crop protection team established a vision to help the poorest people in the world to continue to grow cotton with less risk to their safety and health. According to official figures in Benin alone, 37 people died from misapplication of the older types of cotton insecticide. In looking to enter this new market, the West African DuPont team developed a safer product that reduced application rates by a factor of 10, designed appropriate packaging and then trained officials, distributors, and farmers on the safe use of the product.

Although the sustainable growth transformation and the attainment of zero goals throughout the whole value chain will take time, already the zero challenge is driving new innovations through the business globally. Many DuPont teams are beginning to recognize the opportunities that meeting zero targets presents, turning sustainability challenges into business opportunities. Similar examples are emerging from every DuPont business. The challenging targets are forcing DuPont businesses to rethink products and approaches and come up with new innovative solutions to drive the sustainable growth transformation.

CASE STUDY 49
Cargill Dow *NatureWorks*

The Dow Chemical Company and Cargill Inc. have formed a stand-alone joint venture, Cargill Dow, to manufacture and market polymers for fibers and packing materials derived entirely from annually renewable resources such as corn.

The patented technology to emerge from Cargill Dow is called NatureWorks. The process begins with natural plant sugars derived from agricultural crops and uses a fermentation process to turn these into lactic acid, a common food additive, followed by refining steps to create the polymers. Cargill Dow can now produce a commercially viable plastic that combines performance and cost-competitiveness with the environmental benefits of a renewable raw material source.

NatureWorks can create a wide range of products that vary in molecular weight and crystallinity and are suitable for a broad range of fiber and packaging applications. Fiber and non-woven applications include clothing, wipes, carpet tiles, diapers, upholstery, and interior and outdoor furnishings; packaging applications include packaging films, food and beverage containers, coated papers, and boards.

Using a renewable feedstock presents several environmental benefits. As an alternative to traditional petroleum-based polymers, NatureWorks uses 20–50% less fossil fuel and releases less CO_2. NatureWorks products fit with all current disposal systems and have the option of being fully compostable in commercial composting facilities. Given the proper infrastructure, NatureWorks products could be recycled back to monomer and remanufactured and re-used as a polymer.

Cargill Dow planned to invest more that $300 million in the business and production facility. The USA production plant in Blair, Nebraska—the first of its kind in the world—came on-stream in late 2001 and has an annual capacity of 140,000 tonnes of polymers.

CASE STUDY 50

Conoco *carbon fibers*

From its beginnings as a supplier of kerosene in the western USA 125 years ago, Conoco has grown into a major, integrated energy company. Today, the company is working to increase the uses of crude oil through the production of carbon fibers, which could change the way things are made in the future.

Conoco's carbon fibers can lead to stronger, lighter, and more durable products, opening the door to non-traditional applications in places where aluminum, cast iron, wood and steel currently are used. In addition to strength, this material has a whole range of other properties, such as ionic, thermal, and electrical conductivity.

Conoco's proprietary carbon-fiber process, 12 years in the making, will produce carbon fiber from 'bottom-of-the-barrel' pitch-based materials, thereby transforming a low-value, low-utility product into a high-value and versatile raw material.

The possibilities for Conoco's carbon fibers are numerous. Whether the application uses polymers, metals, cement, asphalt, or exotic cross-material composites, Conoco's carbon fibers will have the potential to enhance performance. Examples include cell-phone batteries that are smaller, more powerful, and longer-lasting than ever before; car-body panels made from plastics that are strong, corrosion-resistant, and light; pre-cast-concrete panels that are one-third the thickness of today's designs; and 'smart' asphalt that is long-lasting and knows when a vehicle is waiting at a traffic light.

'We are confident that our new carbon-fiber venture will result in value-adding solutions that meet the quality, consistency, and reliability demanded by our customers', says Jim Nokes, Conoco's executive vice president for refining, marketing, supply, and transportation.

Conoco's new carbon fiber business is to be known as Cevolution. The first manufacturing facility, with a capacity of 3,600 tonnes, is scheduled to begin commercial production in early 2002. This prototype plant has undergone extensive evaluation and will continue to do so to ensure that future plants are more efficient and environmentally friendly.

CASE STUDY 51

Toyota *hybrid technology*

Through technological innovation, Toyota Motor Corporation has extended its focus from high quality, mass production, and high efficiency to include next-generation transport systems, with the aim of creating modern vehicles that support and promote sustainable development.

Early in the 1990s, Toyota sought to answer two important questions: 'What are the requirements of motor vehicles for the 21st century?' and 'What sort of vision must Toyota have to meet the challenges of the new era?' To answer these questions, Toyota assembled staff members from various departments to evaluate possible themes for future automobiles, with an eye toward developing a totally new type of vehicle.

The group was driven by the notion that a vehicle for the 21st century must set an example by offering solutions to natural-resource and environmental issues. At the same time, these solutions could not interfere with convenience and comfort. The group also wanted a car that would be fun to drive.

They set a target of a 50% increase in fuel efficiency (1.5 times that of existing vehicles). Akihiro Wada, a Toyota executive vice president at the time who was responsible for the project, felt that this was inadequate: '50% is not good enough. Our fuel efficiency improvement target must be 100% (2.0 times that of existing vehicles).' The team's first plans were drastically changed, as the initial technologies being considered would not be capable of reaching this level. Radical innovation was required.

In January 1994 a fully fledged project began. By the end of 1994 the group realized that a hybrid system that Toyota had been developing in a separate project for many years might provide the power-train for such a new type of car. The team's work was unveiled in October 1995 at the Tokyo Motor Show in the form of a car featuring two power sources: a highly efficient gasoline engine and an advanced electric motor.

However, the project team was still faced with many challenges in attaining the goal of a 100% energy-efficiency improvement. Related technical issues, such as battery performance and power-source management, still had to be improved several-fold. It took two years, numerous test engines, and a great deal of effort before this goal was realized.

By the end of 1997 the Prius hybrid sedan was introduced to the market. Toyota had finally made a car that achieved twice the fuel economy but released only one-tenth the carbon monoxide (CO), hydrocarbon (HC), and nitrogen oxide (NO_x) emissions and only half as much CO_2 of conventional cars in its class.

Despite its precedent-setting hybrid technologies, the Prius, now sold in Japan and several other markets worldwide, looks like a conventional car and comes with a price tag similar to that of many popular cars. At its heart is the Toyota Hybrid System (THS), which features an efficient gasoline engine and an advanced battery-run electric motor. One or both are used to maximize fuel efficiency and minimize emissions, depending on driving conditions. The Prius never needs to be plugged in because the THS diverts output from the generator to recharge the battery whenever it is low. Also, a regenerative braking system captures excess energy during deceleration or whenever the driver applies the brakes. This recovered energy is also used to recharge the battery.

Toyota is confident that hybrid technologies hold the key to the future of the car. The company has thus given the development of hybrid systems the highest priority, proof of which can be seen in the release of the Estima Hybrid minivan and the mild hybrid Crown luxury sedan in 2001. However, the company is aware that no single type of vehicle can meet the needs of all, and is therefore pushing ahead with research on a wide range of vehicle-propulsion technologies. Hydrogen-powered fuel cells, which emit only clean water and electricity, may become the ultimate power source of the 21st century. The hybrid technologies developed for and honed in the Prius have great potential to make the fuel cell-powered vehicles of tomorrow even more efficient, ultimately contributing to a more sustainable future.

CASE STUDY 52
DaimlerChrysler *natural-fiber car components*

Ever since launching its first automobiles, Mercedes-Benz has used components made of renewable raw materials in manufacturing its cars. The initial deployment of renewable raw materials at the beginning of the 20th century includes the use of rubber in the production of tires and gaskets and as a binder in padding materials. With the end of World War 2, Mercedes-Benz began to use more and more natural-fiber products in car interiors.

Today, more than 30 components made of renewable raw materials are used in the production of Mercedes C-, E-, and S-Class automobiles. Moreover, tests have shown that natural fibers are suitable both for interior components and for the reinforcement of plastic materials such as external semi-structure trim parts. The engine encapsulations of buses such as Mercedes-Benz Travego and Setra TopClass are made with natural-fiber-reinforced resin. That reduces cost and weight by 5%. The natural-fiber-reinforced engine encapsulations were the first exterior component made by natural fibers worldwide.

Natural fibers such as flax, hemp, kenaf, and sisal provide for great transverse and tensile strength. When embedded in plastic, natural fibers achieve a strength similar to that of fiberglass-reinforced plastics and are thus well suited as a replacement for such plastics.

Through R&D work, DaimlerChrysler has, for the first time, been able to deploy natural fibers within an entire process chain. This includes fiber selection and specification, fiber preparation and processing, component manufacture, materials and component approval, and recycling. This provides opportunities for beneficial technology transfer, as the procedures are transferable to developing countries. The use of locally grown natural fibers for the local production of plastic components is part of the global DaimlerChrysler strategy to increase the local content in different areas of the world.

CASE STUDY 53
Swiss Re *Eco-Portfolio*

The Swiss reinsurance firm, Swiss Re, is offering its investment customers the opportunity to invest in ecologically and socially oriented innovations. Three years ago, Swiss Re started developing a portfolio containing only investments in companies operating in a sustainable manner and creating sustainability-oriented innovations. Today, this portfolio includes 11 direct investments in selected companies and four funds and investment companies with a total of $52 million. Thomas Streiff, head of Swiss Re Group Sustainability Management, states the goal:

> to build up expertise and confidence on a pilot basis before increasingly including sustainability criteria in the normal stock-picking process in the sector-based equity portfolio. But it still has to be significantly demonstrated that in the long run sustainable titles outperform or at least show the same

performance as the traditionally selected ones. Otherwise it will be rather difficult to convince portfolio managers to change their selection approach.

Swiss Re screens the companies selected to ensure that they operate in line with the principles of sustainable development and use technologies and/or manufacture products that provide substantial added value while preserving resources. In assessing companies, equal weight is given to both economic and environmental criteria.

One of the companies that recently passed Swiss Re's screening process is AgraQuest, a US-based company involved in the research, development, production, and marketing of environmentally compatible products for pest control for industry and home use. AgraQuest isolates microbes occurring in nature and tests their effectiveness as pesticides. Micro-organisms suitable for use as pest control are then produced in industrial quantities using a fermentation process.

Swiss Re selected AgraQuest because its competitively priced, natural products provide a viable alternative to chemical pesticides. It has huge market potential in light of the public's increasing environmental awareness, the growing market for organically grown food, and some people's reservations about genetically engineered organisms.

The investment portfolio has included other venture capital projects from companies working in more sustainable ways in both developed and developing countries. Apack, for example, is a German firm producing biodegradable packaging material with a potato starch base. The Moroccan company Sunlight Power supplies electricity generated from solar energy to homes in isolated rural areas not connected to the national grid. Evergreen Solar Inc. provides photovoltaic modules to be used in residential, commercial, and industrial applications in developed and developing countries. Citron Holding AG has developed a process to separate and recycle heavy metals which allows companies to move closer to closed-loop raw-material cycles.

CASE STUDY 54

DaimlerChrysler, Shell, and Norsk Hydro
the Iceland experiment

In Reykjavik, Iceland, a grand plan is being put in motion. The proposal of chemistry professor Bragi Arnason is coming to fruition, and Iceland is now on track to becoming the world's first hydrogen economy.

The Icelandic consortium, Vistorka, is teaming up with three large multinationals—DaimlerChrysler, Shell Hydrogen (a business unit of Shell), and Norsk Hydro—to form Icelandic New Energy Ltd (INE). The INE group, comprising business, government, and academic institutions, is looking to turn Arnason's dream into a reality and facilitate Iceland's transition from a fossil-based economy to a non-fossil-based economy. The three participating multinationals all embraced the idea of making a nation a testing ground for hydrogen vehicles and hydrogen refuelling infrastructure, producing hydrogen using electricity from renewable sources.

Pressure from the supply and price of oil and the global efforts to combat climate change, coupled with the opportunities presented from the revolution in hydrogen fuel cells, provide an ideal opportunity for Iceland to undertake this experiment. And Iceland itself provides the ideal location. The island relies heavily on indigenous renewable geothermal and hydroelectric energy, and the entire energy system is reliant on approximately 58% renewable energy sources. Furthermore, Iceland's population is small and technology levels are high. With a population of only 280,000, the majority of which live in the Reykjavik area, and some 180,000 vehicles, Iceland presents an ideal location as a testing ground for the new hydrogen technology.

If Iceland could turn to hydrogen as its main energy carrier, not only could it be independent of imported fossil fuels but also it could easily reach its Kyoto Protocol commitments on CO_2 emissions. The technical, financial, and political communities in Iceland saw this development as a stepping stone toward their ambition of becoming self-sufficient in energy.

A five-phase development schedule has been laid out. The first phase is a fuel-cell bus demonstration and evaluation project, called the Ecological City Transport System (ECTOS). Under ECTOS, a hydrogen fuelling station from Norsk Hydro is to be erected at a Shell Iceland fuel station for hydrogen fuelling of three DaimlerChrysler city buses to be delivered in 2003 and tested for two years in the streets of Reykjavik. The program is funded by the partners, the government of Iceland, and the European Commission.

In the second phase, all Reykjavik city buses are to be replaced with hydrogen vehicles, and consideration will be given to changing all other Icelandic bus fleets to hydrogen. In the third phase, hydrogen-powered private vehicles are to be introduced. In the fourth phase, hydrogen power units for marine vessels will be introduced, and the fifth phase will see a conversion to hydrogen by Iceland's large fishing fleet.

The outcomes could present major implications for the future of hydrogen power globally. Many other countries are increasing their use of renewable energy sources that can also be used to produce hydrogen. The ultimate challenge for these countries, and for Iceland, is to produce hydrogen and establish an infrastructure to deliver it. The Icelandic partners hope to provide a model for the rest of the world.

Reflecting the worth of the Earth

> **The time to consider the policy decisions of climate change is not when the link between greenhouse gases and climate change is conclusively proven, but when the possibility cannot be discounted by the society of which we are a part. We in BP have reached that point.**
>
> *Lord Browne, BP group chief executive*

The market effectively reflects the financial values of goods and services through pricing mechanisms, but in general it is not very good at pricing environmental assets and services such as a stable climate or rich biodiversity and forest cover. In Chapter 2 we discussed ways to improve this fault in terms of framework conditions. In some countries, governmental interest in establishing framework conditions favoring eco-efficiency and conservation is lower now than it was ten years ago at the time of the 1992 Earth Summit—despite a decade's evidence of the benefits of efficiency and conservation of energy and resources. Business and civil-society groups should do more to encourage our political leaders toward the right market frameworks. Many major companies, for example, have come to accept the reality of the impacts of climate change. In some countries, voluntary emission limits, offset schemes, and other forms of corporate voluntary activities are proving effective, allowing companies to move beyond or ahead of regulation.

Market solutions should be used as part of the package of tools against environmental degradation. Not only are they among the most powerful tools available, but, properly structured, they can be among the least painful. They can create economic opportunities to offset economic costs. Furthermore, market-based approaches tap companies' intellectual wherewithal, experience, and competitive drive.

Some policy-makers, with the support of forward-thinking companies, are taking action to extend the boundaries of the market and turn part of the environmental commons into tradable commodities. Policies are beginning to reflect the fact that economic strength and environmental stability are mutually dependent rather than mutually exclusive.

We do not protect what we do not value. Many of nature's resources and services are currently not monetized. Establishing such prices—in ways that do not cut the poor off from crucial resources—could reduce resource waste and pollution. Proper valuation will help us maintain the diversity of species, habitats, and ecosystems, conserve natural resources, preserve the integrity of natural cycles, and prevent the build-up of toxic substances in the environment. High levels of waste and emissions are signs of poor technology, low efficiency, and bad management of resources. Governments that do not establish efficient environmental management regimes— and the more modern, eco-efficient, and competitive technology encouraged by such regimes—are assuring lack of national competitiveness.

Climate change: facing reality

Environmental issues such as climate change are very complex scientifically. However, they are also complex psychologically. We hate to think that, in going about our daily lives, getting from here to there, heating our homes, using fossil fuels to manufacture products, we may be creating a more dangerous and less predictable global climate.

Thus, when 'contrarians' emerge and tell us that there is really nothing to worry about, we tend to want to believe them, even when they lack qualifications and are in opposition to the main body of scientific opinion. They are published by major publishers and reviewed by major journals. We all want to be urged to awake from the bad dream of 'global warming'.

However, many major companies have come to accept the reality of the impacts of climate change, as described by the Intergovernmental Panel on Climate Change (IPCC), which represents most of the qualified climate scientists on the planet.

'The time to consider the policy decisions of climate change is not when the link between greenhouse gases and climate change is conclusively proven, but when the possibility cannot be discounted by the society of which we are a part. We in BP have reached that point,' Lord Browne, group chief executive of BP, declared in a landmark speech in 1997.

Many companies are acting on their belief that, despite all the problems with the Kyoto Protocol, there is an agreed climate treaty in existence, and it will eventually require action from business. The smart companies will be ahead of the game.

According to the IPCC, global average temperature is projected to increase by 1.4–5.8°C over the next century. New scientific evidence from the IPCC (2001a) suggests that most of the warming observed over the past 50 years is attributable to human activities. A continuation of these trends could double the concentration of greenhouse gases by the end of the century, increase temperatures, raise sea levels, and interfere with atmospheric and oceanic circulation. Effects could also include inundation of coastal areas, loss of forests and coral reefs, endangerment of species, reduction in crop yields, impacts on irrigation, higher levels of air pollution, health impacts as a result of heatwaves, and the spread of infectious diseases (IPCC 2001b).

Reports from the National Academy of Science in the USA have similarly concluded that global climate change is happening and that human activities have an impact. However, the US National Research Council notes that there are still several uncertainties:

> The IPCC's conclusion that most of the observed warming of the last 50 years is likely to have been due to the increase in greenhouse gas concentrations accurately reflects the current thinking of the scientific community on this issue. The stated degree of confidence in the IPCC assessment is higher today than it was ten, or even five, years ago, but . . . uncertainty remains because of (1) the level of natural variability inherent in the climate system on time scales of decades to centuries, (2) the questionable ability of models to accurately simulate natural variability on those long time scales and (3) the degree of confidence that can be placed on reconstructions of global mean temperature over the past millennium based on proxy evidence. Despite the uncertainties, there is general agreement that the observed warming is real and particularly strong within the past twenty years. Whether it is consistent with the change that would be expected in response to human activities is dependent upon what assumptions one makes about the time history of atmospheric concentrations of the various forcing agents, particularly aerosols (NRC 2001).

At the 1992 Earth Summit, the UN Framework Convention on Climate Change (UNFCCC) was signed by 154 governments. The main objective of the Convention is the reduction of greenhouse gas emissions in order to avoid dangerous human-induced changes in climate. To achieve this objective, parties to the UNFCCC adopted the Kyoto Protocol in December 1997. The Protocol calls on 38 industrialized countries to reduce CO_2 and other greenhouse gas emissions from the year 2008 to 2012 by an average of 5%, based on 1990 levels. To reach this target, the Protocol allows international trading of emissions and the use of forests and other carbon sinks to remove carbon from the atmosphere. The Kyoto target is a modest one; the IPCC has estimated that global emissions may have to be reduced by 60–70% to avoid dangerous climate change, but it is a step in the right direction.

The details of the Kyoto agreement have been negotiated over the past four years. In March 2001, the USA declared its intention not to ratify the Protocol, objecting among other things to the non-participation of developing countries in the first round of reductions and fearing that ratifying the treaty would hurt the US economy. The remaining parties were able to resolve their differences and come to a broad political agreement on the most contentious issues at a meeting in Bonn in July 2001. The final details of the Bonn agreement were formally adopted at the climate change meeting in Marrakech, Morocco, in November 2001. Some diplomats predicted that the treaty would be ratified during 2002.

Progressive business leaders are looking to stay ahead of the curve by moving quickly and decisively to address climate change—a problem that many companies expect will most certainly affect their bottom lines. They are choosing to address climate change through voluntary emission limits, offset schemes, internal trading, and other forms of corporate voluntary activity that allow them to make use of market mechanisms to move beyond or ahead of regulation. Not only are market solutions among the most powerful tools available but, properly structured, they can be among the least painful. They can create economic opportunities to offset economic costs. And market-based approaches tap companies' intellectual wherewithal, experience, and competitive drive.

In November 2001, Lafarge of France, the world's largest cement producer, pledged to cut its global CO_2 emissions by 15% from 1990 levels by 2010. This voluntary commitment was the first from the high-emission cement sector and was brokered by the environmental group WWF as part of its 'conservation partnership' with Lafarge. The company plans to achieve the reductions through improved energy efficiency, increased use of waste fuels, and by replacing limestone in cement production with industrial waste products such as steel slag and fly ash wherever possible (*ENDSED* 2001). According to chairman and CEO Bertrand Collomb:

> We are convinced that a global industrial group can only continue to be successful if it operates within the framework of sustainable development with a genuine concern for the environment. This commitment will help Lafarge to prepare for a future carbon-constrained world (Lafarge 2001).

In September 1998 BP, in an initiative with the Environmental Defense Fund (EDF), opened an internal system for trading greenhouse gas (GHG) emissions. In doing so, the company inaugurated internal trading of CO_2 emissions well before climate change negotiators have worked out global permit-trading rules. In the BP program, a flexible market-based mechanism allows individual business units to take competitive cost-cutting measures addressing climate change issues as a precautionary measure. BP's goal is to reduce the company's global GHG emissions by 10% below 1990 baseline levels by 2010. In addition, BP intends to increase its solar energy tenfold by 2010; BP Solar is already the world's largest solar energy company.

Shell has also announced its recognition of climate change treaty realities and a commitment to pump substantial amounts of money into renewable energy. For Shell, which emitted 100 million tonnes of GHGs in the year 2000, any constraints on carbon emissions will most certainly raise the cost of its operations. 'Those constraints will also affect the way customers use our products', says Aidan Murphy, former head of Global Climate Change at Shell; 'Given these factors, it would be insufficient to ignore the risk, and it would not serve our shareholders well' (in Brown 2001).

CASE STUDY 55
Shell
page 236

Ontario Power Generation, a major Ontario-based electricity generator, has taken advantage of an emissions-reduction trading program to offset an increase in its level of fossil fuel use. Also in Canada, Suncor Energy Inc. announced in January 2000 it was investing $100 million in alternative and renewable energy while pledging to cut emission levels for its Canadian operations to 6% below 1990 levels (Suncor 2001). TransAlta, a Canadian integrated energy company, proposed in March 2001 to reduce its net emissions of GHGs in Canada to zero by 2024. It has already reduced its emissions in Canada by more than three million tonnes below 1990 levels (TransAlta 2001).

CASE STUDY 56
Ontario Power
Generation
page 237

Despite the US government's hostility toward the Kyoto Protocol, many US companies have made their own commitments to reducing GHG emissions. DuPont, for example, has committed to reducing its GHG emissions by 65% from a 1990 base, and by 2000 had already cut them by 60%.

Case studies of six international companies published in November 2001 by the Washington-based Pew Center on Global Climate Change (Margolick and Russell

2001) shows that big companies are increasingly setting and achieving tight targets for reducing GHG emissions or the use of energy—often stricter than those contained in the Kyoto Protocol on global warming. Those studied were ABB Inc., Entergy Corp., IBM, Shell Oil Co., Toyota Manufacturing North America, and United Technologies Corp., which together emit as the same amount of GHGs as Argentina:

> By using energy and other resources more efficiently, corporations can reduce production costs and become more competitive . . . At the same time, by creating products that use less energy and produce lower GHG emissions, corporations can differentiate their products in an increasingly environmentally conscious marketplace (Margolick and Russell 2001).

'The aggressive actions on climate change from some US companies may well force the Bush administration to change its stance on Kyoto when the next steps in the Protocol are negotiated around 2005', says Eileen Claussen, president of the Pew Center. She has seen signs of a backlash among members of the US Congress and some parts of US industry. Several senators and congressmen have been pushing for domestic legislation on climate change action. A number of big industrial firms, including even some coal-fired utilities, are concerned that the US stance creates so much short-term uncertainty that they will not be able to make sensible investment decisions in long-lived assets such as power plants. They, too, are pressing for domestic regulation (*Economist* 2001b).

In our view, climate change provides an opportunity and long-term challenge for business to introduce new and emerging technologies and innovative services. Firms that are proactive in emission reductions and/or carbon sequestration should be systematically rewarded to enlist the broadest possible effort. Many of these systems will be developed on a national basis, and will need to ensure that actions, frameworks, and rewards are linked.

Opting for clean development

'The market probably remains the most effective agent for incentivizing sustainable development practices for business', says Wayne Visser, the director of sustainability services for KPMG's operations in South Africa:

> The climate change arena is an excellent example. We believe that the emerging financial market for greenhouse gas emissions trading, largely under the mechanisms of the Kyoto Protocol, will significantly raise the market dynamics of sustainable performance. Likewise, various forms of fiscal intervention (e.g. energy/waste taxes; subsidies for renewables) and financial surety instruments (e.g. environmental rehabilitation trusts) are also extremely efficient market signals that ensure rapid changes in corporate behavior towards sustainable development.

The Kyoto Protocol calls for the establishment of three types of market mechanism, to help the parties to the Protocol achieve their national emissions targets at lowest cost. The first is international emissions trading that allows the industrial (so-called Annex 1) countries to trade up to 10% of their allowable emission level. The second mechanism, joint implementation (JI), offers the Annex 1 nations a way to earn emission credits by funding projects in other Annex 1 countries. A thermal energy project in Romania run by a Swiss entity (company or government) could, for example, qualify as a JI project. The third mechanism, the clean development mechanism (CDM), deals with credits generated by emission-reduction activities of a developed country's entity in a developing country. To be eligible for CDM, a project must be certified by the host country as 'contributing to sustainable development' (IISD 1998b). CDM is conceived as an incentive to industrial nations to export the best clean energy technology. It is expected that CDM will stimulate R&D, create jobs and technology transfer, and allow industrialized countries to gain emissions credits more cheaply than if they had to invest in more efficient plants and machinery at home.

Eugenio Clariond, executive president of Grupo IMSA, an industrial manufacturing company based in Mexico, argues that global climate change presents a significant opportunity for Latin America to improve both environmental and economic development. He says that flexibility mechanisms, and the CDM in particular, will 'open up new avenues of funding and technology transfer among developing countries' (in BCSD–LA 1999).

'The emerging Clean Development Mechanism offers hope for tackling seemingly intractable problems', we argued in the WBCSD's report, *Clean Development Mechanism: Exploring for Solutions through Learning-by-doing*:

> This hope rests upon finding a way to promote foreign investment in developing countries while simultaneously coming to grips with vital issues of sustainable human development and the dangers posed by growing emissions of greenhouse gases (GHGs). However, to achieve this, the CDM will require rules and methodologies that build upon an understanding of how competitive markets and corporate investment strategies can be harnessed to deliver results consistent with the goals of the CDM (WBCSD 2000a).

The prospect of CDM is already leading to innovative ideas. Scientists in Manila are considering the potential of a wind farm that could produce power and be used for carbon credits. Although wind farms are 'just an idea at the moment', they could become a reality with investment through the CDM, says Jose Villarin, the director of the Climate Change Information Center, a research center in Manila:

> Part of the problem is that the CDM doesn't have rules yet . . . But people are willing to take the risk to start these projects before the rules are in place because people want to get involved and trained. We know that if the Philippines delays in this, investment might go elsewhere (*FEER* 2001).

In Brazil, BP is running a small CDM project that contributes to the electricity supply in a rural area by establishing distributed solar systems. The WBCSD is involved in this project by contributing to the high 'first-mover' transaction costs (funded by the UN Foundation) and by disseminating the learnings from that project among all interested stakeholders. The project should also contribute to the development of the 'fast-track' procedure for small-scale CDM projects currently being developed by the UNFCCC by providing first-hand experience of such a project.

In Indonesia, Assistai Semiwan, senior environmental management specialist with the Indonesian state electricity company, is counting on future CDM investments to save a geothermal power plant that has not been economically viable since the Asian economic crisis. She says geothermal power, generated by heat from the country's plentiful volcanoes, 'is very environmentally-friendly, but our problem is very costly. So our geothermal project is not functioning right now. But with CDM money we could bring it back to life' (in *FEER* 2001). Semiwan estimates that the geothermal energy from a single plant could eliminate the 2.5 million tonnes of CO_2 per year produced by a coal-fired plant. In this way, geothermal power could help pay for itself. Other regional projects include an effort to increase the efficiency of a cement kiln in Fiji, develop biofuel cookers for individual homes in Vietnam, and capture methane gas from Indonesian landfills (*FEER* 2001).

The success of trading and offset schemes will depend on companies providing transparent, reliable data about their emissions. To that end, the WBCSD and the World Resources Institute (WRI) have developed jointly the GHG Protocol, a first step toward internationally accepted GHG accounting and reporting practices. The guidelines were developed by the GHG Protocol Initiative, a broad coalition of businesses, NGOs, governments, and intergovernmental organizations. The GHG Protocol is designed to provide GHG information building blocks that can be used as the foundation for meeting the various reporting requirements of national and voluntary GHG schemes. It will also help to minimize the cost of GHG reporting by providing practical guidelines to help companies understand, calculate, and manage their GHG emissions (WBCSD 2001b).

The GHG Protocol will build on already-existing material and best practice and will not attempt to reinvent the wheel. The overall goal is to develop straightforward and credible accounting and reporting standards and guidance for project-based reductions that keep transaction costs at a minimum. For companies, there are two main categories of calculation tools: cross-sector tools and sector-specific tools. Most companies need to apply more than one calculation tool to cover their GHG sources. For example, to calculate GHG emissions from an aluminum smelter, the company would use the calculation tools for (a) aluminum production, (b) stationary combustion (for any import of electricity, and generation of energy on-site), and (c) mobile combustion for transportation of materials, and employee business travel (WBCSD/WRI 2001).

'By applying the GHG Protocol standards, companies can significantly improve the comparability, credibility, and reliability of reported GHG data, and thereby increase the utility of that data. The Protocol will help companies better understand their own position as regulatory programs are debated and developed', says Janet Ranganathan of the WRI (in WBCSD 2001c).

Creating a carbon market

By applying sound market principles, companies can reduce carbon emissions extremely efficiently through trading. Richard Sandor is an economist who pioneered the spot and futures markets in sulfur dioxide emissions for the Chicago Board of Trade. During 2002, Sandor plans to launch the Chicago Climate Exchange (CCX), a voluntary regional GHG trading program. BP, DuPont, and Ford are among the companies participating in the design phase. The scheme will include several energy, agricultural, forest product, and service companies in seven states in the Midwest, together representing 19% of GHG emissions in the region. The companies have agreed to a voluntary cap starting at 2% below 1999 level emissions in 2002, and then ratcheting down 1% annually between 2003 and 2005.

Although the initial focus is regional, the program can extend to all of the USA and can be linked up with other countries. Companies will benefit from participation as they will gain first-mover advantage, help design the protocols, and build managing and trading skills. In addition, companies will increase their reputation among stockholders and potentially gain access to the two trillion US investment dollars that are socially and environmentally screened (*Newsweek* 2001).

Sandor, who currently brokers GHG trades through his company, Environmental Financial Products, predicts that GHG allowances will ultimately constitute 'the biggest commodities market in the world'. A carbon market, explains Sandor, is:

> just a simple adoption of how markets can be used efficiently to allocate resources. Its success will be no different than the success of any market. The market for environmental commodities provides the ability for those who are most specialized in cleaning up the environment to do so (*Newsweek* 2001).

Fortum, the Finnish-based Scandinavian energy company, was among the first companies to experiment with 'external' emissions trading. In 2000 it established a $1.4 million climate fund, aimed at investing in projects to decrease CO_2 emissions in developing countries and in countries with economies in transition. It made its first investment in 2000 by joining the World Bank's Prototype Carbon Fund, which implements the joint projects accepted in the Kyoto Protocol worldwide. Fortum sold 50,000 tonnes of the emission decrease achieved by converting a boiler at its Joensuu, Finland, power plant to a Canadian power company. At the time, it marked the largest emission trade between two continents (Fortum 2000). 'While this is not a huge volume, the project brought us valuable experience in practical implementation of international emissions trading', says president and CEO Mikael Lillius (in Fortum 2000).

Countries and regional governments are moving ahead with their own emissions trading programs for GHGs. The UK government announced in July 2001 the world's first domestic emissions trading scheme with government support of $42 million in 2003–2004 to kick-start the scheme by providing a financial incentive for companies to take on binding emissions targets. In September 2001, DuPont executed the first GHG emission allowance trade, selling 10,000 of its year 2002 GHG emissions allowances to MIECO, a Japanese energy trading and marketing subsidiary of Marubeni Corporation. A leading broker of energy-related products, Natsource, brokered the transaction on a forward basis, as Britain's emissions trading scheme will commence in April 2002 (DuPont 2001).

The International Emissions Trading Association (IETA) was launched in June 1999 to help meet the objectives of the Kyoto Protocol through the establishment of effective systems for market-based approaches. The WBCSD was instrumental in helping to form IETA, a non-profit member organization made up of leading international companies representing a wide variety of private-sector interests. The IETA calls for uniformity in various trading systems to avoid costly divergence (IISD 2001).

CASE STUDY 57
International
Emissions
Trading
Association
page 238

Richard George, CEO and president of Suncor Energy Inc., supports IETA's role as a voice for prospective market participants to ensure design details are resolved to enable an efficient market to develop:

> There is a concern about the ultimate harmonization of national schemes toward development of a truly efficient international market. The creation of the international commodity instruments in the Marrakech accord will assist in aligning national schemes.

The carbon market could generate $10 billion to $15 billion annually, although no one is sure how to set the price of a tonne of carbon credits (all of the six GHGs are converted into CO_2-equivalents; e.g. one tonne of methane is equivalent to 23 tonnes of CO_2 [IPCC 2001a]). George paraphrases Sandor as saying that the development of an international market to trade emissions is 'inevitable and could be standardized and efficient in as little as five to ten years'.

Harnessing the power of technology

A number of companies are working to develop technologies to trap and store CO_2. In July 2001, the US Department of Energy announced plans to spend $25 billion studying methods of capturing carbon gases and storing them in underground geological formations or in terrestrial vegetation such as forests. Its goal is to develop sequestration that costs $10 or less per tonne of carbon; about 30 times less than many options (Houlder 2001b).

BP, Shell, ChevronTexaco, Norsk Hydro, Statoil, and Suncor Energy Inc. (WBCSD 2001d) are six leading energy companies participating in the Carbon Capture Project (CCP), a $20 million joint industry project to research and develop the next generation of CO_2 separation technology and the safe geologic storage of CO_2. Through the CCP, the project partners aim to develop effective methods to capture significant amounts of CO_2 emitted from power generation and industrial sources and store the gas in geologic formations below the Earth's surface. If successful, the project could lead to a notable reduction in GHG emissions across a wide range of industries, not just the energy sector (Suncor 2001).

In addition to renewable energies and energy efficiency, climate-friendly technologies include underground CO_2 storage, also referred to as carbon sequestration. The first step in carbon management is to 'capture' or separate emitted CO_2. The captured CO_2 must then be disposed of or stored. Four types of site could be used: fossil-fuel reservoirs such as oilfields, gasfields, or coalbeds; deep saline aquifers; in above-surface commercial applications such as chemical feedstocks; or in greenhouses (Suncor 2001).

Large amounts of cash have been invested in these technologies. The chemical separation of carbon from hydrocarbons is being undertaken or planned by Texaco at 72 sites around the world. Statoil has been injecting about one million tonnes of CO_2 per year since 1996 from the Sleipner West gasfield in the North Sea into deep saline aquifers. BP and Ford have sponsored a $20 million, ten-year research project at Princeton University on carbon sequestration (Suncor 2001).

Work commissioned by the International Energy Agency estimates that depleted oilfields could store 126 billion tonnes of CO_2. Because injecting CO_2 enhances the recovery of oil—about 70 oilfields worldwide already use the technique—this may even become a source of profit (Houlder 2001b).

Carbon sequestration has been endorsed by the US government as a way to address global warming without having to make radical overhauls to existing energy systems. According to US energy secretary Spencer Abraham, 'The large response and significant cost-sharing from the private sector is a clear message that carbon sequestration is an option worth pursuing' (in Houlder 2001b).

Another way to capture carbon is by planting trees. Growing trees 'lock up' CO_2, cleaning the environment and thus reducing global warming. Companies get credit for their contribution to environmental clean-up and, once an acceptable trading system is operating, they can trade the credit for revenue or use it to offset their pollution. An early example of carbon-offset trading through reforestation occurred in September 2001 when a company headed by Richard Sandor, Sustainable Forestry Management, paid two North American Indian tribes in Montana $50,000 for 'carbon-offset' credits for timber they agreed to grow on 250 acres of burned-over mountainside owned and managed by the tribe. At the time, Sandor declared the deal 'a path-breaking international transaction [that shows] how forestation can advance the global carbon market, and help address climate change while improving the socioeconomic conditions of local communities' (Strommes 2001). Such funds are gaining their impetus from the Kyoto Protocol's rules on land-use, land-use change, and forestry projects, which stress that such projects should favorably address the issues of biodiversity, habitat, and socioeconomic and human development.

The Asia-Pacific region is also poised to benefit from the carbon-offset trade market. For example, Vietnam plans to have an additional 5 million ha of forest in the next 20 years. These could serve as carbon sinks to offset carbon emissions in a developed country. Vietnamese foresters are now working with the Australian government to develop improved varieties of trees that can sequester the maximum amount of carbon (*FEER* 2001). According to Sandor:

> One could see a natural role for Asia as a provider of environmental services through reforestation, or land-use changes, such as reducing the methane produced by paddy rice cultivation, and through investments in clean energy technologies in developing countries that don't already have a lot of fossil fuel infrastructure (*FEER* 2001).

Critics, however, say that using carbon sequestration as a solution to climate change relaxes the pressure to reduce the use of fossil fuels. There are questions as well about the effectiveness of the technology and the safety. In a cautious report issued in 2000, Britain's Royal Society warned that planting new forests could even prove counterproductive. Rising temperatures could kill off the forests, releasing their carbon to the atmosphere over a relatively short time. Researchers in Germany found that, despite absorbing carbon in the 1990s, land sinks (such as forests) had a largely neutral effect on carbon emissions in the 1980s. Some researchers and environmental organizations have also expressed concern that storing CO_2 in the deep oceans could have a detrimental effect on marine life and that sudden releases of stored carbon could harm humans.

These are all legitimate concerns, and a lot more research is going to be needed on all forms of carbon sequestration technology. Ultimately, we consider such technologies a bridge to a more carbon-constrained future, a medium-term solution. If the climate change problem becomes overwhelming, we will need all the help we can get. 'We see climate change as a long-term issue', says Richard George, CEO of Suncor Energy Inc. 'We are assuming that we will collectively learn as we go and adapt to any unintended consequences as they arise.'

Ecosystems under threat

Climate change threatens virtually all ecosystems, but many of these systems are also at risk from other pollutants, economic development, and overuse of resources. These include glaciers, coral reefs, islands, polar and alpine ecosystems, cloud forests, mangroves, coastal wetlands, and grasslands. Freshwater resources are also being threatened by climate change, pollution, and overuse. Water supplies and food production in the tropics may be affected, putting 50 million people at greater risk of hunger by 2100, which may result in mass migration and political instability in the regions hardest hit. Rising sea levels could contaminate water supplies with salt. Such threats pose a serious concern, as fresh water is essential for human health, economic productivity, and social development. Although freshwater resources are still globally abundant, they are unevenly distributed across and within countries. One in five people in the world does not have access to safe and affordable drinking water, and half do not have access to adequate sanitation. About one-third of the world's population is estimated to be living in countries suffering medium-high to high water stress, and the proportion is projected to double by 2025 (Cosgrove and Rijsberman 2000).

Forests also provide a wide range of services to society. These include economic benefits (e.g. timber, pulp for paper, cork, rubber), environmental services (e.g. air and water purification, biodiversity, carbon sinks, erosion control, wildlife habitat), and social benefits (such as employment, recreational opportunities, and cultural values) (OECD 2001d). Frequently, however, the services provided by forests are not reflected in the prices of forest products and are not valued or captured by those who live in or near the forest. Instead, forests are often destroyed to make way for agriculture or ranching. Deforestation (forest clearance followed by land-use changes) and forest degradation (depletion of growing stock, without changes in land-use) are the main factors limiting the ability of forests to provide economic and environmental services. The UN Food and Agricultural Organization estimates that forest loss in tropical countries has been averaging over 15 million hectares per year since 1980, although some of this may recover (FAO 1999).

Biodiversity also offers valuable ecosystem services such as climate change mitigation and a future option value such as genetic material for medical use. But human activities are contributing to biodiversity loss through habitat destruction or alteration, the exploitation of wild species, introduction of exotic species, species homogenization, pollution, and global climate change. Estimates of biodiversity loss in the

21st century are reaching historic levels and are projected to reach as high as a 50% loss in current levels of global diversity (Pearce and Moran 1999).

The Convention on Biological Diversity (CBD), which was negotiated at the 1992 Rio Summit with a view to combating these biodiversity losses, has come under criticism by some leading NGOs. The CBD was intended to provide a legal framework for countries to develop policies, strategies, and action plans, but critics have found that it has led to little progress. The Royal Society for the Protection of Birds (RSPB), Europe's largest wildlife conservation organization, has criticized the convention for lack of focus and a tendency to generate bureaucracy and text instead of results. Yet the RSPB, in calling only on governments to make more of the CBD, overlooks the fact that biodiversity presents business with an opportunity to do more for conservation, says Frank Vorhies, director of the IUCN Business and Biodiversity Initiative. Businesses, especially companies with operations in several countries, can play a major role by adopting corporate biodiversity strategies and action plans based on the objectives and priorities of the convention. In fact, he says, the convention provides a level playing field for addressing biodiversity within multinational corporations. He suggests that companies officially endorse or 'ratify' the convention, perhaps by becoming 'partners' to the convention.

The business sector can connect to the biodiversity agenda in different ways. Those industries that use and depend on biodiversity and natural resources, such as agriculture, forestry, fishing, the extractive industries, and the pharmaceutical industry, have, of course, a vested interest in protecting those resources. But, ultimately, all economic activity and development have potential effects on air, water, land use, and on special habitats. It is to these less directly committed companies that the messages of biodiversity protection must be addressed.

Business can play its part in biodiversity protection at the local level with NGOs and the local community, through such activities as:

- Scientific surveys to map and record biodiversity

- Local biodiversity management implementation projects

- Development of acceptable indicators to measure progress

- Trials of reclamation techniques focusing on habitats and ecosystems

- Research on genetic variation, single species, and ecosystems to develop a better understanding of pressures and adaptability (IUCN/WBCSD 1997)

A recognition that biodiversity must be valued and measured is part of the driving force behind specialty chemicals producer ICI's ambitious biodiversity targets. By 2005, all company sites larger than 10 ha or located close to a sensitive biodiversity region will undertake an ecology survey and develop a management plan. This will involve over 50 sites in four continents over the next four years. For ten years, ICI has been running a Nature Link program in which a Nature Link website (www.ici.com/icishe/naturelink) makes available to a global audience data on more than 2,500 species of animals, birds, insects, and plants found around ICI's facilities worldwide. According to Martin Bell of ICI, by pioneering the concept of an 'industrial reserve', the company seeks to demonstrate that biodiversity preservation is the responsibility of business, too, not just governments or NGOs.

The US pharmaceutical giant Bristol-Myers Squibb is making an effort to support biodiversity through its commitment to purchase and preserve biologically diverse land. The company has an acknowledged self-interest: many important pharmaceutical products, including the cancer drug Taxol, are derived from natural plants and organisms. The company therefore supports natural resource stewardship from both a business perspective and an environmental perspective. By the end of 2001 the company had purchased, for the purpose of long-term preservation, biologically diverse land at least equal in area to the total amount of land occupied by its manufacturing operations worldwide. In addition, it will purchase and preserve land at least equal in size to the total area of land used by any new manufacturing facility. Since 1998 Bristol-Myers Squibb has co-sponsored the preservation of biologically diverse land on the outskirts of Brazil's Pantanal National Park. The Pantanal region is one of the world's largest freshwater wetland ecosystems (Bristol-Myers Squibb 2001).

Putting a price on nature

We do not protect what we do not value. Many of nature's resources and services are currently not monetized. Establishing such prices, in ways that do not cut off the poor from crucial resources, could reduce resource waste and pollution. The services of ecological systems and the natural capital stocks that produce them are vital for human health and quality of life. The world economy is completely dependent on ecosystems. Proper valuation will help us maintain the diversity of species, habitats, and ecosystems, conserve natural resources, preserve the integrity of natural cycles, and prevent the build-up of toxic substances in the environment.

According to Robert Costanza et al. (1997), the value of global ecosystems and services to humanity that are effectively not being costed into our market equation is at least $33 trillion per year. The figure, and the science behind it, have been hotly attacked and debated—as being unsubstantiated, too high and too low. Michael Toman of Resources for the Future, who criticized the work harshly, called the $33 trillion figure 'a serious underestimate of infinity' (Nature 1998).

Such figures are often disputed because putting a monetary value on nature's resources and services is extremely difficult. Important gaps exist in understanding the pressures exercised by human activities on terrestrial and marine ecosystems, in valuing a range of ecosystem services, and in quantifying the health implications of various environmental hazards. Risks of serious or irreversible damage call for precaution in policy-making, yet inadequate information on the size of the risks involved— or on the point where critical thresholds are reached—has often complicated decisions about how much 'insurance' (in an economic sense) is justified (OECD 2001d).

In their seminal 1990 book with Markandya, Blueprint for a Green Economy, which they revisited ten years later in Blueprint for a Sustainable Economy, economists Pearce and Barbier argued that the source of most environmental problems lies in the failure of the economic system to take account of the valuable services that environmental products provide for us. The authors called these 'the missing markets'.

According to Pearce and Barbier (2000), 'Economic importance can be demonstrated by placing monetary values on environmental assets and services, values which reflect human preferences, just as if there was a market. This is the process of non-market valuation.'

Non-market valuation matters for several reasons, they argue:

- It helps to demonstrate the economic importance of environmental assets, placing them in the same political dialogue as economic assets.

- It reminds us that economic activity may increase or decrease those assets. If it decreases them, then it reduces the asset base that supports the whole process of creating human wellbeing. This is the essence of unsustainable development, running down the asset bases on which future well-being depends.

- It helps to avoid the most common reasons for environmental degradation: namely, the failure of environmental services or assets to win in the marketplace with competing economic activity. If land has an economic value for housing, but no apparent economic value in conservation, it is hardly surprising that we develop the land for housing and ignore the impact on the environment.

- It points us toward solutions. If we know what the economic value of an environmental asset is, we can work toward the capture of that value by creating a market for the asset. If we know how people value an asset, we can, for example, find the price that could be charged to those people for using the asset. That price translates to a revenue that, in turn, can be used, at least in part, to finance conservation.

If environmental resources have no market, there are no price signals to alert us to their scarcity or to induce discovery, substitution, and technological change. To the slash-and-burn farmer, there is little benefit in pointing to the many ecological functions served by the forest if he or she receives no income, in cash or kind, from those services. The fact that the trees act as a store of carbon is of no immediate consequence to the farmer, even though it is a matter of great concern in the context of climate change (Pearce and Barbier 2000).

Fresh water is an apt illustration of the importance of non-market valuation (Grosser and Walker 2000). When water is free (from well, river, or pipe), consumers do not place a value on its efficient use or conservation. Eliminating subsidies, and pricing water to cover infrastructure investment, treatment, and delivery costs will go a long way to getting the prices right. This is yet another way of reversing the prevailing externalization of costs. Once the price is right, municipalities and entrepreneurs will begin to invest in new and better ways to provide water services. Customers will be encouraged to save water and save money (Holliday and Pepper 2001). Ways to ensure that the poor have access to water can be found. 'The most important policy recommendation we can make is for the adoption of full-cost pricing of water use and services. It will be the basis for promoting conservation, reducing waste, and mobilizing resources', concluded the World Water Forum in March 2000 (in Holliday and Pepper 2001: 38). 'Water is finite, but demand for water services continues to increase. Equitable water pricing with adequate protection for the poor is one mech-anism to encourage conservation and sustainable use of this most basic of commodi-ties' (in Holliday and Pepper 2001: 38).

> Water is provided free by nature. However, the infrastructure required to capture, clean, deliver, and treat water must be provided by organizations, whether private or public. If the users do not pay, service declines and the poor must turn to more expensive alternative sources (e.g. bottled water) to meet their basic needs (in Holliday and Pepper 2001: 38).

Klaus Töpfer, secretary general of UNEP, believes that full-cost pricing of water will spur technological progress:

> In market economies, technological progress never comes like manna from heaven. It's always about overcoming bottlenecks. We're facing a bottle-neck for development in the declining availability and access to ground-water, and that situation will make both industry and government adopt better water-saving technologies and it will stimulate the demand side to be more aware of limited resources.

Töpfer also points out that water is not only an economic but also a social good. There has to be sufficient quantity of a safe water supply to fulfill the needs of the very poor, who are already paying high prices for water that is often of poor quality. The solution must take into account not only economic instruments but also the social value of water. This will require the political courage to remove or shift subsidies:

> We are subsidizing right now many segments of society which are not all dependent on subsidies while neglecting to help the poorest who do need it. We need a very transparent system of costs and better-negotiated and transparent solutions.

Shaping the right policies

Once we know an environmental asset has economic importance, it is possible to focus on the policies to conserve it. But policies are not effective unless they address the root cause of the problem, which often lies in the structure of the economic system. Hence, economic solutions are required for environmental problems. Policies based on economic incentives give stakeholders financial incentive to conserve rather than destroy. Some steps to create such an economy are listed in Figure 12 (pages 234-35).

Business will be able to contribute greatly in minimizing bureaucracy as we work toward an effective solution for slowing climate change. Business and industry have the key skills and resources to make progress in reducing GHG emissions and provide more energy-efficient consumer products. However, the mechanisms to encourage such initiatives must be efficient and function with low transaction costs. In particular we need:

- Efficient markets with consistent definitions and a compliance system for all three Kyoto mechanisms (CDM, JI and emissions trading)

- Rules and procedures for the mechanisms that are clear, transparent, and simple, to keep transaction costs low and not inhibit worthy projects: that is
  - Ensure low bureaucratic barriers and minimal time delays on CDM and JI projects
  - Ensure full fungibility between the different certificates (which means allowing emission units under all three mechanisms to be treated equally)
  - Provide for sellers' liability
  - Allow private entities to participate directly in all mechanisms

- To avoid two sets of rules (one for the Kyoto parties and one for the USA)

Processes to help bridge the EU–USA divide should be given priority (WBCSD 2001e).

Governments can encourage the use of the CDM through domestic incentives such as tax enhancements for companies that are early movers in the CDM and by setting up registration and accounting systems for the import of certified emission reductions to count against national targets (WBCSD 2001e).

Some policy-makers, with the support of forward-thinking companies, are taking action to extend the boundaries of the market and turn part of the environmental commons into tradable commodities. Polices are beginning to reflect the fact that economic strength and environmental stability are mutually dependent rather than mutually exclusive. For example, tradable or transferable permits are now extending beyond the fields of local and regional air pollution control and regulation of fisheries to other areas. The most obvious examples are tradable permits for CO_2 and other GHGs, but the system is also being applied in the areas of municipal waste management, green energy development, and water.

A number of countries, including Australia, Belgium, Denmark, Italy, the Netherlands, and the USA, are introducing tradable renewable energy certificates (TRECs) as policy instruments to support the development of alternative renewable energy sources in competitive electricity markets. Certificates are issued as a proof that a certain amount of electricity has been generated from renewable sources and supplied to the grid by eligible electricity producers. Therefore, suppliers can buy TRECs from renewable energy producers without having to produce renewable energy themselves (Baron 2001).

A further scheme to combat climate change is the Climate Neutral Network. In this Network, a group of companies are working to reduce GHG emissions.

CASE STUDY 58
Climate Neutral
Network
page 239

With or without government policies in place, business is moving ahead to make its own deals in the pursuit of sustainable development. In November 2001, Hidro-electrica Papeles Elaborados (HPE), a hydroelectric owner and operator in Guatemala, and Nuon, the largest electricity distributor in the Netherlands, completed one of the first international green certificate transactions involving assets in a developing country. It was also one of the largest green certificate transactions to date, with Nuon committing to purchase 100% of the environmental benefits of HPE for the next ten years. The certificates were being transacted from HPE's 8.2 MW run of the river Poza Verde facility in Guatemala and will be used by Nuon as part of its green energy products (EcoSecurities 2001).

What				
● Define the system to be protected	● Define a standard for performance measurement		● Create one or several exchanges to trade these licenses; exchanges can report transaction volume and prices; options and futures can also enhance the trade
● Within the boundaries of this system, establish a protection objective	● The measurement should provide a quality charac-terization of the state of the system	● Create a license to operate that is legally transferable	

Steps	OBJECTIVE	MEASUREMENT	PROPERTY	EXCHANGE
Who	● The performance objective is defined by stakeholder dialogue ● A performance framework is set by voluntary programs or covenants between government, the business sectors concerned, and key stakeholders	● Using the set measurement standard, all relevant actors report progress toward their performance commitments	● Government recognizes and guarantees ownership of such licenses	● A private or public initiative

Example

Carbon sequestration market	National greenhouse gas emission reduction targets	International measurement standards for greenhouse gases	Corporate internal trading schemes	The Chicago Climate Exchange

Figure 12 **PRACTICAL STEPS TO CREATE AN EFFICIENT MARKET THAT DRIVES ENVIRONMENTAL PERFORMANCE**

Source: Holliday and Pepper 2001: 38-39

CAP AND TRADE	PENALTY	ARBITRAGE	NO FREE-RIDERS	COST-EFFICIENCY
• Allocate operational licenses to participants in the system • Total license distribution cannot exceed the protection objective—the cap	• Set a penalty for non-performance • It must be at least related to expected cost of remediation if the protection objective is missed	• Agents have the information and ability to simultaneously purchase and sell licenses in different markets to take advantage of the price differentials • They can also put and call options to trade	• Enforce measurement, reporting, and performance compliance throughout the system to motivate progress through a license-trading scheme	• Drive aggregated costs below the alternative costs in order to mitigate and compensate failure to perform
• If a baseline performance is known for a given period, licenses can be allocated pro rata to baseline performance contribution • Or the public authority raises revenue through an auction of licenses Kyoto Protocol or similar regulation process	• Through periodic reporting requirements or audits a public authority checks compliance • Non-compliers are subject to the penalty and are required to provide compensation	• **Sellers** of licenses expect a higher return from the sale than the discounted cost to operate below their performance allocation • **Buyers** can be expected to enter the market when they have difficulty operating within their performance allocation (due to business growth or efficiency problems); buyers can expect the price of additional licenses to be below the penalty for non-performance	• Government eliminates unfair competition from non-compliers	• Compliers search for the lowest-priced licenses • Innovators maximize their performance at low capital costs so they can release and sell licenses

'These kinds of transactions have the potential to greatly increase market liquidity for environmental values. They will help accelerate renewable energy penetration and convince governments that global carbon reduction targets are achievable', says Jack MacDonald, head of brokerage for EcoSecurities Ltd, which brokered the transaction along with another environmental finance firm, E&Co.

Richard George of Suncor Energy Inc. is confident that, once the rules and infra-structure are established for an international market in GHGs,

> the market will quickly develop and efficiencies will evolve as we've seen with all other commodity markets. Transaction costs will always be a cause for some concern by industry, and getting the balance right between eco-nomic efficiency and environmental effectiveness in the program design is critically important. However, it appears that government negotiators are trying to be conscious of these issues.

BP's Lord Browne notes that:

> Climate change is a matter of public policy—for decision by governments on the basis of political judgements which have to be acceptable to populations and electorates . . . But business can't be passive in the process. We must be alive to our own responsibilities. It isn't enough to ask for acts of leadership from politicians. We can't solve the whole problem but we can make a contribution, and we can test, within our own systems, some of the processes which might have a wider public application (Browne 1997b).

CASE STUDY 55

Shell *the cost of carbon story*

At the heart of the climate change debate lies the issue of CO_2 produced by human activities. It is released into the atmosphere in abundance by individual consumers and industry, mainly as part of flu gas emissions from cars, home heating units, power plants, and factories and is believed to be upsetting the balance in the natural CO_2 cycle and so affecting the global climate. Other greenhouse gases (GHGs) can be equated to CO_2 via a GHG potential ratio (e.g. for methane it is over 20). The concepts put forward below apply equally to them as well.

Industry is being asked to curtail these releases, both directly in its own facilities and indirectly as a result of the energy required by its customers. These considerations are central to Shell's approach to climate change. For example, the company has reduced its own emissions by 10% against 1990 levels and is developing renewable energy and hydrogen businesses.

Reducing CO_2 emissions is not an intractable problem but it is nevertheless a complex one. As a start, a yardstick is required to measure progress, to prioritize efforts, and to give economic meaning to the undertaking. This yardstick is the 'cost of carbon'. For a facility, the cost of abating one tonne of CO_2 can be calculated. This may be the result of a cut in overall production, in which case the abatement cost is directly linked to the loss of production margin. Alternatively, investment may be required at the facility to achieve the result. The capital requirement is now the driver.

In both examples, the cost of abating a tonne of CO_2 production can be calculated, hence giving a cost of carbon (abatement).

Calculating the cost of abatement provides only one side of the equation. Although it can immediately help a company to prioritize projects, it does not put them into any economic context and tell the company how far up its cost curve of abatement measures it should go. For example, should a company do projects with CO_2 costed at $5 per tonne? Should it stop at $10 per tonne or $20 or higher?

The economic context comes from an external driver. This could be a target, imposed either by government or by voluntary acceptance, with penalties for missing it. Alternatively, it could come in the form of an energy usage or emissions tax, such as the Climate Change Levy in the United Kingdom. Either of these will allow the economic benefit of CO_2 abatement to be calculated. It is then possible to put abatement costs into context. However, this will result in significantly different figures for different economic and social circumstances, driven by factors such as the tax regime, the targets applied, and the existing state of the industrial base.

A necessary additional dimension can be achieved by overlaying the equation with a trading system. The purchase and sale of carbon allowances will result in the same per unit cost of abatement for everyone. Abatement can be achieved by internal investment or the purchase of the necessary allowances from a single market. From another perspective, at a given market price, investment (followed by the sale of allowances) may be encouraged where it might not have otherwise taken place. The sale of allowances provides a net inflow of cash to that investor.

Shell has been working in such an environment for some time now. Shell's investment decisions are guided by an expected future cost of carbon and it has been piloting internal emissions trading between several business units. The GHG emission target gives Shell the economic driver to move forward.

Shell is beginning to externalize this approach. It has established an environmental products trading team within its global trading business. That team is starting to use the developing external carbon markets to foster additional investment within the company to further reduce GHG emissions. In cooperation with the company's global business and technical consultancy, the team will be spearheading Shell's use of the clean development mechanism (CDM) in developing countries. Each of these initiatives is driven by Shell's use and understanding of carbon economics. Investment and development efforts such as these allow Shell to implement practical solutions to address the climate change issue.

CASE STUDY 56
Ontario Power Generation
emission-reduction credits trading

The Ontario electricity generator Ontario Power Generation (OPG) made voluntary commitments in the mid-1990s to limit net emissions of GHGs and nitrogen oxides (NO_x) to 26 million tonnes CO_2 and 38,000 tonnes nitric oxide (NO).

To fulfill its obligation to meet electricity demand and to cost-effectively reduce emissions, OPG improved internal efficiencies where possible, invested in technological improvements at the fossil-fueled generating plants and used emission-reduction credits (ERCs) where these proved to be more cost-effective.

An ERC is created by one source that has found a relatively inexpensive way of reducing its emissions below either an actual emissions limit or a regulated or voluntary emissions limit. This reduction is quantified according to a protocol agreed to by participants in the emission-reduction trading market, stakeholders, and regulators and is posted on a publicly accessible registry. This ERC can then be sold to another company, for whom purchasing the credit is more economic than making its own equivalent reduction. The money earned by the first company and saved by the second company can then be used to make further reductions. The result is that overall emission regulations and targets are met or bettered, the environment is improved, and money is saved. The process provides an incentive for companies to make more reductions in response to, or in anticipation of, more demanding regulations and targets.

To meet 2000 voluntary CO_2 and NO emissions commitments, OPG retired 12.6 million tonnes of CO_2 ERCs and 12,500 tonnes of NO ERCs. OPG's first official emissions-reduction trade occurred in 1996 with Detroit Edison. Since then, OPG has participated in over 60 transactions to acquire ERCs, and over 45 internal projects have been identified and reviewed for the creation of such credits. OPG has built up a diverse inventory of CO_2 and NO_x ERCs. These include the purchase of 34,437 tonnes of CO_2 ERCs from energy-efficiency improvements to Toronto's University Health Network. Over a period of two years, the energy-efficiency programs resulted in the hospital using less electricity, natural gas, and steam, reducing GHG emissions. OPG also purchased 1.6 million tonnes of CO_2 credits from Connecticut-based Zahren Alternative Power Corporation. Zahren generated the credits by collecting and burning methane to produce electricity before the gas could be released from landfill into the atmosphere.

All ERC trades conducted by OPG are subject to an independent, third-party assessment that ensures that the credits are quantifiable and are in excess of regulatory or voluntary commitments. To provide additional environmental benefit, all ERCs created and purchased are discounted by 10% so that only 90% of the ERCs may be used to meet emission-reduction targets.

OPG has shown ERC trading to be a cost-effective tool for reducing emissions. OPG's trading experience has highlighted a number of challenges and lessons. These include defining clear ownership rights to emission reductions, standardizing emissions reporting, establishing public and transparent emission-trading rules, and educating stakeholders about the environmental and economic benefits of trading. In addition, a competitive market is needed to establish a commodity price for ERCs.

CASE STUDY 57

International Emissions Trading Association

The International Emissions Trading Association (IETA) is a non-profit organization created in June 1999 to establish a functional international framework for trading greenhouse gas (GHG) emission reductions. The 45 international members include leading multinational companies from across the carbon trading cycle: emitters, solution providers, brokers, verifiers, and legal compliance experts.

IETA members seek to develop an emissions-trading regime that results in real and verifiable GHG emission reductions, balancing economic efficiency with environmental integrity and social equity. The broad membership guarantees a wide range of expertise from representatives of companies in OECD as well as non-OECD countries.

IETA will work for the development of an active, global, GHG market, consistent across national boundaries and involving all three mechanisms of the Kyoto Protocol: the clean development mechanism, joint implementation, and emissions trading.

IETA's strategy for 2002 is to function as follows:

- It will work with partners, as appropriate, in various jurisdictions, remembering that IETA is an international organization. IETA will start establishing cooperation agreements with national and regional bodies such as the UK Emissions Trading Group, the Pilot Emissions Reduction Trading Project, and the Chicago Climate Exchange as well as with other partners such as WBCSD and WWF.

- It will seek to develop components of emissions-trading regimes. It will pick a number of key issues where it will develop original work as well as work in cooperation with other efforts. This will include work on accounting, tax, contracts, registries, validation, and verification.

- It will focus attention on issues such as market mechanisms in general as well as issues that are of special concern to business (integration, etc.). There continues to be the need to promote market mechanisms and trading as one of the solutions that must be available to business in order to minimize societal impact within the framework of sustainable development.

- It will connect efforts and organizations by disseminating information and helping projects connect.

CASE STUDY 58
Climate Neutral Network

A handful of companies are going beyond 'energy efficiency' to seek ways to leave no carbon footprints behind. Their Climate Neutral Network stretches the horizons of orthodoxy for those companies that are trying to reduce greenhouse gas (GHG) emissions.

Over the past three years, the US-based Climate Neutral Network has built an alliance of companies that are learning how to build market share and customer brand loyalty by offering their customers products and services that achieve a net zero impact on the Earth's climate.

Participating companies can become certified as 'Climate Cool' on achievement of complete reduction and offset of all carbon emissions. A company that chooses to become a Climate Cool enterprise agrees to reduce and offset all of the climate impacts for the full spectrum of its internal operations from the point at which raw materials are received to the point at which finished product is delivered. Products or services can also be certified individually as Climate Cool. Product certification requires a reduction and offset of the GHGs generated at each stage of the life-cycle on a cradle-to-cradle basis: the sourcing of materials; manufacturing or production; distribution, use, and end-of-life disposal.

Why do companies participate? Shaklee Corporation, the first company to receive Climate Cool Certification, sees participation in the Network as an opportunity to leverage the company's 40-year history of environmental focus and performance. Participation is a means of branding the organization and not just the individual products. 'We felt strongly about moving beyond past performances and striving just for reductions', says Ken Perkins, environment, health, and safety director. According to Perkins, 'We were attracted by the bold objectives of being climate-neutral. It is not just old wine in a new bottle; the Network is innovative, ground-breaking and distinguishable.'

Organizations in the Network are now actively collaborating to co-design new Climate Cool products and partnerships, and a creative and rapidly expanding company-to-company market is developing. The Saunders Hotel Group, also certified Climate Cool, was seeking lighting alternatives in its program to attain certification for 'cool rooms', its Climate Cool accommodation. Saunders needed to develop a means of reducing the energy consumption of hotel lighting without sacrificing ambience. Philips Lighting worked with Saunders to design alternative bulbs. It came up with more energy-efficient alternatives that were also smaller and lighter in weight. 'This provided an opportunity to plug in new designs', says Paul Walitsky of Philips Lighting. 'The Climate Neutral Network is providing new business opportunities to put products into practice.'

Philips Lighting is also working with US apparel firm Norm Thompson to provide energy-efficient lighting to the Ecumenical Ministries of Oregon. As a result of this and other efforts, Norm Thompson recently received its Climate Cool certification.

The Network more recently began certifying events that achieve a zero emission 'footprint'. This includes a comprehensive calculation of the estimated emissions from an event using the Climate Neutral metrics that closely mirror the WBCSD and WRI Greenhouse Gas Protocol Corporate Accounting and Reporting Standard.

The first certification of this kind was the 2002 Winter Olympic Games in Salt Lake City. This includes measurement of GHGs from such sources as travel to Salt Lake City by athletes, officials, and spectators and transportation around town. It applies also to the events and venues themselves, including even the burning of the Olympic torch. The offsets required were achieved through donations of GHG reductions from DuPont and Petro Source, and the effort was supplemented by the planting of 18 million trees. The reductions that DuPont is donating are from process-related reductions of nitrous oxide, representing reductions beyond their internal commitment. In total, the emission reductions exceeded the calculated emissions footprint of the games by three times.

'By becoming Climate Cool, companies are issuing a leadership challenge', says Sue Hall, executive director of the Climate Neutral Network. 'These exciting precedents are attracting broad interest from many companies who are able to leverage Climate Cool activities for their own objectives.'

Making markets work for all

> **The key point I kept in mind is not how much money a village has to purchase telephone services, but how much money the village can make if the services are made available. The villagers would pay for the phone service from what they make from the phone services.**
>
> *Iqbal Quadir, founder of GrameenPhone, Bangladesh*

Poverty is one of the single largest barriers to sustainability. Poor people are forced to live from day to day to survive. Lacking access to education, safe housing, transport, clean water, sanitation, healthcare, and transport, the 2.8 billion people struggling to live on less than two dollars a day also lack access to property rights, capital, and market opportunities. By 2025 we expect a further 2 billion people to be added to our planet's population; most of these births will occur in the least-developed countries.

Recent history teaches two lessons. First, the developing world will accept no limitations on its perceived needs to turn environmental resources into economic growth. The industrial countries have not provided a role model in this form of development. Second, overseas development assistance is unlikely to increase. Thus both the social and the environmental health of the planet depends on allowing developing countries full access to international markets, in hopes that they can accelerate toward more eco-efficient economies. Only well-constructed markets can offer billions the opportunities they need to move out of poverty. Aid cannot do it alone; welfare cannot do it alone (though both are crucial). Governments cannot do it alone, but they can, and should, establish the structures that allow for this vast movement.

Studies suggest that overall economic growth benefits the poor. Those opposed to markets and trade thus work against the poor. But the fact that a 'trickle-down effect' is so hard to prove demonstrates that the effect is too weak to do the massive job required. Thus business should design new approaches to demonstrate the power of the market to decrease poverty.

Companies need to design and implement ways for markets to bridge the 'afford-ability gap', reaching people in areas where ordinary business models do not work. There will be rewards for companies that creatively step up to this challenge, as unmet basic needs represent market opportunities for those who can deploy the capital and manage the costs to provide solutions at prices the poor can afford. Such market opportunities in poverty-stricken regions include healthcare, water, housing, nutrition, electricity, education, home appliances, and sanitation.

Making the market work for everyone involves two basic measures: enabling access to effective markets and spreading consumer purchasing power. These two measures, representative of supply and demand, go hand in hand. Business is becoming more interested in working to develop partnerships with governments and civil society to demonstrate that markets can help people toward sustainable livelihoods. We need to blend the innovation and prosperity that markets make possible, the security and framework conditions governments provide, and the ethical standards civil society insists on. In poorer regions, business needs to provide appropriately priced products that meet basic needs. This may mean a company adjusting its investment strategies—recouping its return on investment via capital efficiency and high-volume sales rather than by trying to achieve high-margin returns on low-volume products and services.

CASE STUDY 59
Aracruz
page 256

The business case for poverty reduction is straightforward. Business cannot succeed in societies that fail. Poverty wastes human resources—the ability of the poor to contribute to societal development, theirs and others—and undermines market potential—the potential for the poor to purchase goods and services. Smart companies, applying sound business thinking, are already beginning to see the benefits of pursuing poverty reduction. The potential for market expansion, discernible to merchants who see the advantages of dealing with the world's four billion poor, indicates that the best is yet to come.

Meeting the needs of the present

Sustainable development is about meeting the needs of the present without compromising the ability of future generations to meet their own needs. This definition forces us to admit that sustainable development remains elusive. Not only are we far from achieving intergenerational equity; we are not much closer to achieving intragenerational equity either. Not only are we steadily eroding the planet's ability to support us, but also we are faced with a growing gulf between rich and poor in a world where, in spite of all the gains of the global economy, 1.2 billion people still subsist on the equivalent of less than one dollar per day. Measuring poverty in terms of income per capita is only part of the poverty picture, though. Quality-of-life indicators not necessarily correlated with income—such as child mortality, life expectancy, and literacy—also contribute to human development (Panayotou 1998).

The number of poor, and the number of ways in which many are poor, represent one of the great failures of our civilization. Says Mike Moore (2001), director general of the WTO:

> It is a tragedy that, while our planet is blessed with sufficient resources to feed its six billion people, so many are going hungry and so many are living in the misery that poverty breeds. Poverty in all its forms is the greatest challenge to the international community today. We will be judged by our response.

At the September 2000 UN Millennium General Assembly in New York, 189 countries signed the Millennium Declaration, committing to a set of Millennium Development Goals. Chief among their aims is, by 2015, to cut by 50% the proportion of people in extreme poverty worldwide, to improve health, provide education, and to preserve the environment.

Addressing the human development needs of the present must be our first priority, according to Richard George, CEO and president of the Canadian electric utility Suncor Energy. 'All citizens of the world desire clean air, clean water, and healthy, natural ecosystems', he stresses. 'However, before we can aspire to assure this environmental future for all citizens, we need to tackle the problem of global poverty.'

To be sustainable, solutions to poverty must be based on radically new levels of environmental efficiency. With most population growth taking place in the least-developed countries, pressures on the global environment look set to intensify. Given existing technology and products, for all six billion people on the planet to live like the average American we would require the equivalent of three planet Earths to provide the material, create the energy, and dispose of the waste (Holliday 2001a). Future models of growth must therefore be far more environmentally efficient and socially equitable than they have been in the past, for, as economist Lester Thurow (1997: 239) observes, 'there's no point in having a global economy if you don't have a global environment that lets you survive and enjoy what you produce'.

How then can poorer nations and people raise their standards of living while industrial nations maintain their standards of living and both respect environmental thresholds? The answer, according to John Pepper, chairman of Procter & Gamble, is to mobilize markets in favor of sustainability, leveraging the power of innovation and global markets for the benefit of everyone, not just those in the developed world. Says Pepper: 'We cannot condemn developing countries to a life of poverty so those in the developed world can maintain their lifestyles. But neither do we have to presume that the only alternative is for the developed world to reduce its quality of life' (P&G 2001). Instead, Pepper argues, business must 'make markets work for everyone and ultimately make lives better in every part of the world'.

As we argued earlier, the poor need a liberal, open, global market. The economic predicament of the world's poor cannot be reversed by withholding from them the advantages of contemporary technology, the efficiency of international trade and exchange and the social and economic merits of living in open rather than closed societies. The challenge is to use technology and commerce in ways that respect the interests of the poor. The WBCSD has begun a project called 'Sustainable Livelihoods: The Business Connection' to explore ways of making the markets work for all. Among the leaders of this project are the members of the Council's global network of more than 30 national and regional councils and partner organizations, mostly in developing countries.

'Poverty remains the world's most urgent moral challenge', says Peter Sutherland, chairman of BP and chairman and managing director of Goldman Sachs International: 'Eliminating poverty is not only the right thing to do; it is essential to fulfilling the world's growth potential' (Sutherland 1999). Poverty wastes human resources and prevents large numbers of the world's citizens from fruitful participation in the market. For the people and governments of the world's low-income countries, Sutherland maintains, the main challenge of globalization is to avoid marginalization: 'The problem for many of these countries is not what globalization has or has not done to them, but that it threatens to pass them by altogether.' Developing a vision of globalization that is inclusive, has a human face and a strong environmental ethos is our primary responsibility.

The business opportunity

The globalization of the market will not happen unless this is seen to be benefiting the poor. 'If the globalization process is to be deemed a success, the issue of poverty and social exclusion must be addressed', argues McIntosh (1999) in the introduction to *Visions of Ethical Business*: 'If business wants to promote a global economy and free trade, then it has to be able to argue that the benefits will be felt by all the world's citizens, not just the few.' Tackling poverty is not just a moral imperative, it is also in the self-interest of business.

It is not so much that poverty is the business of business, *Visions of Ethical Business* argues, but that business can be a powerful part of the solution to eradicate poverty. According to UN secretary general Kofi Annan (1999), 'many corporations are big investors, employers and producers in dozens of countries across the world. That power brings with it great opportunities—and great responsibilities.' By upholding universal human rights, supporting the precautionary approach to environmental issues and by encouraging the diffusion of innovative, clean technologies, argues Annan, business can play a vital role in promoting the global values of sustainable development.

CASE STUDY 60
Bayer
page 257

A growing number of companies are realizing that there are good business reasons, as well as good moral and philanthropic reasons, why business should address the unmet needs of the world's poor. Promoting sustainable livelihoods for the poor is a powerful way to counteract dissatisfaction with, and demonstrate the benefits of, free trade and open markets. Business, of course, has a vested interest in more open trade and investment, says Niall FitzGerald (2000b), chairman of Unilever, 'but so, too, do ordinary citizens and consumers—particularly in the developing world. Where businesses operate responsibly and sustainably, the very business of "doing business" creates employment, generates new wealth, raises skill levels, and strengthens local economies.'

If companies can design innovative business models that bridge the affordability gaps between poor people and basic needs, they could take advantage of the biggest business opportunity of the 21st century—while solving one of its most pressing moral dilemmas. As C.K. Prahalad (1997: 72) of the University of Michigan Business School observes, 'the biggest bonanza that anybody could have hoped for is to have three and a half billion people peacefully join the global market economy'.

Being an early mover in the world's emerging markets may turn out to be crucial to future competitiveness. Ed Artzt, former CEO and chairman of Procter & Gamble, puts it like this: 'If we don't do it early on globally, someone else will' (in Prahalad 1997: 73). Early targeting of the global market is emerging as a vital aspect of future corporate competitiveness. It is, says Prahalad, about competing for opportunity share rather than market share. And, at the root of it, it is about survival, for 'unless you are growing new markets, new businesses, new sources of profit, you will find yourself on a treadmill, always trying to improve the ever-declining margins and profits from yesterday's businesses' (Prahalad 1997: 65). With established markets in the North increasingly becoming saturated, the fledgling markets and development needs of the South offer the greatest potential for growth in years to come.

As highlighted in Chapter 2, for companies to seize the commercial opportunities of sustainable human development, changes in the governance frameworks of developing countries will be required. As BP's Peter Sutherland (1999) points out, one of the chief barriers to private-sector activity in such countries is that they tend to lack the institutions, human capital, policies, and infrastructure to capitalize on the trade and investment opportunities globalization represents. But it will also require an entirely new approach to doing business .

CASE STUDY 61
BP Solar
page 258

Senegal, for example, has been trying to encourage foreign investment and production that will help it develop. Until recently, however, US chemical giant DuPont notes, companies simply could not figure out business models that would enable them to create shareholder value in an economy such as Senegal's (Holliday 2001a). This is now starting to change. Along with improvements in governance frameworks, new business models are emerging that offer a key to making markets work for all. And the magnitude of the new opportunity is far larger than previously thought.

New business models

One of the clearest calls for greater business involvement in meeting the market needs of the South has come from Stuart Hart at the Kenan-Flagler Business School at the University of North Carolina. Together with C.K. Prahalad, Hart has been a firm proponent of mobilizing the corporate sector to address the needs of those at what he calls 'the base of the pyramid'—the four billion people whose per capita income is less than $1,500 per year (Hart and Prahalad 2002). This vast number represents, in Hart's view, a huge business opportunity that has remained largely invisible to corporate managers.

The fault, he argues, lies with conventional business models, which do not work well in markets that are unorganized, unstructured, and hard to reach. Moreover, where people are poor, unit sales may be high, but gross margins are slim, whereas business has tended to concentrate on high-margin, low-unit sales models. As a result, companies have largely shied away from serving the markets of the very poor. In Asia, for example, DuPont used to maintain a rule of thumb that the company would not invest in building local sales infrastructure until per capita GDP was at least $1,000 (Holliday 2001b). In making such rules, argue Hart and Prahalad, companies have been missing a large potential profit source: 'Contrary to popular assumptions, the poor can be a very profitable market, especially if MNCs (multinational corporations) change their business models' (Hart and Prahalad 2002). The challenge, they say, is to learn to do business differently—'managers who focus on gross margins will miss the opportunity at the bottom of the pyramid; managers who innovate and focus on economic profit will be rewarded' (Hart and Prahalad 2002).

To participate successfully in the emerging economies of the South companies need to turn conventional business logic on its head and reorient business strategies to deal with situations where only a handful of consumers can afford their products, and the majority simply cannot (See Box 8). Being profitable in such markets means thinking differently, producing differently, and learning to bridge the affordability gap by adapting from a situation where a few units are sold at a high price to one where

CASE STUDY 62
SCODP
page 260
many are sold at low cost. Commercial infrastructure must be developed, access improved, healthy markets cultivated, aspirations shaped, and buying power created.

CASE STUDY 63
DuPont
Colombia
page 261
'The real strategic challenge for managers', note Hart and Prahalad (2002), 'is to visualize an active market where only abject poverty exists today. It takes tremendous imagination and creativity to engineer a market infrastructure out of a completely unorganized sector' (see also Figure 13).

Leading companies are already exploring and benefiting from these new 'B24B'—business to four billion—markets. Among the pioneers is South Africa's Eskom, the

---

- Engage with local consumers as well as NGOs and others familiar with the local culture

- Utilize local management that understand the market as well as the capabilities of the company

- Validate financial measurements for success that can account for high-volume sales with low-margin returns rather than simply high-margin returns with low-volume sales

- Tap willingness of senior management to experiment with new business models

- Creatively use the resources of the community to deliver the product or service

- Communicate successes within the company so that successes can be replicated in other markets

- Take a venture-capital-type approach—accept the initial risk to 'seed' new markets in low-income regions in order to contribute to the establishment of a market that can deliver steady returns in the future

---

Box 8 **UNDERSTANDING AND FULFILLING UNMET NEEDS IN EMERGING ECONOMIES**

Source: Holliday and Pepper 2001: 33

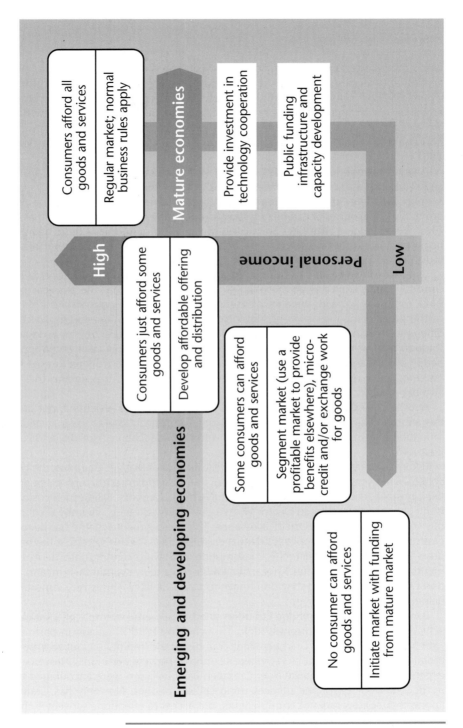

Figure 13 **MAKING MARKETS WORK FOR EVERYBODY:
A SPECTRUM OF BUSINESS OPPORTUNITIES**

Source: Holliday and Pepper 2001: 43

CASE STUDY 64
Eskom
page 262

world's fifth-largest utility, which confronted early on the challenge of linking electrification and social development among South Africa's poor. Faced with a situation
where 65% of households had no access to electricity, in 1988 the company
embarked on an aggressive electrification campaign. Today, over 1,000 new homes
are electrified every day—a rate without parallel in the world. Over 46% of rural
households in South Africa now have electricity, up from 5% in the 1980s (Frankel
2001).

A key challenge for companies entering such markets is how to supply products
and services at a price the poor can afford. Confirms Philip Kotler (1997: 207) of the
Kellogg Graduate School of Management: 'Low-income markets can also be served
profitably. It's a matter of careful targeting, product development and cost efficiency.'
Given better pricing structures and access to capital through microcredit, active participation in the market can offer the poor a better standard of living, but business
must first bridge the affordability gap.

One way of doing this is through the introduction of differential pricing, a route
currently being explored by the pharmaceutical industry under the auspices of the
WHO and the WTO. With the aim of ensuring that life-saving medicines are affordable
to the poor, companies such as Novo Nordisk and Novartis are starting to charge
different prices in different markets according to local purchasing power: for example
through high-volume purchasing, multi-sectoral partnerships, or via licenses between
patent owners and generic manufacturers. For this approach to work on a larger scale,
however, methods will be needed to prevent lower-priced drugs finding their way
into rich-country markets (WHO 2001).

CASE STUDY 34
Suez
page 164

Another approach, pioneered by French company Suez in Argentina, got around
the affordability question by swapping labor for connections to clean water and
sanitation systems, through a participative water service scheme (Holliday and Pepper
2001: 46).

Eskom adopted a different tack in its electrification initiative: changing the billing
system. Many customers live in areas where there is little infrastructure; there are no
fixed postal addresses and people do not have bank accounts. Billing such customers
is difficult, so Eskom offered electricity on a pay-as-you-go basis whereby users could
buy tokens for a given electricity allowance. This pre-payment scheme has been successful: today some 80% of its residential customers opt for this system. It has helped
users to manage their electricity consumption and avoid running into debt. Comments Eskom chairman Reuel Khoza: 'It allows people to live within their means. They
don't have to borrow and they don't have to pay back later. This is very important in
helping them plan their lives.'

Bangladesh's GrameenPhone Ltd offers another powerful example of what can be
achieved by reinventing business logic. Launched by Iqbal Z. Quadir in partnership
with Muhammad Yunus, Grameen Bank founder, the company set out to introduce
mobile telephones to rural areas where telephone services were unavailable or very
expensive. With micro-finance from Grameen Bank, villagers were encouraged to set
up door-to-door telephone services using cellular phones. Not only has Grameen-
Phone created new ranks of entrepreneurs, but access to telephone services is changing how villagers plan and conceive their livelihoods, allowing them to better manage
their incomes and opening up new business opportunities. Farmers, for example, can
now phone ahead to obtain going market prices and therefore decide when best to

sell their produce. Again, bridging the affordability gap was key, and in this case the bridge was micro-finance. Says GrameenPhone founder Iqbal Quadir:

> The key point I kept in mind is not how much money a village has to purchase telephone services, but how much money the village can make if the services are made available. The villagers would pay for the phone service from what they make from the phone service (in Friedman 2000).

In India a similar initiative has been launched by the Usha Group.

Unilever, through its Indian subsidiary Hindustan Lever Ltd (HLL), has reinvented its detergent business, coming up with a new product formulation, a new manufacturing process, and new distribution, packaging, and pricing, all adapted to the base of the pyramid. During the past five years, HLL has registered a 20% growth in revenues per year and a 25% growth in profits (Hart and Prahalad 2002). Moreover, its mother company, Unilever, is now leveraging HLL's experience and business principles in other markets, notably in Brazil, where it has created a new detergent market for the poor based around the *Ala* brand. Crucially, say Hart and Prahalad (2002), serving the base of the pyramid:

> is not about cheap and low-quality products. It is about bringing together the best of technology and a global resource base to address local opportunities. It is about innovation within a clearly defined opportunity space— cost, quality, sustainable development, local knowledge and needs, and volume.

Recognizing the power of digital technologies to reach out to the 'have-nots', WBCSD member companies have set out to apply this logic to the ICT sector, exploring how best to bridge the digital divide through a 'Sustainability through Digital Opportunities' project. The aim is to identify opportunities and linkages between digital technologies and sustainable development and then run a series of pilot projects mapping technological solutions to community needs. The goal is to highlight best practice and create a toolkit for devising business-based approaches to meeting human needs through ICT. Says The Boston Consulting Group's Johannes Lehmann, 'This can't be done with traditional business models. Hence the importance of developing a fresh business approach which responds to specific community needs. This is not about philanthropy, it's good business sense and strategic management' (WBCSD 2001f).

Disruptive technologies

Technologies with the power to disrupt established markets will be at the forefront of the 'new industrial revolution' that is necessary if we are to meet in a sustainable way the needs of the world's have-nots. Disruptive technologies require innovation and, based on past business experience, it is likely that much of this may be carried out not by current industry leaders but by pioneering small entrant companies who capture the market, later dethroning their mainstream competitors. According to Joseph Bower and Clayton Christensen, writing in the *Harvard Business Review*, market leaders tend to have a built-in blockage to disruptive technologies: their investment and marketing methods. These tend to lead established companies to concentrate on perfecting and sustaining the technologies of the present, which appeal to their existing customers, at the expense of investing in the technologies of the future likely to appeal to future customers in emerging markets (Bower and Christensen 1995). This is because most disruptive future technologies fail to pass the usual investment and marketing criteria applied by big companies. 'Using the rational, analytical investment processes that most well-managed companies have developed,' say Bower and Christensen, 'it is nearly impossible to build a cogent case for diverting resources from known customer needs in established markets to markets and customers that seem insignificant or do not yet exist.' In fact, they go on to say, the processes companies use to remain focused on the main customers are so effective 'that they blind those companies to important new technologies in emerging markets'.

To remain at the top of their industries in the global economy, therefore, companies will increasingly need to identify and develop disruptive technologies and learn to manage them strategically in ways that, in the words of Hewlett-Packard CEO Carly Fiorina, 'conserve the spirit of the garage' (Carly Fiorina, speaking on BBC Radio 4, September 2001). To succeed in this, Bower and Christensen (1995) argue, R&D into such technologies will need to be shielded from the very business processes and incentives that drive mainstream markets. They recommend five simple steps for doing this (see Box 9). Acquisitions, strategic alliances, joint ventures, and networks will also have important roles to play, particularly as innovation increasingly takes place globally, flowing from South to North as well as from developed to developing markets. As C.K. Prahalad (1997: 73) points out, when Chinese, Indian, or Indonesian competitors become global, they will not only influence cost structures in new markets, they will also influence new product development.

Three emerging technologies in particular appear to have strong disruptive potential for the markets of the South: biotechnology, ICT, and renewable energy technologies such as photovoltaics and hydrogen-powered fuel cells. While acknowledging that such technologies may be controversial and have yet to make a qualitative difference, India's Tata Energy Research Institute (TERI) has identified five potential applications of biotechnology that could aid development in the south: genetic engineering, bio-fertilizer technology, bio-remediation, enzyme technology, and micro-propagation. 'There is no doubt', TERI claims, 'that the world is on the threshold of a major paradigm shift where these cutting edge technologies will play a significant role in promoting sustainable development' (Pachauri and Batra 2001). Of biotechnology, Klaus Leisinger, head of the Novartis Foundation for Sustainable Development, says: 'To turn a blind eye to 40,000 people starving to death every day is a moral outrage.' We have an ethical commitment, he claims, not to lose time in implementing the technology (in Macilwain 1999).

Poor countries want access to biotech. In response to this desire, Monsanto has reached a royalty-free agreement with Kenya for a transgenic sweet potato and is exploring provision of microcredit to farmers. The company, says Judy Chambers of Monsanto's International Development Program, 'is undergoing a paradigm shift. If we want to reach farmers, we have to completely alter our way of thinking' (in Macilwain 1999). Ensuring that proprietary licensing does not prevent developing

- Determine whether the technology is disruptive or sustaining

- Define the strategic importance of the disruptive technology

- Locate the initial market for the disruptive technology

- Place responsibility for building a disruptive technology business in an independent organization

- Keep the disruptive organization independent

Box 9 **FIVE SIMPLE STEPS TO MANAGING DISRUPTIVE TECHNOLOGIES**

Source: Bower and Christensen 1995

countries from accessing sufficient information and technical expertise to assess such technologies objectively is crucial if they are to participate fully in their application.

Provision of information is more and more the realm of digital technologies, and these, too, offer great disruptive potential for emerging markets. Already, many companies are attempting to cross what has been identified as a 'digital divide' between those who have access to new ICT products and services and those who do not. Hewlett-Packard, for example, has launched World e-Inclusion services, a venture targeted specifically at the very poor at the base of the pyramid. It aims to provide access to health and tele-medicine, to promote education, employment, and greater access to credit, and to broaden access to markets, all via the Internet. 'The Internet and related information technologies hold the promise of rapid, sustainable economic growth that directly benefits everyone on the planet', says CEO Carly Fiorina (in Frankel 2001).

Much depends, however, on how companies such as Hewlett-Packard approach sustainability and the deployment of technology across markets, cultures, and continents. Hewlett-Packard has pledged to sell, lease, or donate $1 billion-worth of products and services via its World e-Inclusion programs, touch 1,000 villages through grass-roots initiatives, and enlist a million partners to help achieve the program's aims. Through this initiative, according to Lyle Hurst, program director, Hewlett-Packard 'is inventing or, through partnership, integrating truly disruptive technology' that addresses head-on challenges such as poverty, lack of infrastructure, illiteracy, and preservation of local cultural and environmental heritage (in Frankel 2001). Cisco Systems, too, is using the Internet to tackle extreme poverty, collaborating with the United Nations on an initiative entitled NetAid, which is promoting 'eAction' as a way to help the very poor.

BP, meanwhile, is seeking to exploit energy-related disruptive technology opportunities that offer superior environmental performance. The group has created a 'low carbon energy' technology program 'to intensify the development of business options that continuously reduce the emissions associated with the production and use of our products' (BP 2000). While this program may lead in many cases to sustaining technologies that offer incremental improvements, it is also pursuing business opportunities in natural gas, renewables, energy efficiency, hydrogen, and fuel cells, many of which have the capacity to become truly disruptive. Where fuel-cell technology, potentially the most disruptive of all, is concerned, the company has established a strategic partnership with automotive company DaimlerChrysler to investigate possible future refueling infrastructure requirements. Such relationships help spread the risk and uncertainty associated with new technologies.

Bangladesh's microcredit pioneer, Grameen Bank, has founded a new venture called Grameen Shakti, specifically to promote renewable energy use in rural areas (Siddiqui and Newman 2001). This initiative combines all three aspects of sustainability—economic development, community development, and environmental development—in a country where the electricity grid reaches only 15% of the population. Grameen Shakti has established a number of programs focused on different renewable technologies: solar home systems, wind power, hydropower, and bio-fuels. Funding for the technologies is provided via Grameen Bank micro-loans.

Financing change

We have seen how pricing and affordability are critical elements in corporate strategies for reaching those at the base of the pyramid. Equally important is the need to create buying power. Where people earn less than one dollar per day, or where they are under-employed and have trouble supporting themselves or their families, companies must first help the poor to break the vicious cycle of poverty if they are to participate gainfully in the market economy. Offering labor-for-service options, like Suez; enhancing the income earning potential of the poor, like Eskom; and providing access to credit, like Grameen Bank, are three ways of doing this. At the macro-level, there is also a need for innovative financing models, through FDI and debt relief.

Credit is a powerful way to free the poor from the cycle of poverty. It can be the linchpin for kick-starting a new business, which in turn helps generate the income the poor need in order to become consumers. Yet, historically, the poor have been excluded from it. In recognition of the need to open up access to credit for the poor, the UN, in conjunction with several major MNCs, has established a target of making basic credit available to the 100 million poorest families worldwide by 2005 (Hart and Prahalad 2002). This marks a sea change in thinking. Commercial credit has been largely unavailable to the poor because the poor tend to lack things such as collateral and mailing addresses. As Hernando de Soto (2000) has pointed out, widespread failure to recognize and value the property of the poor has kept them out of the banking system and out of capitalism in general. Moreover, because the amounts in which the poor deal are so small, transaction costs for catering to the poor are often disproportionately high, creating barriers to entry for financial institutions. Furthermore, because the poor are poor, they have traditionally been considered as a bad credit risk.

Among the first companies to buck this trend and prove that the poor could be not only creditworthy, but profitable, was Bangladesh's Grameen Bank. Set up by Muhammad Yunus specifically to cater to the needs of the poorest in the community, the bank's credit-delivery system has some unique features (Siddiqui and Newman 2001):

- It focuses on women.

- It requires no collateral.

- It depends on group pressure to ensure repayment.

- Loans are repayable in weekly installments throughout the year.

- Eligibility for future loans depends on full repayment.

- Transparency levels are much higher than in conventional banks, to facilitate group management and institutional supervision.

The venture has been extraordinarily successful. By June 1997, total lending had amounted to $2 billion, even though the average loan amounted only to $160, and some were as low as $10. The bank counted some 2.34 million borrowers, spread across some 38,957 villages (Siddiqui and Newman 2001). Most remarkably, the bank boasted a repayment rate of 95%, a figure that would be the envy of most mainstream commercial lenders. Grameen Bank has provided a significant boost to rural development in Bangladesh, and its approach has been emulated worldwide. To date, some 223 Grameen-type financial initiatives have been established in 58 countries (Siddiqui and Newman 2001).

Grameen is not alone. The microcredit industry is growing rapidly worldwide, with loans now reaching around 23 million borrowers (WBCSD 2001g). To assist in its expansion, Deutsche Bank set up in 1997 a Microcredit Development Fund to provide professional banking experience and funding to microcredit institutions seeking loans from commercial banks. The fund has so far loaned $937,500 to 12 institutions in 9 countries. A further $19 million has been leveraged from private financing (WBCSD 2001g). French banker Jacques Attali, meanwhile, has established an initiative called PlaNet Finance (www.planetfinance.org), which makes use of digital networks to create economies of scale in the microcredit field, pool best practice, and lower the transaction costs of micro-lending. CASE STUDY 65 Deutsche Bank page 263

Other players include Standard Bank of South Africa Ltd, whose e-banking business, AutoBank E, now reaches some three million customers through its automated telling machines (ATMs) and to which 50,000 new customers are added every month (Hart and Prahalad 2002). Meanwhile, in a salutary turn of the development tables, the ShoreBank Corporation in the USA is now applying the microcredit model inspired by Bangladesh's Grameen Bank to meet the needs of deprived communities on Chicago's inner-city South Side.

Credit for the very poor still has immense potential for expansion, however. To date, UNDP calculates, global demand stands at an estimated 500 million households, only 3–6% of which are being served (Malloch Brown 2001). Obstacles such as high fixed costs, limited availability of capital, and the difficulty of processing large quantities of information will need to be overcome. Building an infrastructure that gives the poor access to banking and credit is vital if markets are to work for all. Credit, as Hart and Prahalad (2002) have concluded, offers the possibility of breaking the cycle of poverty by opening the prospect of income generation through productive CASE STUDY 66 Banco do Nordeste page 264 employment or new micro-enterprise development. Access to it should, they argue, become a birthright. Moreover, there is money to be made in the process.

Reducing investment risk

We have noted that foreign direct investment (FDI) is now far outstretching official development assistance (ODA) as the prime source of funding for economic growth in developing countries (Jeucken 2001). Says Niall FitzGerald (2000b), chairman and CEO of Unilever: 'In developing economies, where domestic capital is in short supply, international capital is vital—and given the absence of portfolio funds in many markets, direct corporate investment is especially important.'

Innovative mechanisms will be required to reduce the inherent high risks to foreign investors of investing in the least-developed countries, according to François Kaisin, director of quality, environment, and safety at Suez. One innovative initiative in this regard is the African Trade Insurance (ATI) agency, which aims to provide insurance against a wide range of non-commercial risks such as political upheaval, war, expropriation, seizure of goods, exchange controls, and trade embargoes. Launched in August 2001, the agency will provide insurance for exports to, from, and within Africa (*Economist* 2001c). Founded with the aid of the World Bank with the involvement of underwriters Lloyds of London, the scheme aims to encourage more private insurers to do business in Africa. The Multilateral Investment Guarantee Agency (MIGA), the part of the World Bank Group responsible for promoting FDI in emerging economies, is behind the initiative.

There is huge potential for growth and investment in the African region, but this is going largely unfulfilled because of negative perceptions of political risk. Says MIGA executive vice president Motomichi Ikawa, 'by addressing head-on the risk perceptions of firms doing business in Africa, this African-led initiative is an important step in increasing the continent's share of FDI flows' (World Bank 2001b). Ugandan president Yoweri Museveni agrees: 'The ATI is a scheme that is telling investors "please go ahead and trade" and if a coup d'état occurred, you will not lose because we shall cover you' (World Bank 2001b). Over time, it is hoped that the private-sector share in ATI will increase. Overall, the scheme is expected to foster some $5 billion in additional trade for Burundi, Kenya, Malawi, Rwanda, Tanzania, Uganda, and Zambia, the seven participating countries.

Partnering for development

In Chapter 6 we explored the powerful role that multi-sectoral partnerships can play in promoting sustainable development—nowhere more so than in the fledgling markets of the South. The objective of partnerships, the World Bank maintains, is to 'deliver more than the sum of its individual parts', and major challenges such as tackling world poverty cannot be attempted by any one group alone; such challenges require collaboration between a number of different players (World Bank 2001c). BP's Peter Sutherland is convinced of the value of partnerships in making markets work for all: 'The logic of 2000 calls for a new division of labor and new forms of interaction among private investors, national governments, and the international system' (Sutherland 1999).

Increasingly, companies are recognizing that the broader set of responsibilities they face means addressing wider social, economic, and environmental business challenges in partnership with others, such as governments and civil-society organizations. Such relationships are designed to maximize the positive development effects of private-sector investment and distribute more efficiently among the three parties the risks, benefits, and responsibilities associated with the project (World Bank 2001c). Such partnerships tend to be long-term, as they require a high level of mutual trust and a clear sense of aims and expectations, which take time to establish.

CASE STUDY 67
GrupoNueva
and South
African
Breweries
page 265

Unilever is a company that is already exploring the power of public–private partnerships in helping to tackle sustainable development challenges in Africa. The aim of such alliances, according to company chairman Niall FitzGerald (2000b), is to support local economic development, to help raise levels of health and education, to create sustainable solutions to environmental problems, and to improve quality of life in local communities. In Botswana and Nigeria, for example, Unilever is working in partnership with governments, charitable foundations, and other companies to reduce the spread of HIV and AIDS, applying its communication expertise and know-how in setting up distribution networks and offering offices and facilities.

Such partnership is about far more than altruism, claims FitzGerald. It is also about advocacy and about making the case for global trade and investment. 'I strongly believe that further liberalization of international trade and investment, within a clear regulatory framework, has the potential to deliver great benefits, in particular to many of the most disadvantaged people on our planet', says the Unilever chairman. 'If we are to win people's support for further economic liberalization, we need to show people that increasing international trade and investment is actually about spreading prosperity, extending opportunity, increasing consumer choice and raising standards of living' (FitzGerald 200b). Value-added, output-oriented partnerships are one way of doing this.

Novo Nordisk, too, is actively partnering with governments, international NGOs, and local diabetes associations to tackle diabetes in developing countries, through its Leadership in Education and Access to Diabetes care (LEAD) initiative. LEAD projects have included helping governments create national strategies for dealing with diabetes and analyzing the critical success factors for providing sustainable diabetes care in the poorest countries. Most recently, the company has established a World Diabetes Foundation (WDF) under LEAD, with the specific aim of supporting projects that will improve diabetes care among the poor. 'As the world's leading diabetes care company, Novo Nordisk confronts these problems every day', says Lars Rebien Sørensen, president and CEO:

> If left unattended, hundreds of millions of people will suffer and already
> strained healthcare systems will be faced with insurmountable problems.
> Both our own people and doctors who work in developing countries have

raised the red flag and told us that special measures must be taken urgently,
if the diabetes problem is to be prevented from spinning out of control
(Novo Nordisk 2001).

Under the LEAD initiative, Novo Nordisk has undertaken to provide its insulin
products to the public health systems in the poorest countries 'at prices not to exceed
20% of the average price in North America, Europe, and Japan'.

Novartis, meanwhile, has joined ranks with the WHO to provide developing countries with essential new drug-resistant malaria treatments at affordable prices. As part
of the agreement, Novartis will supply a new therapy, Coartem, for use in developing
countries, at a cost of about 10 cents a tablet, and WHO has undertaken to distribute
the drug through governments of malaria-endemic countries and NGOs. The initiative
includes use of packets specially designed for people who cannot read.

Tripartite partnerships such as these offer the most promising approach to the
creation and application of sustainable technologies in the South, according to UNDP
(in Novo Nordisk 2001).

Ultimately, though, the most important partnership that business can forge is with
the poorest of the poor themselves. Reuel Khoza, Eskom chairman, sums up the scale
of the challenge before us:

> If globalization is seen to come in as an imposition from the dizzy heights
> of the North, it will not be accepted. Instead of seeing people as markets,
> companies must learn to see them as human communities who believe in
> being consulted. The only way to ensure globalization with a human face
> is to infuse it with compassion. Companies must be as willing to listen as to
> speak, and they must be willing to consult, for the poor have opinions. We
> must behave as guests with a good contribution to make.

CASE STUDY 59

Aracruz *the Forestry Partners Program*

Aracruz Celulose, the Brazilian pulp producer, operates in the northern part of the
state of Espírito Santo and in the extreme south of the state of Bahia. All of the pulp
produced by the company comes exclusively from planted eucalyptus forests, which
are interspersed with native forest reserves to ensure a balanced ecosystem. Wood
from native forests is not used in the pulping process nor for any other purpose.

The areas where Aracruz runs its forestry activities have been under considerable
ecological pressure as a result of successive cycles of logging, agriculture, cattle
raising, and charcoal burning since the 19th century. One cause of forest loss has been
timber cutting by poor local communities.

In order to develop an alternative source of wood for its pulp mill, Aracruz has
developed the Forestry Partners Program, which is run through partnerships with
local farmers. The Program, introduced initially in 1990, has become an important
supplemental supply of eucalyptus wood for the company's pulp mill. However, the

company's ambitions for this effort go far beyond wood supply. It was designed to play significant social and economic roles by helping local farmers earn a better living, make improved use of under-productive and fallow land, and benefit from a viable and profitable alternative to traditional crops. To help farmers realize these opportunities, Aracruz supplies know-how and partial financing.

The Program involves some 2,152 farmers in 56 municipalities in Espírito Santo, 17 in Minas Gerais, and 13 in Bahia. The farmers grow eucalyptus trees under contract to, and with technical assistance from, Aracruz, which also guarantees the purchase of the harvested wood at market rates. Since 1999, the Program has included several local communities of the Tupinikim and Guarani tribe living near the Aracruz pulp mill.

Participating farmers have generally been able to plant their eucalyptus trees on degraded or fallow land that is unsuitable for other locally grown cash crops such as coffee, beans, coconuts, or papaya, thus giving them an additional source of farm income. Moreover, Aracruz provides comprehensive guidance on environmentally sustainable techniques for managing eucalyptus plantations, helping the farmers preserve the soil fertility on their properties.

Participating farmers are given the option of keeping a proportion of the eucalyptus harvest for their own use, as well as the residues (bark, branches, etc.) that are left over from the harvest process. These residues can be sold to bakeries, brick manufacturers, charcoal makers, schools, and others and serve as yet another source of income from the Program. In fact, the resources involved in the Forestry Partners Program considerably exceed the amount that Aracruz pays to the participants. They include the increased taxes that are collected as a result of the activity and the additional purchase of inputs such as fertilizers and other crop-protection agents. In 2001 alone, the Program involved financial resources of more than $11.8 million. The sustainable cultivation of eucalyptus by independent farmers also generates jobs in rural districts, helping the social and economic development of these regions and combating the exodus of rural manpower.

The Forestry Partners Program is to be expanded further. Greater wood requirements that will result from the scheduled start-up of the Aracruz Fiberline plant in two years' time will require an expansion of Program area. Participants will also be given the option to reserve a percentage of the wood they plant for production of larger-diameter trees. These larger trees will be used in sawmills for the manufacture of value-added solid-wood products.

CASE STUDY 60

Bayer *Integrated Crop Management in Brazil*

Bayer has helped convey information on Integrated Crop Management (ICM) to a large number of farming families in Brazil. Participatory training approaches in communities with an emphasis on children formed the cornerstones of this campaign, which was set up as a pilot project. Results were extremely encouraging.

Bayer began this ambitious project in May 1995 in the area around the city of Santa Cruz do Sul, in the southern state of Rio Grande do Sul. Bayer cooperated with local authorities, the union of agricultural workers, and the farmers' associations to implement the project. The goal was to reach around half of the 25,000 smallholder farmers in the region.

The campaign was based on the basic concepts of ICM. Special attention was given to Integrated Pest Management (IPM), which includes indirect measures of weed, pest, and disease prevention such as crop rotation and monitoring pest populations against threshold levels; it uses direct control through biological, biotechnological, mechanical, and chemical measures. The correct and efficient handling of chemical crop protection products, which is key in IPM, was an important aspect of the project.

The campaign developed new ways to convey information, particularly as many of the beneficiaries could not read or write. A card game was designed, using cards containing pictograms on safety aspects and other visual messages. Trainees and all their family members were involved by, for example, practical exercises to test the water-repellent effect of protective clothing. The campaign emphasized the financial benefits of measures such as getting product application rates right and rinsing of empty containers.

Children are important communicators in regions where they have more education than their parents. The campaign held their interest by setting up a school and a photo competition and by staging a play on the subject of farming and crop protection.

A follow-up survey conducted in July 1998 found that participants' understanding and awareness of the risks associated with handling of crop-protection products had clearly increased since June 1995. Almost half of the population in the project region had been reached, and the networking between the stakeholders increased substantially. Successes included an improvement in the attitude toward protective clothing.

The project proved that farmers will adopt new technologies only if they are given the appropriate incentives, knowledge, and practical skills. The project succeeded because it offered clear financial benefits and used 'learning-by-doing' participatory training techniques and local demonstration projects. Success also stemmed from giving the trainees a sense of project ownership and through using the expertise of all participants: farmers, industry, local authorities, and the agricultural unions.

The experience gained in Brazil has led to similar approaches in Mexico, Guatemala, Colombia, Argentina, and Chile.

CASE STUDY 61

BP Solar *rural development projects*

BP Solar has been supplying equipment and systems to rural development projects for over 15 years as part of the company's commercial business. In remote locations, particularly poor, unelectrified communities without access to the electricity grid, solar products and services can be an effective means of meeting essential needs such as lighting for homes, schools, and community centers, as well as remote telecommunication, fresh drinking water, and vaccine refrigeration.

In the Philippines, BP Solar is engaged in a number of rural infrastructure projects, including the vast Municipal Solar Infrastructure Project (MSIP), undertaken with the Philippine and Australian governments. The MSIP uses solar energy as the 'enabling technology' to allow the Philippine government to target specific needs of remote and poor 'non-electrified' communities, and upgrade basic community facilities. This project has helped to provide health, education, and governance benefits to more than 721,140 poor Filipinos in 11 provinces, 53 municipalities, and 435 villages in the Mindanao and Visayas regions. One of the largest solar contracts in the world, the project cost $27 million. Funding was provided by a grant of 33% from the Australian government plus a soft loan from the Australian government for the remaining 67%. MSIP commenced in November 1997 and was completed in May 2001. BP got involved because of the rural off-grid work it had already undertaken and because of direct interaction with the Australian development aid program, AusAid.

BP Solar was involved in the project from the start, in helping to determine the systems and services necessary to satisfy community needs. The company worked with the governments of Australia and of the Philippines to identify the target communities and to design and implement the programs from beginning to end.

A major component of this project was ensuring its sustainability through delivery of training, social preparation, and community development programs. More than 2,251 villagers were trained under this program. BP recognized the need to complement the delivery of solar systems with training and preparation. 'Without these elements, there are plenty of examples of systems falling into disuse and disrepair, resulting in disillusion in the target communities and leaving them in a worse state than before the systems arrived', said Graham Baxter, vice president for Solar Solutions at BP Solar.

Site surveys and social validations were initially performed at each village to determine the needs of the communities and whether they had the infrastructure needed for the systems (water source, school building, village hall buildings, full-time health worker, etc.). At community assemblies, officials provided an introduction to the project and the basics of solar electricity. This was followed by community organization to form the groups and associations that would ultimately manage the systems. Two people in each community were trained on simple maintenance of the systems. Municipal engineers and operatives were then trained on the more technical repairs and maintenance of the system components. Spare parts were also distributed to the municipality so that the communities could have easy access to replacement parts. After the commissioning and handover of each system, BP conducted three separate follow-up visits to the groups and organizations that were formed.

In total 1,145 packaged solar systems were installed in 435 villages. On completion of the MSIP, the following community facilities had been upgraded and provided with a packaged solar system: 4 district hospitals, 11 rural health centers, 104 village health centers, 260 village potable water supply systems, 6 municipal halls, 201 village halls, 266 schools, and 289 communal area lighting systems for markets and fishermen's wharves.

The MSIP was conceived, designed, and implemented to improve the quality of life for people living in some of the most remote and poorest areas of Mindanao and the Visayas Provinces. BP undertakes such projects because they are good business, both in terms of profitability and in terms of environmental and social contribution. As a result of the MSIP, BP Solar has developed a lot of experience in this form of comprehensive project delivery.

'For BP Solar this can be attractive business', says Baxter. 'We have developed the competences to undertake this work, and there aren't many other energy companies that can do this at the scale we envisage in our future plans.' Rural infrastructure projects are now at the core of BP Solar's business strategy, and in the future the company intends to 'clone MSIP' in other regions.

CASE STUDY 62

Sustainable Community-Oriented Development Program *farmer-sized seed packs*

Kenya is importing food. Its farmers, despite their skills, cannot produce enough to feed themselves and the urban population. Soil has been depleted by years of continuous cropping, and is chronically deficient in nutrients. Thus crop growth is poor, and farms lack organic matter. In some parts of Kenya, despite good rainfall, corn now grows only knee-high, leaving the ground exposed to rain and erosion. Yields are as low as 50 kg grain per hectare, far below the potential yield of four tonnes per hectare .

State and international aid programs have provided fertilizers, ploughs, and tractors on credit, but when the programs end farmers are unable to pay back the loans or continue to maintain the equipment. The size of provisions has also been a problem, with the smallest bags of fertilizer often weighing 50 kg. 'This is an investment of a few weeks of income, and you can only carry it around if you have a bicycle', says Paul Seward, a plant nutrition expert.

Seward has teamed up with Dismas Okello, the local community development expert who formed the Sustainable Community-Oriented Development Program (SCODP). Over the past five years, they have worked closely with farmers in Siaya district to devise a mini-pack project to provide quality seeds and fertilizers at affordable prices. Seward describes the program:

> For 5 shillings (6 cents) you can buy a chewing gum-sized sachet of 250 seeds of the vegetable Sukuma-wiki. For another 10 shillings (12 cents) you get a pack of fertilizer for 150 planting holes. The results are dramatic. A good farmer can earn anything from between 2,000 to 4,000 shillings ($25–50) from using these packs.

Having sold its first kilo bag of fertilizer five years ago, SCODP is now selling 300 tonnes of fertilizer a year to small-scale farmers in affordable quantities. The market potential is for several hundreds of thousands of tonnes.

SCOPD has grown since 1997 to become a recognized and well-supported, successful grass-roots project. Specialist assistance has been provided to SCOPD to address the many pests affecting corn, sorghum, beans, cowpeas, and pigeon peas, including training in crop protection-related issues. Field trials were started in 2000 and are continuing in order to develop solutions for specific pest problems. Crop protection products in small packs and small application devices are now also part of the whole technology package that farmers can access through SCODP. Owing to its success, US Aid for International Development (USAID) and the Rockefeller Foundation are assisting SCODP to extend its approach to other regions in Kenya.

CASE STUDY 63
DuPont Colombia *helping farmers succeed*

Colombia is a potential growth market for DuPont agricultural products and seed, but DuPont was interested in more than just selling products to those few customers who could afford them. DuPont was looking for ways of improving the social and economic conditions of a broader cross-section of growers in Colombia in order to maximize the long-term health of the business. Local DuPont leadership determined that the provision of financial planning and soft credits would be the best approach.

In Colombia, farmers have trouble accessing credit because banks see farming as a high-risk activity and small farmers generally have very few assets that can be used as collateral for bank loans. DuPont Colombia realized that the current system did not help small farmers become successful, so the company initiated a partnership with a group of organizations that focused on identifying the issues and then implementing solutions.

Under DuPont's leadership, the partnership—which includes among others the Ministry of Agriculture, Finagro, the Agrarian Bank, the National Agriculture and Livestock Board, and the State House of Compensation and Security—developed a program that allows for up-front financing so that farmers can afford to purchase the inputs that they need for the season to maximize their yields. DuPont introduced the Integrated Agricultural Plan (PAID, in Spanish) in 1999 to provide farmers with financial and commercial solutions, as well as technical assistance, through an integrated support system. The plan enables farmers to count on financial liquidity through the growing season.

Searching for credit guarantees that were novel enough to meet farmers' needs and at the same time conventional enough to be acceptable to the banks, DuPont worked with the National Agriculture and Livestock Board to use forward contracts. Under such a contract, farmers sell their harvest in advance to different agro-industries in deals agreed on through the PAID system. Farmers are guaranteed a fixed price and payment date in advance, and the buyers are guaranteed a supply at a fixed price. DuPont discovered that this form of farming by contract decreases uncertainty concerning crop sales, allows for adequate financial planning, and lowers commercial risks.

The PAID system provides farmers with credit in the form of inputs required for crop production. Farmers also receive technical assistance throughout the cultivation period. The system emphasizes training and technology transfer to improve farm practices so that little by little the farmers may become more efficient in managing environmental and financial resources. Two training and development centers have been constructed. Training covers the safe use of farm chemicals, and their environmental impacts, working with local communities, and handling and safely disposing of packaging.

In 2000 there were more than 2,000 ha of corn planted under the PAID plan in regions such as Cordoba, and 1,000 ha of sorghum in Atlantico. PAID's success is encouraging DuPont to include rice growers, and to continue cultivating effective financial solutions that will contribute to expanding the agricultural frontier and making international the development of Colombian agriculture.

CASE STUDY 64

Eskom's electrification program in South Africa

Eskom, South Africa's electric utility, supplies approximately 95% of the country's electricity and is one of the lowest-cost producers of electricity in the world, but only a small percentage of South African households have had access to this electricity in the past. Before 1994 only 12% of the rural population in South Africa had access to electricity.

The South African government, the electricity distribution industry, and Eskom committed to connecting 2.5 million households to an electrical supply by 2000. Thus Eskom has been undertaking an electrification program that has seen well over 2 million homes receive electricity since the beginning of the program in 1991. Eskom has made investments of more than 7.5 billion Rand (approximately $1 billion), electrifying 1,000 homes per day since 1995. Over 90% of urban areas and more than 40% of rural areas are now receiving electricity. Thus Eskom has extended its reach and provided basic infrastructure.

Initial problems encountered included cost per connection, a lack of community interaction and non-payment. The company responded with efforts such as community interaction programs and the development of the pre-payment meter. A 50% reduction in the cost per connection was also achieved. Local shops are used as the outlets for the purchase of pre-payment cards.

In order to service remote areas with low population densities, a joint venture between Eskom and Shell was initiated to install non-grid solar home systems. To date 6,000 solar systems have been installed, and the success of the project is attributable to the combined efforts of the private sector, a public utility, Transitional Local Government, and the local rural communities. Local people are also trained to undertake the system installation and maintenance.

Electrification can result in social and economic benefits. The provision of electricity can create jobs and increase disposable income in a community. Electrification of schools and houses is highly likely to improve education and raise productivity levels. The supply of electricity can lead to a decrease in the harvesting of firewood and decrease domestic fuel burning, resulting in a decrease in respiratory disease and providing other health benefits. The relative efficiency of using electricity will reduce the overall emission of pollutants and lead to an improved quality of life.

Eskom has committed itself to a three-year target of a further 600,000 connections, paying even greater attention to rural areas.

CASE STUDY 65
Deutsche Bank
Microcredit Development Fund

Deutsche Bank has established the Deutsche Bank Microcredit Development Fund to fuel the growth and reach of microcredit programs around the world. The fund accomplishes this by fostering durable relationships between microcredit institutions and local commercial financial institutions.

Microcredit institutions are proving to be a revolutionary force in creating opportunities for poor families to start their own business and earn their way out of poverty. Microcredit loans foster self-reliance and community-wide economic development as well as stimulating savings among poor people, allowing them to create and use an asset base that is essential to economic activity. Also, recipients of microcredit are proving to be good credit risks.

Microcredit institutions can be replicated across boundaries of geography and culture; they can serve large populations; and, as a means of organizing communities, microcredit institutions are important vehicles for other positive social developments, such as better healthcare, higher status for women, smaller family size, and civic awareness. However, unless microcredit institutions can become profitable businesses, they will fail to reach the scale necessary to effect true change for the world's poor. The Deutsche Bank Microcredit Development Fund was conceived to combine the interest, abilities, reach, and resources of Deutsche Bank and its Private Bank clients to support the long-term sustainability of microcredit institutions. Since the fund's inception, as a result of the $937,500 in loans Deutsche Bank Microcredit Development Fund has made to 12 micro-finance institutions in 9 countries, an additional $19 million has been leveraged in private financing and cumulative lending capacity to the very poorest.

A loan from the Deutsche Bank Microcredit Development Fund of $75,000 was made to the Society for Helping and Awakening Rural Poor through Education (SHARE), which serves skilled and unskilled, very poor, rural female entrepreneurs in India. This loan, at 10:1 leverage, realizes a $750,000 increase in lending capacity over the average 11.5-month term (equivalent to $780,000 per annum), for a total impact of $3.9 million over the five-year Deutsche Bank Microcredit Development Fund loan term.

SHARE has tripled in size in the last two years, is operationally self-sufficient and has consistently maintained a 100% repayment rate. In an effort to raise funds from commercial sources and to earn profits, SHARE is forming a community-owned, for-profit company called SHARE MICROFIN, which was registered with almost 20,000 shareholders, all of whom are SHARE borrowers.

With loans from SHARE, Hafiza Bee, her husband, and their six children are experiencing new-found hope. Hafiza's relationship with SHARE began in 1988, when she organized four other women to become the first group in their village to participate in the SHARE loan program. With her first loan of Rs 4,000 ($80), Hafiza purchased a buffalo. Sales of three liters of milk a day gave her a sense of achievement as she repaid the loan and also had funds to cover household expenditures. With the additional income, the family could begin to save a portion of the earnings from her father's tailoring business.

Additional loan proceeds have resulted in expanded family enterprises, including new sewing machines for her sons, who are now tailors in the family business. Hafiza began to expand her own hand-stitching and embroidery business, which resulted in her appointment as a teacher of a government stitching center in her village and provided her with a regular monthly salary. Hafiza Bee's positive experience with SHARE is serving as an inspiration to others in the village, and she has become an unofficial guide for those who want to enter the program.

CASE STUDY 66

Banco do Nordeste
new banking models for regional development

In the north-east of Brazil, a region with one-fifth of the country's territory and 47 million of its inhabitants, Banco do Nordeste acts as a development bank. With only 174 branches, the bank oversees 76% of all loans made in the region and is able to make itself present in 1,891 municipalities within its operational area. This high degree of trickle-down is the result of a business strategy that involves working side by side with effective business people, especially small and micro entrepreneurs, identifying economic vocations and investment opportunities, and mobilizing society to participate effectively in the development of its own communities.

To this end, Banco do Nordeste has created special tools such as the development agents program, the mobile branch, and a microcredit program. Under the development agents program, 480 specialists in local development travel around the districts identifying businesses and demand for credit and training, while stimulating the culture of enterprise among regional productive agents.

The mobile branch serves those entrepreneurs who live in more distant locations where there is no bank of any kind. By mid-2001, the mobile bank had made 101,177 stops and served more than 3.7 million clients. Technical and managerial capacity-building precedes all loans, so that business people can invest the resources and manage their businesses more efficiently.

Banco do Nordeste implemented a microcredit program to serve micro and small entrepreneurs with credit and training, mostly in the informal sector and to those often lacking standard loan collateral. After three years, the program had become the second largest in Latin America and the largest in Brazil, both in terms of the number of loans and the amounts invested.

The work of Banco do Nordeste and its business partners in north-east Brazil goes beyond prospecting or maintenance of client bases. It seeks to stimulate business culture and awaken the region's productive capacity so as to make it a more effective partner in the development of Brazil.

CASE STUDY 67

GrupoNueva and South African Breweries *practical solutions to retrenchment*

The 1990s trend of company downsizing has hit workers hard in many parts of the world. The economic crisis in Ecuador and Latin America during the late 1990s resulted in substantial downsizing, and in South Africa increasing unemployment has left many people unable to create sustainable livelihoods for themselves and their families. Some companies are designing innovative approaches to this problem, addressing both lay-offs from their own activities as well as broader unemployment problems in their regions.

GrupoNueva: Business Foundation for Social Development

Amanco, one of GrupoNueva's businesses operating in Latin America, produces and markets integrated solutions for construction, water management, infrastructure, and irrigation. The economic crisis in Ecuador required Amanco to close one of its plants in this country.

Alfonso Campoverde will never forget 14 March that year. He was left jobless, doubting his capacity to go on. But the company did not leave him on his own. Amanco Ecuador decided to support him as a small businessman. By April of 2000 he opened his own metal-working shop. Today, he is the proud owner of his own business, employs three workers, and knows that the business will grow if he can install a new mill and an additional shop. With the resources generated by his own business, he has bought a new house and has been able to expand the existing shop in his old house.

The story repeats itself with 14 other laid-off employees. They opted to set up their own businesses after Amanco Ecuador offered them technical training and economic backing. For the management and human resource personnel of Amanco Ecuador, it was cause for great concern when they had to lay off 111 employees because of the closing of a plant. The human consequences of this ran contrary to GrupoNueva's commitment to social responsibility. In the words of the general manager of Amanco Ecuador, Víctor Aguilera, 'How do we live the importance of human resources, according to our company's values? Is it throwing people out the door or is it finding alternatives for solving their problems?'

The Business Foundation for Social Development (FEMDES) was set up in Ecuador to support social programs from the business sector. In the beginning of 2000, FEMDES established the Program for Small Business Creation with funding from the Avina Foundation. Lasting six months, the Program has two main components. First, a basic two-month training in marketing, administration, and accounting is offered. This process should help each participant create a business idea. Then, during the subsequent four months, the students should apply what they have learned. Participants receive a two-hour visit every week from a tutor who advises them until the business shows a positive cash flow. Also during this part of the Program, FEMDES offers a loan of up to $800 dollars, with a three-month grace period, a preferential interest rate and 24-month maturity. Good results have allowed FEMDES to continue into the second phase of the Program, with a new group of people interested in creating their own businesses.

South African Breweries: Project Noah

In South Africa, South African Breweries (SAB) has set up Project Noah. The Project helps individuals counteract the negative effects of retrenchment, enabling them to build self-confidence, become motivated, determine the options available, make informed decisions about their future, and put these into action. Individuals are counselled prior to retrenchment to identify problems requiring ongoing support during the Noah process.

This first phase requires nine training days aimed at equipping students with an understanding of their circumstances and providing life skills. At the end of this first phase, individuals communicate their goals to the Project Noah team, which then provides personal development plans based on individual needs, strengths, and attributes. A four-week, action-based, business start-up course is then offered whereby individuals are given the opportunity to test ideas and produce business plans.

This is only the beginning of a long association. Extensive backup is necessary, and support is provided for at least a year in order to reduce the risks associated with start-up ventures. Noah also contributes to entrepreneur development, sponsoring specific vocational skills training. A family-support module has also been introduced, where spouses and/or children can also become part of the Noah process.

For SAB, a major inhibiting factor to success has been the inability of many individuals to take personal responsibility. A strong dependency on the structured organizational system exists. However, the company has found that many participants, once they have 'a taste of being an entrepreneur', showed remarkable resourcefulness and tenacity.

Regular feedback is obtained from delegates at the Noah Centers, a database of opportunities was developed and maintained, and an effective communication strategy implemented.

References

Allenby, B. (2001) 'Managing Complexity', www.att.com/ehs/ind_ecology/articles/manage_complexity.html, accessed November 2001.

Allianz (2001) *Environmental Report 2001* (www.allianz.com).

Alston, K., and J. Prince Roberts (1999) 'Partners in New Product Development: SC Johnson and the Alliance for Environmental Innovation', *Corporate Environmental Strategy* 6.2: 100-12.

Andersen, M.S. (2001) 'The Use of Economic Instruments for Environmental Policy: A Half-hearted Affair', Sustainable Development Communications Network, Sustainable Development Gateway, www.iisd.ca/linkages/consume/skou.html, accessed December 2001.

Annan, K. (1999) 'An Appeal to World Business', in M. McIntosh (ed.), *Visions of Ethical Business* (London: Financial Times/Prentice Hall).

Baron, R. (2001) *Renewable Energy Certificates: Trading Instruments for the Promotion of Renewable Energy* (Paris: Organization for Economic Cooperation and Development).

Bartelmus, P. (1999) *Sustainable Development: Paradigm or Paranoia?* (paper 93; Wuppertal, Germany: Wuppertal Institute, May 1999).

BCSD–LA (Business Council for Sustainable Development–Latin America) (1999) *Global Climate Change: A Basis for Business Strategy and Practice in Latin America* (Monterrey, Mexico: BCSD–LA).

Bendell, J. (ed.) (2000) *Terms for Endearment: Business, NGOs and Sustainable Development* (Sheffield, UK: Greenleaf Publishing).

Bhagwati, J. (2000) *The Wind of the Hundred Days: How Washington Mismanaged Globalization* (Cambridge, MA: The MIT Press).

Bower, J., and C. Christensen (1995) 'Disruptive Technologies: Catching the Wave', *Harvard Business Review*, January/February 1995: 45-53.

BP (1998) *What We Stand For: Our Business Policies* (London: BP).

—— (2000) *BP Environmental and Social Review 2000* (London: BP).

Brabeck-Letmathe, P. (1999) 'Beyond Corporate Image: The Search for Trust', presentation to European Affairs Society, Oxford University, Oxford, UK, 30 November 1999.

Bradbury, A. (1998) 'Alive and Sticking', *Tomorrow* magazine 8.6 (November/December 1998): 20.

Bristol-Myers Squibb Company (2001) *On the Path Toward Sustainability: 2001 Sustainability Report* (New York: Bristol-Myers Squibb Company).

Brooks, D. (2002) 'Money Is So Boring Now', *Newsweek*, Special Edition: 'Issues 2002', December 2001–February 2002.

Brown, A. (2001) 'As the Earth Heats Up, Companies Consider Options', *International Herald Tribune*, 21 June 2001.

Browne, J. (1997a) 'Addressing Global Climate Change', speech at Stanford University, Stanford, CA, 19 May 1997.

—— (1997b) 'Global Climate Change: The Policy Options', speech presented to the Berlin Parliament, Berlin, Germany, 30 September 1997.

—— (2001) 'Governance and Responsibility: The Relationship between Companies and NGOs. A Progress Report', Arthur Anderson Lecture, Judge Institute of Management Studies, University of Cambridge, Cambridge, UK, 29 March 2001.

BSR (Business for Social Responsibility) (2001) 'Corruption and Bribery: Business Importance', www.bsr.org/BSRResources/WhitePaperDetail.cfm?DocumentID=180, accessed May 2002.

BSRRC (Business for Social Responsibility Resource Center), www.bsr.org/BSRResources/index.cfm, accessed November 2001.

Buerkle, T. (2001) 'For Top Executives, It's Life on the Front Lines', *International Herald Tribune*, 29 January 2001.

Cable, V. (1999) *Globalization and Global Governance* (London: Royal Institute of International Affairs).

Carson, R. (1962) *Silent Spring* (Boston, MA: Houghton Mifflin).

CEC (Commission of the European Communities) (2001) *A Sustainable Europe for a Better World: A European Union Strategy for Sustainable Development* (COM[2001]264 final; Luxembourg: Office for Official Publications of the European Communities, 15 May 2001).

CMR (*Chemical Market Reporter*) (2001) 'BASF AG Steps up its Use of Eco-efficiency Analysis', *Chemical Market Reporter*, 2 July 2001.

Coleman, G. (2001) 'Time to Teach an Old Dog New Tricks', *Tomorrow* magazine 11.3 (June 2001): 60-62.

Collins, J.C., and J.I. Porras (1994) *Built to Last: Successful Habits of Visionary Companies* (New York: HarperCollins).

Consumers International (1997) *Consumers and the Environment: Meeting Needs, Changing Lifestyles* (London: Consumers International).

Cosgrove, W.J., and F.R. Rijsberman (2000) *World Water Vision: Making Water Everybody's Business* (report for the World Water Council; London: Earthscan Publications).

Costanza, R., *et al.* (1997) 'The Value of the World's Ecosystem Services and Natural Capital', *Nature* 387 (15 May 1997): 253 .

Cowe, R. (2000) 'Say it Loud, I'm Clean and I'm Proud', *Tomorrow* magazine 10.6 (November/ December 2000): 32-34.

Cowe, R., and S. Williams (2000) *Who are the Ethical Consumers?* (Manchester, UK: The Co-operative Bank, 15 December 2000).

CRA/MIT/WBCSD (Charles River Associates Incorporated/Massachusetts Institute of Technology/World Business Council for Sustainable Development) (2001) *Mobility 2001: World Mobility at the End of the Twentieth Century and its Sustainability* (Geneva: WBCSD).

Craig, R. (2001) speech at the European Chemical Marketing and Strategy Association Conference, Berlin, Germany, 10 October 2001.

CSRE (Corporate Social Responsibility Europe) (2001) www.csreurope.org, accessed October 2001.

Dale, R. (2001) 'Groping for Global Ethical Guidelines', *International Herald Tribune,* 6 July 2001.

de Andraca, R., and K. McCready (1994) *Internalizing Environmental Costs to Promote Eco-Efficiency* (Geneva: World Business Council for Sustainable Development).

DeSimone, L., and F. Popoff (1997) *Eco-efficiency: The Business Link to Sustainable Development* (Cambridge, MA: The MIT Press).

de Soto, H. (2000) *The Mystery of Capital: Why Capitalism Triumphs in the West and Fails Everywhere Else* (New York: Basic Books).

Dormann, J. (2000) Speech on Sustainability and the New Economy, Global Ministerial Environment Forum, United Nations Environment Program, Malmö, Sweden, 30 May 2000.

Dow Corning (2000) *Responsible Care Report 2000* (Midland, MI: Dow Corning).

Drucker, P. (2001) 'Will the Corporation Survive?', in 'A Survey of the Near Future', *The Economist*, 3 November 2001.

DuPont (2001) 'DuPont and Marubeni Execute First UK Greenhouse Gas Emission Allowance Trade', press release, 21 September 2001.

Economist (1999) 'The Termite Hunter', *The Economist*, 14 October 1999.

—— (2001a) 'Let Them Eat More', *The Economist*, 14 July 2001.

—— (2001b) 'What Next, Then?', *The Economist*, 28 July 2001.

—— (2001c) 'Insuring Africa', *The Economist,* 11 August 2001.

—— (2001d) 'Now, Think Small', *The Economist*, 15 September 2001.

—— (2001e) 'Survey on Globalisation: Profits over People', *The Economist,* 29 September 2001: 9.

—— (2001f) 'Survey on Globalisation: Grinding the Poor', *The Economist,* 29 September 2001: 10.

—— (2001g) 'Survey on Globalisation: A Crisis of Legitimacy', *The Economist,* 29 September 2001: 24.

—— (2001h) 'Survey on Globalization: Globalization and its Critics', *The Economist*, 29 September 2001: 4.

—— (2001i) 'Fishermen on the Net', Survey on Technology and Development, *The Economist*, 8 November 2001.

EcoSecurities (2001) 'Guatemalan Hydroelectric Facility Enters into Major International Green Certificate Transaction with Nuon', press release, 22 November 2001, www.ecosecurities.com/200about_us/223press_releases/223press_release_19_nov_2001.html, accessed November 2001.

EEA (European Environment Agency) (2001) *Term 2001: Indicators Tracking Transport and Environment Integration in the European Union* (Copenhagen, Denmark: EEA).

Elkington, J. (2001) *The Chrysalis Economy* (Oxford, UK: Capstone Publishing).

Elliott, M. (2001) 'Embracing The Enemy is Good Business', *Time*, 13 August 2001.

ENCE (2001) www.ence.es, accessed November 2001.

ENDSED (Environmental Data Services *Environment Daily*) (2001) 'Cement Giant Commits to Cutting CO_2', *ENDSED* 1096 (6 November 2001).

Environics International (2001) 'Poll Findings Suggest Trouble Ahead for the Globalization Agenda', in *Global Issues Monitor 2001* (Toronto: Environics International).

Eskom (2000) *Towards Sustainability: Environmental Report 2000* (www.eskom.co.za/enviroreport01/index.htm).

F10C (Factor 10 Club) (1997) *The Carnoules Declaration: Statement to Government and Business Leaders* (Wuppertal, Germany: Wuppertal Institute for Climate, Environment and Energy).

FAO (Food and Agriculture Organization, United Nations) (1999) *State of the World's Forests* (Rome: FAO).

FEER (*Far Eastern Economic Review*) (2001) 'Wind of Change', *FEER*, 4 October 2001.

Financial Times (2000a) 'Monsanto Opts to Work with the Grain', www.ft.com (11 April 2000).

—— (2000b) 'World's Most Respected Companies', Special Reports, www.ft.com, accessed October 2001.

FitzGerald, N. (2000a) Speech at the opening of the Unilever biosciences laboratory, Colworth House, UK, 11 July 2000.

—— (2000b) 'Making Globalization Work for All: The Role of Business', speech at the Commonwealth Business Forum, 18 September 2000.

—— (2001a) 'Life and Death of World's Brands', speech at the Annual Marketing Society Lecture, London, 18 June 2001.

—— (2001b) 'Making Globalization Work for Africa: A Business Perspective', speech given at the Southern African Business Association Annual General Meeting, London, 3 September 2001.

Flisi, C. (2001a) 'Seeking a Better Life—And a Safer Planet', *The International Herald Tribune*, 10 May 2001.

—— (2001b) 'Strange Bedfellows: Advertising and the Green Consumer', *International Herald Tribune*, 10 May 2001.

—— (2001c) 'Do Technological Advances Serve Society?', *International Herald Tribune*, 11 October 2001.

FMC (Ford Motor Company) (2000) *Connecting with Society* (Dearborn, MI: FMC).

—— (2001) www.ford.com, accessed December 2001.

Fortum (2000) *Annual Report 2000* (Keilaniemi, Espoo, Finland: Fortum).

Frankel, C. (2000) 'Food, Health and Still Hopeful', *Tomorrow* magazine 11.2 (March/April 2000): 6-8.

—— (2001) 'Let There Be Light Bulbs', *Tomorrow* magazine 10.1 (January/February 2001).

—— (2001) 'Storming the Digital Divide', *Tomorrow* magazine 10.1 (January/February 2001).

Friedman, M. (1962) *Capitalism and Freedom* (Chicago: University of Chicago Press).

Friedman, T. (2000) *The Lexus and the Olive Tree* (London: HarperCollins).

FSC/WWF (Forest Stewardship Council/World Wide Fund for Nature) (2001) www.panda.org, accessed October 2001.

Fussler, C., with P. James (1996) *Driving Eco-innovation: A Breakthrough Discipline for Innovation and Sustainability* (London: Pitman Publishing).

Gallop (1995) *Gallup Omnibus Survey into Investor Attitudes* (London: Gallop, April 1995).

Gladwin, T. (1998) 'Economic Globalization and Ecological Sustainability: Searching for Truth and Reconciliation', in N.J. Roome (ed.), *Sustainability Strategies for Industry: The Future of Corporate Practice* (Washington, DC: Island Press): 29-30.

GRI (Global Reporting Initiative) (1999) *Sustainability Reporting Guidelines* (Boston, MA: GRI).

—— (2000) *Sustainability Reporting Guidelines* (Boston, MA: GRI, 1st rev.).

—— (2001) *Sustainability Reporting Guidelines* (Boston, MA: GRI, 2nd rev.).

Grosser, R., and R. Walker (2000) *Partnerships in Practice: Industry, Fresh Water and Sustainable Development* (Geneva: World Business Council for Sustainable Development).

Gupta, A.K. (2001) 'Rich in Ideas: Grassroots Creativity', *International Herald Tribune*, 11 October 2001.

Hamel, G., and C.K. Pralahad (1984) 'Competing for the Future', *Harvard Business Review*, July/August 1984.

Hart, S. (1997) 'Beyond Greening: Strategies for a Sustainable World', *Harvard Business Review*, January/February 1997: 66-76.

Hart, S., and M. Milstein (1999) 'Global Sustainability and the Creative Destruction of Industries', *Sloan Management Review* 41.1 (Fall 1999): 23-33.

Hart, S., and C.K. Prahalad (2002) 'The Fortune at the Bottom of the Pyramid', in *Strategy + Business*, first quarter 2002.

Heal, G. (2001) 'Survey: Mastering Investment: The Bottom Line of a Social Conscience', *Financial Times*, 2 July 2001.

Henderson, D. (2001) *Misguided Virtue: False Notions of Corporate Social Responsibility* (London: Institute for Economic Affairs).

Henriques, A. (1999) 'Opening up for Business: The Logic of Legislation', in M. McIntosh (ed.), *Visions of Ethical Business* (London: Financial Times/Prentice Hall).

Holliday, C. (2001a) 'Making Markets Work For All', World Business Council for Sustainable Development, speech at the United Nations, New York, 18 April 2001, www.dupont.com/corp/news/speeches/holliday_04_18_01.html, accessed November 2001.

—— (2001b) 'Sustainable Growth, the DuPont Way', *Harvard Business Review*, September 2001: 129-34.

Holliday, C., and J. Pepper (2001) *Sustainability through the Market: Seven Keys to Success* (Geneva: World Business Council for Sustainable Development).

Holme, R., and P. Watts (2000) *Corporate Social Responsibility: Making Good Business Sense* (Geneva: World Business Council for Sustainable Development).

Houlder, V. (2001a) 'Campaigners Learn Lesson of Business Advantage', *Financial Times*, 23 July 2001.

—— (2001b) 'Down-to-Earth Plans for CO_2', *Financial Times*, 9 November 2001.

Hufbauer, G., and T. Warren (1999) *The Globalization of Services: What has Happened? What are the Implications?* (Washington, DC: Institute for International Economics, October 1999).

IADB (Inter-American Development Bank) (2001) 'Environmental Investment Strategy', IADB, Multilateral Investment Fund, www.iadb.org, accessed November 2001.

ICTSD (International Center for Trade and Sustainable Development) (2001) 'Comprehensive Trade Round Broadens Scope of Discussions in the WTO', *Bridges* 5 (14 November 2001) (Geneva: ICTSD).

IFC (International Finance Corporation) (2001) 'Investing in People: Sustaining Communities through Improved Business Practice: A Community Development Resource Guide for Companies', IFC, Environment Division, December 2001.

IISD (International Institute for Sustainable Development) (1998a) 'Redirecting $$$ to Climate Change', *Developing Ideas Digest*, http://iisd.ca//didigest/sep98/sep98.4.htm, accessed October 2001.

—— (1998b) 'Kyoto Mechanisms', *Developing Ideas Digest*, www.iisd.org/didigest/sep98/sep98.3.htm, accessed November 2001.

—— (2001) *Summary of the 5th UNCTAD/Earth Council Policy Forum on Trade and Climate Change: The State of the Greenhouse Gas Market*, Rio de Janeiro, 29–31 August 2001, Sustainable Developments, www.iisd.ca/climate/riopolforum/sdvol56num1.html, accessed October 2001.

ING Group (2000) *ING in Society 2000* (Amsterdam: ING Group).

International Herald Tribune (2001) 'A World Trade Deal', *International Herald Tribune*, 11 November 2001.

IPCC (Intergovernmental Panel on Climate Change) (2001a) *Climate Change 2001: The Scientific Basis. Contribution of Working Group I to the Third Assessment Report of the Intergovernmental Panel on Climate Change* (Cambridge, UK; New York: Oxford University Press).

—— (2001b) *Summary for Policymakers: A Report of Working Group I of the Intergovernmental Panel on Climate Change* (also referred to as *Climate Change 2001: The Scientific Basis*; Geneva: IPCC).

ISO (International Organization for Standardization) (1996) *ISO 14001 Environmental Management Systems: Specification with Guidance for Use* (Geneva: ISO).

Jafferji, G. (2001) 'A Problem that Runs Deep', *Tomorrow* magazine 10.3 (June 2001): 91.

Jeucken, M. (2001) *Sustainable Finance and Banking* (London: Earthscan Publications).

Johansen, D., A. Brown and S. Kalambi (1998) 'Shopping Around', *Tomorrow* magazine 8.6 (November/December 1998): 26-27.

Johnson & Johnson (2000) *2000 Annual Report* (Racine, WI: Johnson & Johnson).

Kador, J. (2000) 'Environmental Evangelist', *Electronic Business Magazine*, 1 September 2000.

Kotler, P. (1997) 'Mapping the Future Marketplace', in R. Gibson (ed.), *Rethinking the Future* (London: Nicholas Brealey): 196-210.

Kuntszch, V. (2001) Speech at the Conference on Responsible Fisheries in the Marine Ecosystem, 1–4 October 2001, Reykjavik, Iceland; reported in *Sustainable Developments* 61.1 (7 October 2001): 6.

Lafarge (2001) 'Global Commitment by Lafarge to reduce CO_2 Emissions', press release, 6 November 2001, www.Lafarge.com.

Lehni, M. (2000) *Eco-efficiency: Creating More Value with Less Impact* (Geneva: World Business Council for Sustainable Development).

Lehrman, S., (1999) 'Developing Countries Look for Guidance on GM Crops Debate . . . As Rockefeller Head Warns of Backlash', *Nature* 401 (28 October 1999): 107.

Lomborg, B. (2001a) *The Skeptical Environmentalist* (Cambridge, UK: Cambridge University Press)

—— (2001b) 'The Truth about the Environment', *The Economist*, 14 August 2001.

Macilwain, C. (1999) 'Access Issues may Determine whether Agri-biotech will Help the World's Poor', *Nature* 402 (25 November 1999): 341.

Malloch Brown, M. (2000) speech at the Meeting of Ministers of Trade of Least-Developed Countries, United Nations Conference on Trade and Development (UNCTAD), Brussels, 13 February 2000.

—— (2001) Statement at Global Meeting on Young and Promising Microfinance Initiatives, New York, 1 June 2001.

Margolick, M., and D. Russell (2001) *Solutions: Corporate Greenhouse Gas Reduction Targets* (Global Change Strategies International; Arlington, VA: Pew Center on Global Climate Change).

Martin, C. (1994) speech at the 1994 World Wide Fund for Nature International Annual Conference in South Africa.

—— (2000) 'How Big is your Footprint?', www.panda.org/news/features/dgstory.cfm?id=2083, accessed September 2001.

McDonough, W., and M. Braungart (1998) 'The Next Industrial Revolution', *Atlantic Monthly*, October 1998: 82-92.

McIntosh, M. (1999) 'Introduction', in M. McIntosh (ed.), *Visions of Ethical Business* (London: Financial Times/Prentice Hall).

Mitchell, M. (2001) 'Petroleum's Limits Prompt Green Solutions', *International Herald Tribune*, 27 September 2001.

Mitchell Moore, M. (2001) 'Green is Good', *Darwin Magazine*, 1 September 2001.

Moore, M. (2001) introductory comment at the Third United Nations Conference on the Least-Developed Countries, Brussels, 14–20 May 2001, www.itd.org/ldc_iii/docs_e/dg.htm, accessed November 2001.

Murphy, D., and J. Bendell (1997) *In the Company of Partners* (Bristol, UK: The Policy Press).

Nature (1998) 'Audacious Bid to Value the Planet Whips up a Storm', *Nature* 395 (1 October 1998): 430.

Nelson, J., and S. Zadek (2000) *Partnership Alchemy: New Social Partnerships in Europe* (Copenhagen, Denmark: The Copenhagen Centre).

Nestlé (2000) *Environmental Progress Report 2000* (Vevey, Switzerland: Nestlé).

Neumayer, E. (2001) *Greening Trade and Investment* (London: Earthscan Publications).

Newsweek (2001) 'Tradable Allowances for Greenhouse Gases May One Day Become the World's Largest Commodities Market', *Newsweek*, 27 August 2001.

New York Times (2000) 'Coca-Cola', *The New York Times*, 17 November 2000.

Novo Nordisk (2001) 'Novo Nordisk Launches International Foundation to Help Combat Diabetes in Developing Countries', press release, 13 November 2001.

NRC (National Research Council) (2001) *Climate Change Science: An Analysis of Some Key Questions* (report by the Committee on the Science of Climate Change, Division on Earth and Life Studies; Washington, DC: National Academy Press).

OECD (Organization for Economic Cooperation and Development) (1976) *Guidelines for Multinational Enterprises* (Paris: OECD).

—— (1998a) *Eco-efficiency* (Paris: OECD)

—— (1998b) *Council Recommendation on Improving Ethical Conduct in Public Service* (Paris: OECD).

—— (2000a) *The Fight against Bribery and Corruption* (policy brief; Paris: OECD, September 2000).

—— (2000b) *OECD Guidelines for Multinational Enterprises: Ministerial Booklet* (Paris: OECD)

—— (2001a) 'About Agriculture, Food and Fisheries', at www.oecd.org, accessed October 2001.

—— (2001b) *Sustainable Development: Critical Issues* (Paris: OECD).

—— (2001c) *Environmentally Related Taxes in OECD Countries: Issues and Strategies* (Paris: OECD).

—— (2001d) *OECD Environmental Outlook 2001* (Paris: OECD).

—— (2001e) *Polices to Enhance Sustainable Development* (Financial Market Trends; Paris: OECD).

—— (2001f) *The Application of Biotechnology to Industrial Sustainability* (Paris: OECD).

Ottman, J.A. (1998) *Green Marketing: Opportunity for Innovation* (Chicago: NTC Business Books).

—— (2000) 'It's Not Just the Environment, Stupid', *InBusiness Magazine*, September/October 2000: 31.

P&G (Procter & Gamble) (2001) *2001 Sustainability Report* (Cincinatti, OH: P&G).

Pachauri, R.K., and R.K. Batra (eds.) (2001) *Directions, Innovations and Strategies for Harnessing Action for Sustainable Development* (New Delhi, India: Tata Energy Research Institute).

Panayotou, T. (1992) *Economic Incentives for Environmental Management in Developing Countries* (Organization for Economic Cooperation and Development [OECD] Workshop Paper; Paris: OECD).

—— (1998) *Instruments of Change* (London: Earthscan Publications).

—— (2000) 'Environment and Development Paper 3: Environmental Sustainability and Services in Developing Global City Regions' (WP-55; Cambridge, MA: Center for International Development, Harvard University, July 2000).

Paulson, H. (2001) 'The Gospel of Globalization', *Financial Times*, 13 November 2001.

Pearce, D., and E. Barbier (2000) *Blueprint for a Sustainable Economy* (London: Earthscan Publications).

Pearce, D., and D. Moran (1995) *The Economic Value of Biodiversity* (in association with IUCN–the World Conservation Union; London: Earthscan Publications).

Pearce, D., A. Markandya and E. Barbier (1989) *Blueprint for a Green Economy* (London: Earthscan Publications).

Pepper, J.E., and A.G. Lafley (2001) 'CEO and Chairman's Statement', in *P&G 2001 Sustainability Report* (Cincinatti, OH: Procter & Gamble).

Petkova, E., and P. Veit (2000) *Environmental Accountability beyond the Nation-state: The Implications of the Aarhus Convention* (environmental governance notes; Washington, DC: World Resources Institute, April 2000).

PIFB (Pew Initiative on Food and Biotechnology) (2001) www.pewagbiotech.org, accessed October 2001.

Pistorio, P. (2001) 'The Gains of Going Green', *The Financial Times*, 25 July 2001.

Porter, M.E. (1980) *Competitive Strategy: Techniques for Analyzing Industries and Competitors* (New York: The Free Press).

Porter, M.E., and C. van der Linde (1995a) 'Towards a New Conception of the Environment–Competitiveness Relationship' *Journal of Economic Perspectives* 9.4 (Fall 1995): 119-32.

—— (1995b) 'Green and Competitive: Ending the Stalemate', *Harvard Business Review*, September/October 1995: 120-34.

Porter, M.E., J.D. Sachs, A.M. Warner *et al.* (2000) *The Global Competitiveness Report 2000* (report on behalf of the World Economic Forum; New York; Oxford, UK: Oxford University Press).

PR Newswire (2001) 'Environmental Leaders in Metals and Mining Sector Enjoy 60% Higher Stock Returns over Past Three Years', *PR Newswire*, 28 August 2001.

Prahalad, C.K. (1997) 'Strategies for Growth', in R. Gibson (ed.), *Rethinking the Future* (London: Nicholas Brealey).

PWBLF (Prince of Wales Business Leaders Forum) (2002) *Creating The Enabling Environment* (London: Prince of Wales Business Leaders Forum Publications, forthcoming).

Rennie, J. (ed.) (2002) 'Misleading Math about the Earth', *Scientific American* 286.1 (January 2002): 61-71.

Reuters News Service (2001) Frankfurt, 19 November 2001, and Tax Analysts, State Tax Notes.

Ribeiro, T. (1997) 'Environmental Taxes: Implementation and Environmental Effectiveness', paper presented at Göteborg Conference, 20–21 November 1997; Copenhagen, Denmark: European Environment Agency.

Rio Tinto (undated) *The Way We Work* (www.riotinto.com/community/policies).

Robins, N. (2000) 'Building Sustainable Markets', in *Trade, Investment and the Environment* (London: Royal Institute of International Affairs).

—— (2000) 'Victims to Victors?', *Tomorrow* magazine 10.3 (May/June 2000): 6-8.

Rodrik, D. (2001) 'Survey on Globalization: Is Government Disappearing?', *The Economist*, 29 September 2001: 16.

Romm, J.J. (1999) *Cool Companies: How the Best Businesses Boost Profits and Productivity by Cutting Greenhouse Gas Emissions* (Washington, DC: Island Press).

Royal Dutch/Shell Group of Companies (2001) *People, Planet and Profits: The Shell Report* (London: Shell International).

Sachs, J. (1998) 'International Economics: Unlocking the Mysteries of Globalization', *Foreign Policy* 110 (Spring 1998): 97-111.

Sampson, G. (2000) *Trade, Environment, and the WTO: The Post-Seattle Agenda* (Policy Essay No. 27; Washington, DC: Overseas Development Council).

Schmidheiny, S. (1992) *Changing Course: A Global Business Perspective on Development and the Environment* (Cambridge, MA: The MIT Press).

Sealord (undated) 'The Seas We Fish', www.sealord.co.nz, accessed October 2001.

Severn Trent (2001) *Stewardship Report 2001* (Birmingham, UK: Severn Trent).

Shapiro, A.C. (1991) *Modern Corporate Finance* (New York: Macmillan).

Shorrock, T. (2001) Inter Press Service, 16 October 2001, http://globalfreepress.com, accessed October 2001.

Siddiqui, F., and P. Newman (2001) 'Grameen Shakti: Financing Renewable Energy in Bangladesh', in J.J. Bouma, M. Jeucken and L. Klinkers (eds.), *Sustainable Banking: The Greening of Finance* (Sheffield, UK: Greenleaf Publishing): 88-95.

Spencer-Cooke, A. (2000) 'Hero of Zero', *Tomorrow* magazine 10.6 (November/December 2000): 10-16.

Spencer-Cooke, A., D. Johansen and M. Wright (1999) 'Milestones and Challenges', *Tomorrow* magazine 9.1 (January/February 1999): 22-25.

Starkey, R., and R. Welford (2001) *The Earthscan Reader in Business and Sustainable Development* (London: Earthscan Publications).

Stevens, R., and D. Rittenhouse (2001) *Innovation and Technology* (Geneva: World Business Council for Sustainable Development).

Stipp, D. (2000) 'Is Monsanto's Biotech Worth Less than a Hill of Beans?', *Fortune* Archives, February 2000.

Streeter, A. (1999) 'Business as Usual', *Tomorrow* magazine 10.1 (January/February 1999): 28-29.

Strommes, J. (2001) 'Tribes on Board with New Program to Plant Trees to Offset Carbon', *The Missoulian*, 4 September 2001.

Suncor (2001) www.suncor.com, accessed December 2001.

SustainAbility (1995) *Who Needs It? Market Implications of Sustainable Lifestyles* (London: SustainAbility).

SustainAbility/UNEP (United Nations Environment Program) (2001) *Buried Treasure: Uncovering the Business Case for Corporate Sustainability* (London: SustainAbility).

SustainAbility/UNEP/PWBLF (SustainAbility/United Nations Environment Program/Prince of Wales Business Leaders Forum) (2001) *The Power to Change* (London: SustainAbility).

Sutherland, D. (2001) 'Europe Tightens Corporate Environmental Accounting Rules', *Environmental News Service*, 5 October 2001.

Sutherland, P. (1999) 'Avoiding Marginalization in the Global Economy', in M. McIntosh (ed.), *Visions of Ethical Business* (London: Financial Times/Prentice Hall).

Sweeting, A. (1998) 'Discuss the Reasons why Asymmetric Information can be a Source of Market Failure: Use Examples to Illustrate your Answers', Economic Research and Analysis (ERA), www. eraweb.net, accessed November 1998.

Teijin (2001) *Annual Report 2001* (Osaka, Japan: Teijin Corporation).

Thurow, L. (1997) 'Changing the Nature of Capitalism', in R. Gibson (ed.), *Rethinking the Future* (London: Nicholas Brealey).

Tocker, R. (2001) Speech at the Conference on Responsible Fisheries in the Marine Ecosystem, 1–4 October 2001, Reykjavik, Iceland; reported in *Sustainable Developments* 61.1 (7 October 2001): 6-7.

TransAlta (2001) www.transalta.com, accessed December 2001.

Turner, A. (2001) *Just Capital: The Liberal Economy* (London: Macmillan).

UNDP (United Nations Development Program) (1998) *Human Development Report 1998* (New York: UNDP).

—— (2001) *Human Development Report 2001: Making New Technologies Work for Human Development* (New York: Oxford University Press).

UNECE (United Nations Economic Commission for Europe) (2001) 'Introducing the Aarhus Convention', www.unece.org/env/pp.

UNEP (United Nations Environment Program) (1999) *Global Environment Outlook 2000* (London: UNEP/Earthscan Publications).

University of Pennsylvania (2001) 'A Quick Guide to the World History of Globalization', www.sas. upenn.edu/~dludden/global1.htm, accessed November 2001.

Upton, S. (2001) *Sustainable Development Nine Years after Rio* (development paper; Paris: Organisation for Economic Cooperation and Development).

Van Dijk, F. (1998) 'Consuming Passions', *Tomorrow* magazine (November/December 1998): 28-29.

Verfaillie, H.A., and R. Bidwell (2000) *Measuring Eco-efficiency: A Guide to Reporting Company Performance* (Geneva: World Business Council for Sustainable Development).

von Weizsäcker, E., A. Lovins and L.H. Lovins (1998) *Factor Four: Doubling Wealth, Halving Resource Use* (London: Earthscan Publications).

Walker Information (1999) *The 1999 National Business Ethics Study* (Indianapolis, IN: Walker Information Inc.).

Wallach, L., and M. Sforza (1999) *The WTO: Five Years of Reasons to Resist Corporate Globalization* (Open Media Pamphlet Series, 7; New York: Seven Stories Press).

Watal, J. (2000) 'Developing Countries' Interests in a Development Round', in J. Schott (ed.), *The WTO after Seattle* (Washington, DC: Institute for International Economics).

Watts, P. (2000) 'Pursuing Sustainable Development: A Shell Journey', Templeton College, Oxford, UK, 15 May 2000.

—— (2001) 'Learning to Make Things Happen: Reflections on Leadership in Complex Global Enterprises', speech at the Windsor Leadership Trust, London, 8 November 2001.

WBCSD (World Business Council for Sustainable Development) (2000a) *Clean Development Mechanism: Exploring for Solutions through Learning-by-doing* (Geneva: WBCSD).

—— (2000b) *Eco-efficiency: Creating More Value with Less Impact* (Geneva: WBCSD, August 2000).

—— (2000c) *Building a Better Future: Innovation, Technology and Sustainable Development* (Geneva: WBCSD).

—— (2001a) 'Case Study Collection', www.wbcsd.org, accessed December 2001.

—— (2001b) *The Greenhouse Gas Protocol: A Corporate Accounting and Reporting Standard* (Geneva: WBCSD).

—— (2001c) 'Accounting for Greenhouse Gases', *Sustain* 17 (October 2001): 11.

—— (2001d) 'Business as a Solution Provider', www.wbcsd.org/projects/solution.htm, accessed December 2001.

—— (2001e) *A Business Perspective on Upcoming Climate Negotiations* (Geneva: WBCSD).

—— (2001f) 'Bridging the Digital Divide', *Sustain* 17 (October 2001): 10.

—— (2001g) 'Microcredit Fund Helps Break the Cycle of Poverty', *International Herald Tribune,* 13 May 2001.

—— (2001h) *The Business Case for Sustainable Development: Making a Difference toward the Johannesburg Summit 2002 and Beyond* (Geneva: WBCSD, October 2001).

—— (2001i) *Stakeholder Dialogue: The WBCSD's Approach to Engagement* (Geneva: WBCSD).

—— (2001j) *Innovation and Technology* (Geneva: WBCSD).

WBCSD/WRI (World Business Council for Sustainable Development/World Resources Institute) (2001) www.ghgprotocol.org, accessed December 2001.

WBCSD/WRI/UNEP (World Business Council for Sustainable Development/World Resources Institute/ United Nations Environment Program) (2002) *Tomorrow's Markets: Global Trends and their Implications for Business* (Washington, DC: WRI).

WCED (World Commission on Environment and Development) (1987) *Our Common Future* ('The Brundtland Report'; Oxford, UK: Oxford University Press).

WHO (World Health Organization) (2001) 'WHO/WTO Workshop on Pricing and Financing of Essential Drugs', press release WHO/20, 11 April 2001.

Wilson, R. (2001) 'Corporate Social Responsibility: Putting the Words into Action', speech made at the Conference on Corporate Social Responsibility, Royal Institute of International Affairs, Chatham House, London, 16 October 2001.

World Bank (1997) *Global Development Finance 1997* (Washington, DC: World Bank).

—— (2000) *Global Development Finance 2000* (Washington, DC: World Bank; www.worldbank.org/ prospects/gdf2000/vol1.htm, accessed December 2001).

—— (2001a) *World Development Report 2000–2001: Attacking Poverty* (Washington, DC: World Bank).

—— (2001b) 'MIGA Helps African Trade Insurance Agency Kick Off', press release, 10 October 2001.

—— (2001c) 'Business Partnerships', www.worldbank.org/business/03partnerships.html, accessed September 2001.

—— (2002) *World Development Report 2002: Building Institutions for Markets* (Washington, DC: World Bank).

WRI (World Resources Institute) www.igc.org/wri/incentives/summ_economics.html, accessed October 2001.

WTO (World Trade Organization) (2001) Ministerial Conference, Fourth Session, Doha, Qatar, 9–14 November 2001, WT/MIN(01)/DEC/W/1.

WWF (World Wide Fund for Nature) (2001a) *Taking Responsibility for the Environment: Europe's Global Leadership Role* (Gland, Switzerland: WWF, April 200).

—— (2001b) www.panda.org, accessed October 2001.

Zadek, S. (2001) *The Civil Corporation: The New Economy of Corporate Citizenship* (London: Earthscan Publications).

Zadek, S., and J. Weiser (2000) *Conversations With Disbelievers: Persuading Companies to Address Social Challenges* (New York: Ford Foundation).

Zadek, S., S. Lingayah and M. Forstater (1998) *Social Labels: Tools for The Ethical Trade* (report of the New Economics Foundation for the European Commission, Directorate-General for Employment, Industrial Relations and Social Affairs; London: New Economics Foundation).

WBCSD publications

World Business Council for
Sustainable Development

Reports

2002 releases
- *Tomorrow's Markets: Global Trends and their Implications for Business*

2001 releases
- *Corporate Social Responsibility: The WBCSD's Journey*
- *Stakeholder Dialogue: The WBCSD's Approach to Engagement*
- *Business and the Rio Decade* (reprinted series of ten sponsored sections published in the *International Herald Tribune*)
- *The Business Case for Sustainable Development: Making a Difference toward the Johannesburg Summit 2002 and Beyond*
- *Mobility 2001* (full report, overview and executive summary)
- *The Greenhouse Gas Protocol: A Corporate Accounting and Reporting Standard* (full report and summary)
- *Innovation and Technology*
- *Sustainability through the Market: Seven Keys to Success*

2000 releases
- *Eco-efficiency: Creating More Value with Less Impact*
- *Contributing to Policy Dialogues. The Clean Development Mechanism: Exploring for Solutions through Learning-by-Doing*
- *Biotechnology Scenarios 2000–2050: Using the Future to Explore the Present*
- *Building a Better Future: Innovation, Technology and Sustainable Development*
- *Measuring Eco-efficiency: A Guide to Reporting Company Performance*
- *Partnerships in Practice: Industry, Fresh Water and Sustainable Development*
- *Turning CO_2 Emissions into Assets*
- *The Wizard of US: Sustainable Scenarios Project*
- *Corporate Social Responsibility: Making Good Business Sense*

1999 releases
- *Corporate Social Responsibility: Meeting Changing Expectations*
- *Energy 2050: Risky Business*

1998 releases
- *Industry, Fresh Water and Sustainable Development*

1997 releases

- *Exploring Sustainable Development: WBCSD Global Scenarios 2000–2050*
- *Business and Biodiversity: A Guide for the Private Sector*
- *Environmental Performance and Shareholder Value*
- *Signals of Change: Business Progress toward Sustainable Development*

1996 releases

- *Environmental Assessment: A Business Perspective*
- *A Changing Future for Paper*
- *Trade, Environment and Sustainable Development: A Briefing Manual*

Periodicals

- *Sustain* (the quarterly newsletter of the WBCSD, since 1996)
- *Annual Review*

Ordering reports

WBCSD
Internet: www.wbcsd.org   E-mail: wbcsd@earthprint.com
Tel: (41 22) 839 3100   Fax: (41 22) 839 3131

Books

- *The Sustainable Business Challenge: A Briefing for Tomorrow's Business Leaders* (1998)*
- *Eco-efficiency: The Business Link to Sustainable Development* (1997)
- *Financing Change: The Financial Community, Eco-efficiency and Sustainable Development* (1996)
- *Changing Course: A Global Business Perspective on Development and the Environment* (1992)

Ordering books

The MIT Press, 5 Cambridge Center, Cambridge, MA 02142, USA
Telephone orders: (1 617) 258 0582   Fax orders: (1 617) 253 1709
E-mail: mitpress-orders@mit.edu   Internet: http://mitpress.mit.edu

* Order from Greenleaf Publishing
Aizlewood's Mill, Nursery Street, Sheffield S3 8GG, UK
Telephone orders: (44 114) 282 3475   Fax orders: (44 114) 282 3476
E-mail: sales@greenleaf-publishing.com   Internet: www.greenleaf-publishing.com

Abbreviations

AF&PA	American Forest and Paper Association	DAC	Development Assistance Committee (OECD)
AIDS	acquired immunodeficiency syndrome	DCI	Danish Consumer Information
AISE	Association Internationale de la Savonnerie, de la Détergence et des Produits d'Entretien (International Association of the Soap, Detergent and Maintenance Products Industry)	DDT	dichlorodiphenyltrichloroethane
		DfE	design for environment
		DJGI	Dow Jones Global Index
		DJSI	Dow Jones Sustainability Index
		ECC	environmental conservation committee (Sony)
ATFS	American Tree Farm System	ECTOS	Ecological City Transport System (Iceland)
ATI	African Trade Insurance		
ATM	automated telling machine	EDF	Environmental Defense Fund (USA)
B24B	business to four billion	EEA	European Environment Agency
BCSD	Business Council for Sustainable Development	EH&S	environment, health, and safety
		EIL	Environmental Impairment Liability (Swiss Re)
BCSD–GM	Business Council for Sustainable Development–Gulf of Mexico	EIONET	Environmental Information and Observation Network (Europe)
BCSD–LA	Business Council for Sustainable Development–Latin America	ELI	Efficient Lighting Initiative (South Africa)
BOTT	Build, Operate, Train, and Transfer (South Africa)	EMS	environmental management system
		ENDSED	Environmental Data Services *Environment Daily*
BSR	Business for Social Responsibility	EPA	Environmental Protection Agency (USA)
BSRRC	Business for Social Responsibility Resource Center	ERA	Economic Research and Analysis
		ERC	emission-reduction credit
CAMBIA	Center for the Application of Molecular Biology to International Agriculture (Australia)	ERU	Environmental Risk and Underwriting (Swiss Re)
		EU	European Union
CBD	Convention on Biological Diversity	FDI	foreign direct investment
CBI	Confederation of British Industry	*FEER*	*Far Eastern Economic Review*
CCP	Carbon Capture Project	FEMDES	Business Foundation for Social Development (Ecuador)
CCX	Chicago Climate Exchange	FIU	Florida International University
CD	compact disk	FMC	Ford Motor Company
CDM	clean development mechanism	FOE	Friends of the Earth
CDSP	Corporate Development Support Project	FSC	Forest Stewardship Council
CEC	Commission of the European Communities	GATT	General Agreement on Tariffs and Trade
		GAVI	Global Alliance for Vaccines and Immunization
CEMA	Cumulative Environmental Management Association (Canada)	GDP	gross domestic product
		GHG	greenhouse gas
CEO	chief executive officer	GIAC	Greater-Kanto Industrial Advancement Center (Japan)
CER	corporate environmental report		
CERES	Coalition for Environmentally Responsible Economies	GM	genetically modified
		GMO	genetically modified organism
CESSA	Cemento de El Salvador SA de CV	GRI	Global Reporting Initiative
CFL	compact fluorescent lamp	GSC	Greening of the Supply Chain (Nestlé)
CI	Conservation International	GSDP	Gerling Sustainable Development Project GmbH
CIS	Commonwealth of Independent States		
CMR	*Chemical Market Reporter*	GWh	gigawatt-hour
CO	carbon monoxide	ha	hectare
CO_2	carbon dioxide	HC	hydrocarbon
CRA	Charles River Associates	HDI	human development index (of UNDP)
CRP	Conservation Reserve Program (US Department of Agriculture)	HFC	hydrofluorocarbon
		HIV	human immunodeficiency virus
CRT	cathode-ray tube	HLL	Hindustan Lever Ltd (India)
CSA	Canadian Standards Association	HPE	Hidroelectrica Papeles Elaborados (Guatemala)
CSO	civil-society organization		
CSR	corporate social responsibility		
CSRE	Corporate Social Responsibility Europe		
CST	Companhia Siderúrgica de Tubarão (Brazil)		
CVRD	Companhia Vale do Rio Doce (Brazil)		

IADB	Inter-American Development Bank	PTMEG	polytetramethyleneetherglycol
ICC	International Chamber of Commerce	PUMA	Public Management Committee (OECD)
ICM	Integrated Crop Management	PVO	private volunteer organization
ICT	information and communication technology	PWBLF	Prince of Wales Business Leaders Forum
IER	initial environmental review	QMS	quota management system (for fish stocks, New Zealand)
IETA	International Emissions Trading Association	R&D	research and development
IFC	International Finance Corporation	RAAC	Ramos Arizpe Automotive Complex (General Motors de México)
IFIR	International Forest Industry Roundtable	RCN	Recycling Chemie Niederrhein
IIED	International Institute for Environment and Development	RSPB	Royal Society for the Protection of Birds
IISD	International Institute for Sustainable Development	SAB	South African Breweries
		SABCOHA	South African Business Coalition Against HIV/AIDS
INE	Icelandic New Energy Ltd	SAM	Sustainable Asset Management (Zurich)
IPCC	Intergovernmental Panel on Climate Change	SCODP	Sustainable Community-Oriented Development Program
IPM	Integrated Pest Management	SFI	Sustainable Forestry Initiative
IPR	intellectual property right	SHARE	Society for Helping and Awakening Rural Poor through Education (India)
ISO	International Organization for Standardization	SME	small or medium-sized enterprise
IT	information technology	SNP	single nucleotide polymorphism
ITQ	individual transferable quota (for fish stocks, New Zealand)	SO_2	sulfur dioxide
		SOE	standard of engagement
IUCN	International Union for the Conservation of Nature (the World Conservation Union)	SPDC	Shell Petroleum Development Company of Nigeria Limited
		SRISTI	Society for Research and Initiatives for Sustainable Technology and Institutions (India)
JI	joint implementation		
kg	kilogram	SSB	Salomon Smith Barney (UK)
kWh	kilowatt-hour	STWI	Severn Trent Water International
LCA	life-cycle assessment	SUV	sport utility vehicle
LCD	liquid-crystal display	SVA	shareholder value added
LEAD	Leadership in Education and Access to Diabetes care	TAC	total allowable catch (for fish stocks, New Zealand)
LMAV	Lower Mississippi Alluvial Valley	TBCSD	Thailand Business Council for Sustainable Development
ME3	Minnesotans for an Energy-Efficient Economy	TEPCO	Tokyo Electric Power Company (Japan)
MIGA	Multilateral Investment Guarantee Agency	TERI	Tata Energy Research Institute (India)
		THS	Toyota Hybrid System
MNC	multinational corporation	TREC	tradable renewable energy certificate
MSC	Marine Stewardship Council	TSRDS	Tata Steel Rural Development Society
MSF	Médecins sans Frontières	TWh	terawatt-hour
MSIP	Municipal Solar Infrastructure Project (BP Solar)	UN	United Nations
		UNDHR	UN Declaration of Human Rights
MW	megawatt	UNDP	UN Development Program
NAFTA	North American Free Trade Agreement	UNECE	UN Economic Commission for Europe
NEMS	Nestlé Environmental Management System	UNEP	UN Environment Program
NGO	non-governmental organization	UNFCCC	UN Framework Convention on Climate Change
NO	nitric oxide		
NO_x	nitrogen oxides	UNICEF	UN Children's Fund
NPI	Nestlé Philippines Inc.	USAID	US Aid for International Development
NRC	National Research Council (USA)	VK	Vodokanal (Russia)
ODA	overseas development assistance	VOC	volatile organic compound
OECD	Organization for Economic Cooperation and Development	WBCSD	World Business Council for Sustainable Development
ONA	Office Neighborhood Association (TEPCO)	WCED	World Commission on Environment and Development
OPG	Ontario Power Generation	WDF	World Diabetes Foundation
OSHA	Occupational, Safety, and Health Authority (USA)	WEF	World Economic Forum
		WHO	World Health Organization
P&G	Procter & Gamble	WICE	World Industry Council for the Environment
PAID	Integrated Agricultural Plan (DuPont)		
PCSD	President's Council on Sustainable Development (USA)	WRI	World Resources Institute
		WSSD	World Summit on Sustainable Development, Johannesburg
PEFC	Pan European Forestry Certification	WTO	World Trade Organization
PEM	proton-exchange membrane	WUP	Water Use Planning (BC Hydro)
PIFB	Pew Initiative on Food and Biotechnology	WWF	World Wide Fund for Nature

Index